D1453179

DATE DUE

SEP 2 5 2018	
OCT 2 3 2018	

BRODART, CO.   Cat. No. 23-221

UNDER THE SHADOW

Under the Shadow

The Atomic Bomb and

Cold War Narratives

David Seed

THE KENT STATE UNIVERSITY PRESS · KENT, OHIO

© 2013 by The Kent State University Press, Kent, Ohio 44242

All rights reserved

Library of Congress Catalog Card Number 2012039121

ISBN 978-1-60635-146-8

Manufactured in the United States of America

Library of Congress Cataloging-in-Publication Data

Seed, David.

Under the shadow : the atomic bomb and Cold War narratives / David Seed.

    p.   cm.

Includes bibliographical references and index.

ISBN 978-1-60635-146-8 (hardcover) ∞

1. American fiction—20th century—History and criticism. 2. Cold War in literature.

3. Atomic bomb in literature. 4. Cold War in motion pictures. I. Title.

PS374.C57S44 2012

813'.54093581—dc23   2012039121

17 16 15 14 13   5 4 3 2 1

For Joanna

Contents

Introduction

The time is one year in the near future. An American professor of physics returns to his hometown after a nuclear war to find it completely flattened. The aggressors are unknown; they are simply the "people with bombs and planes."[1] It seems as if civilization itself has been destroyed—that is, until a piece of uranium isotope is discovered that releases powerful energy from the thought waves of the individual holding it. At this point the novel, Murray Leinster's *Fight for Life,* slides from a disaster narrative into a compensatory fantasy. The protagonist summarizes the nuclear subject as marking the demise of war as we know it. "There can't be an atomic battle," he declares. "There can only be atomic massacre. There can't really be an atomic war. There can only be a contest in destruction."[2] The attack on America is depoliticized into an act of blind force.

The novel was published in 1947, before the Soviet Union developed a nuclear capability, which legitimized its new status as the national enemy. In short, nuclear war is presented as the ultimate act that denies the citizen any option but the sheer need to survive, and this is where Leinster's quasi-magical isotope comes in. Extrapolated partly on an analogy with J. B. Rhine's experiments at Duke University into parapsychology, it restores power to the individual and rescues him from being a plaything of blind chance. What is striking about Leinster's novel is its generic indeterminacy. It was marketed simply as a "novel of the atomic age," but the nuclear subject contorts its narrative, which veers from an unpalatable evocation of ultimate endings into a series of fanciful speculations about the power of the mind to alter the present and maybe also the future.

Leinster's novel represents an early demonstration of one of the main themes in this volume, namely the challenges to expression posed by the nuclear subject and the narrative contortions that resulted.

It has long been recognized by critics and commentators on the Cold War that representations of atomic energy and nuclear weapons were unusually complex rhetorically. This complexity often approached paradox. World War III was depicted frequently in graphic detail, exploiting one of the central tenets of realism that concrete specificity conferred authenticity, but in the hope that the very vividness of these depictions would make the event less likely. The British novelist Martin Amis introduced his collection of nuclear stories *Einstein's Monsters* (1987) with an essay entitled "Thinkability," where he reflected on how very difficult it was to engage with the subject, declaring, "Although we don't know what to do about nuclear weapons, or how to live with nuclear weapons, we are slowly learning how to write about them. Questions of decorum present themselves with a force not found elsewhere. It is the highest subject and it is the lowest subject. It is disgraceful, and exalted. Everywhere you look there is great irony: tragic irony, pathetic irony, even the irony of black comedy or farce; and there is irony that is simply violent, unprecedentedly violent."[3]

The decade of the 1980s saw the recognition of a body of writing about the nuclear subject that demanded critical attention in its own right. Apart from the publication of the first critical studies, a number of special issues of critical journals appeared.[4] In addition, the International Society for the Study of Nuclear Texts and Contexts (ISSNTC) was formed in 1988 to maintain a newsletter surveying scholarship on aspects of the Cold War. It ceased production in 1995.

The rise of what was briefly known as "nuclear criticism" in the 1980s was triggered initially by Jacques Derrida's famous 1984 essay "No Apocalypse, Not Now."[5] In the words of his commentator Christopher Norris, Derrida attacked the "self-deluding premise that strategies of deterrence (or nuclear war-fighting plans) are matters of applied expertise and rational provision. But this is to ignore the *rhetorical* dimension to nuclear thinking, the fact that every new weapons system, every shift in the prevailing policy of "defence," will entail some largely unpredictable change in the way such moves are construed by the "other side."[6] Derrida was not addressing only or even primarily literary material, and his insistence on the priority of discourse connects closely with subsequent studies of Cold War rhetoric which argue that the period was characterized by a war of words. Indeed, he declares boldly that "our thesis is that political rhetoric creates political activity."[7] For Paul Williams, the school of nuclear criticism growing out of this essay addressed a broad range of issues, namely nuclear apocalypse, the relation between literary criticism and the discourse of the arms race, the assimilation of terror into the consciousness of the culture, gender critiques of the arms race, the relation of nuclear weapons to Western technology, and the connections between "nuclear manœuvering [and] military and strategic history."[8] The broad implications of Derrida's essay for nuclear culture as a whole were spelled out by Ken Ruthven in his 1993 study *Nuclear Criticism,* which remains the best introduction to this subject.

Derrida's initiative was followed by a number of works like Peter Schwenger's *Letter Bomb* (1992), which took Russell Hoban's *Riddley Walker* (1980) as typically exemplifying a pattern in nuclear fiction, namely "the traces of a long-past nuclear war are read—or misread—in an effort to decipher its nature. Often the act of reading these traces with a mythological mindset creates an origin which never existed."[9] Schwenger's summary of the nuclear fictional subject is helpful in foregrounding the often cryptic nature of the signs that protagonists have to read, but his approach is directed primarily at self-conscious examples of the genre and at narratives set some considerable time after a nuclear war. Nevertheless, the emphasis by Schwenger and others on the rhetoric of nuclear fiction usefully complements studies like those by David Dowling, which concentrates on the paradigm of apocalypse, and Patrick Mannix, which draws on Aristotelian logic.[10]

The rhetorical focus of nuclear criticism injected a welcome rigor into discussion of works dealing with nuclear war. It also helped to demonstrate how textual the nuclear subject was, a point that can be demonstrated from three sample stories taken from Walter M. Miller's 1985 anthology *Beyond Armageddon.* The first of these, Ray Bradbury's "To the Chicago Abyss" (1963), very clearly demonstrates the importance of absence in nuclear narratives. As its title suggests, the story describes the area around what used to be Chicago, the main sign of a broader absence in the aftermath of a nuclear war. The story focuses on a chance encounter between a youth and an old man, whose statements are lists of the consumer goods long gone. In a sense, he embodies a memory apparently missing in the other survivors, but his lists consist of signs without referents. Nuclear war, in other words, has damaged language itself, severely limiting its expressive range. Erasure of this kind could apply to the United States as a whole. At the end of Philip Wylie's *Triumph* (1963), the United States has been so badly destroyed in a nuclear exchange that not only will it cease to exist as a nation, but its very name will disappear from the map. A second possibility is described in J. G. Ballard's "The Terminal Beach" (1964), where the disused installations for testing nuclear weapons on a Pacific island like Eniwetok are explored by a perverse, death-obsessed character named Traven. Despite the insistent physicality of the concrete bunkers and other buildings, the setting becomes internalized as surreal images within Traven's consciousness and begins to whirl round in a hallucinatory sequence prior to his death. Here the status of the referents becomes destabilized and the objects described take up a position between actuality and dream. Finally, Norman Spinrad's "The Big Flash" (1969) satirically presents nuclear apocalypse as a stage effect promoted by a "freaky" rock group called the Four Horsemen. Spinrad conflates a countdown to a nuclear blast with excitement mounting to a sexual climax in a narrative that exploits an extended pun, once again positioning its descriptions between two apparently disparate fields of meaning.

In these and many other cases, the nuclear subject is presented as so mysterious, so challenging to rationality that it stretches the rhetorical resources of those texts attempting to give it expression. And this problem of expressivity did not originate in the Cold War but began to become evident with the emergence of radium. As Albert I. Berger has pointed out, atomic energy "was the central component of the belief that technological innovation was the principal revolutionary force in the world [giving] promise of actually fulfilling dreams of unlimited power."[11] This only tells half the story, however. Even before the Manhattan Project culminated in the atomic bomb, depictions of radium and atomic energy reflected a deep ambivalence over this power source. On the one hand, it offered unlimited energy, as Berger states; on the other, it could easily reverse into equally unlimited destruction. Robert A. Jacobs has struck a more appropriate note in his conclusion to *The Dragon's Tail* (2010), where he argues that nuclear weapons were perceived as so exceptional that they were positively magical, and as such they presented a unique challenge to understanding.[12]

The destabilizing of rhetoric noted above finds its counterpart in representations of the parameters of time and place in nuclear fiction. As Ken Ruthven has rightly noted, time now contracted startlingly: "The revelation that it took less than three seconds to destroy Hiroshima effects so profoundly a nuclearisation of temporality that . . . fictional accounts of a third world war accordingly stress its brevity."[13] These narratives stress the suddenness of the event, and it is often seen as just that—a single event with such a brief duration that the war is frequently depicted as happening within a single day. However, the sheer scale of destruction that would be unleashed in even a limited nuclear exchange challenges authors' capacity to describe this process, which they sometimes attempt to do through slow-motion effects like running a film at half speed. If the war is brief, its consequences could last for centuries, and we shall see how the landscape itself becomes transformed into a shattered terrain that has to be laboriously explored often in the far future in order to gain an understanding of what happened. Because the prime targets in a nuclear war would be not only military installations but also cities, these cultural centers might be entirely erased, as in Bradbury's story.

Exactly who would do the erasing is sometimes made explicit and at other times coyly hinted at. The enemy is usually presented as an alien aggressive force located elsewhere but capable of striking America where it will. During the late 1940s, once the Soviet Union had become a nuclear power in its own right, there emerged the central dualism of the Cold War, the "two worlds" ideology: "The world is split into two camps. In blunt summary terms, there are on the one hand those who believe in freedom and the dignity of man and on the other hand those who believe in a supreme conquering state to which all men must be slaves."[14] When this ideology is converted into spatial terms, it has the effect of encoding different geographical areas as, in some sense, belonging to one super power or the other. *The Bedford Incident* (novel 1963, film 1965) dramatizes the critical consequences of such territorial presumptions. The action is set in the Arctic, during days with very brief periods of light and with fog and generally poor visibility. It is therefore difficult to gain bearings visually and so the terrain has to be scanned electronically.

Narratives of nuclear war constantly problematize their endings because of the uncertainty over the very possibility of survival. Even in the less bleak accounts society is shown to be so ruptured by war that it can only continue to exist in a fragmented form. In such cases, the narratives engage in a quasi-archaeological process of decoding the traces of the shattered culture. The most pessimistic accounts close with impending death, presenting the reader with an ending whose narrative provenance often remains unclear. As Richard Klein has explained, "The nuclear sublime is that all too familiar aesthetic position from which one anticipatorily contemplates the end, utter nuclear devastation, from a standpoint beyond the end, from a posthumous, apocalyptic perspective of future mourning, which, however appalling, adorably presupposes some ghostly survival, and some retrospective illumination."[15] It is impossible to conceive of an ultimate ending because the very existence of the physical text presumes a kind of survival. Nevil Shute's *On the Beach* (1957) famously presents a nuclear war taking place in 1963 in the northern hemisphere from the perspective of inhabitants of Australia. The war thus seems initially as remote, but later as irresistible, as an act of nature, and the novel concludes with a character settling down to commit suicide. By displacing the war, Shute uses it as an absence, setting up an implicit analogy between fallout and a contagious disease, a sort of radioactive plague that is gradually wiping out humanity.

Endings thus represent the worst case, and if the novel is narrated by a character within the action, the reader is positioned claustrophobically within what appears to be a narrative cul-de-sac. The narrator of Helen Clarkson's much-neglected novel *The Last Day* (1959) has lived through a nuclear exchange seen from the distance of the Eastern Seaboard of the United States and describes its immediate aftermath as a gradual spatial contraction down to the location of her own death. She concludes with fatigued resignation: "At last, worn out by vain weeping, I lay down to sleep in the only place I knew in the whole world that was windless and clean."[16] The pathos of this ending, where the narrator grieves for the demise not just of her loved ones but of the whole earth, is offset by the fact that the novel carries a dedication "to the next generation," which signals to the reader that the novel, like much nuclear fiction, functions rather like a jeremiad, warning an implied public against the very possibilities it describes. A different strategy is followed in Mordecai Roshwald's *Level 7* (1959), where the diary of an operative in an underground nuclear bunker tails off as he approaches death. Because he has been keeping this diary deep underground, its provenance remained unexplained until the restoration of Roshwald's original narrative frame describing the discovery of the diary by visitors from another planet.

Since the end of the Cold War, nuclear criticism has modulated into a more historical mode, where literature is more systematically related to its cultural context, an approach admirably practiced by the historian Paul Boyer. This cultural mapping has been practiced by critics like Albert E. Stone, Daniel Cordle, and, more recently, Robert A. Jacobs.[17] Cordle's 2008 study, *States of Suspense*, for instance, explores the different ways in which nuclear anxiety finds expression in Cold War narratives, fictional and nonfictional. His incorporation of threats to language itself within his discussion testifies to the ongoing legacy of nuclear criticism, and indeed he has argued eloquently that the latter continues to offer important and productive approaches to cultural criticism long after the end of the Cold War.[18] It is a sign of the continuing vigor of criticism in this field that Paul Williams has explored a complex racial subtext to Cold War debates in his 2011 study *Race, Ethnicity and Nuclear War*.

Built on a project I started with my 1999 book, *American Science Fiction and the Cold War*, this study includes more material about and gives more detailed attention to key nuclear narratives. It opens with a discussion of the first novel to describe atomic war, H. G. Wells's *The World Set Free* (1914), and considers the fictional treatment of radium up to the Second World War. Having established this context, I move on in chapter 2 to examine the different strategies used to describe the atomic tests and the bombing of Hiroshima by John Hersey and his contemporaries. Once full-blown narratives of nuclear war took shape from the late 1940s, they participated in an ongoing debate over whether it was possible to survive such a war and how useful domestic or communal shelters might be. This is the subject of chapter 3, whose central figure is the writer Judith Merril. Pursuing the issue of survival, I next examine Pat Frank's *Alas Babylon* (1959), one of the most popular but least discussed of all nuclear novels, relating it to subsequent survivalist writing. Frank's confidence that nuclear war needed a resolute will to cope with it was not shared by Philip Wylie, the subject of chapter 5. Wylie saw himself as a latter-day Cassandra haranguing the American public for its shortcomings, initially in its failure to take civil defense seriously. In his later writings he became pessimistically preoccupied with humanity's capacity for self-destruction, a central theme in chapter 6, which focuses on Walter M. Miller's classic *A Canticle for Leibowitz* (1960), where nuclear technology is presented as triggering a rerun of Western history culminating in yet another nuclear war.

This compulsion is also featured in Bernard Wolfe's *Limbo* (1952), the central focus of chapter 7, which explores Wolfe's complex exploration of the pathology of aggression through a narrative satirizing the very idea of disarmament. The mechanistic streamlining of a war machine is only hinted at in Wolfe and more fully represented in Mordecai Roshwald's *Level 7*. Chapter 8 examines Roshwald's satirical use of one of the most prominent icons of the 1950s, the push button, through a dystopian narrative of how humans become reduced to mere components within a military machine. Chapter 9 turns to the tradition of the hunt in American culture in order to explore the links formed during the Cold War between Moby Dick and nuclear submarines. The focal text in this discussion is Mark Rascovich's *The Bedford Incident* (1963). The issue of control over the military machine returns in chapter 10, this time examining Eugene Burdick and Harvey Wheeler's novel *Fail-Safe* (1962). One of the main ironies of this novel is that its very title identifies a precautionary device that, in the narrative, fails. Control yet again is central in *Dr. Strangelove* (novel and film 1964), where the action is premised on the possibility of a renegade Air Force officer launching a preemptive strike against the Soviet Union. Chapter 11 discusses the absurdist techniques used in the novel and film, including their suggestion of thinly disguised sexual motivations for military action. The next two chapters draw a number of threads together. Chapter 12 surveys examples of narratives that describe postnuclear explorations of the shattered American landscape, sometimes in the immediate aftermath of war, sometimes centuries later. Chapter 13 turns to accounts of World War III, considering future histories of this imagined conflict and also ironic condensations of such a cataclysm into short stories.

The focus throughout this study will fall on the different kinds of narrative used to describe the use of nuclear weapons. Throughout the Cold War there was a constant fear that they might be used but a predictable resistance to the worst-case scenario that they might wipe out all human life. Nuclear narratives in their different ways all evoke massive ruptures to life but then explore possibilities of survival. In this sense, they repeatedly attempt to balance the fears of the time against tenuous hopes for a postnuclear world.

CHAPTER 1

The Atom—From H. G. Wells to Leo Szilard

The discovery of radioactivity in the 1890s would qualify as beginning what Thomas Kuhn calls a paradigm shift in scientific knowledge. In *The Structure of Scientific Revolutions* he uses the term "paradigm" to signify the set of beliefs shared by scientific communities and asks the question, Does the world itself change with paradigms? His answer: "Outside the laboratory everyday affairs usually continue as before."[1] Supposing, however, a writer wanted to incorporate such a discovery into a novel. Kuhn himself recognizes that paradigms exist with slightly different meanings in linguistics and the law and even began speculating on its applicability to the arts. If we take the term to indicate a characteristic or exemplary narrative pattern, then a shift in the scientific sense might carry implications of related shifts in narrative. This is what happens in fiction dealing with the extraordinary forces unleashed by nuclear fission in a context of war. From H. G. Wells's *The World Set Free* on, atomic war does not only kill thousands and cause massive destruction, but it also causes a rupture in the narratives themselves, introducing discontinuities that become important for the narratives to bridge over. Again and again in the postwar period novels dealing with nuclear war are set in a future where the past has to be painstakingly reconstructed by regaining access to history. Typically these novels set up a future retrospect, a future vantage point from which to examine how events have developed from the reader's present to the postwar era of the narrative present.

Spencer Weart points out that nuclear energy tales typically tend to focus on some "tremendous forbidden secret" and, because they deal with one of the most hidden aspects of nature, an "attack upon the secret things in search of mastery."[2] Robert Cromie's *The Crack of Doom*, the first novel to describe an atomic weapon, describes the attempts by Herbert Brande (probably named after Ibsen's obsessed idealist), a scientific genius whose talents include telepathy, to destroy the world with a new device. The novel is narrated by a young medic, Arthur Marcel, whose interest in Brande is stimulated when he tells him roundly, "The Universe is a mistake!"[3] For the rest of the novel, Marcel tries to discover Brande's plan and prevent him from putting it into practice. In other words, the action is an investigation of Brande's mentality rather than the technology of the weapon he has devised, and his logic runs: The atom is the smallest unit in nature but it can be destroyed; therefore, nature is destructible. In fact, strife is a principle of nature, since it is the way life itself emerges, and Brande's fantastic dream is of merging humanity back into the matrix of protoplasm. This "nirvana," as he calls it, therefore represents a kind of atomic mysticism where he doesn't see himself as killing, only returning humanity to the life pool in the universe. Comparing himself with earlier seekers of the principle of life, he uses a characteristic Victorian image of achievement, of attaining the heights: "But we know more than they. We have climbed no doubt in the footholds they have carved, and we have gained the summit they only saw in the mirage of hope."

Although he describes himself as a scientist, Brande actually leads a cult of devoted followers very like the physicist in J. B. Priestley's 1938 novel *The Doomsday Men*. Priestley describes an enormous secret installation in the Mojave Desert; Cromie's hero has chosen a deserted Pacific island. Priestley's scientist's motivation is less clear, but he declares that he wants to perform "one last triumphant stroke, one supreme act of defiance" in deciding the moment of humanity's exit.[4] Shortly before Brande detonates his device, he declares his intention in ringing tones: "I stand . . . I may say with one foot on sea and one on land, for I hold the elemental secret of them both. And I swear by the living god—Science incarnate—that the suffering of the centuries is over, that for this earth and all that it contains, from this night and for ever, *Time will be no more!*"[5] In both novels the discovery of atomic fission licenses the scientist to play destiny with the whole race and forms part of a Promethean dream of power to control one of the forces in the universe and, more importantly, to control or even erase time. In both cases power is appropriated and embodied in the researchers who have uncovered this force in nature. In the quotation above Brande takes on quasi-divine powers that he intends to use to wipe out the limits of mortality: terrestrial life itself. It is a symptomatic irony that the first representation in fiction of atomic energy should show it being used for destruction.

The Crack of Doom is a search narrative based on realist premises of social interaction that Brande is determined to break through. He refuses any limits, whereas, fortunately, our plucky hero and narrator sabotages his scientific formulae and does not prevent an explosion but at least contains it as a local earthquake that destroys the island but leaves the rest of the world intact. The dramatic climax to the novel comes when the narrator and his companions flee the island as it is exploding—or perhaps "erupting," because the analogy with a volcano contains Brande's device within known nature. And this is the same analogy used by the engineer in Karel Capek's *Krakatit* who names his own super-explosive after Krakatoa. We should also note that it is an analogy which problematizes human control of the explosive process. Cromie's sensational title combines two senses of rupture—aural (thunderclap) and spatial, as suggesting a break in the surface of nature.

Cromie's application of the new science is superficial compared to that of H. G. Wells, who used a text by the radio-chemist Frederick Soddy. In his book of lectures, *The Interpretation of Radium,* Soddy waxes enthusiastic about radioactivity because it seems to change one of the projected grand narratives of life: "With all our mastery over the powers of Nature we have adhered to the view that the struggle for existence was a permanent and necessary condition of life." Now, however, there seems to emerge a post-Darwinian possibility of unfettered progress toward a goal of ultimate power, an "unlimited ascent of man to knowledge, and through knowledge to physical power and dominion over Nature."[6] "Mastery," "power," and "dominion" are terms that can slide easily from science into imperial politics. But note here Soddy's excitement over radium as an inexhaustible energy source. For him, radium is a sublime substance giving humanity a glimpse of the forces hidden within the "treasure-house of Nature" and destabilizing matter into a constant process of "flow, continuous change."[7] If we were to render his enthusiasm as a graph, a rising line of constant improvement now replaces the falling curve of entropy.

As early as 1904 Soddy had recognized the military potential of radioactivity when he declared: "It is probable that all heavy matter possesses—latent and bound up with the structure of the atom—a similar quantity of energy to that possessed by radium. If it could be tapped and controlled, what an agent it would be in shaping the world's destiny! The man who puts his hand on the lever by which a parsimonious nature regulates so jealously the output of this store of energy would possess a weapon by which he could destroy the Earth if he chose."[8] At this stage Soddy only phrases the possibility in individual terms. In *The Interpretation of Radium* he briefly mentions the possibility that fission might produce an "explosive incomparably more powerful in its activities than dynamite," but then he quickly moves on to consider the more benign implications of radium. "In the background," he declares, "there has always been the tacit assumption that the supply of fresh energy is only apparently inexhaustible, and that in some remote future a time will at length arrive when the supplies of fresh energy are exhausted and all things will come to a stop and remain at rest for ever."[9] This entropic end to everything is approached by Wells's time traveler when he glimpses the cosmic sunset far into the future in *The Time Machine.* Radium enables Soddy to reauthorize progress as entering a whole new phase with the final ending indefinitely deferred: "We find ourselves . . . at the pinnacle of one ascent of civilisation, taking the first step upwards out onto the lowest plane of the next."[10] Soddy is certainly not giving any sort of dispassionate account of scientific discovery but, rather, a "message of hope and inspiration" to humanity because "radium has taught us that there is no limit to the amount of energy in the world available to support life."[11] *The Interpretation of Radium* is strikingly inspirational for a scientific study, full of millenarian hope for a new postindustrial era soon to dawn. The one thing Soddy does not consider is how radium can be transformed into an industrial process. This was an absence addressed by Wells.

The World Set Free: A Story of Mankind acknowledges its debt to Soddy in an unusually direct way, being dedicated to *The Interpretation of Radium* itself rather than the author.[12] And Soddy returned the compliment by praising Wells's novel in *Wealth, Virtual Wealth, and Debt* (1926). Wells's 1914 novel might seem to belong with *The War of the Worlds* (1898) and *The War in the Air* (1908) as forming a trilogy about modern weaponry.[13] This is the way Roslynn Haynes takes them when she argues that all three novels "warn of the levels of violence to which warfare must inevitably escalate if the resources of technology are turned simply to the task of producing the most efficient weapons possible, without heed to the morality of their use."[14] The problem with this approach is that it oversimplifies the works concerned and ignores the fact that *The World Set Free* is the only novel of the three not to have "war" in its original title and that it carries the subtitle *A Story of Mankind.* In fact, the novel breaks down into four phases: prophecy, application, war, and an aftermath of world government. It is a hybrid narrative, opening as a chronicle of technological development and including extended quotations from lectures and a latter-day sage as well as sections from a bildungsroman of a young man living through the war years. As John Canaday has rightly argued, Wells's book is a multigenre work attempting to "unsettle the assumptions we would associate with any single narrative mode." The constant shifts are thus aimed at unsettling the reader's habits of thought. Wells "obliges us to see [the book] from many narrative perspectives at once, hoping that in this way we may, perhaps, be able to avoid the mistakes made by the inhabitants of his future world."[15]

Wells read and admired Soddy's book, writing him into the narrative as Professor Rufus, whose declaration in a lecture that radioactivity is signalling the "dawn of a new day in human living" continues Wells's opening narrative role as the chronicler of human progress.[16] This is the prelude, set in the 1914 reader's present. The next phase covering the 1930s comes when a visionary scientist discovers a method of releasing and controlling this energy with the result of coal disappearing as a fuel. As these changes take place, Wells's (Soddy's?) utopian hopes of social transformation start to take on a more somber tone, because for every advance there is an unexpected problem. The abolition of coal cleans up the environment but throws thousands out of work. By the end of the section, society has become more polarized than ever by rapid technological change. At this point the action moves into open warfare.

An atomic war breaks out in the mid-1950s that totally shatters European society. Wells's description of what he calls the "last war"—a variation on the catchphrase "war to end all wars" that he helped to popularizes, to his later embarrassment—is introduced by a statement on its sheer illogicality: "Viewed from the standpoint of a sane and ambitious social order, it is difficult to follow the motives that plunged mankind into the war that fills the histories of the middle decades of the twentieth century."[17] And since it is difficult, Wells does not try it. The war that breaks out between Central Europe and the Allies is presented as the inevitable outcome of early-twentieth-century nationalism. In a preface he wrote in 1921, Wells made his thesis clearer: "Because of the development of scientific knowledge, separate sovereign states and separate sovereign empires are no longer possible in the world, . . . an attempt to keep on with the old system is to heap disaster upon disaster for mankind and perhaps to destroy our race altogether."[18] The difference between his worldview at the time of writing the novel and the postwar period is fundamental for Wells, even so early in the century. Whereas in 1913 he saw a general belief that prosperity would increase indefinitely, now "the world is growing accustomed to a steady glide towards social disintegration."[19]

The World Set Free anticipates postwar accounts of actual and imagined atomic bombing in introducing the iconography of bird's-eye charts: "In the map of nearly every country of the world three or four or more red circles, a score of miles in diameter, mark the position of the dying bombs and the death areas that men have been forced to abandon around them."[20] Schematic representations of inner and outer blast areas became a common image after 1945, as did the fragmentation of perspectives on atomic blasts. Here again Wells anticipates this development. We are told that "no complete contemporary account of the explosion of the atomic bombs survives" and so later ages have to reconstruct their narrative retrospectively.[21] This means that the reader gets vivid isolated images or episodes, such as when a palace in Berlin is bombed. We are given the viewpoint of a bombardier looking down on the scene from his plane: "It was like looking down upon the crater of a small volcano. In the open garden before the Imperial castle a shuddering star of evil splendour spurted and poured up smoke and flame towards them [the two airmen] like an accusation. They were too high to distinguish people clearly, or mark the bomb's effect upon the building until suddenly the façade tottered and crumbled before the flare as sugar dissolves in water."[22] In describing a continuing explosion, Wells notes the targeting of a building symbolic of a regime or nation, the representation of apparently solid structures as totally vulnerable to the atomic blast, and also, more importantly, the problem of witness. We are given a firsthand account that is negated by the height of the vantage point as well as by subsequent events. Shortly after this description, the two airmen themselves are blasted into smithereens. Notice, too, the hint of guilt in the phrase "like an accusation." Cromie had chosen a title linking the super weapon with hell. Wells continues this association but separates the construction and use of atomic bombs from any individual. Now he disperses evil into collective national courses of action. He anticipates a designation of the hydrogen bomb in his phrase "Hell Bomb" and describes the atomic bombs on Holland as "falling like Lucifer in the picture," breaching the dykes and causing a new flood of biblical proportions.[23] Wells's reviewers agreed that these sections were the most powerful in the novel. C. L. Graves commented appreciatively that Wells was a "past-master in the conduct of the *debacle,* an expert in Armageddons."[24] The depiction of widespread destruction as a kind of sublime spectacle has led Paul Brians to argue that nuclear war narratives are closest to the disaster genre than any other.[25]

However demonically the atomic bombs are described, the sequel to the conflict was to present a "wave of sanity," as he later recorded.[26] In the wake of the war a small number of idealistic, high-minded leaders take the initiative in forming a world government, which is achieved with amazing speed. Indeed, the only serious obstacle is presented by the King of the Balkans (the "slavic fox"), who tries unsuccessfully to retain two atomic bombs for his own purposes. With this ultimate change in world politics, it only remains for the Russian sage Karenin to construct a liberationist narrative and point out a rather disturbing moral. He stresses how diseased the world was and therefore how strongly it needed its atomic medicine. His metaphor of illness in effect dehumanizes the expendable masses into corruptions of the ideal body politic that will be established by a right-thinking elite. Switching the metaphor, he insists that the bombs "burnt our way to freedom," nevermind the unnamed masses slaughtered in the process. They were dispensable, Karenin implies, and with one eye on postwar city planning he declares, "The great hole in the east of London scarcely matters."[27] Wells clings to his central notion of liberation, but, as Martha Bartter has shown, focuses his hostility to the unplanned society in the city referred to as a place of sin and disorder crying out for "purging."[28] Whereas Soddy recoiled in horror at the thought of nuclear weaponry when he saw the actual destruction caused by the First World War, Wells does not seem to have had second thoughts about his novel, although he felt that the war was a "revelation of the profound instability of the social order."[29]

Wells recognizes that a super weapon raises special problems of control, not to say monopoly. Only two devices could produce enormous destruction and therefore have a threat value far exceeding any previous weapon, as his Balkan king knows only too well. Narratives from the interwar period attach far more importance to this question of ownership than to the technology of such weapons. In *The World Set Free* Wells's military technicians construct their bombs out of an element called "carolinum," and these new elements proliferated in fiction between the wars. In Upton Sinclair's *The Millennium* (play 1914, novel 1924) a scientist discovers an element called "radiumite," which startles those around him with its utopian potential as an unlimited power source: "Here is power enough to turn all the wheels in the country!" one exclaims.[30] But, as in other writers of the period, this hope is offset by a fear of its destructive capacity and of its tendency to slip out of human control. Sure enough, a container of radiumite is accidentally detonated in a "vivid, blinding light" that anticipates by decades the flash of a nuclear bomb.[31] The explosion kills off the entire world's population, all except eleven survivors who can then set up a cooperative commonwealth in the Hudson Valley. Sinclair uses the super weapon to erase the mass of humanity who might obstruct the establishment of this utopia, and it is a measure of how little importance he attaches to its human consequences that he subtitles his novel *A Comedy of the Year 2000*.

In Capek's *Krakatit* the inventor of the new device, who is consciously following in the steps of Rutherford, has a hallucinatory perception that "everything is an explosive." Physical energy shades mental force, as he explains to a companion: "Every thought is a sort of explosion inside the head. When you give me your hand I feel as if something is exploding inside you."[32] The engineer Prokop has internalized the notion of nuclear fission so completely that it has destabilized his sense of reality. Because he totally identifies with his weapon, Prokop himself becomes a valuable military commodity that rival nations try to appropriate. The actual use of such technology stays in the future of Capek's narrative, unlike in Philip Frances Nowlan's *Armageddon 2419 A.D.* (1928–1929, assembled as novel 1962) where it has been applied to guns, transport, and even searchlights. In Captain S. P. Meek's 1929 story "The Red Peril," when war breaks out between the Allies and the Soviet Union the planes of the former carry "vacite" and "uranite" bombs, which are presumed to be irresistible because "both operated on the principle of the disintegration of the atom."[33] But then, in anticipation of the many mirroring effects in Cold War narratives, it emerges that the Soviets have even bigger and better bombs, and their threat can only be countered with great difficulty.

During the interwar period the destructive potential of these new elements vastly outweighed their value as an energy source. Thus, they feature in exotic new weapons like radium-ray pistols or as a power source for military robots. Part of their appeal lies in their mystery. In narratives like E. E. Smith's *The Skylark of Space* (serialized 1928, book 1946) the new form of energy is never fully known but at the same time is dangerous because it might become uncontrollable. Jim Vanny's "The Radium Master," for example, describes what appears to be a radium-powered utopia centered on the "metal city" of Urania in central Africa. This city-state is ruled by a despot with Napoleonic ambitions to rule the world; but when the explorers imprisoned by him turn their radium guns against the city, the latter is destroyed in a massive explosion: "The very bowels of the Earth seemed to be rent asunder while searing rays of radium rose from the fissures that split across the city. Her subterranean passages, a very honeycomb of tunnels, were breaking under the terrific onslaught of radium."[34] The emperor's ambitions are defeated, but the story actually demonstrates a profound ambivalence about radium, which is seen both as an inexhaustible source of power and as a destructive force that can scarcely be contained. The recurrence of such explosions, usually by accident, reflects an underlying anxiety about these elements that anticipates the fears among the scientists working on the Manhattan Project when they were experimenting with the first chain reactions.

By the time of Wells's death in 1946, not only had atomic weapons been well-established in fiction, but they had become a daunting new reality. Wells did live to see his speculations on atomic bombs put into practice on Hiroshima and Nagasaki, and the few recorded comments by him suggest that he shared the postwar gloom over the fact that the only tried and tested nuclear technology was that of the atomic bomb. When asked about the new bomb, he reportedly said, "This can wipe out everything—good and bad—in this world."[35] Little more is known about his reaction except that at the time of his death he was working on a scenario for Alexander Korda's London Films. A memo of 1946 from a company representative that is held in the Wells archive at the University of Illinois explains his purpose and attitude: "Mr H.G. Wells is working very hard upon the scenario of a film to be called *The Way the World is Going*. It is *The Shape of Things to Come* brought up to date with the new ideas and curiosities due to the popularisation of the ideas of the disintegration of the atom and the atomic bomb. He thinks it urgently necessary to dispel many short-sighted, cruel and dangerous misconceptions of the significance of these things. The human situation is grave and tragic, a thing he has been writing and saying for the past half-century."[36] Did Wells intend to revise the presentation of the bomb that he made in *The World Set Free*? We may never know. Not surprisingly, Hiroshima brought a surge of new interest in his 1914 novel. Excerpts were published in the press and an article in *The Nation* even made it sound as if Wells had devised the whole Manhattan Project single-handedly, declaring,

Of course it was H.G. Wells who first perfected the atomic bomb and put it to work. And not only did he put it to work, demolishing most of the world's capital cities and destroying governments, but then he got busy and built an entirely new society. In less time than you can imagine after the last bomb fell, everybody was settling down nicely in a global socialist community under a World Republic; atomic energy, internationally controlled, was performing all the necessary jobs of production, transportation, heating, and such, and the creative energies of mankind were being applied to higher things.[37]

Wells's former mentor, Frederick Soddy, similarly lived to see the use of the atom bomb and warned grimly of its sinister applications, declaring that "the new power science has so light-heartedly and irresponsibly put into the hands of men drunken with conflict . . . is only too likely to prove a boomerang."[38] What Soddy saw at the beginning of the century as a general empowerment was heavily offset by what he perceived to be the political betrayal of the First World War and, even more, by the looming threat of military applications of this power. His 1949 narrative *The Story of Atomic Energy* retains some of his early excitement over what he calls the "sublime conception of energy"; indeed, he describes the development of the uranium pile as the most "god-like scientific achievement of the human brain in all recorded history."[39] His disillusionment emerges largely from his separation of scientific research from the political and economic infrastructure needed to promote it. He already takes the postnuclear future to be a consensus image. "It is universally agreed," he declares grimly, "that, unless positively prevented, the new destructive weapon may destroy anything that can be called civilisation, and again reduce human life on this planet, if it survives at all, to a primitive type of economy, maintained by scattered groups of individual families living directly by cultivation of the soil."[40] This is a far cry from Soddy's optimism at the turn of the century and in fact sketches out a scenario that was to be used again and again by subsequent nuclear war novels. Looking back on his previous hopes, he reflects that the lethal radiation from nuclear fission makes it totally impractical to apply to atomic technology for ships or planes, thereby denying the second phase of *The World Set Free*. What emerges most strongly from Soddy's coda is the sheer difficulty he has in imagining any benign future for humanity. The open perspectives of potential progress he imagined in 1909 have now become replaced by a cautious sense that atomic energy "has not yet advanced beyond the purely scientific stage far enough to warrant any forecast of its technological possibilities."[41] His earlier narrative of a steady progress in achievement now loses its way in an uncertain and ominous future.

Two years before Soddy's history of atomic energy, the American science fiction editor John W. Campbell published his own account, where the political implications of the new energy source are spelled out explicitly. Campbell had already been publishing a series of editorials on nuclear energy. In *Atomic Age* for November 1945 he explained the atomic bomb as representing the "death of every big city . . . the death of an era, and the death of a cultural pattern based on a balance of military power controlled exclusively by big and wealthy nations."[42] In short, it represented a watershed, ushering in new technologies. Although Campbell's evident anxiety over the super weapon was reflected in the fact that he referred to the "Doomsday Bomb," his 1947 volume *The Atomic Story* is designed as a primer for the layman as it outlines the history of scientific research culminating in the atomic bomb. Unlike Soddy, Campbell is relatively unconcerned about the latter, seeing it as a "product" to be tried and tested. When he glances at the bombings of Nagasaki and Hiroshima, he blanks out the issue of radiation and concludes that they were "practically no more than powerful chemical bombs."[43] Where Soddy loses his original utopian hopes for atomic energy, Campbell finds a sign of hope in the present. Giving a new twist to a period label from American literature, he declares, "We are a lost generation—the people who live through the interregnum between the closing of the age of chemistry and the opening of the atomic age."[44] And then he comes to his climactic point, that the United States is uniquely poised to take a dominant role in world politics: "We possess an absolutely irresistible military weapon with which we could conquer every nation on Earth and establish a single world government." This government would be a far cry from Wells's super state, which was modeled on the United States but designed to be truly international. Campbell instead sees American global conquest as the culmination, by "strict logic," of its nuclear monopoly: "By conquering the world right now and establishing American police inspection guards in every city on the planet, we could make sure that no other people would learn how to make atomic bombs."[45] Little did Campbell know that at the very moment when he was publishing this Klaus Fuchs and others were busily transmitting technological secrets to the Soviet Union, which would result in their own test of an atomic bomb in 1949. Although Campbell softens his position by claiming that Americans "do not want conquest," he sees a clear line of development from scientific discovery to political and military empowerment.

Apart from the obvious reaction that Wells had "got it right," there is in fact a close historical connection between his 1914 novel and the atomic bomb through the expatriate Hungarian physicist Leo Szilard. The two men met briefly in 1929 when Szilard told Wells that he was contemplating going into nuclear research as the only way to achieve interplanetary travel. Szilard read *The World Set Free* in 1932 and was particularly struck by its war sections. "This book made a very great impression on me," he recalled, "but I didn't regard it as anything but fiction."[46] The following year Szilard conceived the notion of a chain reaction, and because Wells had given him such vivid images of its military applications Szilard hurriedly patented his invention. He later recorded that "all the things which H. G. Wells had predicted appeared suddenly real to me."[47] Szilard then went on to play a leading part in the Manhattan Project to devise the atomic bomb.

The connections between literature and science explored here are not confined to Wells and Szilard, although their case is an unusually direct example. John Canaday has shown that the scientists at Los Alamos "turned to literature in their descriptions of the work of designing and constructing the first nuclear weapons." This performed a complex function, since "literature provided them with a way of accounting for the strange and threatening aspects of their errand in the wilderness it named and subdued the unknown. It allowed them to submerge previously incompatible elements of their experience—pacifist convictions and military research, for example—within a wide variety of compelling narratives."[48] Canaday's discussion substantiates this general insight that Szilard and his colleagues turned to literature—to the Faust story, among others—to give a narrative form to their activities and to cope with the ambiguities and contradictions in their research.

Despite being a leading participant in the Manhattan Project, Leo Szilard began to have misgivings about dropping the atomic bomb on Japan in 1945, and as he explained in a 1960 interview, "in March, 1945, I prepared a memorandum which was meant to be presented to President Roosevelt. This memorandum warned that the use of the bomb against the cities of Japan would start an atomic-arms race with Russia, and it raised the question whether avoiding such an arms race might not be more important than the short-term goal of knocking Japan out of the war."[49] President Roosevelt died before this memo could be presented, and Truman ignored the advice. After 1945 Szilard turned away from military science and campaigned tirelessly for arms control. In a 1947 article, "The Physicist Invades Politics," for instance, he pointed out the self-perpetuating escalation of the super powers' policy where "both governments consider it their duty to put their countries into the position of winning that war if war should come."[50] Szilard then goes on to spell out a proposal for establishing a world organization to monitor the creation of atomic bombs, a proposal that seemed increasingly quixotic as the tensions of the Cold War deepened.

As if he realized this even while he was campaigning against military escalation, Szilard turned to fiction to articulate his frustrations, and the cycle of interaction between literature and science took one further twist. Among his many postwar activities, in 1946 Szilard traveled to Hollywood to write several scenes for the MGM film about the making of the atomic bomb, *The Beginning or the End*. Although the press kit brochure for the film describes a number of technical advisers who collaborated on this project—figures like J. Robert Oppenheimer—Szilard's name did not appear.[51] When he saw the final film, his opinion was less than enthusiastic.[52]

The major themes of Szilard's stories are the accessibility of reason and the difficulties of rational communication. "The Diary of Dr. Davis" presents entries from a fictitious diary with an anonymous editorial frame dating them from 1948, when John Dewey failed to be elected U.S. president, suggesting the lapse of reason in the electorate. The traumatized Dr. Davis receives a number of visits in the hospital from an American diplomatic envoy to Moscow who reports on meetings with Stalin where he tries to act on his conviction that "something new has come into the world with the atomic bomb."[53] The protagonist functions as an intermediary between the reader and the American diplomat, but in making the character bed-bound, Szilard creates the impression that a willingness to listen to the Russians is tantamount to illness. There is a further complication in the way that the "editor" introduces Dr. Davis: "no single person carries greater responsibility for the fact that the release of atomic energy occurred during the Second World War."[54]

When asked in 1960 whether Americans had a guilt complex because of Hiroshima, Szilard initially said no but then admitted that the fact that John Hersey's *Hiroshima* had such an impact in the United States as compared with Britain was suggestive of this. Otherwise, how can we explain the rationale to Szilard's 1947 narrative "My Trial as a War Criminal"? In this piece Szilard's unnamed narrator is arrested by occupying Russian forces at the end of World War III, forces which demonstrate a liberalism that astonishes him. Szilard evokes a situation that is part alternate history and part reprise of the Nuremberg trials transposed to Lake Success, New York, which was the temporary home of the United Nations. In other words, the situation of the American victors in 1945 is reversed, as they have become the conquered. Szilard himself is put on trial for his part in the events leading up to Hiroshima and documents that might attenuate his role prove to be missing. Szilard's personal guilt, however, shades into a broader American guilt at devising a deadly virus that is dropped on Russia, and even Truman is summoned to trial. In a final ironic twist, the Russians' antivirus vaccine proves useless; deaths and riots follow, and a hasty peace settlement leads to the war trials being abandoned. This ending dissipates the ironic reversal of sides in most of the story, leaving the reader uncertain about what Szilard's point is—to show Russian incompetence? Whatever the answer, the charges of responsibility are left dangling at the end of the story.

"Report on 'Grand Central Terminal'" (written in 1948) is a mock anthropological report compiled by a crew arrived in New York from another planet and headed by the narrator and Xram (i.e., Marx). Their first reaction is one of astonishment: "You can imagine how shocked we were when we landed in this city and found it deserted . . . it turns out—as you have undoubtedly heard—that all life is extinct on this planet."[55] Clearly this is not an alien voice—the speaker has no problems understanding what a city is—but, rather, is a projection of rational inquiry forward to a point after the demise of humanity. How could such a catastrophe have occurred? The investigators then remember having seen some strange flashes on Earth years ago, which signals to the reader that the destruction of humanity was probably caused by a nuclear war. Szilard has transposed rationality from humans on to extraterrestrials as if to imply that it has no place on Earth; the science implicit in the development of nuclear weapons is suppressed and replaced by the more benign practice of anthropology. By leaving New York City apparently unscathed, Szilard erases humanity but preserves the concrete evidence of its culture, thereby allowing the paradox maximum force that an obviously intelligent race has somehow wiped itself out. The fate of humanity is also addressed in "Calling All Stars" (written in 1949), in which a radio message is sent into space by the ultrarational inhabitants of a planet near our own. The message is a query about what they have seen: "We observed on Earth flashes which we have identified as uranium explosions."[56] The message is a double inquiry: Is there life on Earth, and, if so, how could such massive explosions have been caused? There is a deep pessimism underlying this story because it ends on a note of doubt as to whether there are any minds "capable of receiving this message," an obvious enough reference to the receptivity of Szilard's readers. In that sense, "Calling All Stars" embodies the collective purpose of Szilard's fiction as a message "launched" toward an audience of doubtful receptivity.

"The Mined Cities" (1961) was written against a backdrop of escalating tension that would peak the following year with the Cuban missile crisis and Szilard's public speaking at different American universities against the danger of war. The narrative form is that of the "sleeper wakes" pattern, where a character that has been unconscious for eighteen years regains consciousness in 1980. Szilard plays out the role of the sleeper in this piece, which combines a dialogue on disarmament with a prediction of how the Cold War might develop. In the new world he hears that all nuclear missiles have been destroyed except for those buried in an equal number of American and Soviet cities as a mutual deterrent. This has not prevented crises from breaking out, but, when one did, a special direct telephone link was established between both premiers. The hot line was established in 1962 partly at Szilard's suggestion. When the sleeper asks who thought up the mined cities the answer is revealing:

> B. Szilard had proposed it in the *Bulletin of the Atomic Scientists* in 1961, but the idea may not have been original with him. His proposal was presented in the form of fiction and it was not taken seriously.
> A. If he meant his proposal seriously, why didn't he publish it in serious form?
> B. He may have tried and found that no magazine would print it in a serious form.[57]

This passage may suggest Szilard's frustrations stretching back to the abortive memo to Roosevelt, but it clearly indicates a double purpose to Szilard's dialogue-sketch. Ostensibly about strategies to reduce East-West tensions, it also reflects Szilard's difficulties at finding a responsive audience. Readers are thus directed toward the possible impact of the very piece they are reading, and, as if that wasn't enough, the dialogue closes with a brief discussion of the merits of Szilard's short story collection *The Voice of the Dolphins.*

Szilard's major piece in the collection, "The Voice of the Dolphins," grew out of his meeting in 1958 with the biologist John C. Lilly, who in the late 1950s did extended research into cross-species communication between dolphins and humans.[58] Szilard incorporates dolphins into his story to make a comment about humanity; he later stated that "the book is not about the intelligence of the dolphin but about the stupidity of man."[59] The narrative voice Szilard adopts has a clear origin in Wells, even in *The World Set Free,* as Canaday has noted.[60] Taking the reader forward from the historical moment of composition, Szilard describes a nuclear stalemate between the United States and the Soviet Union, with satirical asides on American policy toward Communist China, up to the 1980s, when a general disarmament takes place. A crucial catalyst in this process is the founding in 1963 of the Vienna Biological Research Institute (where Lilly's role is explicitly acknowledged), which is devoted to studying dolphins and their language and where a new food source called Amruss (America + Russia) is devised. It gradually becomes clear that the dolphins are playing an important part behind the scenes in shaping American policy, and the narrator stresses his role as a dispassionate scientific chronicler: "My task here is to appraise the contribution that the dolphins made toward the establishing of lasting peace."[61] Their role is like a parable exposing the inadequacy of political leaders' attention to enlightened scientists and the way the "scientists actually construct the thing to which they submit by training the dolphins in mathematics and the natural sciences."[62] The dolphins are a means to an end for Szilard. Once their aim has been achieved, a virus in the institute kills them off and a fire destroys the library, so that both the experimental subjects and the history of the experiments are wiped out.

The elaborate guises and masks Szilard adopts in his fiction reflect the complexity of his attitude toward the paradox that science was a force for enlightenment but also the means for humanity to destroy itself. His biographer William Lanouette documents Szilard's faith in the powers of human reason and his view that the individuals and elites who run the world only need to be educated to ensure peace. But his stories demonstrate the sheer difficulty, if not impossibility, of that process.

CHAPTER 2

The Dawn of the Atomic Age—
The Bomb and Hiroshima

We have seen that as soon as novels attempted to describe nuclear war, ambiguities and tensions began to emerge between the destructive capability of the new bombs and the utopian hopes invested in radioactivity as an energy source. The title of this chapter borrows from the rhetoric that came into play to describe the atom bomb once it had been successfully tested. H. Bruce Franklin has shown in his *War Stars* that Americans had been fantasizing about a super weapon since the late nineteenth century, and, once fantasy had become actualized in the atom bomb, a profound ambivalence began to run through their reactions to it, which wavered between celebrating it and being horrified at its new destructive power. A consensus rapidly emerged that the success of the atom bomb marked a turning point in the nature of warfare. The issue of *Life* magazine devoted to the Hiroshima bombing exemplifies this, with a feature declaring that "Aug. 5, 1945 is the day men formally began a new epoch in their history."[1]

Paul Boyer has shown in his classic study of the bomb's impact on the American imagination, *By the Bomb's Early Light,* that, even though there might have been popular acceptance of the bombing, the event was very quickly transposed onto the American scene in a whole series of accounts of atomic attack.[2] The two most widely read early commentators on the atomic bomb are William L. Laurence and John Hersey. Although both writers were journalists, they approached the event from the opposite perspectives of producer and victim and, not surprisingly, drew on equally opposing conventions of representation. From the very beginning, the atom bomb presented a radical challenge over how it could be described, a challenge to language itself.

As soon as Roosevelt decided to press ahead with the Manhattan Project, a total clampdown was imposed on all information relating to it. At the same time, however, the director of security, General Leslie R. Groves, invited the *New York Times* journalist William L. Laurence to become the Project's official chronicler. Laurence had already established a reputation as a science journalist, and Groves made the following unusual arrangement: "It seemed desirable for security reasons, as well as easier for the employer, to have Laurence continue on the payroll of the *New York Times,* but with his expenses to be covered by the MED [Manhattan Engineer District]."[3] Part of Laurence's brief was to prepare press releases of the Alamagordo test and the Hiroshima bombing in advance of the events, the latter used by President Truman and Secretary of War Henry L. Stimson. Laurence was an eyewitness at Alamagordo but arrived on Tinian Island too late to be included in the observer plane for Hiroshima, though he did witness the Nagasaki bombing. On the strength of his dispatches he was awarded the Pulitzer Prize for journalism in 1946. Laurence was certainly given a unique journalistic opportunity, earning him the nickname "Atomic Bill," but at the same time he was put in a position where he could hardly afford to be critical of the enterprise. Every dispatch was checked for security issues, which must have meant that Laurence was denied one of the main resources of a journalist—the use of circumstantial detail that gives a story its authenticity.

Laurence was thus caught between revelation and concealment, and one result was for him, as Ken Cooper argues, to "formulate a mythology of the atomic bomb."[4] When Laurence visited the Hanford nuclear reactors in Washington State, he was already formulating a characteristic vocabulary that was to inform his account of the Manhattan Project. He rhapsodized over the "primeval majesty" of the power plants, depicting them as timeless "Promethean structures, which may well stand as eternal monuments to the spirit of man challenging nature, [where] mighty cosmic forces are at work such as had never been let loose on this planet in the 3,000 million years of the earth's being."[5] Through key epithets like "primeval," "Promethean," and "titanic," Laurence abstracts the installations from a specific historical and military context and eternalizes them in a grandiose epic of humanity's drive to uncover the secrets of nature. He casts himself as an apocalyptic witness granted a privileged glimpse of this massive and silent factory complex. But of course the historical context is only temporarily suspended, and Laurence's ringing rhetoric none too implicitly endorses a national undertaking by replacing the lone mythical hero with the United States. Similarly, when Laurence turns his attention to nuclear bombs, his exploitation of the apocalyptic paradigm underlines the patriotic implications of his accounts.

Laurence's description of the Alamagordo explosion is framed in biblical accounts of creation. The countdown is delivered by a "voice ringing through the darkness, sounding as though it had come from above the clouds." With the observation that bombers cannot be seen, it becomes all the easier for Laurence to blank out the enormous technological enterprise of the Manhattan Project and to depict the event as if the observers are witnessing a cataclysm of nature:

> And just at that instant there rose from the bowels of the earth a light not of this world, the light of many suns in one. It was a sunrise such as the world had never seen, a great green super-sun climbing in a fraction of a second to a height of more than 8,000 feet, rising ever higher until it touched the clouds, lighting up earth and sky all around with a dazzling luminosity.
>
> Up it went, a great ball of fire about a mile in diameter, changing colours as it kept shooting upward . . . It was as though the earth had opened and the skies had split. One felt as though one were present at the moment of creation when God said: "Let there be light."
>
> A great cloud rose from the ground and followed the trail of the great sun. At first it was a giant column, which soon took the shape of a supramundane mushroom. For a fleeting instant it took the form of the Statue of Liberty magnified many times.[6]

The dawn is transformed into an apocalyptic spectacle of liberation poised ambiguously between beginnings and endings, birth and destruction. Laurence mythologizes the event by implying that the scientists are repeating the act of creation through the bomb's sudden manifestation of the primal element of light, and the scientific concept of fission is transformed into an opening of nature itself. Laurence's extension of the dawn suggests a multiple beginning, which casts the most positive gloss on the bomb, totally concealing its status as a weapon bringing multiple deaths, an ultimate ending. Through the use of a national icon, the dawn of the atomic age comes to signify a dawn of American military and political supremacy. Laurence does not actually use Henry Luce's 1941 phrase "the American Century," but the implication is clear. For Laurence the Trinity test of 16 July 1945 represented the triumph of U.S. technology and military might. In his books about nuclear weapons, he placed their development within a grand narrative that included the flight of European scientists from Hitler's forces, the discovery of nuclear fission, the organization of the Manhattan Project, and the development of the atomic and hydrogen bombs.[7]

Early comments on the atom bomb reflected an ambivalence. For instance, the editor of the victory issue of *Time* magazine reflected ominously that many might be celebrating but "in the dark depths of their minds and hearts, huge forms moved and silently arranged themselves: Titans arranging out of the chaos an age in which victory was already only the shout of a child in the street."[8] Truman wondered if it represented the "fire of destruction" prophesied in the Bible, but in his public announcement after the Hiroshima bombing declared that it represented a "harnessing of the basic power of the universe." Similarly, press reports expressed satisfaction but fear for the future: "Yesterday we clinched victory in the Pacific, but we sowed the whirlwind"; "we are dealing with an invention that could overwhelm civilization"; and so on.[9] Laurence confines such fears in *Dawn Over Zero* mainly to the countervoice of another observer who sees the explosion as the "nearest thing to doomsday that one could possibly imagine"—in other words, as the ultimate ending, not a new beginning.

Laurence popularized a pattern of iconography (fireball, mushroom cloud, etc.) that recurs in later accounts of bomb blasts and, in the process, highlighted a basic problem of representation: how to articulate action that happens in a millionth of a second and how to capture the sheer scale of the event.[10] Laurence had to rely on the eyewitness accounts of others for Hiroshima. One crew member of the *Enola Gay* stressed the impression of boiling clouds as the mushroom took shape, while another recorded orally the moment-by-moment proliferation of fires and compared the mushroom to a "mass of bubbling molasses."[11] Laurence did, however, see the bombing of Nagasaki and focused his description of that event on the metaphorical transformations of a "pillar of purple fire":

> Awestruck, we watched it shoot upward like a meteor coming from the earth instead of from outer space, becoming ever more alive as it climbed skyward through the white clouds. It was no longer smoke, or dust, or even a cloud of fire. It was a living thing, a new species of being, born right before our eyes.
>
> At one stage of its evolution, covering millions of years in terms of seconds, the entity assumed the form of a giant square totem pole, with its base about three miles long, tapering off to about a mile at the top. Its bottom was brown, its center amber, its top white.
>
> Then, just when it appeared as though the thing had settled down into a state of permanence, there came shooting out of the top a giant mushroom that increased the height of the pillar to a total of 45,000 feet.

The mushroom top was even more alive than the pillar, seething and boiling in a white fury of creamy foam, sizzling upward and then descending earthward, a thousand geysers rolled into one.

It kept struggling in an elemental fury, like a creature in the act of breaking the bonds that held it down. In a few seconds it had freed itself from its gigantic stem and floated upwards with tremendous speed, its momentum carrying it into the stratosphere to a height of about sixty thousand feet.[12]

Unlike the crewman of the *Enola Gay,* Laurence makes no mention of the city being destroyed and concentrates instead entirely on the creation of a new form of life. His awe before this sublime spectacle is given an implicitly sexual articulation through the orgasm and birthing of a titanic monster. In his discussion of the nuclear sublime, Frances Ferguson has argued that "it imagines freedom to be threatened by a power that is consistently mislocated," which would apply to the passage above.[13] Despite Laurence's evident awe at the spectacle of the nuclear cloud, he describes it as a monstrous entity not quite formed but threatening and difficult to locate. The negative implications of his metaphors are held in check by his evocation of the spectacle.

Laurence had few reservations about nuclear weaponry and was undismayed by the testing of the hydrogen bomb in Bikini Atoll. His 1951 study *The Hell Bomb* is significantly less gung-ho than his account of the Manhattan Project, partly because the world situation had changed for the worse. His book was published just after the outbreak of the Korean War, and one of the possibilities Laurence considers is that now the United States might find itself in the position Japan was in just before the bombing of Hiroshima. Accordingly, he denounces unilateral disarmament that would "destroy the shield that now protects civilization as we know it" and expresses his conviction that "good will prevail . . . over the forces of evil . . . that the four freedoms will triumph over the Four Horsemen of the Apocalypse."[14] (His words come to be absurdly echoed by the paranoid officer in *Dr. Strangelove,* who launches a nuclear strike against the Soviet Union.)

No sooner had the bombings of Hiroshima and Nagasaki taken place than General MacArthur slapped a security blackout on southern Japan. Despite this, two journalists managed to get through: the Australian Wilfred Burchett, who reported on Hiroshima, and George Weller, who reported on Nagasaki for the *Chicago Daily News.* Miraculously, Burchett's dispatch reached London's *Daily Express,* which published it on 6 September 1945 under the headline "The Atomic Plague." This report, which has become one of the classics of investigative journalism, was phrased as a "warning to the world" about the atomic bomb and claimed that residual radiation was still claiming victims. It opened: "In Hiroshima, 30 days after the first atomic bomb destroyed the city and shook the world, people are still dying, mysteriously and horribly—people who were uninjured in the cataclysm from an unknown something which I can only describe as the atomic plague."[15] Burchett's grim account of multiple illnesses from radiation poisoning and water pollution, among other causes, carried firsthand authenticity and was implicitly confirmed when he challenged an American officer in a Tokyo news conference who was claiming that stories of radiation sickness were "Japanese propaganda." Shortly after this, Hiroshima was closed to journalists and Burchett was expelled from Japan.[16]

In order to refute this negative report, General Groves arranged for a group of journalists, including the faithful Laurence, to visit the New Mexico test site. Accordingly, on 12 September 1945 Laurence published his own report on this visit to the "cradle of a new era in civilization" under the bold headline "U.S. ATOM BOMB SITE BELIES TOKYO TALES." Unlike Burchett's dispatch, this one is almost entirely the summary of others' views—those of General Groves, other officers, and scientists. Laurence writes entirely as a spokesman for the U.S. Army and concludes that "the Japanese are still continuing their propaganda aimed at creating the impression that we won the war unfairly and thus attempting to create sympathy for themselves."[17] The whole purpose of the article was not to offer the reader news so much as to endorse the official line on radiation in Hiroshima, which was being done thousands of miles from the city itself. There the matter rested until 2004, when the journalists Amy Goodman and David Goodman called for Laurence to be stripped of his Pulitzer Prize on the basis that he collaborated in a U.S. government cover-up of the effects of radiation in the Japan bombings.

Authorities were more successful in controlling George Weller, whose dispatches from Nagasaki were suppressed and remained unpublished until 2005, despite their deliberate avoidance of what he called "horror angles."[18] One reason for this was that Weller quixotically submitted them directly to the authorities instead of trying to smuggle them out. His account tallies with Burchett's in recording the destruction as well as, and more importantly, information about what a Dutch medical officer called "Disease X," the radiation sickness that the U.S. authorities were trying to hide. Looking back, Weller has stressed: "That was a central fact that I wanted to get out—that the effect of the bomb was not fire, not frying of the whole body, except in the cases of those who had the misfortune to be directly under it. It was the death of the platelets. And it was a slow death."[19] Weller collected eyewitness accounts of the bombing from Allied prisoners of war, rarely quoted by the Japanese themselves, and studiously avoided any dramatization of the destruction. Piecing accounts together, he portrayed the city immediately after the blast as a "great, flattened area of industrial slum. It was a sea of rubble, timbers at all angles, cries coming from under them." Then gradually fires start, and "finally it was all one fire . . . Hence the revolting cost of lives."[20] It would be difficult to imagine a starker contrast between this bleak ground-level image and Laurence's awe before the atomic cloud.

The first book to appear about Hiroshima was assembled from a series of reports by John Hersey. In the early months of 1946, Hersey was on assignment in northern China reporting on the American marine bases there and on how peace was affecting rural society. Then he got his opportunity, the chance to produce what was originally planned to be a four-part report on Hiroshima that would end up taking up the entire *New Yorker* for 31 August 1946, be published as a book, and become an immediate best-seller.[21] Before turning to that work, however, we need to consider an intermediary text that Hersey read and used. Several months before Hersey's *Hiroshima*, there appeared in the *Saturday Review* an article by the German Jesuit John A. Siemes entitled "Hiroshima: Eye-Witness," which superficially resembles the narrative of a single individual in Hersey's book. Siemes's account anticipated the broad sequence of Hersey's study in starting with the Japanese expectation of a special weapon on Hiroshima, an hour-by-hour description of the explosion and rescue work, and a conclusion noting the surprising lack of anti-American feeling and speculating mildly on the ethics of the super bomb. Siemes clearly intended to capture the immediacy of the event by writing most of his account in the present tense, but the effect was rather different, as evident in his description of the explosion:

> Suddenly—the time is approximately 8:15—the whole valley is filled by a garish light which resembles the magnesium light used in photography, and I am conscious of a wave of heat. I jump to the window to find out the cause of this remarkable phenomenon, but I see nothing more than that brilliant yellow light. As I make for the door, it doesn't occur to me that the light might have something to do with enemy planes. On the way from the window, I hear a moderately loud explosion which seems to come from a distance and, at the same time, the windows are broken in with a loud crash. There has been an interval of perhaps ten seconds since the flash of light. I am sprayed by fragments of glass. The entire window frame has been forced into the room. I realize now that a bomb has burst and I am under the impression that it exploded directly over our house or in the immediate vicinity.[22]

Siemes awkwardly tries to combine immediacy with precision, but his account only captures some of the sensory impressions that must have run well ahead of any witness's capacity to draw inferences. He gives an effect of running commentary on his own actions, as if watching himself at every second, and the effect of instantaneity is constantly being belied by details that must only have become clear after the event. Nevertheless, Siemes does effectively capture the suddenness of the strike and the resulting confusion.

A progression takes place in Siemes's account from personal glimpses to the assembly of an overall narration. This progression is traced out as a physical journey from the Catholic Novitiate (some two miles outside Hiroshima) toward the center of the city. As the day after the blast dawns, he sees before him a scene of utter devastation: "Where the city stood, everything, as far as the eye can reach, is a waste of ashes and ruin. Only several skeletons of buildings remain. The banks of the river are covered with dead and wounded, and the rising waters have here and there covered some of the corpses."[23] The sublime effects of the bomb blast described by Laurence and others depend on a vertical expansion that dwarfs the observer. Here, by contrast, Siemes gives us a panorama that expands the field of vision laterally toward an unidentifiable horizon. The impact now is not awe but a dislocation arising from the eye's incapacity to see limits to this expanse. And far from being pure spectacle, buildings and inhabitants collapse together in a common reduction to ruin and inert matter. This visual moment is one of the most powerful in an account that had an impact on Hersey, who, when he arrived in Hiroshima, was introduced to Siemes's other witnesses.

In addition to drawing on Siemes, *Hiroshima* was partly modeled on Thornton Wilder's 1927 novel *The Bridge of San Luis Rey*, which Hersey read during a bout of illness on a U.S. destroyer and which uses the disaster of a collapsed bridge over a gorge in Peru to examine the meaning of the catastrophe.[24] A Catholic cleric, Brother Juniper, sets out to try to understand whether the disaster was pure chance or the result of some plan in the universe.[25] Wilder assembles three consecutive narratives of the victims' lives, which all converge on the final moment of the disaster (a method since turned into cliché by disaster narratives). Hersey modifies Wilder's method in a number of important respects. First, there is no Brother Juniper; his role is implicitly woven into the narrative voice. Second, Hersey deals with survivors not fatalities. Third, he counterpoints these characters' destinies against each other in a form of montage. Of course, the analogy with Wilder's narrative could only be approximate, since the bombing was self-evidently a planned act and not an accident.

By 1945 Hersey was known for his journalistic reports on the war published in magazines like *Life* and *Time,* many of which were in novel form, such as *Men on Bataan* (1942) or *Into the Valley* (1943). By 1946, of course, the larger war narrative that Hersey could earlier take for granted had concluded and a new era had come into being. William Laurence made no bones about witnessing a radical historical change, starting his essay "The Atomic Age Begins" as he did: "I watched the birth of the atomic age from the slope of a hill in the desert land of New Mexico." And Spencer Weart has shown that the metaphor of the nuclear bomb as a baby "delivered" from its maternal carrier by male technology very quickly became institutionalized after Hiroshima.[26] And similarly, John Siemes's account of the bombing was already packaged in the *Saturday Review* as an "Atomic Age" byline complete with the famous atomic nucleus logo and punctuated by triumphalist graphics celebrating America's military might.

Hersey made every effort to avoid such triumphalism by focusing on the plight of victims, five Japanese and one German Jesuit. None of the characters appears to have made any contribution to military activity; instead, they are described as civilians with their own domestic and professional worries. In countless ways Hersey familiarizes these characters to his Western readers, only interrupting his narratives to point out instances of cultural difference, like the Japanese treatment of their dead or their concept of shame. Part of the book's polemic consists of the steady accumulation of details that forces the reader to situate herself imaginatively in the victims' daily lives. The narrative method he uses is strategic. For David Sanders, "Hersey's account . . . is strictly limited to the 'visual horizon' of his six survivors; and it so skilfully renders the details of that horizon as to establish suspense for even his best informed readers."[27] Clearly deciding from the beginning that no overview of the bombing was possible, Hersey gives us a montage of victims' impressions, inviting the reader to cross-relate them and draw what limited inferences might be possible.

The first chapter of *Hiroshima* compresses the sort of narrative sequence traced out by Thornton Wilder, where the catastrophe in *The Bridge of San Luis Rey* functions teleologically as an end point marking a sudden termination to their lives. For Hersey's six survivors, however, the bomb blast marked a single sudden disruption to their lives. *Hiroshima* is all about consequences. For instance, Hersey describes the experience of Miss Toshiko Sasaki, a clerk in the East Asia Tin Works:

> Everything fell, and Miss Sasaki lost consciousness. The ceiling dropped suddenly and the wooden floor above collapsed in splinters and the people up there came down and the roof above them gave way; but principally and first of all, the bookcases right behind her swooped forward and the contents threw her down, with her left leg horribly twisted and breaking underneath

her. There, in the tin factory, in the first moment of the atomic age, a human being was crushed by books.[28]

Superficially this passage gives an impression of stylistic simplicity, of paratactic syntax where each event is given the same priority. As in early Hemingway, however, the style masks its own sophistication. The two most frequent verbs in *Hiroshima* are not surprisingly "fall" and "throw."[29] Structures and humans alike collapse, and individuals are literally and metaphorically thrown out of their routine lives into a predicament of common need. Here a series of falls occur within which Hersey, not Miss Sasaki, readjusts the chronology and prioritizes that of the bookcases because of their symbolic potential. Boyer has shrewdly remarked that Hersey quietly recognizes the problematic nature of style in this situation by consistently referring to books as an irrelevance.[30] Indeed, if books are taken as a privileged sign of civilization, then Hersey renders the clerk's fate as an ironic parabolic image of humanity being destroyed by its own culture.

Hersey himself later explained that he had deliberately avoided moralizing or preaching, preferring to "help readers to find their own deepest feelings about this new instrument of killing," and had chosen a "flat style" to avoid giving the reader an overt sense of mediation.[31] But we have already seen how the style covertly guides the reader to take up positions with regard to the bombing. It is this veiled appropriation of his witnesses by Hersey that Alan Nadel has cogently criticized. First, he declares that Hersey is claiming more narrative authority than he is entitled to; then he blanks out the mediation of the witnesses' accounts through interview and recollection; and, finally, he gives no clues about the process of editorial selection that took place in the composition of his account.[32] While Nadel is certainly right that there is a complex process of selection and assembly lying behind Hersey's narrative, there is no way that his reportage could avoid being mediated. Rhetorically, the third person constantly reminds us of the presence of an unnamed observer, but, given the situation, where Hersey was a member of the conquering and occupying forces, it is amazing how little that tension shows itself in his text.

Hiroshima opens with a collective query: How could these six have survived? Here another connection with Wilder emerges. Brother Juniper is haunted in compiling his narrative by the "fear that in omitting the slightest detail he might lose some guiding hint" and as a result attempts a ludicrously encyclopedic account.[33] Hersey's characters are similarly bemused by the "small items of chance or volition" that might explain their own survival—hence, Hersey's extraordinary care to specify their exact positions at the moment of the bomb blast, because a few inches nearer or farther from a window, for example, could be the difference between life and death. Dwight Macdonald totally misunderstood the work when he objected that Hersey had "no eye for the one detail that imaginatively creates a whole" because a whole is exactly what the survivors cannot glimpse.[34] The bomb blast is now apocalyptic not as visual spectacle but in bringing about a sudden and total rupture in their lives, in bringing a disorientation figured through sudden movement. One character is "thrown forward and around and over"; another finds his room reduced to "weird and illogical confusion."[35] *Hiroshima* thus describes a drama of bewilderment where characters are suddenly cut off from relatives, possessions, and habitations and forced, as a result, to search for what is lost.

Although Hersey divides his book into approximate phases, these are chiefly characterized by their narrative *dis*continuity.

> Much later, several men came and dragged Miss Sasaki out. Her left leg was not severed, but it was badly broken and cut and it hung askew below the knee. They took her out into a courtyard. It was raining. She sat on the ground in the rain. When the downpour increased, someone directed all the wounded people to take cover in the factory's air-raid shelters. "Come along," a torn-up woman said to her. "You can hop." But Miss Sasaki could not move, and she just waited in the rain. Then a man propped up a large sheet of corrugated iron as a kind of lean-to and took her in his arms and carried her to it. She was grateful until he brought two horribly wounded people—a woman with a whole breast sheared off and a man whose face was all raw from a burn—to share the simple shed with her. No one came back. The rain cleared and the cloudy afternoon was hot; before nightfall the three grotesques under the slanting piece of twisted iron began to smell quite bad.[36]

In these lines Hersey captures the isolated dependency of a war casualty by using a Hemingwayesque syntax of short simple statements. Because she has been rendered helpless and immobile, Miss Sasaki must wait for help that is rendered by a series of unnamed figures who themselves, like the "torn-up woman," might be casualties. This account becomes a study of absolute contingency where help might or might not come. *Hiroshima* then foregrounds discontinuous images in order to convey the rupturing of perceptions of reality brought about by the bomb. Expectations are always reversed. A shelter turns out not to have offered protection against wounding, and casualties' features become transformed—eyes into tears, mouths into wounds, and so on. "Grotesques" represents a lapse on Hersey's part, obtrusively drawing a conclusion that his understated method makes unnecessary.

The survivors' experience is disabled twice over by their separation from each other and from the virtual inaccessibility of the news media. At the time of the bomb, expectations were rife of an imminent bombing or even invasion by the Americans. Accordingly, the survivors latched on to single characteristics of the atom bomb in order to make sense of their experience. The scale of the blast was reduced to self-scattering bombs; the smell of ionized air to a gas attack; and the flash to magnesium powder (the last of these being dreamt up by a newspaper reporter). The absence of the media is not presented as a simple lack of information but, rather, as another example of an absurd discontinuity between official statements and the survivors' experience: "Even if they had known the truth, most of them would have been too busy or too weary or too badly hurt to care that they were the objects of the first great experiment in the use of atomic power, which (as the voices on the short-wave shouted) no country except the United States, with its industrial know-how, its willingness to throw two billion gold dollars into an important wartime gamble, could possibly have developed."[37] Once again Hersey ironically distances himself from the celebratory descriptions of the beginning of the atomic age as a triumph of American military and industrial know-how.

A passage like this cannot be explained by William J. Scheick's complaint that Hersey uses a double voice in *Hiroshima*: "There seem to be . . . two contrary vectors in the same narrative voice in his account: the existential manner of a dispassionate observer concerned with philosophical insight into humanity and the humanistic manner of a childlike victim dazed in reaction to a traumatizing concrete situation." For Scheick, this is a sign of the postwar period because the latter aspect "at the same time represents the anomie and loss of affect that are Cold-War phenomena."[38] In a sense, Scheick is complaining about a rhetorical doubleness in Hersey's use of third-person free indirect discourse that enables him to move in and out of his survivors' consciousnesses, sometimes using them as temporary angles of vision and at other times describing them as if seen by another. It would be inconceivable for there *not* to be some doubleness in Hersey's narrative voice, since he was attempting the difficult task of describing the experiences of a cultural group until very recently thought of as the enemy for members of the very nation that manufactured and dropped the bomb. Hersey manages this delicate balancing act by distancing himself from the occupying U.S. authorities, drily noting that more information on the atom bomb was circulating in Japan than in the United States.

Etymologically "apocalypse" denotes an uncovering or revelation, which helps to explain why, for all their differences, Laurence and Hersey are profoundly visual writers, although each concentrates on different spatial areas. Laurence scans the skies while Hersey keeps his perspectives fixed at ground level. For Laurence what is revealed is a new entity, a new embodiment of force; while Hersey sees apocalypse in the radical disruption of civilian life. When one of his witnesses tells another that "things don't matter any more," he is identifying a breakdown in the system of commodities that is giving way to greater and more pressing human need. Both Laurence and Hersey present the bomb as a sudden rupture of the natural order. American witnesses to the bomb blast all agreed, for instance, that the flash was like a "super-sun." Hersey finds a more complex set of features that do not rely only on magnitude. Now destruction seems freakishly inconsistent: dress patterns transferred onto the bodies of survivors; the outlines of those near ground zero imprinted on walls; the sudden growth of plants in the ruins. Like Siemes, Hersey works toward a lateral panorama of Hiroshima that suggests in still life a complex continuity rather than a total ending. The human dwellings have been the most thoroughly destroyed ("range on range of collapsed city blocks"), and they establish a background for the surviving structures:

> Naked trees and canted telephone poles; the few standing, gutted buildings only accentuating the horizontality of everything else (the Museum of Science and Industry, with its dome stripped to its steel frame, as if for an autopsy; the modern Chamber of Commerce Building, its tower as cold, rigid, and unas-sailable after the blow as before; the huge, low-lying, camouflaged city hall; the row of dowdy banks, caricaturing a shaken economic system); and in the streets a macabre traffic—hundreds of crumpled bicycles, shells of streetcars and automobiles, all halted in mid-motion.[39]

This image occurs in the book immediately after Japan's surrender, and it totally avoids triumphalism by being focalized through a German Jesuit, through the eyes of one outside the economic and political system of Japan. Hersey implies that the only winner is a commercial structure (and a financial one; the banks are "shaken" but essentially intact) indifferent to the human casualties. The "traffic" in the streets mimics city life as if frozen in a snapshot but is rendered grotesque by the total absence of human beings. Once again we have a tense combination of life and death. The scene itself denotes both destruction and survival; but, even more importantly, it is focalized through a survivor coming to terms with a cataclysmic event.

Here we can locate the key differences between Hersey and Laurence. The latter mythologizes a finite event through rhetoric and imagery that uncritically support America's pride in its military superiority at the beginning of the Cold

War. Hersey, however, stresses how Hiroshima ruptured the lives of his chosen survivors. In 1985 he added a sequel to his original account, "Aftermath," which does not generalize the implications of his original study but modifies it in two important aspects. Early official reports on Hiroshima and Nagasaki, for obvious reasons, attempted to minimize the damage caused by radiation, but Hersey takes Father Kleinsorge as a case study to demonstrate, as Robert Jungk does in his *Children of the Ashes* (1961), that the bombing was an ongoing catastrophe. Kleinsorge endured for the rest of his life a relentless series of painful ailments that constantly baffled the doctors by their seeming illogicality, and he only found relief in death. Hersey also uses the pastor Tanimoto to demonstrate the ironies in media processes. Because MacArthur had forbidden the release of information on the two bombings within Japan, Tanimoto could only campaign about their effects when abroad, specifically when in the United States.[40]

Hiroshima is an open-ended text, explicitly an interim report, and in his coda Hersey looks toward the future when reflecting, "It would be impossible to say what horrors were embedded in the minds of the children who lived through the day of the bombing in Hiroshima."[41] Daniel Cordle has argued rightly that Hersey sees the city "as a fragile environment, suspended forever before a moment capable of shattering it into a post-nuclear world."[42] Exactly what "postnuclear" might mean has been picked up repeatedly by successive novels about the Manhattan Project and the bombings. In 1955 Dexter Masters published *The Accident,* which described the death from radiation of scientists engaged in a secret Manhattan-like project but was dedicated symbolically to the victims of Hiroshima and Nagasaki.[43] Indeed, the slow painful death of the scientist is presented throughout as a single case analogous to the bombings, and therefore the novel intervenes in the ongoing debate about radiation sickness.[44]

Since Hersey's famous reportage, subsequent narratives of the dropping of the atom bomb have attempted to explore the symbolic and psychological importance of the event for American culture. Leigh Kennedy's *Saint Hiroshima* (1987), for instance, describes how a young girl's imagination is dominated by early TV images of nuclear tests and later of Hiroshima itself. A rare exception to this national emphasis has been *The Flowers of Hiroshima,* by the Swedish-born campaigner for nuclear disarmament Edita Morris, which describes how the inhabitants of Hiroshima scarred or diseased by the bombing had become social unmentionables. The novel is narrated by a Japanese woman who lived through the bombing and who has a hallucinatory sense of being accompanied by the ghosts of that time: "Fourteen years ago I ran down these streets with the fleeing throng. For fourteen years they've kept running inside my head, but tonight they're back in

Hiroshima, racing beside me, their faces blackened, their torn skin hanging from their shoulders. I recognize them, like people I've seen in a nightmare. That girl with her whole face burnt away—that man carrying his wife on his back—ran by my side then also."[45] The novel describes the gradual surfacing of these memories and in that sense performs an act of remembrance. Also, the fact that the narrator is Japanese in a novel aimed primarily at a Western readership brings the feelings of the victims powerfully home to the reader.

Jay Cantor's *Krazy Kat* merges the conventions of the comic strip with the novel by making the cartoon character into a witness to American history in the nuclear age. Cantor himself has explained his purpose as being an attempt to "assimilate" the bomb into American culture.[46] The novel, constructed in five "panels," opens with the Alamagordo test blast, seen by Krazy Kat and Ignatz Mouse. This event brings about a symbolic fall from innocence whereby the two characters come to resemble humans, especially in their contradictions. Their actions are described toward the end of the novel as embodying the common human "acceptance *and* the fear of death."[47] Their new perspective on America is ingeniously constructed, but the risk in Cantor's experiment lies in its treatment of violence. Cartoon violence tends to be neutralized by the comic strip format, which shows characters emerging unscathed from disasters. More importantly, the panels have an inevitable effect of containment. The first panel, "The Gadget" (Oppenheimer's term for the experimental device), shows Kat in the foreground reflecting miserably on the bomb blast in the background. This effect is even more visible in the cover illustration to the 1988 Collier edition, which shows Ignatz as a psychotherapist taking notes from a session with Kat who is lying on a couch; between them is a window through which a bomb blast can be seen. Kat is doubly framed as a represented subject by the illustration panel and by the window, which suggests her nuclear psychosis.

Cantor's use of a cartoon figure to comment on the bomb anticipates by several years James Morrow's reinvention of Godzilla in his novel *Shambling Towards Hiroshima*. Influenced by Robert Jay Lifton and Greg Mitchell's reappraisal of the decision to drop the bombs on Japan, *Hiroshima in America: Fifty Years of Denial* (1995), Morrow originally planned a rather moralistic novel but then drew on the Godzilla story to devise "a secret biological-weapons initiative overseen by the Navy in tandem with the Army's Manhattan Project. The Knickerbocker Project reaches its climax in 1945, bringing forth a generation of giant mutant amphibious bipedal fire-breathing iguanas just in time to influence—perhaps—the outcome of the Pacific War."[48] By imagining a monster movie made to persuade the Japanese to surrender by showing a city destroyed by a huge lizard, Morrow pays tribute to the similar movies of the 1950s and also literalizes Susan Sontag's famous argument in her essay "The Imagination of Disaster" that monster films offered oblique ways of commenting on the bomb. Their aestheticization of disaster, for her, offered a morally acceptable imagery of destruction, whereas in Morrow's novel the composition of a Godzilla-like movie is actually designed to forestall the very event that, according to Sontag, would motivate the increased popularity of that film genre.[49]

The ambivalence of Cantor's *Krazy Kat* is shared more dramatically by Lydia Millet's *Oh Pure and Radiant Heart*, which bridges the chronological gap between the first detonations of the atom bomb and the novel's compositional present by showing three leading members of the Manhattan Project—Oppenheimer, Szilard, and Fermi—translated in time to the year 2003. This device confronts the scientists with the ultimate consequences of their research, not only through the many ways in which the bomb has become institutionalized but also when they are taken to Hiroshima and Nagasaki.[50] *Oh Pure and Radiant Heart* assembles a montage of narrative segments and historical interpolations to produce an extended meditation on the symbolic importance of the bomb where three of its designers are interrogated about their motives. Millet's main contrast falls between Szilard, a self-regarding personification of scientific intelligence, and Oppenheimer, whom she sees as later betrayed by America (and Szilard, among others) during the McCarthy hearings. The narrative is filtered through the author's surrogate, Ann, a librarian and historian of the postwar period who enters the novel dreaming of Oppenheimer at the first atomic blast. Oppenheimer himself shifts from creator to casualty as Ann's dream shifts from visual spectacle to destruction. At first, she attempts to naturalize the famous mushroom cloud image into one of growth and protection:

And on the horizon the fireball rose, spreading silently. In the spreading she felt peace, peace and what came before, as though the country beneath her, with its wide prairies, had been returned to the wild. She saw the cloud churning and growing, majestic and broad, and thought: No, not a mushroom, but a tree. A great and ancient tree, growing and sheltering us all. [Then the trope of creation becomes reversed.] At this point in the scene she confused it with the Bible. The man named Oppenheimer saw what he had made, and it was beautiful. But when he looked at it, the light burned out his eyes and turned him blind.

She saw the rolling balls of the eyes when he righted himself to face the tree, and they were white like eggs.[51]

This dream encapsulates the culture's fearful obsession with the bomb. When asked about her subject, Millet explained it as growing from her "fascination with the nuclear sublime," which she then described in the following way: "I mean the poetic and transcendent power of the mushroom cloud as an image and a phenomenon—its terrible beauty. What captivates me is how terrible can be beautiful, how it feels to be floored by something at once dreadful and lovely."[52]

The problem with applying this notion to Millet's novel is revealed in its very historicity, for she recognizes that the visual imagery of the bomb was very limited and largely confined to certain stills and sequences declassified by the security authorities. The powerful opening sequence quoted above is not repeated, since the novel works by a gradual accretion of personal and public details. Indeed, in his discussion of the concept of the nuclear sublime, Frances Ferguson has argued that "the notion of the sublime is continuous with the notion of nuclear holocaust: to think the sublime would be to think the unthinkable and to exist in one's own nonexistence."[53] For Ferguson the very concept of the sublime not only assumes scale but positions itself between absence and presence. The passage quoted in the preceding paragraph renders this ambivalence through a moment of vision that becomes a moment of blinding. The dream figure shifts abruptly from witness to casualty, displacing witness onto the dreamer herself.

Oppenheimer occupies the same special position in *Oh Pure and Radiant Heart* as he does in James Thackara's novel *America's Children,* a carefully researched account of the physicist's life from the beginning of the Manhattan Project up to the removal of his security clearance in the 1950s. Just as early reports of the designers of the bomb presented them as "modern Prometheans," so Thackara deploys the Faust story to give shape to Oppenheimer's extraordinary ambition. The narrative opens with Oppenheimer gazing over the edge of a canyon in the Rio Grande contemplating the "revolutionary dawn" of a new era.[54] Rival perspectives on the new power, which the atomic scientists are presented as stealing from nature, range from the religious to the Marxist to the national. At the Trinity test, Oppenheimer, looking backward, sees a "strange new light" and registers a nonperception among his colleagues: "But no one saw it, no one saw."[55] Despite their intellectual brilliance, the scientists are America's children in the sense that they are innocents abroad, blind to the new security state that their work is bringing into being. Thackara shows not one but three pivotal moments: the Trinity blast, the bombing of Hiroshima (the birth of a "new hell"), and the detonation of the H-bomb. At the moment of detonation, the language shifts into a biblical register: "Then again the bleached white light was upon the face of the firmament."[56] The apocalyptic imagery implies a travesty of nature, but there is a more insidious process at work.

As the "modern power-state" takes shape, America is transformed gradually into a monstrous political entity that devours its own children, and this process explains the final section of Thackara's novel. Here the investigation of Oppenheimer marks a culmination of a power struggle between rival agencies, Stalin's betrayal of the Communist ideal, and many other factors.

The atomic bombings of Hiroshima and Nagasaki remain an enigma in that they are events still being examined for their true significance, and Kim Stanley Robinson has taken them as his prime examples in a meditation on causality and the nature of history, speculating about alternative courses that events could have followed.[57] In his survey of cultural treatments of the bombing of Hiroshima, Boyer has argued that the event has been "linked to the shifting rhythms of confrontation with the threat of nuclear war and with campaigns to reduce that threat."[58] This explains the changes from work to work, but this chapter shows the tensions *within* the works, where different representational possibilities pull against each other and where it usually proves impossible to resolve the narrative into a single perspective on events.

CHAPTER 3

The Debate over Nuclear Refuge

The atomic bombing of Japanese cities not only triggered a whole series of narratives that attempted to describe those events, but it also served a symbolic function throughout the Cold War, which was dominated by fear of nuclear war. Only Hiroshima (and of course Nagasaki, which is usually implicitly included in "Hiroshima") could offer any concrete image of the new bomb's destructive capacity. Thus, Hiroshima serves as a constant reference point throughout Cold War writing long after the development of the hydrogen bomb made it an anachronism.

One of the most debated issues during the Cold War was whether there was any defense against the new bombs, and here we encounter a paradox. In 1953 Murray S. Levine, chairman of the New York Committee of Atomic Information, stated baldly that "there is no defense against the atomic bomb as a bomb" and, as if that wasn't bad enough, "no city in this country is really prepared against atomic attack."[1] This conviction would make nonsense of civil defense measures. Yet the U.S. government could not afford to admit this since it could induce at the worst panic and at the least fatalism toward nuclear attack.

In his survey of the impact of the atomic bomb on American culture, Paul Boyer argues that by the late 1940s civil defense had become a charged political and social issue.[2] Part of the debate included the possible replanning of city layouts with arterial highways to allow for mass evacuation.[3] In 1948 the first Civil Defense planning office was set up and that same year the *New Yorker* correspondent Daniel Lang reported on the Munitions Board survey of caves and abandoned mines that might be used for storage of supplies of food and other necessities. A high-ranking officer told Lang that "people have got to be educated. They've got to become underground-conscious," and he continued that industry should also start considering the construction of underground factories.[4] Finally, in 1950 President Truman established the Federal Civil Defense Authority (FCDA). According to a recent history by Andrew Grossman, the FCDA operations helped promote the "core myth of early Cold War emergency planning: Not only was strategic nuclear war manageable from a civil defense perspective, but it was also no different from a conventional war that the United States could and would "win."[5]

Fear of the atomic bomb led a number of American newspapers to produce special issues describing the effects of an attack. The *Los Angeles Times,* for instance, ran a headline in March 1961 that screamed "Red Alert! What If H-Bomb Hits Los Angeles" and proceeded to describe the destruction that would follow: "Roofs collapse and crash down through upper stories. Walls crack wide and tremble perilously . . . There is no glass in any window, store front or door hit by the blast wave and fires torch everywhere, gutting the wreckage in a smother of smoke."[6] Such "reports" were obviously not designed as fiction, but neither do they read like authentic reports. The use of the present tense in what is essentially a generic description in articles like this one suggests that they offer a kind of future reportage of a dreaded event. Also, the focus in such accounts on blast damage conceals an even greater source of anxiety—radioactive fallout. As Spencer Weart has pointed out, "Fallout was perfectly suited to induce anxiety . . . something that rests upon helplessness and uncertainty, on the feeling that a threat cannot be escaped nor perhaps even comprehended before it is too late."[7] And it was secret in a double sense. Its operation could not easily be perceived, and its publicization was heavily controlled. We have seen how the U.S. government attempted to suppress the facts of radiation sickness in Hiroshima and Nagasaki, but this suppression was widely perceived to be institutional. In a two-part article of 1959 entitled "Fallout: The Silent Killer," Steven M. Spencer surveyed cases where the results of nuclear tests either went awry or were concealed, and he concluded that "radioactive fallout is a silent killer which hides its poisons among the more familiar causes of human illness and death and thus postpones positive identification."[8]

During these years science fiction (SF) stories and novels began appearing that, in their various ways, took issue with this government-promoted minimization of the effects of nuclear war. Whereas the official line broadly stressed limitations of scale and the survivability of such a war, this fiction articulated in narrative form fears of genetic mutation and civic collapse. The debate about nuclear war rapidly turned into a series of speculations about which areas of normal social life would be the first to collapse. Indeed, by 1952 nuclear themes had become so widespread in science fiction that H. L. Gold, the editor of *Galaxy* magazine, complained that "over 90% of stories still nag away at atomic, hydrogen and bacteriological war, the post-atomic world, reversion to barbarism, mutant children killed because they have only ten toes and fingers instead of twelve."[9] The debate over nuclear safety was joined by a number of SF novelists like Martin Caidin and Philip Wylie, who were active in civil defense organizations.[10]

The continuing debate over the consequences of nuclear explosions was entered in 1948 by David Bradley, who wrote *No Place to Hide* in opposition to bland government reassurances that there was no need for the public to worry about fallout. Bradley served as a medical monitor at the Operation Crossroads tests that took place in Eniwetok Atoll in 1946. His account was written for the general reader, carefully avoided all but the minimum of scientific explanation, and followed the sequence of a diary narrative, which privileged his position as eyewitness. His conclusions were stark and uncompromising. First Bradley insists categorically that "there is no real defense against atomic weapons." From this premise he continues: "There are no satisfactory countermeasures and methods of decontamination." Extrapolating this point into the situation of nuclear attack, he virtually denies the possibility of civil defense or even treatment for the injured: "There are no satisfactory medical or sanitary safeguards for the people of atomized areas." Cold comfort indeed for Bradley's readers who lived in the major cities of the United States, although he stresses that Operation Crossroads should not be conceived in national terms: "It is a test conducted by many different people, and a world of men, women, and their children will participate in its results."[11]

Bradley stresses that these are biological not political conclusions, and throughout *No Place to Hide* he constantly draws the reader's attention to the natural of the South Pacific. As Boyer has pointed out, the site of the atomic tests is described as a paradise violated by modern militarism.[12] The atoll is referred to variously as a Shangri-La, a Land of Lotus Eaters, and a Garden of Eden. The splendor of the tropical sunsets, the astonishing wealth of deep-sea life, and the aerial beauty of the atoll all take Bradley's breath away, and he waxes lyrical (and nostalgic) over the harmony of Bikini: "Not so long ago Bikini must have been a beautiful island. It still has areas of palm and pandanus and breadfruit where all is peace and sunshine and the whispering of the trades. The hot sand, littered with shells and bits of crimson coral, the grass and dense undergrowth, the sparkle of the lagoon, and the booming of the surf on the reef give one the impression of complete timelessness."[13] Although Bradley articulates ecological concern in his account, he does not recognize how the very encoding of the Pacific islands as a paradise reflects their appropriation by Western culture. The aerial views he enjoys are not available to the islanders who are a suppressed presence in his narrative. Conspicuous by their absence after U.S. deportation, they represent a displaced colonial Other that continues to be exploited by the military-industrial powers. Even when recognizing this latest phase of colonization, Bradley tends to focus mainly on the territory, not the islanders in question.

This emphasis does not arise from an indifference toward the islanders, however. Rather, it is an aspect of Bradley's use of place within the broader purpose of his book—namely, to bring home to an unconcerned American readership the dangers of nuclear fallout. His denial of refuge anticipates by several years Nevil Shute's 1957 novel *On the Beach*. Historically the Pacific islands have been used as refuge from the pressures of modern life by Westerners like Gauguin and Stevenson. In his description of Bikini, Bradley tacitly recognizes that the pristine harmony of the place has already receded into the past. The Cherry Lagoon represents the effects of this change in its doubleness. On one side remain unspoilt rocks; on the other "all the crud and corruption of civilization" lies spread out along the beach, a line of rusting debris. Similarly, on Kwajalein the military installations from the last war are already rusting into disuse and turning into the ruins that J. G. Ballard would use in his 1964 story "The Terminal Beach." The Pacific atolls, in short, are a hybrid place bearing the traces both of their past and of recent Western interventions in their landscape. Their very names sound remote and exotic, but Bradley uses the atomic tests to close up any sense of distance. Thus, "Bikini is San Francisco Bay." Toward the end of his book Bradley moves from the Pacific tests that, however benign he tries to make them, constitute a kind of assault, if only on the order of nature, to nuclear attack on America by analogy.

What of the tests themselves? They are described as a controlled experiment that fails, although the extent of this failure only becomes evident late in the book. The first test, an air blast, has been awaited with anxiety by all the crews concerned, only to be an anticlimax. There is no widespread destruction, although Bradley seizes the opportunity to meditate on the bomb's use of a "primordial force" in nature. The second test, an underwater one, has a different impact as spectacle. First there comes the flash, and then water spout, which levels off at a certain height: "Where it [the flash] had been now stood a white chimney of water reaching up and up. Then a huge hemispheric mushroom of vapour appeared like a parachute suddenly opening. It rapidly filled out in all directions until it struck the level of the first layer of clouds, about 1800 feet. Here, as though striking a layer of plate glass, this shock wave . . . spread out by leaps and bounds beneath the clouds."[14] Here Bradley draws on what had already become the standard mushroom metaphor of the atomic blast and creates an effect now known as the nuclear sublime. A number of commentators have pointed out the ambiguous spectacle conveyed in early descriptions of such a blast, sometimes encoding the image as a male orgasm.[15] Bradley avoids the crude excitement over the triumph of a male-gendered technology and, as soon as the radioactive rain cloud forms, moralizes it as an "evil curse" hanging over the test fleet.

In fact, the most powerful sections of *No Place to Hide* prove to be the least spectacular and concern the spread of radiation after this second blast. Bradley uses his many visual details to set up by contrast the peculiar threat posed by radiation that can only be detected by special instruments. The traditional traces of war—the smashed superstructures of battleships, abandoned materiel, and so on—bear no relation to the new danger. The sailors discover that scrubbing the decks, for instance, merely allows the radiation to penetrate deeper. The boats look the same but are so dangerously changed that the original plan of sailing the target fleet back to America has to be abandoned. And then there is the damage to the environment. Tests reveal that radiation has contaminated fish and might well spread from species to species in a totally unpredictable fashion, as was later confirmed in part by the notorious case of the Japanese fishing boat *Lucky Dragon*.[16] The naval crews described in these tests function like a public Bradley is trying to instruct. Their incomprehension reflects the need for what is virtually a paradigm shift in their model of reality where a potentially fatal source of danger is so difficult to conceive of. Bradley closes his book with the unmeasured ecological consequences of Operation Crossroads spreading out into the Pacific, and here the significance of his title emerges. It is an adaptation of the spiritual "There's no hidin' place," which denies the possibility of escaping God's scrutiny. Bradley's analogy implies that radiation is a kind of nemesis hanging over humanity that can be neither contained nor resisted.

One of the most famous nuclear war novels of the 1950s, Nevil Shute's *On the Beach,* achieved its fame partly from chiming in with public fears of nuclear fallout. The year is 1963, and a nuclear war has left the entire northern hemisphere polluted with radiation from cobalt bombs among other weapons. The protagonist, an Australian naval officer, is posted on a submarine, one of the few surviving vessels of the U.S. Navy, on a mission to contact possible survivors. Shute's novel gains much of its power from understating the nuclear subject, which is pitted against countless details of a daily life that is about to come to an end. The novel's premise is that it is only a matter of time before winds carry radiation into the southern hemisphere. It stretches plausibility to a breaking point for Shute to state that the first nuclear weapon was launched by the Albanians; but, in a sense, that hardly matters, since the war rapidly escalated to a conflict between the super powers. Also, in keeping with much nuclear war fiction, Shute denies us any coherent story of what exactly happened. The disaster arises out of mounting confusion. The novel's action takes place in the aftermath of this war, describing a search by the submarine to find the source of mysterious radio transmissions from the United States and, more generally, attempts by characters to fill the time before their imminent deaths. Given this inevitability, important roles are played by scientists in predicting symptoms. Thus, one chemist explains that "in the very end, infection or leukaemia may be the actual cause of death. The blood-forming tissues are destroyed, you see, by the loss of body salts in the fluids."[17] The U.S. submarine travels to San Francisco, where again Shute studiously avoids drama: "All they learned was that the bridge was down. The supporting tower at the south end seemed to have been overthrown. The houses visible from the sea around the Golden Gate Park had suffered much from fire and blast; it did not look as if any of them were habitable. They saw no evidence of any human life, and the radiation level made it seem improbable that life could still exist in that vicinity."[18] The care Shute takes not to make impressions too definite contributes to the bleakness of this description (in the 1959 film adaptation San Francisco has survived intact). Within the fiction of nuclear war, house and inhabitant are repeatedly identified; the destruction of one suggests the demise of the other. Thus, the fate of San Francisco is symptomatic of the cumulative fate of humanity. The only relief that can be offered is through suicide pills, and the novel ends with a character taking this pill as she watches the submarine sail out to sea. Apart from its understatement, Shute's method, and that of the film, have a sanitizing effect, as Spencer Weart notes, "by showing none of the physical agony and demolition that a real war would bring, [they] made world extinction a romantic condition."[19]

Shute's novel and Stanley Kramer's film adaptation caused such concern to the U.S. government because of its negative presentation of nuclear war that in December 1959 Eisenhower's cabinet met to discuss the work. The U.S. Information Agency and the State Department drew up a joint memorandum for U.S. officials working abroad of "Possible Questions and Suggested Answers on the Film 'On the Beach.'" The reason for this was twofold. First, the film might "offer opportunities to turn this emotional response into intellectual support of our quest for safeguarded disarmament."[20] And second, it offered a chance to correct two false assumptions: "that a large-scale nuclear war would create effects including radioactivity sufficient to wipe out all life including that at places remote from the detonations; and that people could not or would not take measures to save their lives but would await death passively."[21]

Government objections to the film version of On the Beach were echoed in Allen Brown and Edward Teller's The Legacy of Hiroshima, where Teller insisted that the action had "no relation to any possible future event" and complained that Shute had "disregarded the real facts of life" to serve his pacifist agenda. "Radioactive contamination is treated as a contagion," Teller continued, and indeed the novel draws an explicit analogy with a cholera epidemic. He went on to attack the novel's fatalism, declaring that "the only protection provided against one kind of death is the substitution of a cleaner, quicker kind of death. No one thinks of prolonging lives."[22] However, Teller had his own agenda too. Part of his indignation lay in the fact that *On the Beach* obstructed his promotion of a nationwide civil defense system of nuclear shelters.

Bradley's was not the only popular account of radiation to come out of Operation Crossroads. Richard Gerstell also served as a monitor at the same tests and, encouraged by Secretary of Defense James Forrestal, in 1950 published *How to Survive an Atomic Bomb*. Gerstell was attempting to perform an exercise in reassurance through the genre of the self-help manual framed as an extended dialogue between himself and an anxious citizen. Despite his refrain of "keep your head," Gerstell constantly produces unconscious black comedy in trying to play down the nuclear threat and reduce it to a series of essentially practical problems of housekeeping.[23] When his hypothetical citizen asks, "But is there much chance of our getting bombed?" the answer is rather less than reassuring: "Not much chance. Not on purpose, anyway."[24] Gerstell's description of how a family should respond to nuclear attack only confirms his lack of realism: "In case of air-raid warning, Dad will go around and cover all the windows. Mum will turn off the pilot light in the stove and the light under the gas heater and refrigerator. Brother will run out and shut the garage doors, and collect what little drinking water is needed for storage. Sister will find Bumpy, the pup, and take him down to the cellar."[25] In its military precision, this account totally overlooks the chaos that would be created by nuclear attack. This was later depicted in Philip Wylie's *Tomorrow!* which showed outbreaks of looting, and in Martin Caidin's *The Long Night,* which dramatized the panic to escape a firestorm.[26] Both novels were written by authors actively involved in civil defense organizations. Apart from the psychological factor, Gerstell constantly reveals contradictions or omissions in his account. Everyone should be prepared, but the warning of attack might only give them a few seconds to act. The family unit should stick together, but children will probably have to be evacuated. And, though each household should try to be self-sufficient, survival kits should not include a Geiger counter, because the homeowners will not know how to use it. Finally, unlike Bradley, Gerstell hardly addresses the ecological questions at all beyond simply denying that wildlife would be doomed.

Gerstell's manual and the coda to Bradley are both examples of an emerging postwar genre of hypothetical narrative where writers try to imagine a nuclear attack by transposing aspects of the Hiroshima and Nagasaki bombings and the Pacific tests onto the American scene. The Cornell physicist Philip Morrison produced one of the earliest of these narratives in his contribution to *One World or None,* where he imagined the effect of a single atomic bomb dropping on Manhattan. Ignoring the spectacle of the blast itself, Morrison uses an ideally clear visual point of view that renders the human casualties with graphic precision: "The district near the centre of the explosion was incredible. From the river west to Seventh Avenue, and from south of Union Square to the middle thirties, the streets were filled with the dead and the dying. The old men sitting on the park benches in the square never knew what happened. They were chiefly charred black on the side facing the bomb. Everywhere in this whole district were men with burning clothing, women with terrible red and blackened burns, and dead children caught while hurrying home to lunch."[27] The first general images locate the central blast area for the reader. Then, as Morrison moves on to the casualties, he gives instances of fatalities among the most vulnerable civilians—the elderly and children.

Morrison implies—and it is a general theme of *One World or None*—that there is no viable protection against nuclear attack. The only true defense is the political one of coexistence, hence the title: Either we learn to live together, or we will have no future. This was not the same message put out by John Lear's two "Hiroshima, U.S.A." articles that appeared in *Collier's* 5 August 1950 issue. Once again an atomic bomb drops on Manhattan. Lear made his transposition explicit and drew on John Hersey's *Hiroshima* to give a series of vivid local images, like the man standing at ground zero who is transformed into the "radiant heat etching of a man in the act of wiping his brow" or a Bronx housewife who "went to the kitchen window to see what caused the light; on the way, the windowpane came to meet her, in thousands of slashing bits. Noticing that she was bleeding, she fainted." Transforming a national landmark into a metaphor of America's strength, Lear makes the ruin of the Empire State Building a symbolic comment on the state of the whole country: the building "stared down at the shambles through paneless windows, like a fighting colossus with his eyes blacked and all his teeth knocked out."[28] Lear had a problem of scale, however, which reflected an uncertainty in his purpose. He wanted to bring home the horrors of nuclear attack, and a graphic color illustration—a speciality of *Collier's*—of Manhattan in flames shows the scale of destruction. Yet, the second part of the article was devoted to civil defense measures. *Collier's* sent him to visit the British civil defense training school at Easingwold, near York, and his second article was the result of his experiences. This time the illustrations showed British civil defense crews working in simulated settings of bomb damage that closely resembled scenes from World War II. Taking the British practice as an example, Lear railed against those in America who opposed taking any defensive measures. But his was a broken-backed argument, because he had already dramatized the impossibility of prevention.

From the late 1940s on, a subgenre of nuclear war fiction began to emerge that focused on the symbolic location of an atomic shelter and that repeatedly interrogated the problem of survivability. Household, neighborhood, and local community became synecdoches for the nation as a whole and offered variations on the theme of the garrison state developed during the early Cold War period in the United States. One of the first fictional narratives to incorporate this emerging preoccupation with fallout shelters was William Tenn's "Generation of Noah," which he wrote in 1949 but could not get published until 1951 because editors rejected it as being "too fantastic." Here a sadistic father drills his six-year-old son to run to the family shelter within the three minutes of their warning time. During one of these practices the son trips, is delayed, and as punishment has to recite his future fate: "Then, when the bombs fell, I'd—I'd have no place to hide. I'd burn like the head of a match. An'—an' the only thing left of me would be a dark spot on the ground shaped like my shadow."[29] It is not clear whether Tenn drew on Bradley's book for his story, but certainly the son's "lines" have incorporated the iconography of Hiroshima. The father is an early survivalist who obsessively fits out his shelter with generators, Geiger counters, and other supplies against nuclear attack. When the long-dreaded "judgement day" finally comes, the son is five seconds late entering the shelter, but the father has been so traumatized by the real event that he gathers the whole family together to swear an oath that they will never again punish any human being. Within the opposition the story sets up between the mother's gentleness and care on the one hand and the father's "scientific" method of bringing up his children on the other, it is the latter that collapses under actual nuclear attack. The collapse of the father symbolizes a failure of authority and nerve, and Tenn's title sets up an implicit analogy between nuclear war and an irresistible force of nature, like a deluge.

Andrew Grossman has argued that for political reasons civil defense measures of the early fifties targeted the growing population of the suburbs and also gave a position of central importance to women as "essentially genderless human resources," partly to stress their role managing the home to maximize survival.[30] These issues were fed into the first novel by Judith Merril, *Shadow on the Hearth,* which seems superficially to confirm Kenneth Rose's statement that in civil defense education of the 1950s, "discussions of nuclear war [were] presented in terms as mundane as possible, with only muted references to death, destruction and dismemberment."[31] In fact, Merril used her domestic location without domesticating her subject. For her novel she consulted David Bradley, John Hersey's *Hiroshima,* the Smyth Report, and magazines like *Collier's, Time,* and *Popular Science.*[32] This preparatory reading reflected Merril's conviction that SF was far from fantasy. In an interview of 1971 she declared, "I believe quite firmly that today the science fiction writer is the only writer who is completely relating to his environment. The essence of good science fiction is that it must relate to all knowledge available to the author at that time."[33]

Acting on this principle, Merril wanted to check details with Bradley on radiation: diagnosis time, kinds of nuclear blast, and the timing of symptoms. As evidence of her capacity to do a "reasonably good job" on this subject, she enclosed a copy of her 1948 story "That Only a Mother," which she had written in opposition to the denial by the U.S. Army that infanticides were occurring around Hiroshima and Nagasaki.[34] Published in 1948, the story describes the fears of pregnant Maggie, whose husband is away working at Oak Ridge nuclear enrichment plant. Maggie's fears that her baby may be malformed from radiation transmitted by her husband are brushed aside by the various experts who surround her with reassurances and prescriptions. Merril's title reflects the way in which the male experts infantilize Maggie by not taking her fears seriously, and wrongly in this particular context, since children embody the future. The dialogue between fear and reassurance has been internalized by Maggie herself, who repeatedly censors her thoughts by refusing to articulate the dreaded possibilities confronting her. The story powerfully dramatizes the social imbalance between the medical "authorities" and a female patient and the psychological reluctance to accept the results of radioactive contamination. It demonstrates a reluctance to admit consequences that are realized when Maggie's child is born without limbs.[35] The discussion of mutations within the story is contextualized by references to Hiroshima and Nagasaki.

While working on her novel, Merril wrote to David Bradley in February 1949. Apart from documenting her scrupulous preparation, the letter sheds important light on her general purpose and method. She said that the novel was to be "aimed at the women's magazines" because "women LOVE to read about diseases . . . and also about dangers to their children, homes, and family." While she respected *No Place to Hide,* she described it as a "man's book," going on to say that "few women have read it or will, because the technique you used for relief from strain, the tropical isle stuff, fishing, etc., is men's reading exclusively."[36]

Shadow on the Hearth draws on sources like Hersey, Bradley, Morrison, and others in a selective and original way. First, Merril situates the action in a household in the New York suburb of Westchester when the city is attacked by several atomic bombs falling in the bay near Manhattan that are part of a general attack on the whole country (at least one device has hit the Capitol in Washington). This information is given as a news announcement before the novel's title page, followed by the perception of the blasts registered by Gladys Mitchell, the protagonist, who merely sees a strange flash of light followed by a dark cloud. Merril has no interest in trying to capture the spectacle of the blasts; she's only interested in exploring their consequences for a typical suburban household. In that respect she anticipates a policy government publications were anxious to promote during the 1950s, namely that "the family is the mainstring of civil defense."[37] Morrison's article (unnamed but unmistakeable) has lodged in Gladys's memory, feeding her fears of what has almost certainly happened to her husband who works in the city. Hersey's method of semi-documentary realism is applied in the countless details of home life that give authenticity to Merril's narrative. Even her choice of title reflects an awareness of nuclear imagery.[38] One of the most famous photographs from Hiroshima showed the shadowy outline of a man imprinted on the entrance steps to a bank, clearly repeated in the American context by John Lear and by Ray Bradbury, whose 1950 story "There Will Come Soft Rains" shows an outline of human figures imprinted on the side of their house by nuclear blast.[39] Apart from their traditional connotations of threat, shadows in the nuclear context hint at the grim irony of a technological device destroying humans so completely that it only leaves a two-dimensional trace.

Merril makes no attempt to identify or demonize the attackers, although no reader of 1950 could fail to draw the inference that the bombs had been launched by the Soviet Union. In contrast with earlier science fiction accounts of alien attack, the most famous being H. G. Wells's *War of the Worlds, Shadow on the Hearth* literally domesticates the theme of attack. Merril herself was a former Trotskyite and in 1950 a member of the United World Federalists.[40] Although she saw her book as a "very political novel," its politics emerge from the management of public information about the results of attack. She approached the issue as a medical problem, highlighting "diagnosis," "treatment," "timing of symptoms," and "detectability" in her working notes for the novel. The attack itself is seen as an anonymous physical force to which the citizens must respond as best they can, and, not surprisingly, she gives doctors special status in her narrative.[41]

Although popular writing on the nuclear threat tended to privilege the family, Merril uses the household in a symbolic as well as realistic way. To get a sense of how this operates, we need to consider a news announcement made over the radio by the governor of New York, who declares: "There will be no more attacks. A screen of radar shields every inch of our borders, from below sea level to the far reaches of the stratosphere. Nothing can get through. We are living inside a great dome of safety, our whole nation protected by the great network of warning devices."[42] In *One World or None* Louis Ridenour declared radar obsolete, and Merril retains this perception as an irony in the order of her events. The announcement comes after multiple attacks have demonstrated the failure of this early-warning system. The governor uses the figure of a protective dome created by military technology over the American nation, but Merril's novel actually dramatizes the penetration of a series of symbolic interiors by the atomic bombs and their resultant fallout. If we consider the house as a key site of family life, the daily routine of that life has been radically damaged by the presumed death of Gladys's husband. If we think of it next as a physical protective space, the house offers refuge to a scientist who proves to be very helpful to the family. Here the house is differentiated from the nation that has black-listed him.[43] Similarly, when looters attack the house, their successful repulse contrasts with the nation's apparent helplessness before nuclear attack. In short, circumstances force a radical change on the function of the house and on Gladys's lifestyle.

Within the novel, official ideology is based on a series of concentric spaces: radar puts a "roof" over the nation, the nation over the state, the state over the household, the household over its members. Merril's novel belies this protective layering at virtually every point. Officials and official information are subjected to a constant ironic scrutiny. Soon after the attack two figures in antiradiation suits arrive at Gladys's door: a doctor and a neighbor now acting as local warden. The moment they lift their visors, they cease to be (in the eyes of Gladys's younger daughter) men from Mars. Echoing an identical moment with a tractor driver in *The Grapes of Wrath,* Merril makes a similar point about estrangement: "The simple act of revealing their faces changed them from fictional monsters to human beings."[44] As in Steinbeck's novel, the revelation of features situates the figures within a set of relationships. Not only does the warden supply Gladys with verbose mimeographed instruction sheets, he also patronizes her constantly and offers himself as a comforting substitute for Gladys's missing husband. Here an important principle emerges in Merril's narrative: No information is introduced without that information or its supplier being questioned. A fugitive physicist, for example, tells Gladys of the dangerously misleading suggestion her other visitors were promoting that urine analysis could be performed instantly in the latter's truck. How to respond to the crisis is shown to be a shared predicament where opposing points of view have to be debated or tested.

The most moving point in the novel comes when Gladys realizes that her youngest daughter has suffered radiation poisoning from a contaminated toy.

Thus, nation, house, and body prove equally vulnerable to radiation. Out of this situation of common need, the house ceases to be a private dwelling occupied only by the Mitchells and turns into a communal space offering shelter to neighbors. David Dowling has glossed this aspect of the novel negatively: "The novel proceeds like a situation comedy, with the living room as the set and many entrances, exits, and visits from neighbours and officials."[45] This description fails to take into account the crucial fact that staying in the house is a necessity imposed by life-threatening circumstances. The simulation of family and social life continues against a background of new dangers and urgencies where domestic spaces change correspondingly. It is absurd to refer to "visits" without recognizing the total change in outside life that Merril depicts. Counterpointed against Gladys's activities inside her house, Merril inserts nightmarish sections dealing with an unnamed man's experiences at the hands of the emergency services. Within the topography of the novel, "outside" signifies darkness, chaos, and threat. Furthermore, the superficial resemblance between Merril's narrative and a situation comedy reinforces its purpose in making nuclear attack familiar to the reader.

As these transformations are taking place, Gladys's role and self-image are changing. The most immediate consequence of the attack is that she becomes estranged from the "script" of domestic life, which recedes into an "old worn-out film"; a shopping list contains words "from another world." Later in the novel, when the police bring in the family maid for questioning, the situation reminds Gladys of a "grade-B gangster movie." Thus, at many points Gladys registers the strange resemblances that intermittently characterize her experiences. One fundamental change that takes place is a revision of her role within the household. Gerstell's conservative and traditional allocation of roles assumes an unlikely stability in the family situation Merril addresses head on. One symbolic event that shows the change taking place occurs when Gladys, donning her husband's work shirt, decides to fix a gas leak herself. At a later point she thinks back speculatively about the events on the day of the attack and reflects, "*If Jon were here . . .*" but then catches herself: "That was silly too. All the ifs were silly. Jon wasn't there. The other time, the other war, it was different."[46] Throughout the novel, Gladys engages in an extended dialogue with her own thoughts and with the voices she hears around her. In this way she quietly interrogates her own situation, gradually becoming a more articulate critic of the emergency procedures being implemented. As she takes charge of her household she becomes increasingly restive of "experts." When the scientist and a doctor discuss her daughter's illness, she silently complains, "Why did they have to talk in code?" And she defies the authorities by not taking her daughter to the hospital as recommended. This debate over how to deal with the current situation of crisis takes place during the countless practical tasks in the house that lend the novel its realism. *Shadow on the Hearth* received an exceptionally positive review in the *New York Times* that compared the novel to Huxley and Orwell and praised Merril for her characterization: "Indeed there's so much about the standard operating procedure of housework in the story that it is frequently impossible to believe that a war is really on."[47] Conversely, in the novel it is equally impossible to forget that domestic life has become transformed by the national crisis.

Merril's originality in *Shadow on the Hearth* lay in her attempt to imagine a female viewpoint on nuclear attack as it impacted family life and the life of a neighborhood. The novel is framed by radio announcements of the beginning of the attack and the end of the subsequent war. In other words, there is an official narrative of unprovoked attack (implicitly modeled on Pearl Harbor) followed by war and national triumph. The official announcement closes off this narrative with the national anthem, but Merril's narrative refuses this closure.[48] Her editors at Doubleday imposed a change to the novel's ending that contradicted the whole drive of her narrative, namely having Gladys's husband return home and thereby reestablish the fractured family unit. It was not until the 1966 reprint that Merril could restore her original text, which is significantly more open-ended. Despite the ending of hostilities, Gladys reflects, "Isn't anything safe? Not the rain or the house? Not even a little blue horse?" Characteristically, the last line of the novel is a rejoinder in an unfinished dialogue: "'But the war's *over*,' she said."[49] The novel leaves the reader questioning the irreversible loss of security experienced by Gladys and, by implication, countless other citizens.

Throughout her career, Merril remained preoccupied by the nuclear threat. She refused to share her fellow novelist Robert Heinlein's faith in nuclear shelters. Partly because he was then living near the underground NORAD complex at Colorado Springs, Heinlein had built a shelter for his family in 1961 "as an act of faith, as an example to others."[50] Merril did not follow suit, and later in the sixties she renounced her U.S. citizenship in protest over the Vietnam War. From 1967 to 1981 she was an active member of the Canadian citizens' group Hiroshima-Nagasaki Relived, and during a 1986 interview she recorded her disagreement with Heinlein and Poul Anderson on nuclear attack: "If you talk about holocaust, you come down to the fact that from what we now know, there is no aftermath."[51]

Merril's novel was adapted for television and appeared under the title *Atomic Attack* on the *ABC Motorola TV Playhouse* in 1954.[52] A voice-over introduces the action: "The play you are about to see deals with an imaginary H-bomb attack on New York City and with the measures that civil defense would take, in such an event, for the rescue and protection of the population in and around the city. It is the prayer of every one of us that such imaginings shall remain forever fictions."[53] This introduction was probably designed to avoid the panic created by Orson Welles's dramatization of *The War of the Worlds*, but it inevitably has the effect of reassuring the viewer that the action is a kind of make-believe. In contrast, Merril's novel uses the methods of realism to impress the reader with the likely possibility of nuclear attack. A second difference lies in the play's tendency to make its points explicitly, whereas the novel constantly positions the reader to draw out the implications of previously routine acts like eating and playing. Thus, the play establishes the typicality of the family from the start in showing the hubbub of a breakfast scene. When one of the girls complains, "Oh why can't we be like other families, a nice normal group of people?" the mother replies, "We are . . . normal as oatmeal and apple pie."

The scenic construction of *Shadow on the Hearth* made its dramatic adaptation relatively straightforward, though at the cost of losing much of the novel's psychological dimension.[54] Close-ups of the mother suggest her thoughtfulness in dealing with the attitudes of other characters, who each personify different ways of reacting to the current crisis. For example, the science teacher admits to her that he recoiled from physics when he realized that science was being directed into weapons of mass destruction. The mother, unnamed and therefore more determined by her family role, is contrasted with a hysterical neighbor in a dialogue between practical action and despair. As a new ethic of mutual help emerges, the mother makes this explicit: "I know this much now, that we'll oftentimes do things for others that we'd never dream of doing for ourselves." Such commentary on each episode makes the play more didactic than the novel.

The other major difference between novel and play is in the latter's use of radio announcements. The novel contains occasional news flashes that give characters hints of external but primarily domestic information. The play, by contrast, punctuates the action with announcements about the American response to the (still unnamed) enemy's assault. Where Merril kept revealing ironic gaps between official statements and the situation of Gladys's household, the play suggests an uncritical parallel between the national military campaign and the experiences of the characters. Success in one coincides with success in the other. The end result is that the play risks arriving at a crude notion of triumph. When the radio announcer states that "the enemy's will and ability to fight have now virtually been broken," the daughter Ginny asks, "Are we winning?" Gladys's reply, the last line in the play, shows unambiguous confidence: "Not yet, darling, but we're going to." The novel gradually questions characters' presumptions of security. The play identifies the external enemy with the internal danger of despair and shows a congruence between national and personal goals that will be resolved at an imminent point of victory.

In 1958 Merril told Philip Wylie that her novel was appearing on civil defense reading lists and that *Atomic Attack* was being shown in civil defense and Atomic Energy Commission programs.[55] This would have struck a chord with Wylie, who, from 1945 through the late 1950s, when he realized the destructive potential of the H-bomb, was a tireless campaigner for civil defense projects at the federal and local levels. In 1950 he proposed the "Miami plan" for local civil defense organizations, and in his 1951 article "A Better Way to Beat the Bomb" he proposed that each city should train its own civil defense personnel who should be prepared to move to neighboring cities if need be. However, Wylie expressed most concern at the "failure so far of the average citizen to assimilate what has been told, to infer what that means, and to deduce what might happen and what he *could* be ready to do that he *could* arrange rapidly and *could* pay for."[56] Wylie's repeated target in his writings, fiction and nonfiction, was the morale of city dwellers under nuclear attack. He planned to make a film on this subject, to be called *The Bomb*, which was enthusiastically supported by General Vandenberg among others, but this never materialized. Instead, Wylie chose the medium of fiction to warn the American public against its apathy with his 1954 novel *Tomorrow!* which describes the bombing of twin midwestern cities modeled on Minneapolis and St. Paul. Wylie dedicated the work to the staff of the Federal Civil Defense Authority, one member of which reviewed the novel and recommended its promotion among civil defense officials.[57]

Wylie's conviction that civil defense measures would be effective if only the public were properly educated was not shared by other writers of this period. Two of his novels from the fifties, for example, demonstrate a cultural difference between the United States and Britain over the use of the subway as a potential place of refuge. Where underground stations in London served as improvised shelters during World War II, the New York subway in *Few Were Left* and *The Rest Must Die* becomes the site for a release of violent impulses that play themselves out in lurid twilit settings suggestive of a collective unconscious finding expression. Andrew Grossman has shown that Project East River, an elaborate civil defense project centered on New York in the early fifties, included recognition that mob action might well be one result of nuclear attack, a result serious enough for the authorities to consider how to isolate and disable the ringleaders.[58] Harold Rein's *Few Were Left* describes the sheer incomprehension of the few survivors who crawl through the tunnels looking for means of survival. As they head uptown, they encounter a larger group run militaristically by the self-styled "Co-ordinator." At this point the novel shifts toward political parable as a character tries to compete with the Co-ordinator over whether the surviving remnant should live in slavery or freedom. When his attempted rebellion against tyranny fails, the novel ends with the protagonist being stoned to death. This bleak ending culminates an unrelievedly pessimistic view of urban attack where the city tunnels present to survivors not a refuge but a confusing maze.

Rein shows this tyranny to be a gradual result of the chaotic postwar circumstances of New York. K. F. Crossen (writing as Richard Foster), in *The Rest Must Die,* however, foregrounds the issue of law and order as soon as the bombs drop. Foster describes the same terrain as Rein—the darkened tunnels, the stalled trains, the near impossibility of access to the surface—but this time dramatizes the speed with which civilized restraint collapses. The cover of the novel proclaims, "The law of the jungle was supreme," and the narrative describes a mounting surge of violent hostility between the survivors, some of whom attempt rape while others commit suicide in despair. The tunnels become divided up into gangland areas where armed struggles take place: "The battle with the people who were living on the Long Island tracks was in its second day, but no one had any doubts but that it would soon be over. Cut off from regular food and water supplies they could not last long. Five times they had rushed Gimbels basement and five times had been beaten back. Each time, the number of dead was appalling, especially on the part of those from the Long Island tracks. Not many were killed from Gimbels because they had all the advantage of position and more guns."[59] The combat is presented as a form of rivalry over looting that implicates all survivors and dramatically reverses the civil defense imperative of cooperation. Earlier spokesmen, like Gerstell, presented a utopian vision of family members (and, by implication, members of the national family) working harmoniously together, whereas Foster draws on the naturalistic tradition of social Darwinism to depict a kind of spontaneous and fragmented civil war that breaks out. The collapse of social order is a reflection of the destruction of the city. New York has become a wasteland: "In every direction there were blackened and broken bits that once had been buildings and had sent up smoke signals of help until there was nothing more to burn. In the distance there were ghosts; here a wall standing in dark splendour and there a shell representing some corporate tradition. And that was all. There was nothing else."[60]

The work of the novelist James Blish, who served in the Civil Air Patrol during the 1950s, engaged with issues of nuclear civil defense throughout that decade. He, too, attacked what he saw as a deceptive fashion in shelters. His 1953 story "First Strike" describes an America where such shelters have become routine, but, the narrator wonders, "Just how much 'shelter' [they] would have provided in the event of an actual atomic raid was not even an open question. Like all summer shelters, it was really a flimsy affair." The shelter's very existence reflects ironically on the passivity of the public, exactly the kind of passivity that Merril's *The Shadow on the Hearth* questions: "During the Cold War of 1950–1962 . . . most Americans allowed themselves to be pushed about by the civil defense authorities without the slightest emotional conviction that anything might happen to *them*."[61] The figure of a protective shield that U.S. radar establishes too late in *Shadow on the Hearth* becomes a literal container in "The Box," in which Blish describes the erection of a huge gray membrane over New York City.[62] This "barrier," "screen," or "box" has gone up so suddenly that it causes mass panic in the city. In a sequence of reversals, the device is revealed to be fatal because it prevents air from penetrating the membrane, thereby slowly suffocating the city; and the "experiment" on New York proves to be a covert form of attack by a devious enemy bent on trying out this technology on its opponent.

Blish further wove his skepticism about nuclear shelters into his 1958 novel *A Case of Conscience*. During his revisions to the original short story, he encountered James W. Deer's article on the "shelter race" in a 1957 issue of the *Bulletin of the Atomic Scientists*, which presented a depressingly fatalistic image of the cycle of arms production and defense measures: "The play has begun, and we are the actors. The end is implicit from the nature of the beginning. Within the framework of fusion bombs, guided missiles, and shelters, there is nothing we can do but go ahead and play out our part in the preordained ritual."[63] Deer locks human action into a script over which the agents have no control. From a future-retrospective vantage point frequently used in SF, Blish extrapolates an "international shelter race" from 1960 to 1985 that is triggered by nuclear weapons but then drawn out by the sheer scale of the project. This extended crisis drives human society underground.

> Defensive though the shelter race seemed on the surface, it had taken on all the characteristics of a classical arms race—for the nation that lagged behind invited instant attack. Nevertheless, there had been a difference. The shelter race had been undertaken under the dawning realization that the threat of nuclear war was not only imminent but transcendent; it could happen at any instant, but its failure to break out at any given time meant that it had to be lived with for at least a century, and perhaps five centuries.[64]

Where Deer posits a nuclear narrative so truncated and obvious that the end is clear from the beginning, Blish extends his fictive history over centuries and presents the shelters as a multiple form of imprisonment. The underground world has become a form of hell and the shelter economy an entrapping commercial imperative that virtually excludes change. This is Blish's version of the military-industrial complex, and it is a measure of his gloom about the Cold War arms race (which by the time of his narrative has extended into a worldwide situation) that the underground society can only be mediated to the reader through an enlightened visitor from another planet. The novel exploits the now-familiar iconography of nuclear defense narratives in its very title, where, as David Ketterer has argued, "case" signifies container rather than instance: "The various containers of one kind or another and the images of containment which permeate the novel all serve to illustrate its central ambiguities. To what extent do containers (including conscience, if it is one) protect and screen the contained from the external truth of reality?"[65] Once again, a defensive measure proves in Blish to have entirely negative consequences in inducing mass neurosis among the novel's underground society.

By the 1960s fictional treatments of nuclear defense had reduced in number and had also veered toward the absurd and satire, as if the subject was no longer accessible to "straight" description. In John Cheever's 1961 "The Brigadier and the Golf Widow," a well-appointed bomb shelter has become an integral part of a suburban garden, for instance. A number of factors played their part in this change. First, there had been a gradual loss of public confidence in the efficacy of fallout shelters despite President Kennedy's campaign to promote them.[66] Second, a "crisis fatigue" may have set in after a decade of increasingly outmoded civil defense practices, an overemphasis that was reflected in the subjects of fifties SF. Then there were the political developments in the Cold War, especially a relaxation of tension following the death of Stalin. And, last, the rise of black humor in the United States was historically related to a growing credibility gap between official statements and actuality that came to a head during the Vietnam War.

Gina Berriault's *The Descent*, the novel and film *Dr. Strangelove*, and Leonard C. Lewin's *Report from Iron Mountain* all question the rationality of nuclear confrontation between the super powers.[67] Berriault satirizes the fashion for shelters as a collective self-deception; *Dr. Strangelove* lampoons the arms race as a distortion of the sex drive; and Lewin inverts the relation of peacetime to war by presenting the latter as a new norm. The debate over civil defense even entered *The Twilight Zone* TV series when an episode called "The Shelter" was screened in 1961. Here a false alert triggers such extreme panic among the neighbors of a doctor who has built a fallout shelter that they turn on each other with an unbridled hostility that could easily lead to murder.

Berriault ridicules the whole culture of shelters as an obsession with image. The protagonist of *The Descent* is a history teacher appointed by the president to be

Secretary for Humanity under the Secretary of Defense, but what exactly his brief is remains mysterious. The year is 1964; the arms race is running toward crisis; and the shelter business is booming. But the promotion of shelters and the circulation of government civil defense booklets are presented as part of a collective exercise in distracting the public from the real horrors of nuclear attack. Priority items in the shelters include games and coffee dispensers; and when Hiroshima is visited, for instance, commemoration of the dead takes second place to a lascivious performance before the American troops by Miss Massive Retaliation. An evangelist puts a superficial gloss on the use of shelters by reversing the direction of movement, proclaiming that "man's descent into the bowels of the earth shall be known as the great descent that was the ascent."[68] Berriault satirizes the whole culture of nuclear shelters as self-deceptive, and the novel ends with yet another shelter put under rush construction because, as the timekeeper at the site explains, "our shelter programme means we're aiming to start a war, get our people underground and send the missiles over. [The boss] says they're using it as an excuse to attack *us*. The first one over in this kind of war has the advantage, you know."[69]

From the very beginning, then, skepticism has informed American fictional accounts of refuge from nuclear war. The physicist Freeman Dyson has argued that the fallout shelter program could never have succeeded because it was perceived to be blatantly inadequate and socially divisive and as promoting an unacceptable image of the United States attacking one population while keeping its own safe. Apart from economic and political considerations, he finds the ultimate impossibility of the program to be its contradiction of a national ideology of "freedom under the open sky," where the very idea of underground would be anathema.[70] Boyer has further suggested that interest in civil defense lapsed after the end of atmospheric nuclear tests.[71]

Historically, American science fiction has tended to celebrate the potential of new forms of technology—hence the recurrence of the inventor as a character in these narratives—but in the novels described here, nuclear attack is the main, and of course negative, expression of technological achievement. On the whole, these writers describe scenarios where attack is anonymized and depoliticized as an abstract force triggering essentially domestic situations of crisis and conflict. This is not to say that the narratives are apolitical, only that their politics focuses on issues like survival, the efficiency of the emergency services, and the control of information. Essentially, they present versions of skepticism or pessimism about survival that suggest a deep unease about the possession of nuclear weapons throughout the Cold War period.

CHAPTER 4

Do-It-Yourself Survival

In fiction dealing with civil defense, an important dimension of self-help supplemented the activities of local organizations, and Pat Frank's *Alas, Babylon* is a classic in this field. Never out of print since its original publication in 1959 (and 1960 adaptation for the television series *Playhouse 90*), it has remained one of the most widely read novels of nuclear war and yet, paradoxically, one of the least discussed.

In the September 1960 issue of the *Bulletin of the Atomic Scientists, Alas Babylon* was reviewed positively as an "imaginative study of civil defense and organization."[1] Albert Stone, one of the very few critics to even mention the novel, declares that it "created neither intimate portraits of domestic fears nor graphic urban demonstrations of mass terror and brutality."[2] The novel has in fact been the victim of its own understated style, which some critics have mistakenly taken to mean that Frank was unduly softening the impact of nuclear war.

Frank began his career as a journalist, served in the Office of War Information, and only turned to writing fiction after the war. His first engagement with the nuclear subject was with *Mr. Adam* (1946), where an explosion at a plant making atomic bombs sterilizes all males except one. Paul Boyer has described the novel as a "satire on postwar America" through the lens of sex.[3] It is, however, *Alas, Babylon* that is remembered for Frank's powerful intervention in the contemporary debate over nuclear war. Surveying the field in 1960, Frank himself reflected that the "writer should not be inhibited by the secrecy that mantled the birth of the bomb or the mystery, much of it official and stupid, that has clouded subsequent development." He continues, reinforcing his point about the sheer size of the subject, that the "novelist who chooses a nuclear subject should not be awed by technical complexities, but the facts he sets down on paper must be accurate."[4]

Frank puts this position into practice in *Alas, Babylon,* which reduces technical information to a minimum and which concentrates on those aspects of a nuclear strike, like fallout, that impact survivors most directly.

The novel describes the experience of nuclear war in the small town of Fort Repose, a fictionalized version of Lake Beauclair in the Mount Dora area of central Florida, where Frank was living when he wrote the novel. The former's idyllic name belies its strategic vulnerability in being situated near a number of important military installations, in particular McCoy Strategic Air Command (SAC) base just outside the city of Orlando. The novel focuses most of its narrative on problems of survival in the aftermath of the nuclear strike as experienced by the protagonist Randy Bragg, a former platoon commander in the Korean War who assembles and organizes a group of survivors to cope with the problems posed by worsening food shortages and marauding gangs. The novel was written with the clear purpose of bringing home to an American readership the probable nature of nuclear war, since, as David Brin states in his foreword, "the H-bomb is beyond the imagination of all but a few Americans," never having had the experience of war on their own territory.[5] To reinforce the message of his novel, in 1962 Frank published a nonfictional work about civil defense, *How to Survive the H-Bomb and Why,* which functions partly as a retrospective commentary on *Alas, Babylon,* sometimes explicitly so.

Frank's title is taken from Revelation 18.10, where an angel witnesses the destruction of the city of sin: "Standing afar off for the fear of her torment, saying, Alas, alas that great city Babylon, that mighty city! for in one hour is thy judgment come."[6] The title phrase is used as a private family signal between the protagonist Randy Bragg and his brother Mark, an officer in SAC intelligence, that war is coming. The phrase is used in a telegram, then checked out by the town librarian, who finds its biblical origin. In other words, Frank leaves us in no doubt about the significance of his title, which feeds broadly into his narrative. In the biblical chapter, Babylon is destroyed within one hour just as the United States suffers destruction mainly in a single day. The sinners suffer plagues, just as America falls subject to radiation sickness and the fruits of the earth either disappear or become contaminated. Frank even depicts a family that obsessively hoards valuable jewelry as a hedge against future prosperity without realizing that the jewels have become irradiated. And so the signs of wealth are not merely negated, as in the Bible, but actually bring death to their owners. This is not to say that Frank is indulging in a biblical moral fable, but rather, like Steinbeck's use of Exodus in *The Grapes of Wrath,* he is signaling differences from the Bible. There is no guiding providence and no external mechanism of punishment. The crowning irony in Frank's title lies in the fact that humanity has brought its own destruction on itself.

The ordering of *Alas, Babylon* is geared closely to the shifts in circumstances following the bombing of cities and military bases in Florida. Elsewhere Frank had described the state as "one big landing field, a center of air bases."[7] Roughly two-thirds of the novel depict the aftermath, while the first four chapters proleptically explore the small-town community working against the fragmentary news reports of a mounting crisis in the Middle East. Frank implicitly ties every detail of Fort Repose to the impending strike, not least the differences between Randy's old but very solid house in contrast with a newcomer's lavish one-floor "rambler," with its huge plate-glass windows. In a nuclear war these would be a "death trap," Frank warns.[8] Nuclear war figures as a subject for discussion between characters. One couple is in denial, the husband because he thinks the Pentagon whips up scares to secure appropriations and his wife because the subject is "horrid." Ironically, the best prepared character for what develops seems to be Randy's young nephew. As his mother explains, "All their lives, ever since they've known anything, they've lived under the shadow of war—atomic war. For them the abnormal has become normal."[9] But he is the exception to the general rule that most characters simply assume life will carry on as before.

The political crisis that mounts during the first chapters grows out of Soviet ambitions to penetrate the Mediterranean and their launch of another spy satellite. Randy has an inside source of information from his brother, who points out that, as the crisis comes to a head, no reports appear in the newspapers. This absence makes events in the Mediterranean seem all the more remote from public consciousness. Randy's brother Mark takes Soviet expansionism for granted and attributes the crisis to a failure of national will on the part of the United States, a perspective on the Cold War shared by the novelist Robert Heinlein. Specifically, the war is triggered when a U.S. fighter fires a missile at a Soviet plane (initially just a "bright blip" on American radar screens), which then goes off course and strikes a train in the Syrian port of Latakia, causing a massive explosion from stored ammunition.[10] As happens throughout *Alas, Babylon,* Frank is concerned to bring out the unique features of nuclear war, one of which is the rapid speed of events: "Now, the critical factor in warfare was time, measured in minutes or seconds."[11]

When the nuclear strike comes, survivors quickly designate it "The Day" because it is over within twenty-four hours. This is the first difference from any earlier war. The second is the complete absence of any visible enemy. In short, nuclear attack is presented as a massive rupture, one of the most dramatic moments coming when Randy and his companions witness a nearby blast. Frank uses paragraph spacing to pace the visual perception of the moment:

A stark white flash enveloped the world . . .

A thick red pillar erected itself in the southwest, its base the unnatural sun.

The top of the pillar billowed outward. This time, the mushroom was there.

There was no sound at all except Peyton's whimpering. Her fists were pressed into her eyes.

A bird plunged against the screen and dropped to earth, trailed by drifting feathers. Within the pillar and the cloud, fantastic colors played. Red changed to orange, glowed white, became red again. Green and purple ropes twisted upward through the pillar and spread tentacles through the cloud.

The gaudy mushroom enlarged with incredible speed, angry, poisonous, malignant. It grew until the mushroom's rim looked like the leading edge of an approaching weather front, black, purple, orange, green, a cancerous man-created line squall.[12]

The first casualty in this scene is the small girl Peyton, who was facing the flash and becomes temporarily blinded. While Frank's main concern is to get across the shifting spectacle of the blast, we have already seen how the novel foregrounds a biblical analogy through its title. In this scene, the pillar and the cloud ironically echo the divine sign in the sky that guides the Israelites toward the promised land in Exodus. Here the image is threatening and apocalyptic, signaling an end to the order of American society, even of nature itself. From the very first Trinity test blast, comparisons with the sun had become routine in nuclear descriptions, and Frank's is no exception. The shifts in color and shape are presented as a violation of natural order possessing a travesty life, as if some monster had come into being. Comparing the cloud with a weather front places the phenomenon in time also, as if it is approaching the observers, as if the worst is yet to come. Thus, the two casualties here also function as small precursors of the inconceivably large numbers of deaths already taking place. The temporary blindness of the girl, and presumably the bird too, even implies a retrospective irony, commenting on the West's blindness to the full implications of the arms race. Randy measures the distance of the strike from the bomb blast, concluding that it was MacDill air force base in Tampa.

The Day is full of endings, some more dramatic than others. Although Frank makes apocalyptic statements like "with the use of the hydrogen bomb, the Christian era was dead," endings are serially drawn out through chapters 5 and 6.[13] The first general casualty Randy perceives as he drives into town is civic order. A hotel collapses into chaos because the guests have no conception of what is happening. The mailman makes his last delivery. More ominously, a group of convicts, without their guards, carry guns. And then there is the fate of the dollar. In the first wave of panic buying, Frank hints at the gradual loss of value of currency. The first chapter devoted to The Day culminates with a run on the bank and the suicide of the bank manager, whose death symbolizes a shift in the region toward a "barter and trust" economy.[14] Fort Repose, like any small town, is dependent for its services on deliveries from the urban centers that were the first targets in the nuclear strike. Accordingly, Frank points out its fate: "With the Red Alert, all these services halted entirely and at once. Like thousands of other towns and villages not directly seared by war, Fort Repose became an island."[15]

Frank uses three geographic levels in the novel. First he sketches out the political geography of key areas like the Mediterranean with potential flashpoints noted to establish the likelihood of nuclear war. Then at a regional level he releases details about the strategic installations in Florida that would make that state a target. (In fact, he had been working on an assignment about SAC centers in Florida shortly before starting the novel.) And then, at the greatest level of specificity, there is the local geography of Fort Repose itself, which is described through a series interlocking social relationships as much as terrain. For Frank, the locale should offer a model of community survival through the pooling of shared skills. This town only experiences the consequences of nuclear war once cities like Orlando and Miami have been destroyed, through the disruption to services. Although he assembles an amazingly versatile group of characters to keep the community going, Frank actually dramatizes the sheer dependence of a town like Fort Repose on state-run facilities like electricity, water mains, and a highway network. In *Tomorrow!* Wylie constantly drew the reader's attention to the gap between local and national knowledge to show the lack of preparedness in his cities. Frank stresses a similar information gap to show the chaos in the state as a whole.

> The people of Fort Repose had no way of knowing it, but establishments on the arterial highways leading down both coasts, and crisscrossing between the large cities, had swiftly been stripped of everything. From the time of the Red Alert, the highways had been jammed with carloads of refugees, seeking asylum they knew not where. The mushroom cloud over Miami emptied Hollywood and Fort Lauderdale. The tourists instinctively headed north on Route 1 and A1A, as frightened birds seek the nest. By nightfall, they would be stopped outside the radioactive shambles of Jacksonville. Some fled westward toward Tampa, to discover that Tampa had exploded in their face.[16]

The discontinuity between state and local community brought about by the rupture of services makes it impossible for Frank to incorporate this scale of description into the details of his narrative. What he does show is the total failure of civil defense (a key concern for Wylie) and, even more strikingly, the isolation and ignorance of his chosen town. The distance of Fort Repose from any major city or highway has the effect of sanitizing Frank's narrative so that consequences only impact the town gradually and selectively. In an ironic twist, the survivors discover that the whole state of Florida has been designated a contaminated zone, so that even when they make contact with the national military authorities, they are not offered release from their restricting community.

Throughout *Alas, Babylon* Frank maintains a tension between the local experiences of the survivors in Fort Repose and the fragmentary glimpses of what is happening in what remains of the nation. The key medium for Frank in supplying the latter was radio. In *How to Survive the H-Bomb* he states that "only radio can be depended on to reach the great mass of the people swiftly and simultaneously."[17] In the novel, however, he partially contradicts himself. There, news reports are minimal and fragmented. When Frank shifts the locale of the action to the aircraft carrier in the Mediterranean, where the crisis occurs, he is giving the reader direct access to events that would be unknown to the vast majority of Americans. Randy's brother Mark also supplies special access to unfolding events that would be limited to a small elite, even among the military. In short, Frank's urgency to give a picture of the crisis that leads to war unconsciously demonstrates the inadequacy of the public news system. Even at the point of Red Alert, there is little in the news because public warning time would be so short and could simply induce panic.

But once the attack takes place there are emergency announcements over the radio in line with the CONELRAD (Control of Electromagnetic Radiation) system established in 1951, whose purpose was originally twofold: to provide an emergency information service to the public (as it does briefly in *Alas, Babylon*) and to prevent Soviet bombers from using radio and TV stations for establishing their bearings during an attack. As ballistic missiles replaced bombers, however, CONELRAD became obsolete, a point noted by Frank in 1962, and the following year the system was replaced.

Alas, Babylon is one of the very few works to describe the working of this system; it is also featured in the 1962 film *Panic in Year Zero!* where the experiences of the Baldwins, a Los Angeles family, are described under nuclear attack.[18] The action roughly parallels that of *Alas, Babylon,* though in a much simplified form. As law and order collapse, a Darwinian principle emerges of survival at all costs, especially with the help of firearms. As the Baldwin family heads for the relative safety of the hills behind the city, their transistor radio enables them to keep in touch with what is happening around them. While details of damage remain sketchy at first, the announcer declares, "Your duty is to stay alive. There are unconfirmed reports of looting. Proceed with caution and good judgment."[19] As in Frank's novel, the radio here reinforces the Baldwins' emerging instinct for survival and gives them intermittent guidance. The film was sensationally promoted as showing the end of civilization and a collapse into the law of the jungle, but the radio messages, especially the last one, offer a tenuous hope of reconstruction: "Authorities report that many areas are responding to discipline, but effective control has not yet been established in many rural and mountain sections of the state. People in such areas are urged to maintain caution and vigilance. Emergency centres are operating in the following towns and cities—for San Diego and vicinity—Los Angeles— Malibu."[20] The system has clearly not broken down completely.

The major CONELRAD announcement in *Alas, Babylon* does not give advice but partly echoes a pivotal date in American history. The acting president confirms what Randy and the other characters had suspected when she declares, "Fellow countrymen. As all of you know by now, at dawn this morning this country, and our allies in the free world, were attacked without warning with thermonuclear and atomic weapons . . . The toll of innocent lives taken on this new and darker day of infamy cannot as yet even be estimated."[21] U.S. defense policy during the Cold War was planned consistently as a response to a first strike from the enemy, and the major precedent for this stance was the Japanese attack on Pearl Harbor. On 7 December 1941, President Roosevelt announced war with Japan in what became known as his "Day of Infamy" speech, which is clearly echoed in Frank's novel.[22] In the latter the enemy is not named, but it is clear who the aggressor is. For Frank's characters this is an academic question, because their priorities lie entirely in the detailed practicalities of survival.

Alas, Babylon realizes a scenario that Frank had earlier sketched out in his 1956 novel *Forbidden Area,* where the United States and Soviet Union have achieved "H-parity" (parity of nuclear weapons) but where the United States is testing ballistic missiles, which will decisively shift the balance of power. A Pentagon think tank is directed to speculate on likely Soviet intentions, and one member predicts that their only hope of triumph would be a "one-day blitz. In one day they must create a hundred Pearl Harbors."[23] In *Alas, Babylon* Frank is not concerned with military strategy or the feasibility of such a strike. His use of a historical allusion is sufficient to demonize the aggressors as implacable foes. A retired admiral seeks to find lessons in historical commentaries like those of Gibbon and Toynbee, but such speculation is too general and abstract to shed a meaningful gloss on the novel's action, which tends to concentrate on what Frank calls the "imperative present," the day-by-day engagement with the practical problems of survival, like rigging up a water supply from an artesian well.

If nuclear attack ever takes place, Frank writes that most survivors would find themselves in a "gray zone where we can live or die as we determine. So I think it is fair to say," he concludes, "that each man decides, in part, his own destiny."[24] His characteristic appeal to the will is reassuring, but in his novel one unexpected effect of the CONELRAD broadcasts is his characters' increased sense of isolation. An aerial survey of the country assesses the destruction, confined mainly to the eastern half of the country, and those worst hit are designated "Contaminated Zones": "It is forbidden for people to enter these zones. It is forbidden to bring out any material of any kind, particularly metal or metal containers, out of these zones. Persons leaving the Contaminated Zones must first be examined at check points now being established."[25] And the whole of Florida is one such designated zone. Far from strengthening the survivors' links with the country as a whole, this measure serves to exacerbate their problems by cutting them off from other regions. The coda to the novel only ambiguously softens this isolation.

Once the attack on America has taken place, the rest of the novel explores the possibilities of survival. Frank was writing polemically against works like Nevil Shute's *On the Beach* and other "prophecies of complete doom" which imply that there is no possibility of meaningful action in a nuclear war. Like Heinlein, Frank saw such a crisis as a "time of personal decision," and throughout his companion volume, *How to Survive the H-Bomb,* he stressed the critical importance of practical individual action.[26] The same emphasis is written into *Alas, Babylon,* where survival depends on constant improvisation to cope with shortages and mutual help. As the shortages worsen and people begin to die, a grim message of the survival of the fittest is discussed by the characters, but Frank refuses to depict his as a slide into savagery. Rather, the characters use animals and other creatures as useful models from which lessons can be learned.

The Day is the major turning point in the novel because the entire fabric of American life is ruptured. In *How to Survive the H-Bomb* Frank discusses the fate of the "marvels of the supermarket." "Some will vanish in a moment, and some in thirty days, but all will end," he warns. "They will end because electricity will end and electricity is at once the muscle and nervous system of the continent."[27] The first part of the Florida system to collapse is the network of roads crammed by tourists trying to flee to urban centers that no longer exist. Along the way they empty the supermarkets of goods, but the worst is yet to come. Emergency and shortwave radios maintain some contact with the outside world, until Orlando suffers a strike: "The lights went out in the room, the radio died, and at the same time the world outside was illuminated, as at midday. At that instant Randy faced the window and he would always retain, like a colour photograph printed on his brain, what he saw—a red fox frozen against the Admiral's green lawn." Frank internalizes technology to convey an instantaneous image of a human being glimpsing another living creature within a context of death. Once again the moment is symbolic: "Thus the lights went out, and in that moment civilization in Fort Repose retreated a hundred years."[28]

Throughout the last chapters of the novel, Frank maintains a tension between endings and a tenuous continuity with life before The Day, between the rupture of the attack and ways in which characters cope with their new circumstances. For instance, they find new sources of food in the local wildlife—fish, armadillos, quail. (Although here, in retrospect, Frank admitted an error, since radioactive fallout would not be selective and would have included the local fauna far more severely than he shows. As he recognized, "there will be few, if any, shelter 'arks' for animals."[29]) The careful balancing between before and after The Day can be seen embodied in the protagonist Randy Bragg. In so far as he teaches the others skills of survival, he acts at times like a surrogate of Frank himself. And because he is already in the Army Reserves, this "legitimates" his new role as local militia commander. He is the organizer of the novel, the citizen-soldier ideally suited to step into the new emergency situation, but only if that new role can be validated through the pre-Day institutions. He thus embodies a combination of authority and improvisation, which depends largely on his prior military experience.

The reemergence of the military at the end of *Panic in Year Zero!* offsets the apocalyptic title and promises a restoration of civic order. The coda to *Alas, Babylon* is less straightforward. The characters see a plane flying over their area in a fresh survey of the terrain, and then a helicopter lands with officers in radiation suits carrying Geiger counters. This is their first contact with the outside since The Day, and the helicopter offers them a chance of escape to a less dangerous region. But they decide against acting on this. Frank totally denies any triumphalism in his ending. The characters hear that the United States "won" the war, but does it matter? The concluding lines to the novel read: "The engine started and Randy turned away to face the thousand-year night."[30] Does this imply a decision to confront human fate, however grim? Frank has shown in considerable realistic detail that, however ingeniously the characters improvise with what they have, their supplies will gradually dwindle away. Their decision not to leave thus resembles a choice of slow suicide. Despite the bleakness of this ending, the novelist

David Brin has acknowledged the impact of *Alas, Babylon* on shaping his own 1985 postnuclear novel *The Postman*. Brin sees Frank's novel as a protosurvivalist work, but one that avoided the extremes of macho triumph or unrelieved gloom.

> Pat Frank certainly criticized some contemporary attributes that he saw in his fellow countrymen—shortsightedness, political myopia, and slowness to correct racism, for example. But he also perceived the majority of them as basically good, capable of cooperation and deserving—if possible—a second chance.
>
> In his novel, the characters are not *only* knocked down by cruel fate. They get to stand up. He lets them try and rebuild.[31]

The writings of Frank and Heinlein on postnuclear survival appeal to the national traditions of the handyman and of self-help in suggesting ways to build a family shelter in a "cabin." As early as 1946 Heinlein was discussing issues of nuclear attack. In his essay "How to Be a Survivor" he recommends "training in various fundamental pioneer skills," essential practical skills that would come into play in life outside a city.[32] Years before any official survival handbooks, Heinlein was combining practical tips with recommendations about morale. Throughout the essay he insists on a continuity between the founding of the United States and the methods needed for national survival. Recovery from nuclear attack thus becomes an atavistic duty to keep alive the spirit of the original pioneers, and Heinlein makes no bones about his national rallying cry: "If you plan for it, you can survive. If you study and plan and are ready to organize when the time comes, you can hope not only to survive but to play a part in winning back lost freedoms."[33]

Heinlein's 1964 novel *Farnham's Freehold* enacts a number of these patriotic values in describing the fortunes of a nationally emblematic family during a nuclear attack. The novel was published shortly after the international crises of the early 1960s that led the Kennedy administration to promote a program of shelter building. The 1961 Department of Defense brochure *Fallout Protection* contained advice on constructing and stocking a family shelter with the aim of being self-sustaining for at least two weeks, all of which has been put into practice by Heinlein's protagonist, Hubert Farnham. From the very first line of the novel, when he has his radio tuned to the emergency frequency, Farnham demonstrates a state of preparedness; he is ready to step into the role of leader to his miniature community of family and neighbors, which he does with military precision (like Heinlein, he is an former naval officer). Once the nuclear bombardment starts, Farnham also adopts the role of tutor to his group, educating them about radiation and the use of their supplies, raising the possibility of biological attack, declaring, "The communists won't smash this country if they can kill us without destroying our wealth. I wouldn't be surprised to learn that bombs had been used only on military targets like the antimissile base here, but that New York and Detroit and such received nerve gas."[34] Whatever the true facts, their communication with the outside world is broken for good.

The group inside the shelter represents a surviving remnant of the nation. As if the point wasn't obvious, Farnham's safe combination is the date of America's Independence Day. After being shot forward in time to a future dictatorship by African Americans, the family manages to return to the novel's present, where the narrative concludes with an enduring image from American history: the frontier trading post. In his coda Heinlein presents his characters as a collective embodiment of national endurance: "They lived through the missiles, they lived through the bombs, they lived through the fires, they lived through the epidemics."[35] The point Heinlein makes is that they survived against all the odds, and their final "freehold" is a synecdoche of the reconstituted nation.

Heinlein's narrative offered an example of the triumph of the will. Its internal logic suggests that Farnham wins because he wants to. In a similar spirit, the ecologist Bruce D. Clayton published *Life After Doomsday*, a self-help manual for how to equip a home shelter and take elementary precautions against nuclear attack. Clayton was writing polemically against what he called the "disarm or die" approach to nuclear war as well as against the disinformation about nuclear attack he felt was being foisted on the public. His handbook supplements and fleshes out a general criticism he had made of discussions of disarmament in the *Bulletin of the Atomic Scientists*, where he attacked the rigid mind-set that clung to the "no survivors myth," among others. Describing Shute's *On the Beach* as technologically impossible even with the current stores of nuclear weapons, he pleads for a rational approach to the issue, an approach he developed in *Life After Doomsday*.[36] It is striking that Clayton concludes his volume by citing three SF novels to exemplify the need for a remnant of books in coping with nuclear war: Walter M. Miller's *A Canticle for Leibowitz*; Jerry Pournelle and Larry Niven's *Lucifer's Hammer* (1977), which describes how a comet strikes Earth; and Wells's *The Time Machine*. From the first of these, he explains, "the Leibowitz project is my informal attempt to see that the knowledge essential to civilization's recovery after a nuclear war will be available when it is needed."[37] Miller would have been bemused by a novel written against the very presence of nuclear weapons being used in the process of surviving a nuclear war.

Descriptions of self-help preparations for nuclear attack resurfaced during the debate over Ronald Reagan's Strategic Defense Initiative in the 1980s and were strongly supported by Heinlein, among others. Dean Ing co-edited with Jerry

Pournelle *Mutual Assured Survival* (1984), one of the key documents supporting SDI, and wrote his survivalist beliefs into *Pulling Through,* which combined
within the same volume a narrative of nuclear war with extensive advice on how
to build and stock a fallout shelter.[38] Ing had earlier contributed a series of articles
on nuclear survival to the journal *Destinies* where he supplies details of how to
construct an air supply system. This practical advice was designed to lift the
reader's morale. At the end of the essay he declares that "it's enough to know you
can live under pressure."[39] These kinds of appeals to handyman skills as a means
of containing the nuclear threat by posing questions of practical know-how take
their cue from the 1977 government brochure *Protection in the Nuclear Age,* which
Ing cites with approval but by the 1980s had come to seem increasingly ludicrous.
The novelist Frederik Pohl pointed out Ing's unconsciously negative lesson:
"If you read Dean Ing's brilliant novel you will see how, with only moderately
optimistic assumptions, perhaps as many as one-third of the American people
can survive a nuclear war and enter into an existence of twelve-hour, seven-day
drudgery, with few amenities and an excellent chance of grisly disease."[40] Praise
for a survivalist novel ironically questions the very value of that survival.

Pulling Through tells the story of a latter-day bounty hunter who survives a
nuclear attack on the United States partly because he is prepared. His home in the
Mount Dora valley north of San Francisco doubles as a shelter, with all the necessary
stocks of food, ammunition, etc.[41] The trigger to nuclear confrontation, as in *Alas,
Babylon,* arises from a crisis with Syria; and when the strike hits San Francisco the
position of the narrator's home enables him to get a panoramic view of the Bay:

> Now the entire region, miles across, lay half-obscured under a gray pall like
> dirty fog. Winking through it were literally thousands of fires, some of them
> running together by now. Black plumes roiled up from oil storage dumps,
> and as I watched, a white star glared in the bay, hurling debris up and away
> in all directions. Even faster than the debris, flying away in what seemed a
> mathematically precise pattern, a ghostly shock wave expanded through the
> smoke, fading as it spread from its epicentre. In the paths of the debris, spidery
> white traceries of smoke fattened into a snowy mile-wide chrysanthemum
> that hid the source of that mighty blast.[42]

This visual spectacle of destruction plays a crucial role in validating the narrator's
care in preparing his home against the worst eventuality. It is also a spectacle that
he scrutinizes scientifically in an attempt to estimate blast limits, wind direction,
and so on.

The blast of "Doomsday," as it is called, induces the narrator's urgency to fix up a basement tunnel, air supply, and other necessities in his sister's house nearby. Unlike Frank, Ing minimizes the psychological impact of the bombs so as to concentrate on practical activities necessary for survival, and all the time the narrator consults his radiation meter to check for danger levels. Another difference from Frank lies in Ing's graphic depiction of different forms of radiation sickness. His narrative reads like a discursive guide to shelter construction and care of the contaminated, and it even includes mention of government publications on shelters, although coming too late for the characters within the narrative.[43] The conclusion to the novel comes with an endorsement of the narrator, his new wife, and the people like them: "So it's my wife Kate, more than any of us, who'll be the key to the future of this country. We adults are survivors by definition; our first priority now is to make our next generations expert at pulling through."[44] For the reader, this immediately cues the second section of the volume, which rejects the argument presented by the physicist Freeman Dyson, among others, that the sponsoring of shelters could actually encourage nuclear war. In other words, through the very act of reading we become members of Ing's future and well-prepared generations.

Ing's confident survivalism was not shared by Tim O'Brien, whose 1985 novel *The Nuclear Age* describes the experiences of a child of the nuclear age. The narrator William Cowling has grown up under the shadow of the bomb, constructing a home shelter in his childhood and protesting it as a student, and in the novel's present is driven by sheer dread to dig a hole in his garden. During the composition of the novel, O'Brien explained, "there is another real bombshelter. No metaphor, no image. Real! Real!" The novel was to be about survival, but "we *won't* survive if we can't stop thinking of nuclear weapons as mere metaphors."[45] Unlike Heinlein, who presents survival as a matter of will and patriotic commitment, O'Brien uses his narrator to assault comforting illusions that distract from the physical immediacy of the bomb. Thus, he complains that "the world . . . is drugged on metaphor."[46] Whether Cowling's hole is expressing anything beyond his futile and obsessive search for a shelter, and thereby demonstrating the pathology of the nuclear age, is part of the finely tuned ambiguity of O'Brien's novel.

By the 1980s such ambiguity might have been expected, but even as early as 1959, *Alas, Babylon* only sustains its account of communal self-help by suppressing some key effects of nuclear war. In the following chapter we turn to another neglected novelist of the Cold War, Philip Wylie, whose fiction reflects an initial, if ambiguous, commitment to civil defense that gradually slides into overt skepticism.

CHAPTER 5

Philip Wylie on the State of the Nation

Although he was one of America's most popular writers of the 1940s and 1950s, Philip Wylie is not widely read today. During the Cold War, however, he was an important commentator on the fears of nuclear war, and his fiction from this period, especially the novels *Tomorrow!* and *Triumph,* offer two of the most graphic accounts of America under attack.

Wylie's studies in psychology and evolutionary biology at Princeton, together with his lifelong interest in science, gave him an intellectual grounding that shaped his postwar career. Although he earned a living as a freelance writer, he prided himself on his expertise in different fields. His stance as a "lay authority" (his own phrase) on civil defense, nuclear weapons, and a host of other subjects reflected his conviction that postwar American life was shaped at every level by science and technology, and he was indignant over the absence of the latter in leading novelists like Hemingway and Faulkner. Wylie contributed to a 1953 symposium on science fiction with an essay entitled "Science Fiction and Sanity in an Age of Crisis," where he railed against pulp SF for producing "wild adventure, wanton genocide on alien planets, gigantic destruction and a piddling phantasmagoria of wanton nonsense."[1] According to Wylie, there were only a few writers, like Wells, Olaf Stapledon, and Aldous Huxley, who addressed the reader's mind.[2] SF can use the principle of extrapolation to bring the reader's dread to the surface, he argued, identifying one possible reason for the repeated emphasis on destruction in his fiction.

> The proper function of the science-fiction author—the myth-maker of the twentieth century—would be to learn the science of the mind's workings and

therewith to plan his work (as many "serious" writers do) so it will represent in *meaning* the known significance of man. Logical extrapolations from existing laws and scientific hypotheses should be woven into tales congruent not with our unconscious hostilities and fears but with the hope of a subjective integration to match the integrated knowledge we have of the outer world . . . For the reader not only projects himself into each tale he encounters, but he considers it, whether he is aware of the fact or not, from the allegorical standpoints. It becomes a parable to him.[3]

Throughout his career Wylie saw his role as addressing national shortcomings, sometimes striking the stance of the nation's conscience, which tended to give his writings a didactic or polemic urgency. He achieved fame with his attack on American infantilism and hypocrisy in his 1942 best seller *A Generation of Vipers.* As Clifford B. Bendau has argued, "Using the intellectual evangelism he inherited from his father, he mercilessly exposed the sin of self-deception."[4]

Wylie saw the Cold War as a period of extended crisis. In a story written shortly before the end of World War II, he first explored the possibility of a super weapon. "The Paradise Crater" (1945) is set in 1965. Despite the fact that the Allies won the war, a secret Nazi organization is using a cavern in Colorado to build uranium-237 bombs. Unusually for Wylie, the Soviet Union is an ally, not an enemy.[5] The advent of the atomic age signaled two things: a massive increase in the destructive potential of military weaponry and a loss of freedom of information, since severe security restrictions were put on scientific research. He combined these two anxieties in his 1946 story "Blunder" set in the 1970s after the "Short War" between Russia and the United States has left the Eastern Seaboard a wasteland. Two scientists plan to explode a bismuth bomb in an abandoned mine in Scandinavia. Their calculations have been published in a journal that other physicists read and note with horror a crucial error in their calculations. Security restrictions prevent this information from reaching the scientists, however, and the explosion bursts out of control, creating an apocalyptically named "omega ray" that destroys Earth. By the end of the story, the planet can only be viewed from Mars, which thereby renders rather absurd one of the scientists' comments on their experiment: "If this goes wrong . . . it's justice! It will teach the whole idiotic world that you cannot monopolize knowledge!"[6] The moral, however, will fall rather flat if there is no surviving humanity to learn from it.

For Wylie, the Cold War was defined through one prevailing emotion: "We live in a midnight imposed by fear—a time like all dark ages."[7] Until the mid-1950s he saw a prime role for civil defense as informing the public and therefore in some measure diffusing that fear. In 1949 he was invited to join the new Federal Civil Defense Authority as an expert consultant; there he devised a defense program for American cities and during the following years wrote passionately against what he felt to be a lack of national preparedness. In the 1951 article "A Better Way to Beat the Bomb," he sharply criticized plans to build underground shelters and replan the layout of cities because time was running against them. Rather contradictorily, Wylie suggests that the inhabitants of big cities should be willing to leave at a moment's notice, but at the same time he attacks government plans for evacuation, taking as his precedent London during World War II. The main point of his article, however, is to criticize the "failure of the average citizen to assimilate what has been told, to infer what that means, and to deduce what might happen and what he *could* be ready to do."[8] This upbeat message conceals an ambivalence in Wylie's writings on civil defense, however. Evidently feeling honor bound to make practical recommendations, his only models could be taken from the last world war, and these, as he recognized, had become obsolete by 1950. Moreover, the imminent production of the H-bomb and intercontinental ballistic missiles simply underlined that obsolescence. This ambivalence runs through Wylie's novels about nuclear war.

During a December 1945 congressional hearing, Robert Oppenheimer was asked how easy it would be to detect a smuggled atom bomb in a major American city. To Congress's consternation, Oppenheimer replied that the only reliable tool would be a screwdriver, meaning that every crate would have to be opened to be absolutely sure that no device was there. This reply, which has gone down in the folklore of the atomic age, was echoed in the physicist E. U. Condon's contribution to Dexter Masters and Katherine Way's 1946 collection *One World or None,* where he declares that "twenty-thousand tons of TNT can be kept under the counter of a candy store."[9] Condon was unconsciously reinforcing the paranoia of the times by arguing that a bomb encased in a wooden box would be undetectable in the next room and that it could be smuggled into the country either in parts or whole by boat.[10] Wylie addressed exactly these possibilities in *The Smuggled Atom Bomb* (serial 1948, novel 1951), which initially plays down the melodrama of the subject by focusing the action on a typical middle-class family living in southern Florida whose lodger is suspected of being a spy by a young member of the household who conveniently happens to be an expert on locks and on chemical analysis. Prying into the lodger's cupboard, the protagonist finds a mysterious heavy, metal object resembling the "segment of a big egg." Taking a scraping, he discovers that the metal is none other than uranium-235, but he is unable to prove this because he loses the sample. In the meantime, the object has disappeared from the lodger's room. The "investigation" stalls temporarily but then extends gradually up the security hierarchy from the family to the FBI and military intelligence. The conspiracy is finally traced to a warehouse in Manhattan, and bombs are subsequently discovered in other American cities. Wylie confirms the seriousness of the threat by describing the accidental detonation of a bomb off the Florida coast, an event without any narrative justification beyond bringing home to the reader the full force of the plot. The political motivation of the conspirators is left implicit throughout, but the conversion of citizens to their cause is described by an FBI agent as a "hollowing out": "They reach the insides of patient, peaceful, law-abiding guys! . . . Rot out their hearts! And yet leave their outside just like always."[11] The attack from within can be conducted against individuals or the nation; the effect is the same. Wylie's emphasis on the untrustworthy nature of appearances plays to the paranoia of the early Cold War, a strategy later followed by works like *The Invasion of the Body Snatchers,* where the alien transformation of small-town citizens leaves them superficially unchanged and therefore indistinguishable from "authentic" humans.

The Disappearance represents one of Wylie's first attempts at applying nonrealist narrative methods to the Cold War situation. On a certain day, the members of one sex "disappear" from the other, and the novel subsequently alternates between sections dealing with the newly isolated men and women. Each sex is thus compelled to recognize the gendered nature of their world, especially women's recognition of how masculinist in impulse the arms race is. One character immediately rationalizes the catastrophe as predictable "ever since those atom boys got fiddling with the forces of nature." An old man "with nasty eyes" in a Miami crowd rationalizes the Disappearance as the "Last Judgement of American capitalism."[12] Although he is ignored within the scene, divine judgment, at least as metaphor, is written into Wylie's first two section headings: "The Hand of God" (on the bizarre disappearance) and "Armageddon" (on its catastrophic consequences). The novel actualizes Armageddon in the nuclear war that breaks out after the Soviets detonate a mine in the San Francisco Bay.[13] Chicago, New York, and other cities suffer the same fate once the war breaks out, and, although a large number of cities are also destroyed in the Soviet Union, Wiley reserves the most spectacular nuclear panorama for the transformation of the American landscape around Chicago:

> In the "total" area of destruction, a region roughly forty miles in radius, little remained of man or his works. The bomb used to cause the ruin was on the order of five hundred thousand times as powerful as the most potent pluto-

nium bomb . . . Approximately twenty-eight hundred square miles of city, suburb and farm had been flattened and driven from twenty to two hundred feet below their former level. The hammered urban pancake had instantly melted. Planes flying high over the resultant immensely radioactive area immediately after the blast saw it as a majestic saucer, here cherry-red, there white-hot, everywhere incandescent.[14]

Much of the impact of *The Disappearance* lies in such bird's-eye images of erasure or in the spectacle of urban ruin. Wylie simply reinforces his conviction of implacable Soviet hostility by evoking pathos from images of American destruction without even considering the parallel consequences for Russia of an attack by the Americans. As the novel progresses, it is revealed that the Soviets had planned their attack from mines long before the Disappearance and that the bomb dropped on Chicago was a "scientific monstrosity" of a "plutonium-tritium-lithium missile" known among the Soviets as "a Lenin." The novel shows women to be infinitely better diplomats, capable of cutting through the polarities of Cold War ideology and thereby avoiding atomic war, but Wylie simply does not have the space to do more than suggest the roots of aggression that were to be probed at length in Bernard Wolfe's *Limbo* and *Dr. Strangelove*.

Where *The Disappearance* attributes social and political ills to gender separation, Wylie's 1955 novella *The Answer* draws on Christian mythology for its parable of the arms race, which drew appreciative comments from both Eleanor Roosevelt and Bernard Baruch.[15] The work opens on an American aircraft carrier during "Mike," the first H-bomb test, which destroyed Elugelab in the Marshall Islands. The actual blast is described in a visual set piece:

A hundred-times-sun-sized sun mottled itself with lesser whiteness, bulked up, became the perfect sphere, ascending hideously and setting forth on the Pacific a molten track . . . The thing swelled and swelled and rose; nonetheless, instant miles of upthrust were diminished by the expansion. Abruptly, it exploded around itself a lewd ring, a halo . . . The fireball burned within itself and around itself, burnt the sea away—a hole in it—a hole in the planet. It melted part way, lopsided, threw out a cubic mile of fire this way—a scarlet asteroid, that . . . The mushroom formed quietly, immensely and in haste; it towered, spread, and in the incandescent air hurtled at the watchers on the circumference. In the mushroom new fire burst forth, cubic miles of phosphor-pale flame.[16]

As in earlier evocations of the nuclear sublime, this spectacle is a visual event detached from its natural context which has a dynamic of its own that is partly sexual, partly Promethean. The purpose of the image is clearly to establish the power of the nuclear subject that functions as the starting point for the parable. All goes well with the test until, on a nearby island, a casualty is discovered who turns out to be a dead angel, though is suspected of being an extraterrestrial, Gabriel, or a Soviet "biological device." Then a second parallel explosion takes place in Siberia with the same results. The Russian premier has an apocalyptic reaction: "In the angel he saw immediately a possible finish to the dreams of Engels, Marx, the rest. He saw a potential end of communism and even of the human race."[17] Each angel then challenges the ideology of the opposing sides, ironically recalling the common Christian origins of American and Russian cultures. The angelic corpses pose a practical problem of information management and a broader problem of understanding. The forthright Russian reaction is to attach the remains to another hydrogen bomb and blast them to smithereens. On a Pacific island it is finally revealed that the angel fell to earth with a gold book containing the message "love one another" in different languages.

To a large extent, this parable is built on parallels between the two sides, but the apparent evenness of comparison is undermined by the description of the Russian premier as a wily oriental despot with a "Mongol face and eyes as dark and inexpressive and unfeeling as prunes" and American officers as the embodiment of righteous strength—"anvil shoulders, marble hair, feldspar complexion." The revelation of ideologically controlled hatred as a transformation of fear is a diagnosis directed only against the Russians, so *The Answer* proves in that sense to be a skewed fable. On the surface it recommends mutual respect and a recognition of parallels between East and West; but the subtext uncritically polarizes each regime along a series of oppositions between humanity and despotism, reason and repression. Communism functions throughout Wylie's fiction as an alien force, not an alternative creed. Indeed, Wylie collaborated with the psychologist Robert Lindner on an essay on "psycho-politics" that describes communism as a mental illness, and a 'round-the-world trip he made in the midfifties was expressly designed to show Americans that communism was an aggressive ideology whose "target is the intellect of every living person; where people cannot be persuaded, the target becomes the heart, nerves, sanity and the body of each of us."[18]

In his 1954 essay "Panic, Psychology, and the Bomb," Wylie attacks the civil defense strategies of the time for their denial that a nuclear attack would cause widespread panic. On the contrary, he insists, panic is already being registered indirectly through forms of suppression or displacement, like the UFO craze. With the evidence of Hiroshima, he shows survivors who remember the spectacle of the blast and the horrific sight of casualties and who fear that another bomb might fall. Wylie continues with a 1954 statement that sheds direct light on his Cold War fiction: "Movies and TV have given the American public no adequate idea of the mere spectacle of the bomb, its sky-filling, multi-hued aftermath, the peculiar ruins and the cubic miles of rolling dust—not to mention a city a-fire."[19] In 1951 Wylie had contributed to a special issue of *Collier's* magazine devoted to a "Preview of the War We Do Not Want," which combined text with emotive graphics.[20] Thanks to his Q-level (maximum) security clearance from the Atomic Energy Commission (AEC), Wylie must have been virtually unique among American writers of the time in having witnessed nuclear test detonations firsthand, and he was determined to convey their visual immediacy to his readers, to fill the gap he felt had been left open by the media.

Accordingly, in 1951 he began working on a film of a nuclear attack on America that "was devised to satisfy certain vast gaps in general public knowledge concerning atom bombs, their dangers, and how to deal with them if they are used by an enemy on our cities."[21] His plan was to supplement existing civil defense strategies and provide an educational component. During the preliminary stage of his planning, he secured approval from the Air Force head General Vandenberg, the secretaries for Air and Defense, and the chairman of the Atomic Energy Commission. Despite his skill in securing clearance at the highest level, the project never came to fruition, except as the novel *Tomorrow!* Nevertheless, the existing manuscript treatment gives us a clear indication of how Wylie wanted to depict the bombing. Having established sequences showing the day-to-day lives of his characters living in twin Midwest cities loosely modeled on St. Paul and Minneapolis, Wylie planned to accelerate the pace of shots against the background of air raid sirens getting louder and suddenly falling silent. Then would follow the blast sequence, a rapid montage of shots for which Wylie expected technical help from the AEC.

First should come the burst, a shot taken over a miniature of both cities.

Then a closer shot of a fireball forming. Maybe the AEC will let us have one. These pictures, multi-colored, magnificent, could be superimposed over a picture of the city.

Then, back on the miniature, the down-blast of atomic fire and heat and radioactivity—which hits the area in the middle and spreads out in a few seconds at least a mile in every direction. In this shot you can't see what the rainbow-hued rain of violence does. Everything is merely obscured in fire and formidable light.

Next—a new series of fast shots showing what happens as the various items of blast, heat and radioactivity hit our main characters . . .

These shots are very short and taken from the center of the cities out, so that we almost feel the camera is following the race of the bomb effects as they spread.[22]

The following shots essentially repeat parts of the blast, at first without survivors and then showing people fleeing the destroyed areas.

The problem with Wylie's sequence lies in a tension between his intention to educate the public and the quasi-documentary method he outlines. The same problem arises in *Tomorrow!* In order to film atomic explosions, very high film speeds were needed that were well beyond the normal limits of human vision. Despite its speed, the sequence functions like slow motion, in a way not dissimilar to the famous urban explosion in Ray Bradbury's *Fahrenheit 451*: "For another of those impossible instants the city stood, rebuilt and unrecognizable, taller than it had ever hoped or strived to be, taller than man had built it, erected at last in gouts of shattered concrete and sparkles of torn metal into a mural hung like a reversed avalanche, a million colors, a million oddities, a door where a window should be, a top for a bottom, a side for a back, and then the city rolled over and fell down dead."[23]

Throughout the novel there have been radio warnings that another war might break out, and this image is the culmination of the military activity signaled by the jets roaring overhead. Bradbury's orgasmic image of destruction paradoxically figures itself as a reconstruction or, more correctly, an inversion, a surreal deconstruction of the city into its own materials. In contrast, Wylie's sequence separates out mini-phases of the bomb's detonation in order to make sense of an instantaneous event. There is a much starker difference between the two accounts, however. Bradbury describes a dissociated society where political and military activity takes place outside the consent or even interest of the citizens, whereas Wylie shows how nuclear fear and civil defense measures penetrate every level of his twin cities of Green Prairie and River City so thoroughly that civilian and military roles are constantly blurring into each other.

Tomorrow! grew out of Wylie's film project and also out of work he had done for the Federal Civil Defense Authority (to whose members the novel was dedicated) on the psychological effects of the atom bombing of American cities. The novel describes the atom bombing of the twin cities and was written with a very specific aim. When Wylie sent President Eisenhower an advance copy, he described its purpose as being "to supply the intellectual and emotional means to the public for facing what might have to be faced in reality someday." More specifically, in an essay of 1954, he explained: "In my currently best-selling novel, *Tomorrow!*, I have predicted that USA, under atomic blitz, might panic and stampede simply because our people will not learn the lessons and the facts that their government, through FCDA, has tried for years to teach them."[24]

A crucial role is that of the editor of one of the local newspapers who publishes a trenchant editorial addressed to a "sleepwalking nation" on the public's inability to confront its own fears of atomic holocaust—clearly a surrogate for Wylie. Such fears of Armageddon, the editor argues, are nothing new and date back at least to the Middle Ages. What *is* new is a collective dissociation of deep-rooted anxieties from civilized reason: "Thus a condition is set up in which a vast majority of the citizens, unable to acknowledge with their minds the dread that eats at their blind hearts, loses all contact with reality." There is an absolute congruence between the editor's words and Wylie's narrative comments, such as the following: "It was a time where Americans once again refused to face certain realities that glared at them with an ever-increasing balefulness."[25] Wylie repeatedly contrasts the willful ignorance of his characters with the awareness of the narrator. Another crucial difference from Hersey's narrative is Wylie's engagement with the psychological issue of expectancy. And there is no sharp separation of civilians from the military, since each of the main families described has members in the army. The editor conflates the two roles of social commentator and victim. In fact, he is one of the first to die in the blast: "It was a Light of such intensity that Coley could see nothing except its lightness and its expanding dimensions. It swelled over the sky above and burst down toward him. He felt, at the same time, a strange physical sensation—just a brief start of a sensation—as if gravity had vanished and he, too, were a rushing thing, and a prickling through his body, and a heat. And he was no more."[26]

Wylie awkwardly sets up the point of view of an eyewitness with the clear purpose of conveying the horrific immediacy of the blast, but the very pacing of the prose, which acts like slow motion, contradicts the suddenness of the moment. Just for a second Wylie invites the readers to imagine their own nuclear deaths. Of course, the editor's death is simply the first of many, and Wylie presents a relentless series of images designed to force the reader to confront the most horrific sights. Although the growing mushroom cloud is compared to Technicolor newsreels at one point, this description of corpses certainly would not have appeared in any news report: "They were mostly blackish, but some were scarlet and some had faces and bodies that looked exactly the way a steak looked when it caught on fire. And some . . . weren't exactly dead, or completely dead. A few in cars were opening and closing their mouths or moving their arms feebly."[27]

Tomorrow! foregrounds the possibility of attack in its first chapters as a subject for debate, confronting a public dread that Wylie describes elsewhere as a "repressed super-hysteria." Ironically, scientists have rendered apocalypse possible, as pestilence and famine, and the novel's title self-evidently insists on the imminence of disaster.[28] At the beginning of the novel Wylie outlines the history of the "sister cities" as a microcosm of America itself, in effect narrating a series of beginnings (the establishment of settlements, trade, industry, and so on). Counterpointed against that narrative, the section headings supply an apocalyptic "bomb-time" counting down from the disaster-point ("X-day minus 90"). The designation of the day of attack by the sign "X" and subsequent references to this event as "It" indicate a suppressed referent that is immediately comprehensible but never spoken. It is also symbolically appropriate and consistent with other narratives of the period that the attack comes on Christmas Day—in other words, it presents an attack on a Christian way of life. The UK edition's title of C. M. Kornbluth's 1955 account of a Russian invasion is *Christmas Eve* (U.S. edition *Not This August*), and Alfred Coppel's postholocaust narrative *Dark December* also pivots around the Christmas season. The obvious implication is an ironic perception of a celebration of peace being the occasion of warfare.

Also, *Tomorrow!* traces out the psychological reactions to each phase of disaster. When "Condition Red" is announced, it produces "the sound of thousands upon thousands of people—men and women and children—in absolute panic, in total fear, in headless flight, being trampled, being squeezed to death, having ribs caved in and legs broken, screaming, trying to escape."[29] This total collapse into animal fear has been identified by Guy Oakes and Andrew Grossman as typical of Wylie: "Irrational, uncontrollable, rampant, and stampeding mobs reappear throughout Wylie's Cold War fiction . . . once the organized monopoly of force that backs up legal sanctions is destroyed, the social order collapses."[30] The novel's dwarfing perspective, the sounds of lament, and the sudden coming of the "Light" encode the spectacle as a travesty of the Day of Judgment, where enlightenment is replaced by an erasure so complete that even the rudimentary distinction between animate and inanimate is lost. Wylie's evocation of such a negative spectacle runs completely against his civil defense training, which was supposed to instil determination and rational responses.

Wylie's exploration of human reactions to the catastrophe—the fragmentation of perception, struggle of emergency services, outbreak of looting—gives way to a continuation of combat that lifts the scale of destruction on to an altogether different level. When Russia requests surrender, America responds by exploding a "dirty" H-bomb (coated in cobalt) in the Baltic. This can only be imagined through a hypothetical external observer on Mars: "In the ensuing dark, a Thing swelled above the western edge of Russia, alight, alive, of a size to bulge beyond the last particles of earth's air." When Russia surrenders, we are told, "The last war was finished. The last great obstacle to freedom had been removed from the human path."[31]

The novel is based on the ideological premise of the Soviet evil empire, which means that it cannot conclude on its main local focus. The shift to world war demonstrates the inadequacy of Wylie's narrative starting point and implies the incipient obsolescence of his main subject. The editor of the *Bulletin of the Atomic Scientists* objected that Wylie's ending might induce a smug triumphalism in the reader, to which Wylie responded: "To attract the readership I wanted, I had to invent a victory bomb (which I knew to be technically silly) and I had to show America restoring itself, complete with juke boxes."[32]

Coincidentally, with the publication of *Tomorrow!* Wylie made contact with the writer and rocket specialist Martin Caidin, who had been working for the New York State Civil Defense Commission and from February of 1955 had begun to serve as consultant to the Air Force Missile Test Center. At the time of their first contact, Caidin was completing a novel on the same subject as *Tomorrow!*—namely, the atom bombing of an American city and its struggle to survive. Originally called *This City Lived,* this "documentary-novel," as Caidin described it, was published in 1956 with the title *The Long Night.*[33] The city in question, Harrington, is modeled on New York, and the narrative covers much the same ground as *Tomorrow!* with the difference being that an elaborate civil defense organization is already in place and works effectively after the bombing despite the widespread panic. Unlike Wylie, Caidin describes the immediacy of the blast through the fate of a single character:

> The shock wave and the blast arrived. The steel fist pounced savagely on the small recreation hall. Charley Bowers, still transfixed, blind, before the window, received full force the impact of the shattering glass. The jagged shards erupted into the room, preceding the blast which for a fraction of a second hesitated against the outside walls. The glass erupted toward Charley Bowers with bullet-like speed. There was not even sufficient time for blood to begin to flow before his body was lacerated into pulpy slivers. The shock killed him almost instantly.[34]

As in Wiley's novel, the description carefully paces the syntax to give a slow-motion effect necessary for the reader to understand the process. This passage gives only a brief segment of a longer event which begins with the flash that burns

Charley's eyes. By the time we read of the window's implosion, he is already dead, in effect, and there follows immediately the full force of the shock wave that destroys the building. Where Wylie's disparate accounts of blast victims imply that sheer chance plays the major role in survival, Caidin's description has a simple protective point to make: In case of nuclear attack, avoid windows. However, the development of the hydrogen bomb and of intercontinental ballistic missiles was already rendering obsolete Caidin's account of survival, which draws parallels with World War II events like the Allied bombing of Hamburg, thereby inevitably normalizing nuclear attack for his readers.

By the end of the 1950s, Wylie had become convinced that the proliferation and sophistication of H-bombs had rendered civil defense impossible. In a 1960 letter to the editor of the *Bulletin of the Atomic Scientists,* he explained that if H-bombs held by both super powers were ever used in an all-out war, "no conceivable form of defense and Civil Defense would prevent such a war from pretty much wiping out life in the Northern Temperate Zone."[35] As usual, in his writings Wylie homed in on perceptions of likely scenarios and in his 1960 article "Why I Believe There Will Be No All-Out War" attacked the "belief, almost as absolute as a religious faith, that they [the leaders] and the rest of the people of the land must have a change to 'win' any war—whatever the megatonnage of weapons used against it, whatever their numbers, and however swiftly they are missile delivered."[36] This naive triumphalism, he argues in the article, is based on serious errors of judgment. It presupposes that nuclear shelters will offer refuge when they really will become death traps, that there will only be a single nuclear assault, and that large-scale evacuation would be possible, whereas panic would cause chaos. And, as if all these factors were not bad enough, fallout would reduce the whole country to a "death chamber." Thus, Wylie totally negates any possible value for civil defense by denying the very possibility of nuclear victory. He accordingly shifts the discourse of warfare into nonmilitary areas like loans and education, while insisting that the worldwide struggle against communism is "the only real war in which we and our children and, probably, theirs will be embattled—the so-called war for men's minds."[37]

From the mid-1950s on, Wylie struggled to balance his implacable hostility toward Soviet communism with his recognition that the hydrogen bomb had raised the nuclear stakes so drastically that any talk of victory was problematic. He wrote his 1963 novel *Triumph* against a trend in nuclear war fiction as described by one character:

There were also lots of prophetic books and movies about total war in the atomic age, and all of them were practically as mistaken as plain people and politicians and the Pentagon planners. In all of them that I recall, except for one, we Americans took dreadful punishment and then rose from the ground like those Greek-legend soldiers—Jason's men—and defeated the Soviets and set the world free. That one, which came closer to reality so far as the Northern Hemisphere is concerned, showed how *everybody on earth* died.[38]

This one exception has been identified by Paul Brians as Shute's *On the Beach*.[39] Although there is no such resurgence in the conclusion to *Tomorrow!* that novel, nevertheless, describes a just war to ensure the freedom of the surviving remnant and concludes with a massive imbalance between the devastation of the Soviet Union and the regional destruction of the United States.

In *Triumph* Wylie radically alters his sense of an ending to undermine the very possibility of survival. The novel opens with what promises to be a weekend party at the home of the millionaire Vance Farr. The group that gathers is an ethnic mixture that again suggests a microcosm of the United States, and Farr's house is built at the top of a Connecticut hill that is steeped in history. Farr has fitted out the tunnels under the house as a nuclear shelter so elaborate as to be an absurd denial of a national civil defense system. The second irony is the house's name, Uxmal, since it resembles the stepped pyramids of the Mayans, an extinct civilization. A considerable portion of the novel is taken up with the psychology of the group in Farr's shelter after nuclear war breaks out, and here a structural problem presents itself. Wylie pursues the possibility of survival in shelters. Yet he is equally concerned with conveying to the reader the sheer scale of destruction in a nuclear war. Initially, then, there is a formal separation between chapters dealing with the shelter and those dealing with the outside world.

When describing the explosions of the bombs, Wylie is cautious to avoid the paradoxes of *Tomorrow!* and makes a strenuous effort to describe the complex unique nature of the bomb blast:

"The burst of a nuclear weapon is curiously different from an ordinary explosion. An observer, providing he has adequate protection for his eyes and is far enough away to survive, at first merely *senses* some tremendous event in the air. There occurs a not-really-seen but shocking awareness, as if of an invisible leap, or as if the air itself has been smitten by a colossal but unseen fist." Out of his attempt to capture its uniqueness, Wylie writes one of the most sophisticated descriptions of the nuclear blast. Although the blast would be perceived through the senses, Wylie shows how it challenges the ordering of the senses and even the capacity of language to articulate it. The first overall sensation of an event gives way to the extraordinary light—both brilliantly white and shifting through multiple colors.

Then the sound is not a momentary blast, "so it is not like the shuddery thump of a land mine or the geysering bang of a torpedo or the boom of a shell. There is no sudden noise. When the noise comes, it is infinite, enduring, and more a *compression* than thunder—thunder augmented beyond belief."

The city map that Wylie printed in *Tomorrow!* kept the bomb blasts on a human scale. Here, however, the extent of the destruction is conveyed through nonspecific plurals and through the reversal of materiality so that the insubstantial (air) becomes hard and all buildings desubstantialized: "In a roughly circular area, miles across, underneath this thing, all buildings will have been vaporized. Farther out, for more miles the thrusting ram of steel-hard air will topple the mightiest structures and sweep all lesser edifices to earth, as if their brick and stone, girders and beams were tissue paper."[40] The future tenses in these parts of chapter 3 make it clear that the descriptions are nondiegetic and are presenting a typical hypothetical case whose rhetorical force depends on the cumulative use of terms like "millions," "myriads," and "multitudes." As such terms mount up, the event seems so unavoidable that hypothesis turns into narrative certainty.

Farr and his guests are still down in their shelter, however, experiencing such blasts through the mediation of technical recording equipment. The latter offers Wylie the means to link inside to outside. A surviving TV station in Central America transmits film of explosions taken for posterity ("the surviving world needs to know") by an aircrew that subsequently dies of radiation. As the survivors in the shelter gather before the screen, holocaust becomes media spectacle, the camera panning across unrecognizable, lunar landscapes. Even when a small town seems to have escaped damage, the total absence of life suggests that it has been deluged in fallout, and the town thus becomes a poignant image of a lost civic order. The progression in the novel's evocation of destruction is outward and expansive so that after a second nuclear strike the entire northern hemisphere is reduced to a pock-marked wilderness swept by radioactive clouds.

Both *Tomorrow!* and *Triumph* describe scenarios of nuclear attack where the United States reacts to preemptive strikes from the Soviet Union. In the latter case the ostensible flash point is given rather anachronistically as an invasion of Yugoslavia by "volunteer" troops, a fantasy deriving from the 1949 Cominform call to overthrow Tito's regime. The U.S. defense system is attacked constantly by the narrator and later by Farr, speaking as Wylie's surrogate, for missing obvious inferences, for failing to design a coherent plan, and above all for missing the ideological premise of Soviet communism: that their leaders "had always been willing to pay *any* price whatever to conquer the world."[41] Unlike the Americans, the Russians have a "fiendishly planned" long-term strategy whereby state-selected members from all walks of life will be housed in massive underground bunkers. The Yugoslav crisis turns out to have been stage-managed so as to catch the Americans off-guard and launch a first strike that destroys two-thirds of the country. A second strike saturates the entire western hemisphere with deadly radiation. The few surviving U.S. submarines destroy the underground bases but are themselves destroyed in the process. Wylie then adds a sardonic epitaph: "The doctrines of Marx, Engels, Lenin, Krushchev, Merov, and Grodsky were finally undone . . . at the cost of half a world and of the vast majority of people who once called themselves free and civilized."[42]

The irony here is ambiguous, since it could be directed solely against communism but the novel also attacks the U.S. government's use of war games and routine "doomsday" scenarios in its defense planning. East and West are both (unequally) indicted for their militarism and materialism. Clearly there is no suggestion here of transforming apocalypse, only of national erasure. One of the survivors recites Psalm 23 as he emerges, metaphorically encoding the shelter as the "valley of the shadow of death." And other parallels present themselves. The protagonist of the novel, a brilliant physicist, reflects on the radioactive plasma contained in "bottles" in a research establishment, and of course the nuclear holocaust is depicted as the bursting forth of this material from "vials of wrath." The novel shadows the figures of apocalypse in other respects, and always with the deity as an absence. In the Book of Revelation God comes in a cloud, while the mushroom cloud here functions as a secularized sign of destruction. The thunder, lightning, and devastating fire similarly signify military technology spiraling out of human control. And, as already suggested, the alignment of nations cannot be read as the godly confronting the ungodly, because part of Wylie's purpose is to show his own nation's slippage into worshiping the false god of materialism.

However potent the external threat is from Russia, Wylie ultimately writes into the novel America's status as a super power as a negative quality, since the failure of the United States to anticipate war results in worldwide destruction. At the end of the novel, Farr and his companions are rescued by helicopters from an Australian carrier and taken away from an America that will have "no name." Ultimately, Wylie's title is sharply sardonic, since the novel traces out the erasure of America from the face of the earth. By the 1960s Wylie had become completely disenchanted with Pentagon strategists' attitude toward nuclear war. Like Stanley Kubrick with *Dr. Strangelove*, Wylie attacked the routine discussion of "mega-deaths" as a sanitizing term and also Herman Kahn's "doomsday machine," insisting that the United States could not possibly defend itself against an all-out nuclear strike. In 1968 he described Secretary of Defense Robert McNamara's "thin shield" of antiballistic missiles as an expensive scheme that would only benefit the arms industry. Far from offering greater security, the ABMs "amount only to an escalation of the standing stalemate," he insisted.[43]

Shortly before his death in 1972, Wylie's interest had shifted to ecology. In 1970 he agreed to write an episode for the television show *The Name of the Game* about a future America where everyone has to live in airtight underground cities, a script he then rewrote in novel form as *Los Angeles: A.D. 2017.* Drawing on H. G. Wells's *When the Sleeper Wakes* (1899), Wylie's protagonist falls asleep in the early 1980s and wakes in 2017 to discover that Los Angeles has become a subterranean city run on commercial lines ("USA, Incorporated") with strict security guards. Apart from Wylie's borrowings from Huxley and Orwell to evoke a brave new world of streamlined technologies, where defectives and criminals are "erased" and where citizens are classified from A to D, many of the images in the novel could apply to the aftermath of a nuclear attack. The first thing the time traveler sees is policemen in protective clothing, then an arid landscape littered with rusting vehicles, and finally a Los Angeles rebuilt underground, as if realizing the civil defense plans of the early Cold War. In a "historical" video showing how the present situation came into being, he sees a gigantic bulldozer pushing over piles of corpses in the street. The analogies with nuclear war are left implicit in this narrative, unlike in *The End of the Dream.*

The End of the Dream is one of Wylie's most experimental works structurally; it is a polyphonic novel on ecological disaster with a broad variety of narrative means included within its chronicle sequence ranging from passages from fictitious histories, news articles, and excerpts from radio and TV programs. Wylie's method owes much to Wells's *The Shape of Things to Come*, a work he viewed with considerable respect. There is, however, a stark difference between the end points of their respective histories. Wells saw history (that of Britain and America) as evolving toward an ultimate world state that would mark the triumph of rational social organization, whereas Wylie carries out an autopsy on the future demise of America more in the tradition of Orwellian dystopias.[44] As his very title suggests, the United States has ceased to exist by 2023, the present of his novel. The dream of a "proper heritage" for America that Wylie saw as opening up with the dawn of the atomic age has now collapsed.[45] In place of Wells's Simon Raven, Wylie uses the editor Willard Gulliver to assemble a collage of different voices that collectively articulate the environmental anxieties of the country (Gulliver himself witnesses Black Valentine's Day, a massive blackout in New York and the Northeast), but this role is then picked up by a whole series of different characters. One of the underlying premises of Wylie's novel is that nature is a whole system that knows no boundaries, and Wylie takes care to situate his characters geographically so as to relate them to the entire nation. Thus, a Vietnam veteran in Kentucky helplessly watches as his children are boiled alive in the local river polluted by a nearby nuclear reactor. On the whole, the media in Wylie's novel perform a positive function in transforming local events into national news. The vet's voice is channeled through a TV documentary, later transcribed in the text. Wylie reserves a special status for investigative journalism in this context. He pursues a populist method of assembling instances of eyewitness accounts, letters, notes on a mysterious green slime, etc., that dramatizes ecological inquiry as a spontaneous and collective undertaking, not the hobbyhorse of a few cranks. Diversity of voice carries its own special plausibility and, if anything, tends to understate the apocalyptic dimension of what is being described. Radio announcements during the blackout tersely give only the bare facts of the attendant air crashes, or a nineteen-year-old Floridian gives an interview account of an invasion by predatory wormlike creatures from the sea ("vibes")—both of which play down scale and concentrate instead on the immediate practicalities of avoiding death.

As early as 1947 Wylie had declared, "Today, freedom has disappeared from the face of the earth."[46] For him, one of the defining characteristics of the atomic age were the restrictions imposed by the newly formed security state on the circulation of any information that might relate to the production of nuclear weapons. Wylie's postwar writings return again and again to the political right of the American people to know, and *The End of the Dream* is ultimately concerned with the circulation of knowledge. As the Cold War proceeded, Wylie developed a perception of a general self-protective secrecy maintained by the establishment, which he attacks throughout the novel. A newspaper editorial makes the point about a potato blight: "No means of silencing those who had the facts seems to have been too cunning, illegal or unethical, even criminal in many cases."[47] The specific case polemically challenges the reader's identification of government with legality and aligns industry with officialdom and secrecy. It is no coincidence that Wylie several times refers to Richard Nixon, whose presidency was marked by running battles with the press. While for convenience I have been referring to this work as a novel, Wylie casts his future history in the form of a quasi-journalistic exposé, a future-retrospective work of reportage designed to reveal to the reader how the United States destroyed itself.

Throughout his narrative, Wylie draws on a pool of images of nuclear apocalypse to articulate the disasters that are now not the result of an enemy but of Americans themselves. In other words, American technology has turned against its own land with catastrophic results. Wylie's imagistic continuity between nuclear attack and ecological disaster had already been exploited by Rachel Carson, one of his sources, in her 1962 classic report on pesticides, *Silent Spring,* which opens with a "Fable for Tomorrow," describing a midwestern town rendered ghostly by pollution:

> The roadsides, once so attractive, were now lined with brown and withered vegetation as though swept by fire . . .
>
> In the gutters under the eaves and between the shingles of the roofs, a white granular powder still showed a few patches; some weeks before it had fallen like snow upon the roofs and the lawns, the fields and streams.
>
> No witchcraft, no enemy action had silenced the rebirth of new life in this stricken world. The people had done it themselves.[48]

The enemy is relocated within the home environment, although Wylie attributes specific responsibility to the military-industrial complex first named by Eisenhower in 1961. Again and again Wylie presents actual and hypothetical military projects as a series of attacks against the environment. Carson singles out pesticides as the prime destructive agent; Wylie stresses radioactive waste.

In the novel's early pages, discussion of possible disasters essentially repeat the civil defense orthodoxies of the early 1950s that were the subject of Wylie's attack in *Tomorrow!* A New York teacher claims that the citizens would behave with fortitude in any crisis, but shortly afterward a Manhattan warehouse full of toxic chemicals explodes. Fear of a firestorm raises the local emergency to "Condition Red," the same level as for a nuclear attack. The absence of official statements about the fire creates panic across the city, and after the main explosion the radio switches to emergency information only, another analogy with the nuclear aftermath. Air traffic is so badly disrupted that planes have to crash-land in the sea and, in a graphic anticipation of 9/11, one plows into a high-rise apartment block. As fuel leaks down the side of the building, it ignites, illuminating the spectacle of surviving passengers and residents trying to find their way to the ground. The Manhattan fire is the first of many disasters, but the 1979 explosion that destroys Cleveland is the one where the nuclear analogy is made the most explicit. A local newspaper reports:

> At 10:10 this morning Cleveland was devastated by an explosion so cataclysmic it was attributed to an atomic bomb. A ring of fire as much as two miles across now rages on the perimeter of an area of total ruin and thousands of smaller fires elsewhere in Greater Cleveland are still burning. [Analogies with

Hiroshima and Nagasaki are admitted as logical, then refuted, and finally the newspaper returns to the comparison.]

The blast was actually "atomic" in its force . . . the blast at "ground zero" had a force of twenty-one kilotons, plus or minus two.[49]

It seems as if the only way of making sense of the disaster is through the nuclear analogy. Ironically, it is revealed that the explosion took place on the Cuyahoga River running through the city, which had become polluted by leakage from a chemical plant "doing work essential for national defense" and caught on fire on 23 June 1969. Wylie's graphic descriptions of cities being destroyed echo some of the most sensational warnings of nuclear attack in the 1950s. The trailer to the film *Invasion USA* (1952), for example, invites its viewers to "SEE NEW YORK DISAPPEAR! SEE SEATTLE BLASTED!" and Wylie is appealing to the same sense of spectacle, without any reassuring reestablishment of normality.

If nature is perceived as a system with its own homoeostatic balances, then the early displacement of the biblical threat "vengeance is mine" from the voice of the deity indicates that Wylie is dealing in secular apocalypse. For Robert Howard Barshay, Wylie in this novel "saw himself as a Hebrew prophet dealing with the Protestant themes of grace and damnation."[50] Biblical allusions underpin this progression through the fall of towers (a high-rise block in New York explodes during a blackout), plagues, and a river of flames (symbolically marking the transition from the seventies to the eighties), culminating in an "Antarctic Gehenna" triggered off by pit fires. One of the pivotal scenes in the novel presents mass deaths in a New York overhung by a toxic cloud.

What I saw was almost incredible. The crowd on my side of the street at a distance of four blocks and beyond had become dwarfed. It took a moment to understand that incredible phenomenon. It was as if everybody had suddenly become two feet tall. And this strange endwarfing was spreading. The standing masses were serially shortening—and then it was plain.

They had fallen.

They were falling like wheat cut by an invisible reaper, one that was approaching. They were, I knew, dead.[51]

This passage makes it clear that Wylie is drawing on a Christian tradition of apocalypse far older than the Cold War. Apocalypse, however, should have two phases: the destruction of the old order and the introduction of the new. In Christian apocalypse, the breakdown of the current world order is a herald to a new spiritual dispensation, but here and throughout the novel Wylie shows civic order collapsing without any alleviation. This was characteristic of Wylie's writing on the bomb in general. Despite his ardent campaigning for civil defense, he retained a quasi-religious fascination with spectacles of destruction implicitly moralized as the results of human failings. This underlying pessimism about humans' ability to control nuclear technology was shared by Walter M. Miller Jr., who imagined nuclear war as such a massive rupture to culture that it resulted in a rerun of history itself.

CHAPTER 6

Cultural Cycles in Walter M. Miller's
A Canticle for Leibowitz

We have seen in the fiction of Philip Wylie the fascination with the "prospect of the postholocaust social collapse."[1] Indeed, without making any of his works overtly religious, Wylie's favored stance as a writer was that of a latter-day Jeremiah, grimly warning the nation of its shortcomings. For an explicit engagement with religious issues we turn to Walter M. Miller's *A Canticle for Leibowitz*, which avoids the clichés of barbarism by presenting the aftermath of nuclear war as a rerun of the Dark Ages and which traces out a historical sequence through its three books until the novel ends at a point where nuclear war breaks out again.

A Canticle for Leibowitz was composed as three novellas: *A Canticle for Leibowitz* (1955), *And the Light Is Risen* (1956), and *The Last Canticle*.[2] It is not unique to dramatize the aftermath of a disaster as historical repetition. Postnuclear narratives by many authors ranging from Aldous Huxley to Neal Barrett Jr. show how the population has reverted to pastoral tribalism. Nor is it unique to use historical repetition as an ironic comment on the present. Philip K. Dick does as much in *The World Jones Made* (1956), which describes the rise to power of a demagogue as a replay of political events in 1930s Germany. Miller, by contrast, establishes a whole series of resemblances in his novel in order to describe how the history of the West evolves in cycles. Critics of the novel have tended to concentrate on Miller's religious themes at the expense of the novel's textual intricacies. William Senior, for instance, sees distortion everywhere in the narrative and infers a rather bland message, namely the "uncertainty of life in this world," but scarcely comes to grips with the rhetorical nature of that uncertainty.[3] *A Canticle* is a very rare example of the postnuclear genre where the cataclysm has a direct impact on the novel's own textual condition.

Miller's 1952 story "It Takes a Thief" (retitled "Big Joe and the Nth Generation") anticipates some of the central themes of *A Canticle* in depicting a posthollocaust world where books have disappeared, surviving only as "memorized ritual chants." Earth has been destroyed, and the protagonist, a member of the scattered Mars colony, has been nailed up, as if in crucifixion, for stealing one of these chants. When he is unexpectedly released, he attempts to penetrate the lost archive (Fermi, Einstein, and others have become a pantheon of "ancient gods") housed in vaults guarded by priests and a monster named Big Joe. The latter turns out to be a robot programmed to attack anyone who steps on certain floor tiles before the entrance: "A creature of metal . . . he had obviously been designed to kill. Tri-fingered hands with gleaming talons, and a monstrous head shaped like a Marswolf, with long silver fangs."[4] Once inside the archive contained within the computer, the protagonist finds the records of the "Blaze of the Great Wind," and the story ends with an expectation that this force can be re-created.[5] On a small scale, here we encounter themes Miller would expand and develop in *A Canticle*: the loss of knowledge, the tenuous preservation of literacy by oral transmission, the priests' guardianship of the archive, and the privileging of technology within that body of lost knowledge.

A Canticle opens with a discovery within a wasteland around the year AD 2600. The context is a new Dark Age where one Brother Francis, a novice from the nearby Leibowitz Abbey, is performing a Lenten fast. An aged man appears out of the desert and shows him a rock that will complete the shelter he is building. When he removes this rock a "cave" is revealed that proves to be the remains of a fallout shelter from an earlier era. Within the cave Francis finds a metal box containing a number of documents: a shopping list, a racing form, a note to a friend, and a blueprint. Inside the lid is a message with the following postscript: "I put the seal on the lock and put TOP SECRET on the lid just to keep Em from looking inside."[6] Here the reader is positioned as a vicarious recipient of a message posted during wartime, where the sender was trying to keep a loved one from disturbing information. Opening this Pandora's box thus carries connotations of the release of dangerous knowledge. Francis is a member of a monastic order devoted to preserving the traces of a literacy that has been lost. Other members of this same order have been committing works to memory, the "bookleggers." In Bradbury's *Fahrenheit 451* the memorizers are evading the dominance of a centralized state and, for Susan Spencer, the ending of that novel suggests that the text will prevail. By contrast, in *A Canticle* "the monks' painstakingly reconstructed 'literacy' turns out to be a world of signifiers with no corresponding signifieds to give them concrete meaning."[7] Furthermore, the bookleggers are acting in opposition to a popular wave of hostility against literacy. Although their title punningly associates them with illegality, they are acting within a world where civic order has broken down, indeed where they, and the Catholic remnant in general, are attempting to reconstitute some sort of order.

The contents of Francis's box can be construed as an enigmatic and perhaps random collection of metonymies, parts of a whole narrative and culture that have disappeared. Like the sporadic references to nuclear technology in Russell Hoban's *Riddley Walker,* the found objects have no context that would give them meaning. Francis's documents tease the reader toward an act of interpretation, but their narrative context—how they came to be left in the shelter—is never recovered. Instead, the blueprint, signed by one I. E. Leibowitz, becomes incorporated into the abbey's archive by being copied and "illuminated"—another pun, since no light is shed on the meaning of the document itself. Cut off from the culture that produced what might be no more than a box of junk, Francis assumes a "fallout" to be some kind of monster, a comical example of the incomprehension described above. The blueprint accordingly remains a puzzling textual object, and considerable parts of Books I and II of the novel revolve around possible processes of interpretation. It is a double entity, with writing on its reverse, and when Francis makes an illuminated copy the back becomes a mirror image of the front. However, the copy is stolen by robbers, since its apparent value is greater. Then, in Book II, the scholar and scientist-to-be, Thon Thaddeo, demonstrates the new discipline of rational analysis by examining texts, considering that the Leibowitz documents are "probably forgeries." Book I thus depends on a skillfully maintained strategy of estrangement whereby a neo-medieval perspective (the new present) is directed against the traces of nuclear technology relatively familiar to readers of the 1950s but now rendered as an enigmatic past.

In Book II Miller lines up a series of dialogues between the spokesman for the new science and representatives of the tradition of preservation. The tension here lies between the rival approaches of analytic use and a reverential reification of texts as pious objects. As Rose Secrest has argued, the very pace of Book I is slow, as befits an age "concerned with meticulosity and preservation because there was no sophisticated technology."[8] With the reemergence of science, the pace quickens. The growing opposition between analysis and reverential preservation closely resembles the confrontation between William of Baskerville and the authoritarian librarian in Umberto Eco's *The Name of the Rose* (translation 1983), which similarly describes a cultural watershed—the period when literacy is threatening to extend beyond Church control. In short, the texts within each of these novels are firmly situated within a system of preservation, interpretation, and controlled access. Thaddeo makes a utopian claim for an era of enlightenment he sees as imminent: "Tomorrow, a new prince shall rule. Men of understanding, men of science shall stand behind his throne, and the universe will come to know his might. His name is Truth. His empire shall encompass the Earth. The mastery of Man over the Earth shall be renewed. A century from now, men will fly through the air in mechanical birds."[9] This claim is striking in two respects. It addresses the future and does so in terms of conquest; but the claim is naive, since he ignores the political systems that will embody this supposed truth, and Miller makes this irony clear by presenting the rising prince in Book II as an illiterate cynic.

Miller demonstrates an attitude toward the media similar to that advanced in Harold A. Innis's *Empire and Communications,* where it is argued that each medium of communication tends to create monopolies of knowledge and therefore power. The ecclesiastical monopoly depended on parchment, for instance, and was then undermined by paper.[10] In contrast with the indiscriminate preservation of the archive by Miller's clerics, the copying of material as described by Innis involved choice and thus became a political act.[11] *A Canticle* does not refer to trade so much as the network of communications that underpins the Church's authority in Book I, the printed promulgation that symbolizes secular political authority in Book II, and the jealous control of information by the modern state in Book III. Here a polylinguistic printing machine, an early form of computer known as the Abominable Autoscribe, constantly goes haywire, producing a typographical jumble or a reversed text.[12] In a Joycean play on words, the culture of the letter only produces litter. And as if to deny any technological progress the machine is described in exactly the same terms as Francis's blueprint, as a collection of "squiggles" and "thing-umbobs."

Apart from the irony of impending war marking the climax of modern history, this section of the novel again and again discredits the official news media as actually concealing information from the citizens. In that respect, the regime exemplifies a position Miller formulated in the 1980s, when he wrote:

> There will be two sides in Megawar, all right, but the two sides are not going to be the two nations. One side is the two mutually hostile governments, who have become politically, economically, and militarily dependent on each other's hostility to keep stud generals and defence contractors and commissars busy; that side is the mad, transpolar duality which may at any time commit itself and the human race to the *casus belli* when the odds are infinite. The *other* side in the Megawar is the rest of the human race.[13]

As in *Nineteen Eighty-Four,* the prevailing regime maintains a permanent state of crisis and only makes announcements when a leakage of information has made them unavoidable. These announcements constitute a narrative that is viewed with considerable skepticism because of the credibility gap between official statements and private experience, an irony common to much American science fiction of the 1950s. The discourse now is characterized by Cold War polarities between power blocs, "us" against the enemy: "In a surprise attack, the space forces of the Atlantic Confederacy last night struck at three concealed Asian missile sites located on the far side of the moon, and totally destroyed one enemy space station known to be involved in a guidance system for space-to-earth missiles. It was expected that the enemy would retaliate against our forces in space, but the barbarous assault on our capital city was an act of desperation which no one anticipated."[14] Hostilities in the novel are clearly linked to American foreign policy of the 1950s through such contemporary euphemisms as the phrase "police action," which was used by President Truman to describe the Korean War. And with the World Court of Nations Miller glances sardonically at the impotence of the United Nations.

At every point in its narrative, *A Canticle* demonstrates an awareness of how texts are constituted, circulated, and validated. The radio announcements of Book III in a sense parallel the papal declaration on Leibowitz's sainthood, which only occurs after a prolonged interrogation of Brother Francis's "visitation," while the radio announcements occur after government decisions hidden from the average citizen. Miller's novel, then, is not only postmodern in its fictional chronology but also in its methodology, which anticipates that fiction of the 1960s and beyond referred to as "historiographic metafiction." For Linda Hutcheon, this fiction—exemplified in the United States by the writings of Coover, Heller, Pynchon, and others—situates itself in "the 'world' of discourse, the 'world' of texts and intertexts."[15]

Walker Percy has been one of the few critics to recognize this dimension to the novel, which he has compared to a "cipher, a coded message, a book in a strange language."[16] Decoding is an important activity in Miller's short stories as well as in *A Canticle.* In "Dumb Waiter" (1952) an American city's central computer goes on functioning long after an atomic war has emptied it, and the robot cops that maintain a grotesque semblance of civic order can only be stopped once the central computer program has been identified. In "Dark Benediction" (1951) the shells of meteorites that have brought plague germs to Earth carry an encrypted account of the evolution of these "neuroderm" parasites.[17] The very text of *A Canticle* is charged with half-concealed meaning. Interestingly, this intricacy seems to have been added to the text of Miller's three original novellas when he was revising them for publication as a single novel. In the original version of Book I, Miller limits his wordplay to a rather forced, realized passage of V words, where the initial letter carries a clear symbolism for Brother Francis: "The parting words of the pilgrim tumbled back to him: 'May you find a Voice, as y' seek.' Voice indeed, with V capitalized and formed by the wings of a descending dove and illuminated in three colours against a background of gold leaf. V as in *Vere dignum* and *Vidi aquam*, at the head of a page of the Missal. V, he saw quite clearly, as in Vocation."[18] The passage is too explicit for the character who inflates the event, metaphorically at least, into a repeat of Christ's baptism, signaled in Matthew 3.16 by the descending dove of the Holy Spirit. In the novel, Miller reserves such symbolistic cross-references for the more intellectual analysts and builds a comedy of incomprehension around Francis.

A Canticle repeatedly foregrounds certain signs as if to promise the reader meaning and then destabilizes those signs through ambiguity and repetition. In the original version, the old man who meets Francis is described naturalistically as one of the "black specks" shimmering in the heat. The novel's text revises this image into an unstable sign, a "wiggling iota of black," which punningly plays on the letter sign and "iota" as denoting the smallest distinguishable item. Furthermore, Miller stresses such differences as those between old and new English that revolve around vocabulary, Hebrew and English, and the special status of Latin. When the old man writes two Hebrew letters on Francis's rock at the beginning of the novel, the action establishes the major motif of the cryptic nature of signs. Russell Griffin has given one of the most thorough accounts to date of the interconnections between signs in *A Canticle,* which he explains as Miller's medievalism.[19] Thus, he has shown how Miller glosses most important names in the novel, develops parallels between Joshua and Jesus "often ironically," and so on. Griffin very helpfully identifies the textual density of *A Canticle* but does not bring out the problematic nature of such connections. As often as not, the connections raise more questions than they answer. For example, the ritual of sacrifice and the role of the scapegoat are clear in the Old Testament as symbolic atonement for guilt. In chapter 15 a steer's blood is drunk by a tribal chieftain as a sign of his military prowess, to the disgust of the Christian observers. In that same section a goat with a bald head might just be a mutant but is later crowned (converted into a religious effigy). While the poet sees Leibowitz as the scapegoat, the abbot wonders at the old Jew's identification with the fate of his people. In other words, the symbolism of images and rituals is open-ended and frequently a matter of debate within the text. The most complex example of this self-analysis occurs with a central complex of light imagery.

Throughout, Miller plays on the figural opposition between light and dark to articulate the limits of human understanding. The master narrative lying behind Book I is the story of the redemption, whereby mankind is led out of darkness to a "place of light," as Brother Francis imagines it. The latter's excavation of the battered metal box from the radiation shelter is at once an act of salvage and a metaphorical saving of the documents it contains, which anticipates the ultimate salvation. Light, therefore, in this section of the novel, suggests the possibility of cultural change and carries retrospective postlapsarian ironies of loss. The historical inset explains that the present age is an "inheritance of darkness" where humans are caught in a limbo "between dusk and dawn." The light/dark opposition is one of the most deeply embedded metaphors in the language, extending into a whole range of domains of experience. Miller sets up the following pairs in Book I, which are then destabilized later in the novel: belief versus paganism; civic order versus barbarism; understanding versus ignorance. As the saving remnant on the American continent, the monks see themselves as the guardians of the light of faith, but light is also used to define their social group against the threatening nomads who surround them.

In Book II the analogy between the novel's present and the Dark Ages establishes an expectation of cultural change, a new Renaissance; but expectancy is written into the opening chapters negatively as the imminence of war or—even worse—of "the remorseless, the mindless." Most of the action in Book I takes place in bright, clear light, whereas in Book II many scenes occur in semi-darkness. The metaphors of enlightenment now figure as mundane metonyms in the repeated action of kindling a flame. The climax to this motif comes when a scholar visits the abbey and witnesses the invention of electric light. This scene is shot through with symbolism. The lamp has replaced a crucifix in the only appropriate niche. It is demonstrated one morning (suggestive of the dawn of a new era) and possesses a brightness to rival the sun's (the first character in Book II is a priest named Marco Apollo). The trial takes place in a basement, and one observer exclaims that the effect is "hellish." But the ironies of this scene are even sharper. In order to situate the event within the rituals of the abbey, the monks recite the first verses from Genesis as they are beginning the experiment. The latter thus straddles the sacred and the secular as a cultural watershed, partly a travesty of the primal creation narrative and partly a recovery of lost knowledge. As usual in this novel, Miller signals such ambiguity with wordplay. An incautious monk who gets a shock from the machine exclaims "Lucifer!" which is for Russell Griffin a sign for "destructive technological knowledge," since its literal meaning, "light-bearer," has become overlaid with satanic connotations.[20] By Book III the phrase "Lucifer is fallen" has become a coded signal like the title phrase in Pat Frank's *Alas, Babylon,* secularized into a warning that a nuclear war has broken out.

Miller sets up countless obstacles to reading history as linear progress by inverting his images, shifting contexts, and introducing reversals. The lamp that rekindles the light of science goes out and is replaced once again by the crucifix, and Miller's choric comment on that era ("after the generations of the darkness came the generations of the light") puns on "generation" and erases its creative meaning by ending that section on a note of war and death. In Book III a travesty revelation occurs when the "brighter and brighter" light of a nuclear bomb blast shines through the confessional door at the abbey. It is appropriate at this stage in the novel for such symbolism to be interrogated by the abbot: "Fire, loveliest of the four elements of the world, and yet an element too in Hell. While it burned adoringly in the core of the Temple, it had also scorched the life from a city, this night, and spewed its venom over the land. How strange of God to speak from a burning bush, and of Man to make a symbol of Heaven into a symbol of Hell."[21] The changes to the sense of sight reflect this puzzlement. Characters have driven themselves blind poring over manuscripts in poor light, and by Book III this physical difficulty of seeing has become a collective environmental problem as radioactive dust clouds drift across the landscape, not only obscuring vision but bringing death. The fact that each section of *A Canticle* ends with a death carries obviously grim implications for characters' attempts at coming to some understanding of events in this novel.

A similar symbolic extrapolation of light occurs in Daniel F. Galouye's 1961 novel *Dark Universe,* which also describes a postnuclear holocaust world but from the perspective of distant survivors who live permanently underground. Because their visual sense has atrophied, they communicate aurally through "clinkstones." Sight, however, is not forgotten; it has become internalized as a deity, and the predicament of the tunnel dwellers has become rationalized as a second Fall, as the result of a primal wrong. The protagonist at one point thinks back to the scriptural tuition he received from their Guardian of the Way: "So compassionate was the Almighty that when he banished man from Paradise, he sent parts of Himself to be with us for a while. And he dwelled in many little vessels like this Holy Bulb."[22] The discourse replaces the deity with light and the devil with radiation, resulting in an internally consistent version of Christian polarities in which the traces of electronic technology from the upper world (bulbs particularly) function as icons. The lexicon of references to sight represents correspondingly the verbal traces of a lost domain to experience inscribed culturally as sacred myth. The tunnel dwellers have mythologized the original world as a lost place of light and demonized radiation as the "Twin Devils Cobalt and Strontium."

Dark Universe narrates the tortuous journey of the protagonist up to the surface. The novel at times resembles romance in describing Jared's confrontation with alien "zivvers" (Hebrew *ziv,* meaning "light') and irradiated bats; any creature who can communicate without clinkstones challenges his sense of reality. As Jared explores the links between light, eyes, and sight, the most horrifying discovery comes when he reaches the surface, where he finds light literally and metaphorically through a series of discoveries.

> Light was not in Paradise.
> It was in the infinity of Radiation with the Nuclear monsters.
> All the legends, all the tenets were bitterly misleading.
> For man there was *no* Paradise.
> And, with the Atomic Demons roaming the passageways at will, humanity had reached the end of its material existence.[23]

Jared experiences negative revelations that despiritualize his world. His entry into a secular existence coincides with him beginning to see and also with him learning the history of his situation. Characters on the surface explain that underground survival complexes had been built as refuges against a nuclear war. All had functioned well except his own, where there was a failure of lighting. The inmates suffered an extreme fate: "When your people left their basic chamber they left knowledge and reason behind."[24] In other words, they became metaphorically blind. *Dark Universe* can be read as an ironic, negative parable about nuclear refuge and misdirected faith in technology.

Galouye's novel is more comfortable to read than Miller's because it starts from severely limited perceptual horizons and works its way toward an end point where, thanks to a happy collaboration between science and psychology, its antecedent narrative can be reconstituted. *A Canticle* denies any such progress. Although its historical moments change, the novel never focuses on a single consciousness and always shows comprehension to be a desired goal rather than an achieved state. Miller's characters are always embedded within different institutional and cultural processes that they articulate or repeat, hence the novel's denial of origination. Northrop Frye has pointed out that the Genesis story demonstrates the primal power of the divine Logos since forms of life are spoken into existence.[25] In *A Canticle,* however, human articulation follows and travesties the divine script, just as physical experiments are exercises in *re*discovery. Once again, this factor is written explicitly into the novel, for example, in the recurrence of representations of a human face with an enigmatic smile. Characters typically ask themselves, "Where have I seen that before?" "Before" does not refer to any individual memory but, rather, signals a condition of the text itself that is packed with the traces of earlier cultural periods or of earlier phases in its own unfolding. Because Miller's narrative recapitulates Western history, it is literally true that everything within it has already been said.

Biblical metaphors and typology are based on a codified system of correspondences between the worldly and the spiritual or of progression from type to antitype. But Miller repeatedly deconstructs such correspondences. He personifies the duplicitous shifting nature of signs in the bizarre figure of Mrs. Grales, an old woman in Book III who sells tomatoes and who is virtually the only important female character in the novel. As a mutant, she has two heads and thus two names. "Grales" resembles "grail," while her other name, Rachel, evokes the proverbially beautiful wife of Jacob. Mrs. Grales keeps her second head wrapped; indeed, it is not clear that it is alive until nuclear war breaks out and she seeks its baptism. The five slivers of glass embedded in her body by a nuclear bomb blast resemble the stigmata, but there is no warrant for reading them as spiritual metaphor rather than metonymy. Similarly, the monk Joshua has a nightmare about this woman, where a surgeon has threatened to cut off the "deformity" of the Rachel head before it becomes "malignant":

> And the Rachel face opened its eyes and tried to speak to Joshua, but he could hear her only faintly, and understand her not at all.
> "Accurate am I the exception," she seemed to be saying, "I commensurate the deception. Am."
> He could make nothing of it, but he tried to reach through to save her. There seemed to be a rubbery wall of glass in the way. He paused and tried to read her lips. I am the, I am the—
> "I am the Immaculate Conception" came the dream whisper.[26]

This fantasy contains a message that only emerges through a kind of verbal slippage from "exception" through "deception" to "conception." "Deception" increases the ambiguity of the communication, which is grimly ironic since a mutant is claiming the quality of transcendent beauty possessed only by the Virgin Mary; "immaculate" signifies "spotless." As soon as Rachel utters her words, she is killed, thereby inverting one meaning of "conception." Miller leaves the door ajar to reading this episode as a travesty vision of death rather than life by synchronizing it with the outbreak of war.

Joshua's nightmare can be read on a number of different levels: psychologically, as a fantasy of guilt; as symbolizing the tension between medical and clerical power; or as a travesty of mystical visitation. Umberto Eco has explained the medievalism of Joyce in terms directly applicable to Miller, clarifying the shifting and ambiguous nature of signification in both writers: 'In the medieval symbol, the signifying—signified relationship is clear because of a homogeneous culture. The homogeneity of a unique culture is lacking in the contemporary poetic symbol as the result of a multiplicity of cultural perspectives."[27] How much more must this be the case for a novel like *A Canticle,* which spans a series of historical periods where quite different cultural conditions prevail? It is possible that in the Janus figure of Rachel/Mrs. Grales Miller embodies the hybrid qualities of humanity, which at that point in the novel had reached a destructive climax.

One important consequence of Miller's method is that his main characters all become readers but suffer from a lack of competence in varying degrees. The deity provides an ideal standard for contrast as the "inscrutabilis Scrutator animarum" (the inscrutable scrutinizer of souls). Such total access is unavailable to the mere human figures, who are constantly found in the posture of examining signs and texts for their meaning. In the chapters following his experiences in the desert, Brother Francis engages in dialogues with others about hermeneutics (was it natural or supernatural?) and narrative accretion (the result of oral transmission and inflation). In other words, once again the novel foregrounds the difficulties of processing and stabilizing texts. There are obvious metafictional implications in such episodes, which Miller focuses in Book II by introducing his only explicit allusion to other science fiction. The scientist Thaddeo is examining the documents of the archive to try to understand the origin of mankind. He stumbles across a "fragment of a play, or a dialogue," describing the creation of a servant species that revolts against its own creators and jumps to the conclusion that present humanity is descended from this new species. Clearly the work referred to is Karel Capek's 1922 play *R.U.R.* (which ironically describes the creation of mechanical replicants virtually indistinguishable from humans), but the monks do not know how to classify the fragment ("probable fable or allegory'). Thaddeo sees its importance as opening up speculative thought—and here Miller in turn opens up a function for his own novel—whereas the abbot takes it to be a scurrilous attack on the past, and the scene collapses into a nondialogue, with Thaddeo's assertions of the need for scientific progress alternating with the abbot's recitation of the temptation from Genesis. The contrast between scripted and open utterance seems clear at this point, but embedded within the intertext is another work that forms a connecting link between twentieth-century SF and the Bible: *Frankenstein,* which describes a scientist's attempts to rival the prerogative of God in creating a new species, shadows the Genesis story (particularly as retold by Milton), and stresses the destructive consequences of pride in terms very similar to Miller's own account of the holocaust. Each speaker is bounded by his own historical and cultural horizon.

The Catholic Church has been referred to so often that it must be clear by now that it occupies a privileged position within the novel, reflecting Miller's conversion to Catholicism soon after the Second World War. Even the title denotes a "song or prayer derived from the Bible, which is used in the liturgical worship of the Church."[28] The title thus situates us within a set of cultural practices, and Book I shows a world structured chronologically by the Catholic calendar, hierarchically by the monks and clergy, and ritually by the liturgy. The Church is the "caretaker of human society."[29] The survival of the abbey from one historical era to the next is paralleled linguistically by the persistence of Latin as a universal language of the sacred, a possibility difficult to maintain since Vatican II. Just as the canonization of Leibowitz in Book I leads to his inclusion in the Church calendar, so the holocaust has become incorporated within the litany of the saints ("from the curse of the Fallout, O Lord deliver us"). As the novel progresses, the power of the Church gradually diminishes, a change signaled at the beginning of Book III by one of the most ironic sections of the novel: a "liturgy of man," a hybrid form combining secular pageant with liturgical elements. This Audenesque sequence reduces the liturgy to a secular performance where the voice of the centuries is delivered from a high-kicking chorus line. The human life span is compressed into a couple of brief lines, and mythic figures are diminished—Eve to a farm girl in a bawdy joke and Lucifer to a traveling salesman. Desire becomes a recurrent infantilism, a pursuit of utopian dreams that can never admit change: "Generation, regeneration, again, again, as in a ritual, with blood-stained vestments and nail-torn hands, children of Merlin, chasing a gleam. Children, too, of Eve, forever building Edens—and kicking them apart in berserk fury because somehow it isn't the same."[30] Each of the three books carries scenes that raise the question of the Church's authority: the canonization ceremony in New Rome; the lighting of the lamp where science and religion jostle for precedence; and a debate between the abbot and a doctor on the ethics of euthanasia for war casualties. The abbey does not function as a location of value so much as a site for a continuing debate about truth.

The title, then, should not be taken to imply a privileged stability in the Catholic liturgy. Nor could it, since it incongruously links the liturgical term with a Jewish name. Canonization does nothing to reduce the ambiguities surrounding Leibowitz and his "relics." A similar ambiguity is evident in Anthony Boucher's

1951 "The Quest for Saint Aquin," which evokes a postholocaust scenario with striking resemblances to *A Canticle*. In Boucher's story, the world is now ruled by the Technarchy. The pope commissions Thomas to set out on a quest for Saint Aquin, which he does riding a "robass" (a robotic ass). As Miller does in *A Canticle,* Boucher juxtaposes ancient and modern and draws out resemblances between his narrative and the Bible. Thomas thus notes parallels between himself and Christ and, even more so, with Balaam, but the latter story remains an enigma, "as though it was there to say that there are portions of the Divine Plan which we will never understand."[31] An extended dialogue between Thomas and the robass raises the issue of means and ends: Why not tell the lie that Aquin has been found if that results in greater belief? When Thomas finally locates the body of the saint, it turns out to be a robot. The story thus can be read as a parable of spiritual inquiry which shows that search as physical action, while Miller frequently casts inquiry in the form of dialogue.

In the Boucher story and in Miller's novel, recovery promises a confirmation of meaning but proves to be virtually impossible. The situation in *A Canticle* is particularly complex because of how Miller treats the past. Sections of the novel shift into a different register when Miller writes as a chronicler from notional points in the future. Book I, for example, gives an account of the holocaust in a kind of new scripture scrupulously free of vocabulary with specific historical references. The narrative includes pastiche biblical phrasing and rhythms and describes the holocaust through analogies with the flood (explicit) and the destruction of Sodom and Gomorrah (implicit). The three main phases of destruction are the Flame Deluge (an "unleashing of the hell-fire"), the Fallout ("great clouds of wrath"), and the Simplification (initially a collective revenge against those held responsible and then an "insane frenzy of mass murder and destruction"). Miller repeats the narratives and imagery of the Old Testament, recapitulating the fall of Babel by showing the sequel to disaster as a state of linguistic division: "In all parts of the world men fled from one place to other places, and there was a confusion of tongues."[32] Miller names his new scripture the Memorabilia, the archive of surviving texts and narratives from the past. But one rhetorical principle involved in Miller's use of the trilogy structure is that no segment of his text is exempt from modification by other segments. Thus, although the tone of this narrative mimics the authority of the Bible, it is radically altered in Book II as a more drawn-out study of political ambition. This account, which exists in different versions, purports to describe the past but is actually predicting the possible consequences for humanity of princely ambitions being realized in that section of the novel. Finally, in Book III Miller rhetorically distances himself from humanity, giving a symbolically external and quasi-scientific description of the new era: "There were spaceships again in that century, and the ships were manned by fuzzy impossibilities that walked on two legs and sprouted tufts of hair in unlikely anatomical regions."[33] Miller cleverly offsets the possibility of technological progress by describing mankind as a freakish species carrying only a verbal trace of humanity ("manned").

A key term in this passage is "again," one of the countless indicators of recurrence that fill the novel, where readers have to revise their sense of the real at the opening of each section. At the beginning of *A Canticle* we have a pretechnological world evoked through the descriptive details of the desert, which is then disrupted by Francis's discovery of documents familiar to us from contemporary technology. Our assumptions about history invite us to read the Dark Age as a distant precursor of the latter era; but the fact that the documents are the traces of a vanished civilization forces us to reverse this perceived sequence. Time, therefore, functions in a variety of different ways in this complex novel. Dates give us linear time; recurrences and resemblances suggest cycles; and the constant presence of the old Jew adds another pre-messianic time scale again. As if that wasn't enough, early scenes recede into the past of the text itself, undergoing a constant process of revision and modification. The Poet, a satirical commentator in Book II, has become Saint Poet of the Miraculous Eyeball by Book III, an example typical of a process at work throughout the novel.

We must therefore read among a whole series of historical resemblances. The popular wave of anger manifested in the Simplification represents an attempt to wipe the historical slate clean and has been shrewdly compared by Dominic Manganiello to Hate Week in Orwell's *Nineteen Eighty-Four*.[34] The regime in Orwell's novel manipulates history by reifying information and disposing of it down the "memory hole." In *A Canticle,* however, the mob wants to erase the past and start fresh, making the world anew in an ironic echo of one of America's cherished slogans. This attempt is exactly what the novel as a whole resists, hence its privileging of terms of recall and resemblance. When Brother Francis takes his document to Rome, the pope praises him for acting as the memory within the body of the Church. Throughout *A Canticle* Miller strikes a fine balance between the need to retain history and a recognition of how history is subject to a constant process of revision and distortion. The artifacts and texts from earlier periods can only be assessed within specific sign systems (what Miller calls "knowledge systems"), which are themselves historically bounded. The construction of three narratives dealing with quite distinct periods and the allusions to other eras thus foregrounds this historical relativity. The reader is thus led to make a series of recognitions in the novel. Take two examples. In Book II a prince proclaims himself supreme head of the state, taking on the title of "defender of the faith," an echo of Henry VIII; again, toward the end of the novel, monks demonstrate against the use of euthanasia machines by carrying placards that read "ABANDON EVERY HOPE YE WHO ENTER HERE." These words from the portal to Dante's Hell encode the machines as devilish and implicitly assert the Church's unique role as an asylum. Second, the use of colored stars to identify the war casualties clearly echoes the Nazis' genocide, now transposed onto America. Miller relates the construction of nuclear technology to a new militarism. For instance, in his 1956 story "Vengeance for Nikolai" Russia has been invaded by a neo-fascist America with its own Blue Shirt movement.[35] Remember that the setting of A Canticle is America, specifically the Utah desert, on which the entire history of the West is replaying itself.

The grimmest implication of repetition in the novel is the suggestion that history consists of a cyclical script determining human behavior from era to era. As the abbot in Book III reflects with despair, "Are we doomed to do it again and again and again? Have we no choice but to play the Phoenix in an unending sequence of rise and fall?" rehearsing a list of empires that have since disappeared into oblivion.[36] Many critics have noted this emphasis on repetition, but Walker Percy adds the crucial consequence for the traces of these worlds: "When one age dies, its symbols lose their referents and become incomprehensible."[37] The "fallen" nature of human discourse emerges through an explanation supplied in Book II: "For man was a culture-bearer as well as a soul-bearer, but his cultures were not immortal and they would die with a race or an age, and then human reflections of meaning and human portrayals of truth receded, and truth and meaning resided, unseen, only in the objective *logos* of Nature and the ineffable *Logos* of truth."[38] The implication of this passage is that truth is never lost; it's simply hidden. Historical repetition can thus be seen as a process of recovery, not merely fated recurrence. Each section of the novel, however, returns to the elusive Logos by ending outside human action with buzzards (Books I and II) and, finally, a shark. Each section carries as its penultimate ending a death, and in Book III it may be the death of humanity as a whole. Concluding with other natural creatures draws our attention to mankind as a species uniquely cursed with a death wish.

At the end of Book III a spaceship carries an ark of survivors into space, following a trajectory into a notional future that Miller did not see fit to pursue in his sequel. The desire for happy endings persists. On the last page of the novel, a shark instinctively avoids the fallout of radioactive ash and heads out into the deeper, cleaner area of the ocean. Robert Scholes and Eric S. Rabkin argue that this conclusion is quite hopeful because the shark is a survivor, the sea is the matrix of life, and the fish is a traditional icon for Christ.[39] The latter point is a particularly curious one to make, since Miller has shifted the narrative outside any such signifying system so that the shark can scarcely be anything other than metonym and still carries strongly predatory connotations.

In his introduction ("Forewarning") to his 1985 anthology of holocaust stories, *Beyond Armageddon,* Miller revises the notion of Logos as a form of rationality that displaces humanity: "Logos *does,* in a way, create the object-world, as a dark mirror between us and the One."[40] He makes it clear that he was drawn to this Taoist position in recoil from the apocalyptic foreign policy of the Reagan years, and he criticizes Marxism and Christian fundamentalism alike for having as their agenda the destruction of the other. From the perspective of a ruptured cultural holism, he argues:

> I point to the West's idolization of Logos, not to disparage science, for this idolatry preceded modern science by many centuries, but to preface the assertion that sometimes the use of reason is so inappropriate as to be either laughably or criminally insane, and that we need to learn to sacrifice reason when it's crazy to be rational. [He goes on to cite sex as one such occasion.] Death is another subject inaccessible to reason, and so Dr. Strangelove, who insisted on using reason when the world faced global extinction, was also funny. Strangelovian logic is hilarious even in a straight Air Force study of the post-Megawar viability of paper money.[41]

A Canticle for Leibowitz achieves much of its impact by relativizing such agendas and destabilizing the signifying systems that underpin culture.

Rumors persisted for years that Miller was working on a sequel to *A Canticle,* but this work only appeared one year after his death in 1996, having been completed by the novelist Terry Bisson.[42] *Saint Leibowitz and the Wild Horse Woman* describes the period known in *A Canticle* as the new Dark Age in America. It is the thirty-second century, and America has fragmented into different tribal areas with a landscape still marked by traces of a nuclear holocaust. A pit is named "Meldown," also known as the "Navel of the World" and the "devil's hole," and areas are populated by "gennies," the genetically handicapped mutants similar to figures described in the early fiction of Poul Anderson and Judith Merril. The protagonist is a young novice monk named Brother Blacktooth, whose fortunes shadow those of an elusive older figure introduced as the Red Deacon, who becomes Vicar Apostolic for the area and who coordinates the local tribes' uprising against the oppressive empire of Texarkana. Blacktooth's main task at the beginning of the novel is to translate into the demotic a "scholarly but highly speculative attempt to reconstruct from the evidence of later events a plausible history of the darkest of all centuries—the twenty-first."[43] This is one of the very few metafictional references in the novel, and it marks one of the main differences between *Saint Leibowitz* and *A Canticle*. In *A Canticle* he speculates at length about how written records might be preserved and passed on to later generations, about the fragmentary nature of historical materials, and about the cyclical nature of history. *Saint Leibowitz,* in contrast, flattens out its action into an orderly sequence tracing the growth of Blacktooth toward manhood. As such, it lacks the speculative dimension that informs Miller's extended meditation on the consequences of nuclear war in *A Canticle for Leibowitz.*

CHAPTER 7

The Pathology of Warfare in Bernard Wolfe's *Limbo*

Once the Soviet Union demonstrated that it possessed an atom bomb in 1949, the nuclear arms race got under way, and there was real danger that such atomic weapons might be used against China during the Korean War, as General Mac-Arthur recommended in 1951. The following year Bernard Wolfe published his novel *Limbo*, which presented a satirical parable on the roots of war in human aggression and which is unique in nuclear war fiction because of the sheer breadth of its intellectual reference. In his afterword he explicitly denied a predictive dimension to his novel: "Anybody who 'paints a picture' of some coming year is kidding—he's only fancying up something in the present or past, not blueprinting the future. All such writing is essentially satiric (today-centred), not utopic (tomorrow-centred). This book, then, is a rather bilious rib on 1950."[1] This was a year filled with debate over the new hydrogen bomb, an increase in American civil defense measures, and a virtual acceptance that a third world war was inevitable. Against such a background Wolfe pitted his sardonic black humor.

The novel is set in the year 1990 in the aftermath of the Third World War, which broke out in 1972. The enormous devastation of the war has reduced the habitable land area of the eastern and western United States. The country has become reduced to the Inland Strip, since all seaboards have been laid waste, and a confederation loosely analogous to the Soviet Union has emerged called the Eastern Union.[2] The protagonist is Dr. Martine, a medical officer who fled during the war to an uncharted island in the Indian Ocean where he has been performing experimental lobotomies on aggressive locals. When a group of Americans with prosthetic limbs visits the island, Martine decides to return to America, where he finds to his amazement that facetious remarks he made in a wartime journal have been taken seriously and, in the wake of the war, developed into an international movement, "Immob" (i.e., Immobilization), dedicated to the eradication of human aggression by voluntary amputations ("Vol-amp") and their replacement by prosthesis. The novel traces Martine's gradual discovery of this movement and reaches its climax at the prosthetic Olympic Games when the Eastern Union team guns down the judges and war breaks out again, this time on a smaller, containable scale. This war comes to an end with the death of the Western premier and overthrow of the Eastern Union regime by its citizens, and the novel concludes with Martine returning to his island.

Limbo is a text of its time in that it places the threat of nuclear war at the center of its action, Martine's search to find out what is happening in the world about him. It is, in short, a novel of attempted diagnosis combined with political enquiry, an appropriate first work from a Yale psychology graduate who served for a time on Trotsky's staff in Mexico and then held a series of posts as editor or correspondent for a number of periodicals. *Limbo* has been routinely mentioned in histories of dystopias and more recently within the context of cybernetic fiction.[3] True, a few lone voices have spoken up on behalf of Wolfe. J. G. Ballard, for one, has recorded his great respect for the author's "lucid intelligence" that so impressed him that he began to write fiction himself. And Carolyn Geduld has done an outstanding job of explaining Wolfe's interest in Freudian psychology.[4] Recently there have been some signs of a rise of interest in Wolfe, who is now being read as a precursor of cyberpunk, but the risk there is of forgetting the period of unparalleled world crisis out of which the novel grew: It was published in the same year that the United States detonated its first H-bomb in Eniwetok Atoll.

Not surprisingly, Wolfe took the arms race and human aggression in general as his subject, but he chose an unusual and unfashionable method in his approach. The dust jacket of the first edition promised the reader that *Limbo* was a "novel of action, suspense, adventure, science-fiction and sex." For once this description did not overstate the case, since the novel constantly disconcerts the reader by moving from genre to genre. In fact, it belongs within the mode of encyclopedic narratives identified by Edward Mendelson and exemplified in works such as *Moby-Dick* and *Ulysses*. For Mendelson, this genre is itself multigeneric and inclusive: "Encyclopedic narrative identifies itself not by a single plot or structure, but by encompassing a broad range of qualities."[5] *Limbo* does exactly this. It includes within itself, among other genres, the novel of espionage, journal, dystopia, and narrative of scientific experiment. It covers an extraordinary range of texts, from ribald jokes up to summaries of brain mapping and the origins of game theory. In his afterword Wolfe describes his work modestly, as a "grab bag of ideas," but this totally understates the subtlety and complexity of novelistic expression he has given these ideas. For sheer intellectual reach *Limbo* could be compared to Thomas Pynchon's *Gravity's Rainbow* (1973), which applies a similar late form of Freudian thought to criticize Western science as being death-oriented and which culminates in the Hiroshima bombing.[6] It is consistent with his syncretic method that Wolfe should draw on such cultural commentators as Arthur Koestler, Norbert Wiener, and Lewis Mumford.[7] *Limbo* marshals its materials around a probing and bizarre analysis of Cold War aggression, and it constantly foregrounds the human body as the site of this enquiry.

The opening episode presents an image of cultural unity—the tropical island with its indigenous inhabitants—which is then progressively fractured in a number of ways that look forward to the processes of the novel as a whole. The island has served as a refuge for Martine from the horrors of nuclear war, but it is already compromised by colonial/scientific appropriation in an experimental animal research station. Also, the natives practice a primitive form of lobotomy to achieve "peace," an operation Martine himself adopts. The island is visited by a group of American "amps" (amputees) wearing prosthetic limbs. Lobotomies and amputations constitute the first examples of a "proliferating series of divisions" that run throughout the novel.[8] Sometimes these divisions carry with them the promise of a newfound wholeness, but in practice they simply function as the prelude to yet more divisions. Even the United States survives as the trunk of a country that has lost its extremities. Constantly alert to the metaphors embedded within political discourse, Wolfe suggests a tacit analogy between the hemispheres of the brain and the East-West polarities of the Cold War.

Wolfe probably extrapolated his notion of prosthesis from Freud's *Civilization and Its Discontents*. Reflecting on how the gods embody an "ideal conception of omnipotence and omniscience," Freud concludes: "Man has, as it were, become a kind of prosthetic God. When he puts on all his auxiliary organs he is truly magnificent; but those organs have not grown on to him and they still give him much trouble at times."[9] In 1930 Freud saw an approximate realization of qualities that had traditionally been viewed as unattainable. He presents prosthesis as simultaneously marking a technological advance but also as increasing humanity's unease with that progress.

It is typical of Wolfe's novel to map its intellectual connections through quasi-realist detail, like the name of the boat that carries Martine back to America—the *S.S. Norbert Wiener*. By the late 1940s Norbert Wiener, the main founder of cybernetics and an acknowledged source for Wolfe, saw that the science of prosthetics was developing rapidly and immediately linked these changes to the dystopian tradition: "It makes the metaphorical dominance of the machines, as imagined by Samuel Butler, a most immediate and non-metaphorical problem. It gives the human race a new and most effective collection of mechanical slaves to perform its labor."[10] At the beginning of the next decade, Wiener's evident realization that the military-industrial complex was appropriating such sciences sharpened his anxieties about the immediate political future of the United States, which he saw as sinking into a sinister machine age dominated by a "threatening new Fascism dependent on the *machine à gouverner*."[11] In her indispensible analysis of *Limbo*, N. Katherine Hayles argues that Wolfe extrapolates on Wiener's fears that cybernetics might be turned to military use and that the novel shows that "under the stimulus of war the machine component, no longer limited to mimicking an organic limb, is hardwired into the human nervous system to form an integrated cybernetic circuit."[12] For Hayles, Wolfe attempts to straddle humanity and technology through a rhetoric of "hyphenation," linking the two fields until they finally pull apart in the novel's denouement.

One of the central features of cybernetic progress in *Limbo* is the design of new and powerful computers. Wolfe's novel, like Kurt Vonnegut's *Player Piano*, places its action in the years following World War III, and both novels emphasize the central role of computers in planning and conducting that war. Vonnegut's EPICAC takes over these human functions as if it were itself human: "EPICAC I had been intelligent enough, dispassionate enough, retentive enough to convince men that he, rather than they, had better do the planning for the war that was approaching with stupefying certainty."[13] The computer has thus taken over both the functions of the government and economic planning, supporting a huge industrial corporation modeled on General Electric, where Vonnegut worked after World War II. EPICAC is not a single entity but an expanding serial computer constantly increasing in sophistication and correspondingly reducing human decision making in the military-industrial process.

Wolfe similarly foregrounds the importance of the national computers of East and West, which this time actually conduct the war, but he also contextualizes the war as a culmination of a historical process—a development by each super state into a technological monolith—that outstrips the language of each culture, which degenerates as a result into a "constant gush of slogans and catchwords."[14] The war occurs because their languages are deemed to be incompatible:

> In 1970 Russia and America simultaneously came to a hallucinated decision: they, and not merely their vocabularies, were such diametric opposites that they could not exist side by side on the same planet. So the Third, the global EMSIAC

war, broke out. And this was the most grotesque irony in human history, for the EMSIAC war proved only one thing: that the cybernetic-managerial revolution had been carried to its logical end and now Russia and America were absolutely and irrevocably alike. In fact, it was precisely in preparation for the global showdown of the EMSIAC war a war predicated on the assumption that the two had nothing in common that they had come to be mirror images of each other. For each was now the monster that Wiener had warned was coming: the totally bureaucratized war machine in which man was turned into a lackey by his own machines. And each was presided over by the super-bureaucrat of them all, the perfect electronic brain sired by the imperfect human brain.[15]

Behind the polarities of Cold War discourse, Wolfe locates a crowning irony: the homology between the two super states, which Norbert Wiener had noted with deep gloom.[16] The world war, therefore, also occurs at a particular phase in the process of mechanization where the national computers (given identical names) displace the human brain and attempt to fulfill their own agendas of rationalized expansion. Where Vonnegut's computer survives into the postwar period and extends its "nervous system" into a series of ever larger models, in Wolfe's narrative the war comes to an end because each side bombs the other's computer. Both novelists were capitalizing on contemporary cultural commentary that diagnosed a mechanization of the present. Mumford, for instance, an ardent supporter of disarmament, described the atomic age as being "machine dominated" and in his plea for humanistic renewal, *The Conduct of Life* (1951), wishfully pushed this "domination of the machine" into the past: "Whereas the mark of the machine age was the dehumanization of man, the new age will give primacy to the person."[17] Wolfe anticipates such later novels as Mordecai Roshwald's *Level 7*, where a nuclear war breaks out because of errors in the defense computers, and D. F. Jones's *Colossus* (1966), where a super computer takes over American foreign policy and then links up with its Russian equivalent, totally excluding humans from the exercise of political power. The destruction of the two computers in *Limbo* appears to signal that humans have regained control over their own actions, but that turns out not to be the case, as is proved by the Immob movement.

The latter can be seen as an elaboration of an idea Wolfe sketched out in a preliminary narrative called "Self Portrait," published in *Galaxy Science Fiction* in November 1951. Set in 1959, this tells the story, in journal form, of a scientist named Parks who secures a post at the Institute for Advanced Cybernetics Studies. His immediate project is to design efficient prosthetic legs for a Korean War casualty, which he finally manages by dividing up the laboratory work on a more efficient basis. Parks is an utterly humorless researcher and therefore in no way a prototype for Martine. The only ironic or facetious voices in his journal belong to others, and they make two suggestions that ridicule Cold War confrontations. The first is the proposal that each country's computer should calculate when hostilities could begin, and on that day a ceremony would take place: "In each capital the citizens gather around their strategy machine, the officials turn out in high hats and cut-aways, there are speeches, pageants, choral singing, mass dancing—the ritual can be worked out in advance. Then, at an agreed time, the crowds retreat to a safe distance and a committee of the top cyberneticists appears. They climb into planes, take off and—this is beautiful—drop all their atom bombs and H-bombs on the machines."[18] This event, commemorated as International Mushroom Day, would happen simultaneously in each capital. Afterward, the scientists would go back to their laboratories to devise new series of super weapons that would result in future Mushroom Days. This description partly echoes James Agee's satirical sketch "Dedication Day" (1946), which describes the unveiling in Washington of an arch of fused uranium to signal the importance of the discovery of atomic fission. What gives the event an ominous dimension is the smoldering beneath the monument of the Eternal Fuse, as if the whole ceremony was being performed over a bomb.[19] Both this satire and the imagined commemoration look forward to the Olympic Games Peace Day in *Limbo*.

The second proposal in "Self Portrait" makes a facetious application of game theory to the Cold War, once again involving computers. Casualties for each side would be calculated in advance, and then volunteers would be called for to undergo amputations in return for compensation. That way the conduct of a war would be simulated without using any actual arms. The voluntary amputation program in *Limbo* is essentially an elaboration on this basic idea, but one far richer in its self-contradictory symbolism. We could best think of it as a movement aimed at controlling aggression, since "cybernetics" literally denotes the science of guidance or control. "Vol-amp" attempts to regain control of the impulse that produces war and is articulated as reason attempting to reimpose itself on human conduct. In his examination of the psychological impact on America of the atom bomb, Paul Boyer suggests it induced fear of "death of a new kind, death without warning, death *en masse*." This fear was particularly unsettling, he continues, because it introduced the irrational into human destiny and also challenged American confidence in progress, producing the "sense that the meaning of one's existence—at least in social and historical terms—was being radically threatened."[20] This impotence was expressed by Lewis Mumford as an atrophy of humanity into mechanical figures. For him humanity had become a "race of moral robots," and he insisted that "the main task of our time is to turn man himself, now a helpless mechanical puppet, into a wakeful and willing creator."[21] The suppressed fear of death lies at the heart of *Limbo,* although Wolfe's depiction of prosthetics and mechanization generally is rather more complex than a reflection of human helplessness; it often embodies the very opposite—a dream of power.

The Immob movement in *Limbo* can be seen as an absurdist extrapolation of fears of uncontrolled technological development and perceptions of a dissociation of the populace from political processes. It also suggests that the desired opposite to mobilization involves not only an avoidance of militarism but of mobility itself. The scheme itself is subjected to ironic scrutiny by Martine, its unwitting inventor, who serves to reveal its resemblances to earlier movements as well as its paradoxical nature. The contradictions in the scheme become more and more obvious as the novel progresses, since artificial limbs prove to be more efficient "arms" than their originals and the movement professes a question contradicted by its own moral fervor. When Martine hears a public speaker whipping up enthusiasm for amputations, he thinks he sounds like a cross between a salesman and a politician. The meeting that follows contains two analogies, one American and the other Russian; it seems to be a gathering of a religious cult, and, also, the recruits "were about to sign their own Moscow confessions and death warrants." The conflation of resemblances from both cultural poles of the Cold War takes an added twist from the fact that a kind of conscription is taking place. Most absurd of all is that society's self-mystifying abuse of language. The public speaker impatiently brushes aside verbal difference as hair-splitting: "Pros are such good Immobs that we refuse to make a fetish of any word at all."[22]

Words were largely responsible for World War III in Wolfe's future history because cultural discourse had lagged behind technological and political change. Now, once again, words become separated from actuality, and nowhere is this more obvious than in the campaign slogans, which vary from unrecognized puns ("War Is on Its Last Legs") or miniature revisionist texts ("Arms of the Man"). The new conjunction attempts to separate humanity from its own extensions by altering the phrase from the opening of *The Aeneid* ("Arms and the man I sing"), which was further popularized by Bernard Shaw's 1894 antimilitaristic play about the Balkan Wars, *Arms and the Man.* Needless to say, the possibility of epic combat is totally excluded from Wolfe's narrative. The very title of the novel makes a bad pun (limb-o), and the dust jacket of the first edition carried within concentric rings (an image already associated by 1952 with bomb blasts) the icon of the triskelion, three bowed legs joining at the top of the thighs, an image therefore of detached limbs. Apart from the novel's wordplay, which is constantly deflecting the reader from one semantic field to another, the novel's graphics (a pen stroke taken from *Tristram Shandy,* for instance) remind us of the text as a physical construct and play on the relation between metonym and metaphor. Allusions to Joyce's *Finnegan's Wake* strike the appropriate note. A drawing in Martine's notebook, for instance, shows a machine with an operative in the driving seat. Behind his head there is a hypodermic needle and in the foreground a larger version of the same image resembling a roller. The reads, "point there, somewhere," another pun on "point" signifying purpose, perhaps an indication of direction, but both possibilities reflecting Martine's search for meaning.[23] He is very far from the sage that he has become in his absence.

He is, however, a child of the atomic age. Martine was born within minutes of the first Alamagordo bomb blast, and Wolfe uses him as a linking device between the psychological and political dimensions in the novel. Martine's return to America involves him in an investigation of his own personal past and the recent history of his country. This investigation of results in the gradual revelation of the grotesquely misdirected idealism within the Immob movement. Martine—who for Geduld is primarily a "talkative spectator"—returns to his world as a stranger to find an apparent new world order operative.[24] Immob society has established itself on a basis of universal pacifism, but Wolfe exploits the traditional dystopian ironies of the result not matching the intent and of the new system bearing many similarities to the old regime supposedly superseded. The Inland Strip contains a society with a very marked hierarchy where prosthetic limbs are the most conspicuous signs of status. It is riddled with party oppositions and has merely internalized the language of political supremacy into attempts to "master" or "control" the body through rigorous exercises. The outward and visible sign of the new order is a Wellsian city named New Jamestown after William James, author of the 1910 essay "The Moral Equivalent of War," in which he proposes a national militia working against nature.[25] New Jamestown is a concentric symmetrical paradise of order that Wolfe, through Martine's eyes, represents in bodily terms: "It was all too hygienic and prissy, a bit too meticulously scrubbed behind the ears, too well-groomed, too goddamned aseptic."[26] If this city represents the apotheosis of a puritanical resistance to disorder, the enormous industrial complex beneath the capital of Los Alamos represents the triumph of the Taylorian industrial system.

The main implication of these ironies and of the novel's black humor is that humanity is denying its own nature in such schemes as the Immob movement. This was recognized early by one of Wolfe's few commentators. Chad Walsh declares that *Limbo* demonstrates the following moral: "Man is not dangerous because he has teeth that can bite and hands that can hold a rifle or press a guided-missile button. He is dangerous because of his mind and spirit."[27] Geduld puts more or less the same point more specifically: "Modern man is vetoing ambivalence in favor of consistency. In trying to force a two-sided world into a one-sided pigeonhole, he is being more than just damaging; he is being suicidal, for the ultimate consistency, in theory, is the frozenness of death."[28] This ultimate end point is hinted at in the self-contradiction of Immob being a movement and in the introjection of aggression as a violent impulse against the human body. It might seem that the Freudian polarities of Eros and Thanatos merely essentialize the stark oppositions of Cold War politics, but Wolfe steadily undermines this possibility by revealing a similarity, even homology, between East and West. Once again Norbert Wiener offered him a way forward in *The Human Use of Human Beings* (1950) when he disposed of the Russian bugbear (pun intended and written into the novel: "Russian bear never reigns but it paws"): "To a large extent, this enemy is not Russia, but the reflection of ourselves in a mirage. To defend ourselves against the phantom, we must look to new scientific measures, each more terrible than the last. There is no end to this vast apocalyptic spiral."[29]

In order to move out of this vicious circle, Wolfe tracks Cold War rhetoric and social behavior to their roots in the collective psyche and finds symptoms of a death wish in the "lure of the One," which is phrased with careful political symmetry: "the communist yearning for the oblivion of the proletarian herd or the American yearning for the oblivion of the Jonesian herd."[30] As if wanting to distance himself from such balances and the finely tuned ironies of the novel, Wolfe, in his endnotes, stresses that such a sarcastic examination of political power would never have been permitted in the Eastern bloc. And in his notes to his novel about the Trotsky assassination, *The Great Prince Died,* he launches a whole attack on modish leftism: "Left-bound intellectuals have arrived at such a nicety of discrimination that they . . . will defend the masses only against blows from the right; all blows from the left, however vicious, they will take and dress up as caresses."[31] Although this was written some years after *Limbo,* Wolfe stays consistent with his earlier novel in making the body the site of political experience.

The title of *Limbo* is at once a pun on prosthetics and an allusion to that region in Christian mythology near to hell, described in *Paradise Lost* as the "Paradise of Fools." Traditionally the term denotes a state of neglect or transition between phases. As one figure in the novel points out, the current technological situation has put human desire one step further from the real so that they engage in metagestures: "Now, in the cybernetic limbo, men grasp for the instruments of grasp."[32] The title anticipates the novel as a whole in playing on different areas of meaning, and the perception of semantic difference occurs through low puns. Freud clearly supplied Wolfe with the rationale for such wordplay. In *Jokes and Their Relation to the Unconscious* he identified three main techniques that resemble those operative in the dream work: condensation, recurrence (the multiple use of the same material), and double meaning. The last of these items was elaborated by Arthur Koestler into a whole theory of jokes that, he argued, depended on "bisociation"—in other words, a recognition of doubleness. He defines a joke, therefore, as the "intersection of two *independent and self-contained logical chains.*"[33] It depends on suddenness and on the listener's capacity to respond to semantic alternatives. Different mental systems—what Koestler calls "operative fields"—therefore meet at the moment of a joke, which Koestler describes metaphorically as a "junction." Most of his examples and discussion revolve around double meaning ("a mental concept is simultaneously perceived under two different angles"), but there is no intrinsic reason within his theory as to why a joke should not include a perception of three or even more dimensions of meaning.[34]

Wolfe assimilated this post-Freudian interpretation of humor so thoroughly that *Limbo* contains no single stable frame of semantic reference. Propositions are always relative and provisional, subject to constant modification; and this instability frequently clarifies the novel's political themes. We can see this technique at work in one of the earliest episodes of the novel, where Martine is performing a lobotomy on an African woman. Here as everywhere else in the novel, Wolfe is picking up on a subject that had become a matter of controversy by the early fifties. Although lobotomies were more and more widely performed, there was considerable opposition to an operation that many felt "converts patients into docile, inert, often useless drones."[35] The controversy revolved around the problem of medical risk and the broader issue of whether a supposedly therapeutic operation was actually being used for administrative convenience or even social coercion.[36]

This controversy manifests itself as a series of disruptions to Martine's consciousness by a recurring, apparently nonsensical phrase. But this "nonsense" turns out to be charged with a meaning he has been suppressing because it is so unwelcome, namely an obsession with death. The title phrase from Shakespeare's *Measure for Measure* flits through his mind as he glances at a work depicting the masked operation of authority (Martine, too, is literally masked for the operation) and then initiates a series of repetitions that deforms the line from the negro spiritual "Massa's in the Cold, Cold Ground":

1. Measure's in the cold, cold ground
2. Massa in the cold, cold groan
3. Masseur in the cold, cold groin
4. Messiah's in the cold, cold ground[37]

The original line relates the embodiment of racist authority to death. The first variation suppresses the power term, suggesting instead the demise of proportion. The second substitutes a sign of pain or grief for death, suggesting this time the suffering that Martine is supposedly trying to cure. The third revision changes both key terms when Martine realizes that the operation has destroyed the woman's sex drive, metaphorically rendering her body a place of death. In other words, the distortions of the original line make manifest Martine's latent doubts about the operation and render it an exercise of colonialist violence against the member of a subjugated race. This is confirmed by Wolfe's reference to the islanders' ancestors as "X-men" and "X-women," former humans under erasure. The final occurrence of this line in the novel comes at a point where Martine has finally confronted (and subdued?) a megalomaniac impulse in himself.

The verbal substitutions just discussed represent the emergence of suppressed opposite views of the lobotomy and of Martine's dealings with the African islanders. As such they exemplify the principle on which the discourse of *Limbo* is based, namely that of ambivalence. Wolfe even makes it a principle of nature: "every cell contained a seething mixture of Eros and Thanatos; ambivalence was its glue." A tension between opposing impulses is historicized by summaries of Nietzsche and Freud and then written into the text again and again as a series of dualities. For instance, Mandunji Island contains two narcotic weeds, one inducing tranquility and the other stimulation. The Immob leaders Theo and Helder represent the political polarities of idealism and realism. And so the list could go on. Every instance in the novel presumes its opposite, which will appear sooner or later; and that opposite will in turn produce new polarities; and so the process continues. That is why Wolfe includes reversible paired terms like Dog-God and palindromic names like Ubu. Vonnegut uses the same device in *Player Piano,* which reverses a human activity (piano player) to something purely mechanical. But Wolfe extends this device into the whole rhetoric of *Limbo,* so every proposition implies an opposite counterproposition.

The novel demands that the reader be constantly alert to such variations of verbal connotation and register. Since Martine returns to America after eighteen years of absence, he is utterly estranged from the new culture he encounters and therefore, like the reader, scrutinizes recurring terms and slogans for their meanings. This process of decoding involves a recognition of the transferability of language from one domain of experience to another. And, as usual, this is made explicit in a statement that anticipates the wordplay of *Dr. Strangelove:* "The rhetoric of love is remarkably like the rhetoric of war."[38] The same proposition is implied in Martine's lobotomy operation, which is described as "firing" "bullets" of strychnine into the brain.

Words themselves, therefore, become unstable signs. When Martine visits the Immob academy in America, a lecturer warns against confusing words with referents. The solution, he declares, is "to understand that the word is not the object, eloquence is not photography, sound does not equate with substance."[39] When the novel shifts temporarily into the genre of spy fiction, that shift only makes explicit a general tendency within the language of the novel. A Communist agent in Wolfe's 1957 espionage thriller *In Deep* philosophizes about this dimension to language, arguing that "communities are based on the common acceptance of words and their meanings: they're cemented by language." Spying, however, induces "moments of eerie doubt as to whether the cover words mean *anything*." This notion of verbal disguise is embodied particularly in Martine, who separates himself into a series of selves in his notebooks (Mark I, II, etc.) and who negotiates his way through the novel by adopting different aliases, such as Lazarus (back from the dead) and Brigham Rimbaud.

Martine's notebooks constitute a journal and as such bear his witness to nuclear war. However, we have seen how one journal is distorted into a kind of holy script, and the reader constantly suspects that Martine himself may not be exempt from the pathological effects of the war. In other words, we read for symptoms, just as we doubt the deadpan journal of Wolfe's "Self Portrait." The physicist Leo Szilard also experimented with journal fiction in this period. "The Diary of Dr. Davis" purports to be the first entries describing a mission to Stalin by an American emissary. The Soviet premier tells the American that "doing away with atomic bombs would not necessarily make for peace."[40] Szilard clearly intends the diary to express the need to understand the Soviet perspective on these weapons, but, at the same time, he places an ambiguous frame around the entries, which have been published in 1980 after later world wars have broken out. Furthermore, the publisher's foreword casts doubts on the mental state of the diarist, describing his text merely as a "remarkable document." Ultimately, Szilard's diary, like Martine's notebooks, fails to prevent the dreaded outcome of war and may only serve to demonstrate the ambiguous mental state of its author.

Here we encounter a paradox in *Limbo*. Despite Wolfe's blatant conservatism in presenting sexual roles, his novel anticipates the practice of postmodernism in destabilizing verbal signs, moving across different genres, and handling Martine's notebooks, which represent the core of the novel's text. Not only do they give us brief glimpses of World War III, they also contain Martine's reflections on his own expressions. In other words, the notebook sections are the most self-conscious parts of the novel. Each entry is followed by Martine's retrospective examinations of his own words, the implicit desire for a readership in posterity, and his own half-conscious motives. The order of notebook entries is also crucially important: an excerpt from Mark II describing Martine's return to America; his discovery at the end of Part 4 of his original wartime notebook (Mark I) published in book form; a retrospective assessment of himself and the Immob movement (Mark II again); and, finally, a brief conclusion. In Mark I Martine is confronted with his own private journal made public as an Immob text and "canonized" by explanatory footnotes from the Immob leader Helder. Martine devotes part of the text to an imaginary dialogue between himself and Babyface, a war casualty (whose name ironically echoes that of the bank robber Baby Face Nelson). At the end of this dialogue, Martine facetiously proposes a way in which people can overcome their fear of helplessness before the larger processes of war (the "steamroller") by volunteering to be amputated. The program could function as a recruitment campaign, with accompanying slogans reminiscent of *Brave New World,* but is now directed toward pacifism:

> It would have to be suggested that the volunteers wouldn't be hurting themselves but actually doing themselves and the world some good. You could easily do that with a few well-chosen slogans, such as—oh, I don't know, slogans to the effect that there's no demobilization without immobilization, pacifism means passivity, arms or the man: anything that makes a wound into some kind of boon. And then, of course, as you've suggested, you could offer special inducements to the recruits: cash awards, bonuses, pensions, hero status, medals and decorations, membership in exclusive clubs, leisure, women, all in proportion to the degree of amputation or other forms of crippling. How many men were actually clipped in World War II—25,000, 30,000 on our side alone? How many in World War III—many hundreds of thousands around the world? Hell, you could round up millions of volunteers if you just put a heavy enough stamp of social approval on it and offered enough juicy come-ons. You'd get precisely the same results that you get from war now, except that everybody would be happy and feel himself the dignified master of his own fate. And, secretly, revel in the enormous amount of pain he'd arranged for.[41]

To Martine's horror he finds that a joke has become reality. His ironic suggestion has become institutionalized in an international movement, and he himself has been mythologized as its founder. In short, Immob has been established on the basis of a misreading of his text. It is as if the Irish have literally started eating their own children in response to *A Modest Proposal.* That is why Wolfe peppers his text with references to Dostoyevsky, Gide, Joyce, and Mann, all novelists specializing in complex ironies.

The centrality of a joke in a novel dealing with such a sobering subject as warfare has been more than some critics could stomach. In his review of *Limbo,* Philip Wylie praised the satirical ideas and the solution but objected to Wolfe taking "non-classical liberties with scientifiction, so that his story as a story is almost childishly implausible."[42] Paul Brians argues that *Limbo* "represents the farthest extreme of antipacifist muscular disarmament fiction" and rejects an ironic reading.[43] David N. Samuelson has been one of the very few critics to date to admit the power of the novel's black humor and argues that "this central absurdity [the voluntary amputation program] functions straightforwardly as an estranging device."[44] In fact, its functioning is quite complex, since the whole emphasis on amputation actualizes a metaphor embedded in such routine expressions as "disarmament" and "lay down arms." The punning is as obvious as representing Immob fanatics as refusing prosthesis and therefore needing to lie in baskets—becoming basket cases. Such jokes drain off the solemnity of the pacifist movement and render it absurd. Yet Wolfe's central complex of metaphors skillfully combines political and psychological analysis.

The human body thus functions throughout *Limbo* as a holistic image that the very title of the novel tugs against by suggesting synecdoche. So the central pun on "arms" bears directly on the historical moment when Wolfe was writing. The phrase "arms race" was first used in the 1930s to describe the competition between military powers. In the postwar period the phrase took on an extra urgency when applied to weapons of mass destruction, and its use was accelerating in the early 1950s. The cause of disarmament is described by Wolfe as growing from error (misunderstanding Martine's journal), confusing means with origin (limbs with aggression), and pursuing self-contradiction in designing prosthetic limbs even more powerful than the originals. Scott Bukatman finds in *Limbo* an anticipation of postmodern SF that treats the body as the site of exploration and transformation, which helps explain Martine's spatialization of his African lover's body as a colonized terrain for him to explore.[45] The body as trope, however, goes through many more permutations. The diminished American landscape is figured as a torso with two truncated arms. And the whole concept of the body politic lies behind Wolfe's depiction of the functioning of post–World War III society. Once again Norbert Wiener underpins the analogy when he draws comparisons in *Cybernetics:* "It is certainly true that the social system is an organization like the individual, that it is bound together by a system of communication, and that it has a dynamics in which circular processes of a feedback nature play as important part."[46] The relation of body to society, then, can be read at various points as synecdoche, metaphor, or systems analogy.

Wolfe's novel is constructed over a fear specific to the period of its publication. As N. Katherine Hayles has pointed out, "War, acknowledged or covert, is the repressed trauma that threatens to erupt throughout *Limbo*."[47] When Martine returns to his national and local origins in the central sections of the novel, his actions suggest a search for origins as a move toward understanding the pathology of his present. But the psychosis within the novel is collective not individual. For Freud, the aggressive instinct is a given impulse in the psyche at odds with the restraints of civilization and one that can unpredictably break through those restraints. This is exactly what happens in Part 6, ironically titled "Games." Historically, the Olympic Games were held in London in 1948 without the Soviet Union—and then in Helsinki in 1952, this time with their participation. Subsequent history has shown that they offered an avenue for channeling Cold War rivalry into the nonmilitary sphere. There is, however, a second dimension to "games" discussed by Wiener toward the end of *The Human Use of Human Beings,* where he explains that "the concept of war which lies behind some of our new government agencies, which are developing the consequences of von Neumann's theory of games, is sufficiently extensive to include all civilian activities during war, before war, and possibly even between wars."[48] Wiener's abiding fear yet again is of a mechanization of international policy in pursuit of triumphalist aims. At this point in *Limbo,* the arms race becomes explicitly militaristic.

The prelude to the Olympic Games is an accusation made on television by Vishinu, the Eastern Union delegation leader, that an ostensibly innocent visit by "Strippers" (members of the Inland Strip, or America) to Mandunji Island was in fact to prospect for colombium, a rare metal needed for the manufacture of prosthetic limbs. Vishinu tries to corroborate this charge by catching Martine in a "honey trap," a sexually compromising situation with a nubile Eastern agent. During the games themselves the Unionists win all the events, and there follows a ceremony where the Strip leader, Helder, praises the nonmilitary value of the games only to have his words thrown back in his face by Vishinu: "Your imperialist crimes can no longer go unpunished. You are traitors, saboteurs, terrorists, schemers, and you will be dealt with as such . . . We have knocked you off your smug thrones cybernetically. Now, for the sake of everything we call Immob, we must knock you off your imperialist thrones too."[49] With this, he gives a signal to his team members, who then raise their prosthetic arms and gun down the Western judges.

A clear set of analogies emerges here. In order to construct arms the super powers need a rare metal. The games combine an attempted transposition of military rivalry on to peaceful competition à la William James, but the ceremonies can also be read as a parody of the United Nations, where Vishinsky (Vishnu) made a name for his constant denunciations of Western imperialism. The games represent a literal arms race whose competitiveness is evaded by the naive Theo. The games themselves at once parody the jockeying for power and also enact the overturning of the American presumption of technological supremacy. Vishnu's team, in its perfect discipline, resembles an "electrified centipede" in how it coheres into a single body, and its use of prosthetic weapons restores the concept of military extension "to arm" while the biological limb has become elided. To compound the political reference—this time to the 1936 Munich Olympics—the Union team members hold out their arms in unconscious imitation of the Nazi salute.

What we have been considering as a doubleness of language can now be seen as a duplicity of behavior. The pacifist movement patently fails because war is going on behind the scenes. The last sections of the novel contain revelations that confirm this perception, not least Helder's admission that he has secretly retained weapons and placed agents in enemy territory. Within the series of identifications Wolfe constructs, one emerges between Martine and both Helder and Theo, as if the latter represent two sides (pragmatic realism versus idealism) of one consciousness. Martine is thereby drawn into the internal politics of the Strip just as his decision to grow a beard that makes him resemble General Smuts implicates him in colonialism.

The grotesque analogy between the Union team and an electrified centipede exemplifies Koestler's proposition of humor occurring at an intersection between semantic chains. Wolfe plays on the proximity between the concepts of team and body (the latter in the sense of a collectivity) and concretizes the metaphor through a creature that combines singularity and multiplicity. It also specifically links these figures with war, since Martine argues in his notebook that "each war brings the human race a little closer to the insects, whose lives are all 'it' and no 'I'; at the end of the war people feel less human and more insectlike."[50] Insects, therefore, offer one means of expressing the dehumanizing processes of war. This instance, however, is not a self-perception but, rather, a realization by Martine of a sinister dimension to the team's discipline that is compounded by the epithet "electrified," which suggests that they form a collective technological simulacrum of life. The team now becomes linked with a mechanizing process cast in a negative light throughout *Limbo* and one associated specifically with the totalitarian centralism of Stalin. In Wolfe's later novel on the killing of Trotsky, *The Great*

Prince Died, the assassin's fanatical mother gives him a disingenuous lesson in believing in his own acts: "If *their* will . . . moves you like a robot," she tells him, alluding to his directors in the Politburo, "then you do your work out of weakness, not strength!"[51] But it is exactly that kind of unquestioning robotic obedience that she is trying to induce in her son. Similarly, the members (etymologically, the "limbs") of the Olympic team move in absolute obedience to Vishinu's signal, and their latent connection with warfare becomes overt and explicit once they gun down the judges.

Fleeing the scene of the gun battle, Martine finds himself in the nerve center of the Inland Strip, a huge underground industrial complex on the site of Los Alamos. The super factory represents an ultimate triumph of cybernetics, which Wolfe writes ironically into the text through echoes of the human body:

> Flame-geysering blast furnaces and spark-showering open hearths and incandescent kilns, close by them many thin-lipped mouths from whose spinning cylindrical dentures spewed flat sheets of steel and aluminium, and, just beyond, to mould those metals, row upon row of planers and shapers and drillers and bevelers and stampers and buffers and riveters and welders; all the sleek devices invented by men to supplement their own puny fingers and teeth, and to muscle these super-biters and super-hammerers, to supply the super-biceps, atomic power plants everywhere. It was Willow Run and Oak Ridge and Hanford rolled up in one.[52]

This is a composite facility, combining the functions of a wartime bomber factory, the Atomic City that once served as the base for the Manhattan Project, and a nuclear production site with multiple reactors. As well as a bureaucratic labyrinth, the complex is compared to a massive externalized nervous system taking its orders from an electronic "brain." In other words, it represents the ultimate military-industrial complex of the atomic age. Everything seems clinically sterile—until it is attacked by fifth columnists. Martine is still gazing at the complex when he sees mushroom clouds rising over the complex, which have reduced the site to a shambles.

Limbo concludes with Martine's flight from the Inland Strip and returns the reader in the last chapter to the uncharted tropical island. War has not ended; it is simply happening elsewhere. Some of the earliest prosthetic arms were designed
• for battle casualties, but in the last section Wolfe shows how the replacement limbs have themselves been designed as weapons, thereby enacting a perverse circularity of function. Wolfe's surrogate within the novel, Martine, performs

tortuous acts of wordplay and ransacks the fields of psychology, cybernetics, and many others to try to find meaning to his experiences. The novel shows repeated attempts at mapping, whether of the body, the brain, or a truncated United States; but at the same time it warns the reader that "the map is not the territory."[53] This warning against confusing the codified representation with the thing itself applies equally well to language, which is comically destabilized throughout *Limbo*. Words sometimes mutate, as happens more startlingly in Russell Hoban's postnuclear novel *Riddley Walker* or as puns point toward diverse semantic fields. Martine's search for meaning ultimately can be read as symptom, as the pathological workings of the mind in the atomic age. Wolfe's novel also explores the consequences of technological extensions to the human body.

CHAPTER 8

Push-Button Holocaust in
Mordecai Roshwald's *Level 7*

In *Limbo* Bernard Wolfe expressed sardonic doubts about a technologized defense system running out of control. One of that novel's main ironies lies in the complete inability of the protagonist to affect not only political events but even the fate of his own notebooks. We turn now to narratives that describe the consequences of automation for nuclear defense and examine the problematic role of the human operative within such a highly sophisticated electronic system.

John W. Campbell, who edited the SF journal *Astounding* (later *Analog*) from 1937 to 1971, used his journal to promote a greater awareness of science, including articles like that by the émigré German rocket engineer Willy Ley on the introduction of orbital missiles.[1] Campbell adopted the role of intermediary, channeling new discoveries in nuclear physics to the public. Indeed, in an essay he contributed to a 1953 symposium he argued that science fiction uniquely could "provide for a science-based culture" and, since "the atomic bomb represents one of the points at which physical science directly impinges on sociological science," the SF novelist can combine these two main areas of culture in his work.[2] Campbell displaces any reservations about scientific progress onto human operatives in his *Astounding* editorial for January 1950, "The Real Pushbutton War," where the really dangerous "button" is the trigger to ingrained habit: "These carefully taught pushbuttons are the only kind that are really dangerous to Man: the metal and plastic kind aren't any good at all, the great intercontinental bombardment rockets, the subcritical masses of uranium and plutonium are all useless—unless a man who has been carefully taught is there to push them. And the man won't be, unless a whole population has been carefully taught, with plenty of pushbuttons installed in that deadliest of all weapons—the human mind."[3] Essentially,

Campbell is warning that the danger in sophisticated technology lies not in the technology itself but in the internalization by operatives of mechanistic processes.

Several years later a number of stories began appearing in print that engaged this crucial issue. J. F. Bone's "Triggerman" (1959) is set in an underground defense bunker manned by General French, the "man who could push the button that would start World War III!"[4] When a DEW (Distant Early Warning) Line radarman spots a "bogey" on his screen, missiles are launched to intercept it, but without effect.[5] Everyone assumes that the Russians have devised a new weapon when the missile hits Washington, destroying the Capitol, and French is urged to launch retaliatory bombs. But the whole story pays tribute to French's logic and therefore, by implication, to the military screening process he went through. His finger hovers over the button, but he is the only one not to yield to the war hysteria around him, and he is ultimately justified when it is revealed that the "missile" was a meteorite and its landing an act of God. French and the system lying behind him are both vindicated for their embodiment of reason.

Similarly, in his 1960 story "Pushbutton War" Joseph P. Martino, a research scientist in electrical engineering, demonstrates complete confidence in the Western military system. Harry Lightfoot serves as a U.S. fighter pilot at an Arctic defense base, where the skies are monitored constantly for missiles: "[The Launch Control Officer] sat in a dimly-lighted room, facing three oscilloscope screens. On each of them a pie-wedge section was illuminated by a white line which swept back and forth like a windscreen wiper. Unlike a windshield wiper, however, it put little white blobs on the screen, instead of removing them."[6] Martino presents the difficulty of distinguishing meteorites from missiles on the radar screens as a practical problem, not a danger. When a red alert sounds, Lightfoot takes off. Every aspect of the launch process functions smoothly, as does the interception of the weapon, and Martino leaves no doubt about either the enemy (the missile was launched in Central Asia) or about its purpose: "This one . . . was carrying the complex mechanism of a hydrogen bomb. Its destination was an American city; its object to replace that city with an expanding cloud of star-hot gas."[7] The story describes an idealized harmony between operation and equipment. Pressing the launch button is a critical but essential moment for Lightfoot; the transition from manual to autopilot is smooth, and he returns to base with the satisfaction of a job well done. Martino keeps his focus throughout on the technical details of the action and by so doing contains the subject, blocking out its wider implications. We hear nothing about possible American retaliation or about similar missiles launched elsewhere.

Broadly speaking, these stories demonstrate confidence in the smooth working of the U.S. military system, but a more skeptical counterposition was being articulated in the same period, where overconfidence in technology was seen as a broader failing in American society. Lewis Mumford, for one, questioned the crude identification of technological development with progress in *The Pentagon of Power* (1964), where he warned that the paradox of automation lay in our loss of control over the pace of the process. This posed the greatest danger in what he termed "technics," a danger exacerbated by hidden motives transforming capability into compulsion: "Why is the secret motto of our power-oriented society not just 'You can, therefore you may,' but 'You may, therefore you must'?" For Mumford, automation presents a danger to humanity in its "displacement of the human mind" from decision making, and he cites with particular approval a satire that, as we will see, played its part in shaping the image of the nuclear operative—*Brave New World,* where the characters are "deliberately fabricated for the purpose of keeping every part of existence, above all human potentialities, under centralized scientific control."[8]

Mordecai Roshwald's *Level 7* was published in 1959, a period when the arms race seemed to be rushing forward remorselessly, when the United States and the Soviet Union were locked in a rivalry over satellites, and when fears were growing that nuclear war could be triggered accidentally. These fears had been dramatized as early as 1946 when the physicist Louis N. Ridenour published his play *Pilot Lights of the Apocalypse,* which describes the outbreak of such a war in an underground control center beneath San Francisco. The system is explained to the visiting U.S. president as keeping the defense board well away from the counterattack because "they don't have time to think." The bunker is totally reliant on electronic means of communication through teletype machines, sensors triggering different-colored lights according to danger levels, and switches that can launch nuclear missiles currently orbiting Earth. Suddenly the room shakes and a red light appears that seems to show that San Francisco has been destroyed. A hysterical officer rushes to the counterattack console and launches missiles before he can be stopped, from which point an increasing series of red lights signals the destruction of other cities. In a desperate attempt to stop the process, the Americans transmit the message "THERE IS NO REPEAT NO WAR," but the play ends with destruction: "The room rocks, the lights go out. With a dull, powerful rumble the roof caves in."[9] The very brevity of Ridenour's play makes an ironic point about the speed of this destruction. His title, in a further irony, suggests coming revelation, whereas the final image marks the end of all communication.

Level 7 addresses such fears in its description of an accidentally triggered nuclear war from the viewpoint of an operative in an underground nuclear control bunker. Roshwald has explained the origin of his novel: "I became involved in fiction writing through concern about the menace to humanity from nuclear armament, as well as out of a sense of disenchantment with some aspects of modern life." Without rejecting the SF label, he is careful to distinguish his own fiction from more sensational narratives: "The science fiction I have written is very much colored by social, political and cultural concern. Indeed, science fiction is for me a *form* of expression rather than an objective in its own right. In this sense I would classify it with such books as Swift's *Gulliver's Travels* or Huxley's *Brave New World*, rather than with some modern stories dealing with inter-stellar warfare, monsters from distant planets, and the like (unless such stories are used as parables)."[10]

Roshwald originally planned to introduce his narrative through the framing device of a report from the Martian Institute for Archaeological Excavations in the Solar System, but this was cut from the text and only restored in the 2004 edition. This is the same device as that used in Leo Szilard's 1961 story "'Grand Central Terminal,'" where an interplanetary expedition has been exploring a New York emptied of all human life, and in the novel version of *Dr. Strangelove,* which introduces the narrative as a documentary about the primitive worlds of antiquity. In all these cases, scientific rationality is displaced from Earth onto a culture from another planet, as if to imply that Earth has destroyed its own life in a final act of madness. This preamble to *Level 7* explains the provenance of the narrative as a found manuscript, but at the same time it sheds doubt about its authenticity, stressing the contradictory nature of the narrator: "On the one hand, he seemed to have been intelligent enough to express himself in intelligent symbols of considerable complexity. On the other hand, however, his story about the deliberate attempt of the people of the Earth to exterminate each other for no clear reason, the amount of work, energy and organization used to this end, makes no sense at all."[11] If they had a culture, how could they have destroyed themselves? And might the diary simply be the fantasies of an individual without any social reference? By raising these questions in advance, Roshwald nudges the reader toward speculating about the relation of the diary narrative to the moment of its publication. The Martians' puzzlement over its nature anticipates a reader response that might not otherwise occur, since the diary mode is one that privileges interiority and reader identification with the diarist. Roshwald himself has subsequently explained that in his novel "the whole scientific and logical edifice is exposed as a failure."[12] *Level 7* ruptures the identification of military technology with reason, revealing it to be the ultimate destructive force.

The abstracted, self-enclosed world of *Level 7* represents Roshwald's attempt to isolate for ironic scrutiny the way certain elements of modern technology can run under their own momentum and quite independent of human control or decision making. The setting, an underground bunker, symbolizes the "warfare state," where the United States is described as being run through a combination of politics, the military, and big business.[13] Roshwald embodies this combination in the smoothly functioning but totally anonymous miniature world of the bunker. Everything about this "Taylorized" society is organized on the basis of collective efficiency; the meals are served, in an echo of Chaplin's *Modern Times,* on a conveyor belt; and over everything are heard the commands of the ubiquitous loudspeakers, prefaced with "attention please, attention." Roshwald took care to make *Level 7* as free from cultural markers as possible so that, in theory, it could be read by East or West as a warning against nuclear war. In an essay of 1961, "Who Will Bury Whom?" he questions the meaning of oppositions like "East and West," "Dictatorship versus Democracy," or "Atheism versus Christianity" and argues that "the real thing is automation."[14] Roshwald read the ongoing dispute between the two super powers as a latter-day version of the ludicrous domestic dispute in Swift's Lilliput, over which end of their egg they should break, that spills over to international relations with Blefuscu. By adopting such an external perspective, Roshwald implies that Cold War confrontation can only be viewed objectively from the outside. Thus, readers of *Level 7* are led to recognize a crucial technological feature of their own culture. This avoidance of projecting a specific identity onto the installation he describes in the novel helps to explain his narrator's growing suspicion that the enemy has identical installations, and it also reflects Roshwald's ironic view of Cold War dualities. His novel was initially dedicated equally to Eisenhower and Krushchev, and in his original afterword he stressed that *Level 7* was "*not* neutral in the sense that it accuses both. It is submitted for the benefit of the West and the East."[15]

Essentially, Roshwald saw the technology he describes in *Level 7* as resulting from a general tendency he observed during the 1950s toward uniformity in American life, which he had planned to analyze in a study to be called "America: The Dream and the Nightmare." Although this was never completed, he did publish an essay in 1958 that indicates early planning for his novel. In "Quo Vadis, America?" which takes its cue from David Riesman's notion of "other-directed" behavior in *The Lonely Crowd* (1953), a person who is other-directed in effect gives up the faculty of individual choice and becomes an "imitating anthropoid." Roshwald attributes this social characteristic to the amazing mobility of American life that inevitably detaches the individual from family and place, and he concludes that the United States faces a danger less obvious than the bomb but nonetheless of great importance:

Atomic warfare is not the only menace of the atomic era! The loss of individual norms in moral issues, the admiration of unjust power, the lack of tradition, the disruption of family, education without principles—these are dangers which can be called spiritual, though they cannot be disconnected from the material and physical aspects of human civilization. To warn against these and to fight them may be a second front in the fight for human survival, but it may be the first front in the fight for human dignity.[16]

The military protagonist in *Level 7* is an extreme case of such mobility because he is totally separated from any family or domestic context and is subject to arbitrary decisions of an anonymous bureaucracy.

In his essays Roshwald addresses the encroachment of spheres in human activity, such as the intrusion of commercialism on friendship. He attributes this to a latter-day pioneer ethos of free enterprise and concludes that this is one of the less obvious signs of American democracy at work.[17] More importantly for his novel, in another article Roshwald describes the United States as a Fordist culture based on the principle of "efficient organization." The desire to organize replaces spontaneity with "mechanical behaviour." When his impressions of America were still fresh in the fifties, he has recalled that they "seemed to point to a uniformly happy, efficient and self-sufficient society, verging on automata or robots."[18] While American uniformity reminded Roshwald of the society described in *Brave New World*, when he taught that novel at the University of Minnesota the students failed to see any kind of dystopian dimension to it. However, Roshwald himself saw ominous signs of a loss of humanity: "Where emotional and intellectual spontaneity are replaced by predictable reactions and exceptions are not tolerated human behaviour comes to resemble the motions of machines. The human machines may be more intricate than the inanimate ones, but then the modern machines and robots are reaching high degrees of sophistication as well."[19] This mechanization of human life was a major theme in American science fiction of the fifties. As we saw in Kurt Vonnegut's *Player Piano* and Bernard Wolfe's *Limbo*, both works satirize the loss of human initiative by investing the hand and arm with a special symbolism focusing on this central problem of control.[20]

Roshwald discusses a process where the methods of industrial production are fed into American society as a whole, producing a hypertrophy of organization. His argument approaches that of Aldous Huxley in the latter's 1958 collection of essays, *Brave New World Revisited*. Whereas Huxley admitted that in his 1932 novel the "completely organized society" seemed a remote possibility, this possibility was being realized in contemporary American life and declared that "too much organization transforms men and women into automata, suffocates the creative spirit, and abolishes the very possibility of freedom."[21] Huxley attacked the social ethic, which he saw as emerging from the increased commercialization of American society and from the "hidden persuaders," to borrow another title catch-phrase from the fifties, of the media, political propaganda, and advertising. By a slightly different route he arrived at a very similar conclusion to Roshwald's—that the individual in America was being swamped by a whole series of social and cultural processes. The experiences of the protagonist in *Level 7* are thus symptomatic of society as a whole and of a military-industrial organization in particular.

Like *Brave New World, Level 7* describes an institutionalized and regimented world. In Huxley's novel biology is destiny, since characters have been genetically designed for specific social roles. One difference Roshwald introduces lies in the absence of names. His narrator is designated X-127, thereby situated within the class of "Push-Button Officers." Like the characters in Yevgeny Zamyatin's dystopia *We* (translation 1924), the narrator is an anonymous cipher within an official hierarchy, where choice is made by others; X-127 and his colleagues simply carry out orders from "above." Huxley and Roshwald both describe societies serviced by labor-saving devices and punctuated with announcements over loudspeakers. Equally, both writers evoke an ethic of collectiveness where characters are benignly coerced into acting according to group norms parodied in *Level 7* through the talks on "Know Thy Level." The tangible sign of this acquiescence is the drug Soma and the pills that X-127 and others take with their food. In addition to echoing Huxley, Roshwald also parodies 1950s American psychology through slogans like "get adjusted" and arguments that take away the real anxieties of living underground by dismissing them as "symbolism."

The question of psychological health emerges at a number of points in *Level 7*, always with the implication that such "health" supports the status quo. X-117 experiences such a traumatic surge of guilt that he commits suicide, and that individual death has a much stronger impact on the narrator than the millions he reports in the outside world. And X-127 himself experiences a mental collapse just before war breaks out. What happens at such points is that Roshwald turns the notion of health against its enforcers and implicitly questions the sanity of the whole military system. In his diary, X-127 records an intermittent dialogue between rival perceptions of his situation. A typical example occurs when he is reflecting with considerable pleasure on his own importance within the Push-Button section but then wonders who is above him: "There must still be the Command itself, naturally, whatever it may be."[22] The comment is absolutely typical in that X-127 has the intelligence to notice discrepancies in the system but at the same time possesses such a strong faith in the latter's rational organization that he shrugs off his doubts. Because he has so thoroughly internalized the values of the regime, he can only express his criticism or fear obliquely, through dream or story. A series of nightmares mentally enact situations forbidden by his superego. He dreams of drowning in a lake that gets deeper and deeper; he imagines himself walking in a city under attack and being surrounded by travesty corpses ("grotesque brown rubber dummies"); and he imagines being with his parents during an atomic blast.[23] Even the stories he and others write ostensibly for children depict the atomic fears that the regime tries to suppress. The story of Gamma, Alpha, and Ch-777 anticipates the seepage of radiation later in the novel, figuring a rise toward the higher levels as a move toward death; "The Story of the Mushroom" draws on one of the most famous Cold War icons, here presenting the nuclear threat as a monstrous growth that finally explodes into millions of death-carrying particles. These stories and the narrator's nightmares symbolically break through the abstraction of the regime, which attempts to focus power in the apparatus of the bunker.

Erich Fromm's 1955 study *The Sane Society* similarly discusses the emergence of a feeling of "push-button power" induced by electronic consumables like television.[24] We live, he insists, in a world of numbers, abstracted from physical reality, and he even cites a case identical with X-127: "In modern war, one individual can cause the destruction of hundreds of thousands of men, women and children. He could do so by pushing a button; he may not feel the emotional impact of what he is doing, since he does not know the people whom he kills; it is almost as if his act of pushing the button and their death had no real connection."[25]

This is exactly what happens to X-127 when called to action by the loudspeaker. The whole system is directed toward an outcome—nuclear war—referred to merely as "it." X-127 obediently pushes his button and then watches his electronic screen with fascination. After the second strike the image becomes more satisfying: "Aesthetically the picture was quite pleasing. Red blobs and blue and yellow spots, some on the red blobs and some outside them. But the colour was still restricted to Zone A. The other zones remained white, like a continent waiting for an explorer to map it."[26] Although X-127 reminds himself that the first button he punches launches only "one-to-five megaton rockets," the overwhelming impression conveyed in his description is one of abstraction. The blobs and spots come to resemble a grotesque work of art, an electronic spectacle. Technology estranges the operative totally from any observable human consequences, an effect incorporated into the narrator's language. "It" suggests a suppressed referent, either nuclear attack or the order to press the button. By remaining relatively unmoved by this abstract spectacle, X-127 is fulfilling the function that he has been trained for, but he then begins to wonder if he and the others in his bunker are unfeeling monsters. This is one possibility Roshwald addressed in his 1960 essay "Training the Nuclear Warrior," where he speculates that the nuclear triggermen might be caught between a dangerous conditioning and an inadequate hostility. Because of their physical insulation, they will probably never see the enemy except through electronic screens, in which case conditioning becomes essential to instilling a suitably negative image. However, that conditioning could in itself be dangerous, because "a few angry men might start off an atomic world disaster."[27] In *Level 7* X-127 might be simply functioning as an extension of the military machine, but at least he gradually comes to reflect on whether this is the case, however late in the day. His function, if not his subjective life, reflects what Roshwald was later to call a "computer mentality," a naive reliance on war games models that he saw as affecting the conduct of the Vietnam War.[28]

As the war progresses in *Level 7*, the narrator learns the grimmest irony of all: that it was triggered by accident. The enemy declares over the radio that its first launch of missiles was the "outcome of a technical failure." That is bizarre enough, but then X-127 hears that the command he received was given through a device called an "atomphone" working "for safety's sake" on a principle similar to a seismograph and designed to circumvent human error. Thus, a process of escalation was set in motion over which no one had any control whatsoever. As X-127 remarks, "The progress of the war resembled the chain reaction going on inside the atomic bomb itself!"[29] The novel thus approaches a possibility that Roshwald had only speculated on in "Training the Nuclear Warrior": "In an age of automation, it is not inconceivable that rockets might be made to retaliate automatically. If a trigger-pulling apparatus could be developed which would register and react to a nuclear bomb exploding within a certain radius, but which would remain insensitive to ordinary explosions and earthquakes, not to speak of nuclear mishaps on a neighboring firing-site (are there more qualifications needed?), the human factor could be eliminated altogether."[30] The whole point of *Level 7*, of course, is to foreground, not eliminate, the human factor. X-127 is a figure on the verge of obsolescence within the system; hence, one of the many ironies in the novel is shown through his misplaced pride in a function that could just as easily be carried out by a machine. As we shall see, he only comes to realize the enormity of what has happened when it is too late for him to save his life.

Roshwald presents the main part of his novel as a sequence of diary entries that trace a process whereby X-127 gradually develops an identity distinct from his official role and function. The running dialogue between critical and acquiescent parts of his consciousness noted earlier becomes progressively more difficult to resolve. Put simply, he starts as an organization man and ends up an individual. Roshwald himself has explained this method as aiming at two objectives: "I chose X-127 to tell the story, or to write the diary, because I wanted to tell it from the inside. I also intended to create a desensitised, dehumanised individual who complements the apparatus of an automated weapons system."[31] By giving him an official designation rather than a name, Roshwald represents him as a true organization man and also avoids situating his protagonist within American culture. As he has subsequently explained, "The push-button officer and his colleagues can be equally Americans or Russians, as indeed the weapons systems and deployment of the two opponents have, broadly speaking , been the mirror images of each other."[32]

Level 7 was published during a debate in the United States over civil defense, specifically about the provision of nuclear shelters. In 1956 the Holifield Committee reported on the inadequate state of affairs, and the following year James W. Deer, a civil defense coordinator for Portland, Oregon, contributed his impressions to the *Bulletin of the Atomic Scientists* in an article entitled "The Unavoidable International Shelter Race," which Roshwald originally planned to incorporate as an appendix to *Level 7.* In his essay Deer tries to give imaginative expression to how the United States would look if it really was prepared for nuclear attack along the lines recommended by the U.S. Navy. The country would then consist of around a hundred "city-states."

> The city-states themselves will for the most part be underground . . . Each city-state must be self-sufficient, and not dependent on central control. It must have its own nuclear power generators. It must be capable of sustaining itself in a state of indefinite siege, in a world where normal agricultural pursuits can no longer be carried out because of world-wide radioactive contamination. This means an initial large store of food is required, to be supplemented by underground hydroponic tank farming. Complete air filtering systems will be required, to filter out poison gas and germs, because gas and germ warfare is to be expected.

This is Deer's prediction for a period of at least twenty-five years. The irony in his title arises from his perception of the competition between each power bloc. One race gives way to the next and, after intercontinental ballistic missiles, why not a shelter race? Exactly the same extrapolation is made more ludicrously when, after proposing the use of mine shafts as nuclear shelters, Dr. Strangelove insists that the West may suffer from a "mine shaft gap." Stressing a tit-for-tat logic of response between East and West, Deer goes on to evoke an inevitable, unchanging cycle of events: "The play has begun, and we are the actors. The end is implicit from the nature of the beginning. Within the framework of fusion bombs, guided missiles, and shelters, there is nothing we can do but go ahead and play out our part in the preordained ritual. Fusion bombs, guided missiles, and shelter on one side and only fusion bombs and guided missiles on the other must be regarded as an unstable situation."[33]

Deer's description of self-supporting underground installations anticipates the techniques of survival used in Roshwald's nuclear bunker, which, as a command facility, we assume would be a place of maximum security. However, news begins to filter down that people at Level 2 are dying, probably from a polluted air supply. X-127 now begins to extrapolate what might be happening beyond his bunker: "This means that the world population is quickly being reduced to those living in the deeper levels, the ones fitted with self-sufficient air-supply systems. The enemy must have shelters with this equipment too, but I suppose none of the allies and neutrals could afford it."[34] Unlike Deer's scenario, which is relatively static, the situation worsens toward the end of *Level 7* as radiation gradually seeps down from the upper levels. In contrast, the thoughts of X-127 symbolically rise toward the surface and the outside world. Indeed, one couple decides to make what will almost certainly be a fatal expedition outside the bunker and report by radio the spectacle of destruction they are witnessing. In their final transmission they mythologize themselves as the doves from Noah's Ark that didn't come back and formally bid farewell to the devastated Earth. The last entries of X-127 evoke an entropic decline toward death as supplies run out, the radio ceases, and the differences between outside and inside gradually attenuate. At one point he goes to get lunch, but "the place looked like a battlefield. Corpses scattered around everywhere. But not a wound to be seen."[35] Even the simplification of the narrator's syntax has become a symptom of his impending death.

The ultimate irony in *Level 7* only emerges at the end of the novel, although there are many hints earlier: Not even the deepest level of the nuclear bunker is safe from fallout. Roshwald thus drew on the debate over nuclear shelters and made the symbolism of underground an integral part of his polemic against nuclear war. He has explained the meaning of his title: "Hebrew mythology, or rather mysticism, assumes the existence of seven levels of heaven and seven levels of hell. The deepest level of hell was an obvious choice of venue for my story."[36] In fact, the level where most of the novel's action takes place is a space onto which a number of possible meanings are projected: dungeon, ultimate refuge, hell, or elitist pinnacle. Martha

Bartter has pointed out that "reversal is Roshwald's primary trope, and the upside-down underground world his primary metaphor."[37] X-127 is promoted but travels *downward,* and the topsy-turvy hierarchy of the different levels resembles an inverted pyramid. Inversion in itself suggests a reversal of logic, and throughout the novel X-127 struggles to convince himself that "high is bad, low is good." Similarly, his descent into the complex is the physical correlative of his estrangement from human values and his commitment to a mechanistic mentality.

When it was published, *Level 7* carried endorsements by two leading campaigners in the antiwar movement: Bertrand Russell and the chemist Linus Pauling, who in 1958 published his own antinuclear statement, *No More War!* and submitted an antinuclear petition to the United Nations signed by more than 11,000 scientists. The novel received very positive reviews from Frank Kermode, V. S. Naipaul, and others. One of the most enthusiastic came from J. B. Priestley, who had already endorsed it as the "best statement there has been so far on the ghastly imbecility of nuclear armaments." Priestley had campaigned for nuclear disarmament since the mid-1950s and had written a TV play on the subject, *Doomsday for Dyson.* In 1957—the year Roshwald began composing *Level 7*—Priestley published "Britain and the Nuclear Bombs," an article that played a part in the formation of the Campaign for Nuclear Disarmament later that same year and where he notes the phases of a seemingly endless arms race (bombs to ballistic missiles to nuclear submarines) and protests against the danger of accident: "The more elaborately involved and hair-triggered the machinery of destruction, the more likely it is that the machinery will be set in motion, if only by accident." This might involve "push-button arrangements to let loose earthquakes and pestilences and pronounce the death sentence of continents." Elaborate technical machinery and risk of accident are two central themes of *Level 7,* as is the question of neurosis. As Priestley wrote, "The catastrophic antics of our time have behind them men hag-ridden by fear, which explains the neurotic irrationality of it all, the crazy disproportion between means and ends."[38]

It is not surprising that Priestley had such a positive reaction to *Level 7,* because it did give expression to so many of the concerns he had been expressing for years. He noted the multiplication of ironies in the novel and praised what we might call its imminent realism. Commenting on Roshwald's evocation of an underground military community, he wrote: "For this is the kind of world we are already trying to create. Indeed, I am convinced myself that unless we rid ourselves very soon of nuclear weapons, Level 7 and the rest will come into existence." Drawing a comparison with Kafka, Priestley next drew the reader's attention to Roshwald's apparently neutral style: "Writing quietly and easily, wearing a poker face, he allows us to draw our own conclusions."[39] Priestley's review has the special value of combining political insight with the sensitivity to technique of a practicing novelist.

Among the writers who supplied endorsements for *Level 7*, Bertrand Russell gave one of the most direct and forceful, declaring, "I wish that it could be read by every adult in both the Eastern and Western blocs. With admirable skill it brings home to the reader the madness of present policies and the utter disaster to which they may lead." Roshwald's London publisher, Heinemann, at its own initiative, sent a prepublication copy of the novel to Russell, and the endorsement was the result. Since the end of the Second World War, Russell had been vociferously campaigning against the nuclear arms race. According to his biographer Alan Ryan, the testing of the H-bomb in Bikini Atoll on 1 March 1954 was a pivotal event in Russell's life and one that encouraged him to cofound the Campaign for Nuclear Disarmament in Britain at the end of 1957.[40] The connection between Russell and Roshwald dates from the midfifties, with Roshwald praising the stories in Russell's *Nightmares of Eminent Persons and Other Stories* (1954) for their concern with the plight of mankind. This collection was described by Russell as "signposts to sanity" and presented a series of fantastic culminations to dominant fears. It is a sign of the anxieties of the 1950s that the period should be defined in terms of fear, and a number of Russell's sketches engage with the question of East-West confrontation. Thus, Stalin dreams he has fought and lost World War III; Eisenhower dreams that McCarthy has been elected and has created a totalitarian power bloc in the West that exactly mirrors that of Stalin's successor; and Dean Acheson fantasizes that a right-wing superpatriot has taken over the United States but has actually fallen victim to the Soviet Union, which takes over the country. In all these cases Russell shows the holders of powerful positions to be potential victims of their situation, and, as Roshwald was to do in *Level 7*, he chose the medium of fiction because it could be "more true to life . . . especially in fear-ridden societies" and also because it had the advantage of enabling him to "develop a point of view dramatically in complete purity and to the logically utmost point."[41] Specifically, he felt able to express warnings of imminent danger through the medium of fiction.

In 1959 Russell published an ironic parable called "Planetary Effulgence" in which he satirized the arms race and the militarization of space exploration that he noted in *Common Sense and Nuclear Warfare* in the comments of a U.S. general who thought that the moon would make an effective nuclear base. In these works Russell creates an effect that we find in *Level 7* and many other novels of the Cold War: a mirroring or congruence between the attitudes and practices of each super power. Russell expresses this in a compact and symmetrical statement: "The West thinks the Kremlin wicked, and the East thinks Wall Street wicked."[42] In his parable Russell assembles instances of doubling. He sets his action initially on Mars, where a power struggle is taking place between the Alphas and the Betas. This struggle is extended when they attack Earth, itself in the grip of a struggle between blocs. Then Mars is attacked by Jupiter, where the opposition falls between the Alephs and the Beths. By giving these peoples a minimal mathematical identity, Russell draws the reader's attention to the relationships and uses a device similar to that employed by Szilard. Like Russell, Szilard campaigned for disarmament after the Second World War and actively supported Russell's Pugwash Movement, which gathered world scientists to protest against the bomb. Szilard produced a series of SF stories designed, like Russell's and *Level 7*, to galvanize public opinion. In "Report on 'Grand Central Terminal'" (1961) Szilard presents an account of creatures from another planet visiting New York and being astonished to discover that, despite all the signs of an elaborate culture, human life has ended. One of the visitors speculates that humans have been wiped out in a war, but the narrator is very reluctant to accept this explanation because it is so paradoxical. How could a species use the necessary intelligence to destroy themselves? Szilard displaces the rationality that should be possessed by humans onto extraterrestrials, just as Russell uses Mars to set up an external and therefore detached perspective on the Cold War arms race.

"Planetary Effulgence" is followed in Russell's *Collected Stories* by a companion narrative, "The Misfortune of Being Out of Date" (1962), which is located on another planet and which describes a nuclear "competition" that destroys the Moon. At this point the powers turn their eyes elsewhere: "The Solar System, so the zealous Governments on either side decided, is too small for our cosmic warfare. We cannot hope to win a decisive superiority over our dastardly foes, unless we find a means of enlisting the stars."[43] Russell presents each side as an unthinking reflection of the other locked into an ideology of inevitable escalation where all of space becomes commandeered as a site for nuclear confrontation. During the voyage of the space ships, a new regime comes into place on Earth, a world government that has rejected the polarities of the Cold War. On their return to Earth, neither crew finds any motive for living, and the two groups kill each other in despair. The use of interplanetary travel here, in Szilard, and in Herman Wouk's "mirror satire of nuclear confrontation," *The "Lomokome" Papers* (like Roshwald's original version of *Level 7*, an "edited" narrative), is essentially a distancing device that forces the reader to take up a perspective symbolically outside the familiar pattern of Cold War confrontation.[44]

Published at the end of the 1950s Russell's polemic *Common Sense and Nuclear Warfare* protested the "march towards insane death." Russell insisted that he was writing from a nonaligned position of concern for humanity and stressed that his argument should appeal equally to East and West. Indeed, Russell only speaks as a realist when he quotes massive figures for probable deaths from a nuclear war, partly to question the very notion that such a conflict could be won in any conventional sense. Notwithstanding the reassurances that the U.S. Federal Civil Defense Authority was putting about, Russell stresses how fallout could spread across a whole hemisphere. The booklet still makes a valuable companion to *Level 7* and Roshwald actually made it required reading for one of his courses at the University of Minnesota. Among the different dangers Russell identified was that of war accidentally breaking out, exactly the possibility Roshwald was addressing in his novel: "The present readiness for instant retaliation makes it possible for some wholly accidental misfortune, such as a meteor exploding an H-bomb, to be mistaken for enemy action . . . Many things more probable than collision with a meteor might initiate a war that no Great Power had intended."[45] This possibility had been explored in Peter George's novel *Red Alert* (UK title *Two Hours to Doom*), which was to form the basis for *Dr. Strangelove,* where an unhinged American general launches a preemptive strike against the Soviet Union. Yet another alternative scenario, that of technical error, was dramatized in Eugene Burdick and Harvey Wheeler's novel *Fail-Safe.* In 1961 Russell published *Has Man a Future?* where he poured scorn on the efficacy of nuclear shelters against the H-bomb: "What life in the shelters might be like has been vividly portrayed in a book that has not received the publicity which it deserves: *Level 7* by Mordecai Roshwald."[46]

Roshwald wrote one further novel on the nuclear theme, *A Small Armageddon,* which was inspired by his viewing of the 1959 Carl Foreman film *The Mouse That Roared,* in which a tiny bankrupt country declares war on the United States. In Roshwald's novel the executive officer of a U.S. nuclear submarine, the *Polar Lion,* kills the commander in a drunken brawl and then proceeds to hold the vessel for ransom, demanding a supply of alcohol and nubile young women for his crew. The new commander acts out a dream of total power: "Nuclear submarine meant power. It was the real seat of power. It could destroy, without fearing retaliation; it could annihilate, yet remain safe from vengeance."[47] The language of strategy, the vocabulary of bluff and counterbluff, gets transposed here onto the U.S. government and its own supposed forces in a ludicrous standoff that results in the bombing of a California city—but only after it has been evacuated. The complication in the action comes when a second U.S. officer, this time the commander of a missile squadron in the Air Force, sets himself up as a divine instrument for purifying the country. In his letter to the American president he declares: "We have been chosen by the Lord to be His soldiers in order to save America from sin and death. The Lord has entrusted us with His mighty rockets to save this people from eternal damnation. In God's name we proclaim a Nuclear Crusade for the eradication of sin from American soil."[48] Roshwald parodies the language of the religious Right here and also, in the contrast between the two acts of rebellion, demonstrates the contradictions within American culture—its material plenty and its puritanism.

Like *Dr. Strangelove,* this novel suggests sexual origins to the rebels' dreams of power, and it received an endorsement by the SF editor Tom Boardman Jr., who claimed that the novel was a "comic adventure in the traditions of *Dr. Strangelove.*" Certainly Roshwald's novel centers on a similar irony that the U.S. military has to swing into action to control the freakish actions of its own machine, but there is a difference. In *Dr. Strangelove* the enormity of nuclear war is never minimized but is allowed to overshadow the desperate actions of the human agents to prevent that disaster from ever happening. In *A Small Armageddon* the dropping of a nuclear bomb on a California city is described from a distance and reduced from a disaster to an inconvenience. Roshwald sets up two ironic twists to conclude his novel. First, the rebels destroy each other (and Boston in the bargain), and then further copycat actions take place. Neo-Nazis seize U.S. bases in West Germany, and a small African country acquires three H-bombs. What might happen as a result takes us beyond the end of the novel, which, in that sense, refuses closure to the nuclear subject. Russell wrote to Roshwald in January 1962 to express his appreciation of the comic methods of the novel. "Although the events related in it are fantastic," he stated, "there is no reason whatever why they should not actually happen."[49]

Plans in the 1960s for making a film version of *Level 7* made progress to the point where a company had secured the rights and J. B. Priestley had written a script; but the scheme fell through due to lack of financing. On 27 October 1966 and 29 April 1967 an adaptation of *Level 7* was shown on BBC TV in the second *Out of the Unknown* series, which, like Rod Serling's *Twilight Zone* in the United States, consisted of self-contained episodes based on works by such figures as John Wyndham, Isaac Asimov, and Ray Bradbury. The script for the *Level 7* episode was written by Priestley, perhaps based on his movie script, and directed by Rudolph Cartier, who had earlier directed the 1954 BBC TV dramatization of *Nineteen Eighty-Four.* The adaptation selectively highlights a number of themes from the novel. The ironic use of hierarchy, for instance, is introduced through the figure of a general, an authoritarian figure who looms in the background of the action. The automation of the human figures is made explicit when a character exclaims, "We're pupils of the tape!" And loss of human control is symbolized in the paralysis of the protagonist's right arm, the limb he uses to press the button. Where Roshwald presents the narrator's mother as a tenuous humanizing influence, the adaptation gives him a wife who restates her love for him after the bombs have fallen. The episode fades out on the two characters as if they embody a human warmth already destroyed while a machine spills command tapes from its metal guts.

The stories from *Astounding* described at the beginning of this chapter, "Triggerman" and "Pushbutton War," each end with a reestablishment of the status quo. Dangers have been evoked and neutralized or otherwise contained. Ridenour's play, in contrast, concludes with the destruction of the set: the reality containing the action. Although it is extended through the last section of the novel, the denouement of *Level 7* is even bleaker in tracing out the gradual seepage of radiation down to the narrator's level. The narration gradually fades away with the narrator's vitality. On the last pages he is totally isolated, still trying to measure time and still hearing music over the speaker system. Vision goes and then the language attenuates into the white space of the page: "I cannot see Oh friends people mother sun I I."[50] The separation of the words reflects the narrator's estrangement from all human contact brought about by the military-industrial system within which he has been living. In this ending Roshwald austerely leads the reader into a cul-de-sac where there is no relief from the widespread destruction caused partly by his narrator. *Level 7* has earlier shown the military-industrial system as a deforming force on the narrator, and it is grimly consistent for this deformation to extend to his language as the novel ends with his dwindling assertions of selfhood. The narrator is thus the ultimate casualty of the technology he has been appointed to operate.

CHAPTER 9

Whales, Submarines, and
The Bedford Incident

The action in *Level 7* was almost entirely subterranean, the underground bunker suggesting not only refuge but a distancing from real-life consequences. We turn now to a surface narrative. Mark Rascovich's 1963 novel *The Bedford Incident* draws on the American tradition of hunt narratives, specifically that of *Moby-Dick,* with consequences vastly greater because of the new Cold War context.

The commission of the first nuclear-powered submarine, the USS *Nautilus,* in 1954 radically transformed the conduct of sea warfare and inevitably introduced a new source of East-West tension since the new subs could travel under the surface of the sea for days on end.[1] *The Bedford Incident* deals with a military engagement between an American destroyer and a Soviet submarine in the Denmark Strait between Iceland and Greenland. The USS *Bedford* has the duty of patrolling that area to find signs of Soviet submarines trying to monitor the microwave emissions of NATO DEW line (Distant Early Warning) stations. This line of radar installations, completed by 1957, stretched across the Arctic from the Aleutian Islands, across Canada's Northwest Territories, and, by 1961, across Greenland to connect with the Faroe Islands and the Iceland defense system. This was in theory a multinational construction, but in practice the United States played the leading part in its construction and implementation. Thule Air Base in Greenland, positioned strategically midway between New York and Moscow, was one of the largest units within a network of radio, radar, and other installations.[2] Adam Piette has noted that "in many ways, the Arctic came to symbolize the Cold War, secret, inaccessible, bitterly cold, hiding within its wastes enormous bases such as Thule in Greenland, incredible surveillance systems and mind-numbingly powerful weaponry."[3]

Frank Herbert's *The Dragon in the Sea,* probably the first novel to make a nuclear submarine its subject, powerfully conveys the hidden quality of naval strategy by describing the claustrophobic intensity of serving on such a sub. The novel is set in a future where America is locked in a war with the Eastern Powers to find fuel. Atomic submarines have been stealing oil supplies from Eastern Power wells using submarine tugs, but the expeditions have been failing regularly because Eastern Power forces have been guided to the subs through spy-beam transmitters planted secretly on the vessels. On one desperate effort to break out of the spiral of sabotage, the *Fenian Ram* sets out for Novaya Zembla carrying Ensign Ramsey, an electronics expert as well as a psychologist whose brief is to observe the conduct of the crew under pressure. Ramsey is, in both senses, a reader and decoder of signals.[4]

The novel focuses centrally on the tensions and suspense that mount as the *Ram* runs the undersea gauntlet near the coasts of Norway, Iceland, and Greenland. As in all submarine narratives, the drama emerges through the crew's responses to electronic signals of approaching enemy craft. Indeed, the enemy is attenuated to an anonymous threatening "them" who have to be avoided at all costs, and on one level Herbert skillfully captures the fluctuations in the mood of the crew and the technical difficulties of operating a nuclear power source. The novel was originally marketed by Doubleday as a futuristic thriller dealing with attempts at sabotaging the nuclear pile, the betrayal of their position to the enemy (a spy-beam device is discovered on board), and even the suspicious death of a crew member.[5] However, there is a deeper, even more claustrophobic level to the action that concerns security and combat fatigue. The war between East and West has been dragging on for years, and the resulting sheer exhaustion could persuade an officer to commit sabotage in his search for mental relief. Security is the major factor, however. The *Ram* is a miniature security state where every crew member is encouraged to spy on the others. As the crew slides into collective paranoia, one officer even speculates that the enemy is part of each individual without any external existence.

Commander Sparrow comes under maximum pressure to execute the mission and also to hold the crew together. As Ramsey observes him at critical points, he exclaims to himself: "He's like a piece of machinery . . . Great God in heaven, what went into making a man like that?"[6] The answer is, of course, the U.S. military machine. And Sparrow rationalizes the tensions in his command by attributing a mythic significance to the submarine, hence Herbert's title, which is taken from Isaiah 27.i: "In that day the Lord with his sore and great and strong sword shall punish leviathan the piercing serpent, even leviathan that crooked serpent; and he shall slay the dragon in the sea." For Sparrow, the submarine is paradoxically an embodiment of the ungodly that has to be smitten, whereas the Cold War encoding of the narrative would be as a courageous venture against an unscrupulous enemy that is ultimately outwitted. In fact, Sparrow proves to be more articulate than Ramsey about his own psychological situation, arguing that the navy has trained the crew to adapt to submarine conditions through behavior that would elsewhere be described as psychotic. The tension between Sparrow's and Ramsey's competing explanations finds its counterpart in broader unresolved oppositions that grow stronger as the novel develops. In addition to the ambivalence over the relation of the *Ram* to godliness, the submarine is presented as a womb and a death machine, and the running analogy "between the depths of the ocean and the depths of the human psyche," noted by Peter Nicholls, produces Freudian and Jungian interpretive possibilities that risk introverting the action away from any political dimension.[7]

The emergence of the nuclear submarine into a modern system of national defense was dramatized in relation to a more defined external enemy in the 1959 film *The Atomic Submarine*. Set in the near future, the film opens with a gesture toward the peaceful use of atomic energy to transport goods under the Arctic ice cap, but the main action is triggered by the mysterious destruction of a number of vessels by a saucer-shaped submersible that seems itself to be powered by nuclear energy. Once one such attack has been shown, the film cuts to the Bureau of Arctic Defense, a location that demonstrates that the whole of the Arctic has become assimilated into a military system directed by the United States. The admiral planning a response to this crisis enumerates some of the effects:

1. Complete disruption of communications with DEW line warning stations.
2. Destruction of four surface vessels, largest 10,000 tons.
3. Radioactivity in the Arctic waters, floe ice and bergs.[8]

This resembles nothing less than a nuclear attack mounted by this strange craft. The most sophisticated U.S. submarine, the *Tiger Shark*, is fitted out and dispatched against the hostile vessel, against which its torpedoes prove to be useless. The last resort is to fire an ICBM missile against the craft as it rises above the North Pole, and this confrontation supplies the visual climax to the film: "In one corner of the frame, the saucer rises swiftly. But as it comes to centre frame, in from the opposite corner comes the ICBM, heading straight and true for the saucer. They meet. The explosion is tremendous—a mighty, nuclear fireball, great chunks of debris hurled sizzling into space in all directions, a booming, pounding after-shock wave, then a great sweeping mushroom cloud. After this . . . nothing but empty sky."[9] There is no such reassuring erasure of the enemy in the conclusion to *The Bedford Incident*. The threat in the film is presented by a flying saucer transposed into the ocean depths. For present purposes, it is historically significant that the Arctic is transformed into a battle ground where the fate of humanity itself is at stake. Drawing on the stereotypes established in science fiction films of the 1950s, the saucer contains an intelligent enemy with apparently superior technology whose aim is to find the planet "most suitable for colonization."[10] In other words, it exactly reinforces the Cold War perception of the enemy as ruthless, sophisticated, and imperialistic.

The designation of the Arctic as an area of Cold War confrontation was reflected in its assimilation into the discourse of the frontier. A 1963 article in *Life* magazine described Arctic installations as the "North American defense frontier" and, just in case readers missed the analogy, insisted that these were not unmanned posts: "Though the northern frontier is primarily a warning zone, alerting defences thousands of miles away [like NORAD headquarters at Colorado Springs], there are also defenders right on the frontier."[11] This kind of report presented the DEW line as a new frontier inscribed across the Arctic and thereby made it easy for the reader to perceive these installations as a continuation of the practices necessary to preserve national security. Such an assimilation had a certain topicality under the presidency of John F. Kennedy, who had accepted the Democratic Party's presidential nomination in 1960 by declaring, "We stand today on the edge of a New Frontier—the frontier of the 1960s—a frontier of unknown opportunities and perils—a frontier of unfulfilled hopes and threats."[12] In his survey of modern versions of the frontier in the United States, Richard Slotkin has glossed this statement as a rallying call: "Kennedy's role was to 'alert' the public to its danger and to summon it to join him in an act of heroic self-sacrifice."[13] He argues that Kennedy's speech gave political validation to the role of the patriotic warrior, precisely the role maintained with pride by the commander of the *Bedford*.

The official practice of patrols like the *Bedford*'s was one of surveillance, to monitor the movements of Soviet submarines or surface craft disguised either as trawlers or weather ships. As was usually the case throughout the Cold War, the practice of one side mirrored that of the other. Thus, U.S. subs probed the shore areas of the Soviet Union while their counterparts prowled areas like the Denmark Strait. If a submarine was found within territorial waters, the practice was for it to be forced to the surface, observed as closely as possible for its intelligence potential, and then sent on its way. This is what happened to a U.S. sub off Vladivostock in 1957 and also in 1959 when a Soviet submarine was detected within Icelandic waters by the USS *Grenadier* and forced to the surface. The main operational contrast is that between territorial waters, where Soviet submarines can be stopped, and the open seas, where no action is permitted. Thus, the two overt political and ideological oppositions on which the narrative is based—between the Soviet Union and NATO and between the open sea and territorial waters—run counter to each other. It is a practice that Rascovich and Lloyd M. Bucher, captain of the surveillance ship *Pueblo,* which was seized by the North Koreans in 1968, differentiate from spying:

> Electronic intelligence gathering in international waters does not fall into that category, whether the ships involved choose to be disguised or not, the only purpose of such disguise being to keep the opponent from knowing where his secrets are being pried into, and it will likely remain henceforth an accepted military technique conducted under the universally accepted principle of the freedom of the high seas. But the ground rules are strict. One does not purposely invade territorial waters, which is not only technically unnecessary, but likely to cause an international incident. One does not act or look provocative, which is why conspicuous armed warships such as destroyers or cruisers are seldom used.[14]

Both these rules are broken in *The Bedford Incident,* which describes the actions of a U.S. destroyer and the violation of Greenland territorial waters by a Soviet submarine.

In *The Dragon in the Sea* and *The Atomic Submarine* the subs are named after animals, as if to attribute to them a life of their own. In *The Bedford Incident* the Soviet sub under pursuit is nicknamed "Moby Dick." This no mere detail but, rather, an overt reference to an American classic that took on a special significance during the Cold War when it became interpreted as a parable on power. The artist Gilbert Wilson began a series of murals on *Moby-Dick* in the late 1940s, but it was his essay in the August 1952 issue of the *Bulletin of the Atomic Scientists* that explicitly linked the classic with the Cold War by opening with the following declaration: "The White Whale as a symbol bears disturbing resemblance in our times to the atomic bomb [or rather] the power within the atom." Wilson mythologizes the whale as the dragon in the sea, a "tremendous embodiment of force," which poses a problem for humanity in, namely, how to employ it: "If we approach the tremendous elemental force in the atom with hostile and destructive intentions as Ahab approached the White Whale, perhaps we too are doomed." In what Wilson presents as a unique analogy reinforced by his mapping together of the final confrontation with the whale and the Bikini Atoll nuclear tests, the tale of Ahab's quest becomes a parable of the dangers of "unrestrained free enterprise" and of "that huge, terrible and dark side of life which is so difficult to countenance and explain."[15] In common with many commentators on the Cold War, Wilson simplifies the action of *Moby-Dick* so as to externalize and thereby explain the inexplicable. The main thrust of his essay is psychological, as if he is interpreting the atomic bomb pathologically, not as emerging from a complex set of external circumstances. The internal composition of the atom's negative and positive ions gives him a neat analogue for the contrasting moral possibilities in its use.

If we jump forward ten years, we find a second argument relating Ahab to the then-current super power confrontation. Ray Bradbury, at John Huston's suggestion, wrote the script for the latter's 1956 film adaptation of *Moby-Dick,* whose credits sequence presents a chart of the Pacific highlighting Eniwetok Atoll, the site of nuclear tests. The experience had such a deep impact on him that, in 1962, when he came to write an introduction to Jules Verne's *20,000 Leagues Under the Sea,* he devoted at least as much attention to Melville's novel as to Verne's. In his famous comparison, "The Ardent Blasphemers," Bradbury concludes that Verne's protagonist ultimately shows more respect for the natural order of creation than does Ahab. In that sense *Moby-Dick* is for Bradbury a contemporary work with a clear, if implicit, relevance to the Cold War. "If I assay right, we in America are just emerging from a period inclining toward the Melvillean. We are tempted to hurl our sick heart into God's face," he declares.

> The world *will* change, at any rate, through outright fury, neglect, or through the mild but dedicated blasphemy of such as Nemo.
>
> Ahab might explode a hydrogen bomb to shake the foundations of God.
>
> But in the fright-flash of illumination, at some distance, we would see Nemo re-perusing notes made in mathematical symbols to use such energy to send men to the stars rather than scatter them in green milk-glass and radioactive chaff along the shore.[16]

Bradbury allegorizes the relation between the two novels as a contrast between the uses of power. On the one hand we have an obsessive, ultimately self-destructive drive; on the other a rational exploration of science that appears more benign and more in keeping with an American tradition of ingenuity and inventiveness. For him, the choice facing the United States is stark: Ahab or Nemo? The opposition is unanswerable and irrelevant to the Cold War since Bradbury excludes major contextualizing factors by individualizing the choice as one between individuals and not systems. Like Gilbert Wilson, he presents the issue in terms of pathology, thereby excluding any consideration of the U.S. military establishment as an organization operating under its own impetus.

The use of *Moby-Dick* in this period extended beyond literature and film. Lewis Mumford's *The Pentagon of Power* drew on the novel to underpin his diagnosis of the military-industrial hierarchy within America, an emerging "collocation of institutional and technological forces." Here he sees in Ahab an anticipation of the "Khans" (probably a pun on Herman Kahn) of the global Pentagon and argues, "Through his own mad reliance upon power, [Ahab] had become dominated completely by the creature that had disabled him."[17] In fact, the whole relation of *Moby-Dick* to the Cold War has become a major and complex issue in American studies. In their reassessments of classics of American literature, recent critics have tended to oppose a Cold War interpretive consensus that divorced literature from its context and that followed the political polarities of that period. For Donald Pease, "Its clear opposition between 'our' genuine freedom and 'their' totalitarianism presumes at once to define the only true political question and to decide it—as an ideal opposition."[18] The process is one of simplification, since the contradictions within a complex work like *Moby-Dick* are lost, and also of reduction to a single pattern. For Pease the American Great Tradition, then, was crucially shaped by and then reinforced as a Cold War dissociation of politics from culture. For William V. Spanos, even more specifically, such critical readings reinforced a belief in American exceptionalism that led directly to the Vietnam War. Both critics share an impatience with a simplistic reading of *Moby-Dick* as a struggle between tyranny (Ahab) and free reason (Ishmael) where the survival of the narrator signifies a triumph for freedom.

It is in Rascovich's novel that the most sustained parallels with *Moby-Dick* occur. A running analogy is drawn in the novel (but not its film adaptation) between the movements of the *Bedford* and the pursuit of Moby Dick by the *Pequod,* where NATO has replaced the whaling business as the collectivity ostensibly regulating the voyage of the individual boat. The captain of the *Bedford* has, like Ahab, allowed his duties to become driven by an obsessive concern to hunt down an individual enemy. Ironically, he himself draws the analogy with Melville's novel, even as he is enacting a role like Ahab's. For the benefit of the journalist Munceford (and also to make the analogy absolutely explicit), Captain Finlander briefly orders his ship to pursue a terrified whale. More worryingly, an officer tells Munceford that in practice it is often very difficult to distinguish a whale from a submarine because they interfere with sonar. Thus, at a very early stage in the narrative the reader is warned of the possibility of error, with the appalling consequences that might follow.

The analogies with *Moby-Dick* help to encode the action of the *Bedford* as a hunt and to dehumanize the Soviet sub into a kind of military animal that is fair game to the Western pursuers. Captain Finlander takes pride in this role, which he describes to the visiting journalist Munceford as an unavoidable paradox: "We are hunters—*stalking* kind of hunters—who track by ear a foe who is also intently listening to *us* . . . As captain, I must key all my men up to an intense fighting pitch . . . Then, if we get a contact, I must key them to an even finer pitch so they hang on, close up and drive in for a kill they know will end in nothing but the dull mockery of an anti-climax."[19] The notion of a hunt transforms the actions of the *Bedford* from a patrol, which would imply a repeated movement across a designated area, to an end-directed narrative. Whether related specifically to *Moby-Dick* or not, the very notion of a hunt sets up the narrative expectation of a kill, however much Finlander tries to deny this. Reinforcements of the hunt analogy prove to be far stronger in the novel than do denials. For example, the first sign of the expected Soviet sub is its garbage, its "droppings." There is absolutely no trace in *The Bedford Incident* of Melville's lyrical evocation of sea life. Instead, technology is all, and whales are only referred to as an obstruction to military strategy since they cannot be differentiated from submarines by the sonar.

Finlander is a former WWII destroyer captain marked by a scar across his throat from when his boat was sunk by a U-boat. Like Ahab, he has internalized his earlier injury as a personal fate located in the Denmark Strait projected onto a Soviet sub that he has encountered several times and that his crew now refers to as Moby Dick. Finlander explains his actions as different from other Cold War practice: "We're not here to make faces at Commies over a wall . . . Here we *hunt* Russians. Here we have our enemy and, more than accepting his challenge, go after him without any inhibitions of containment policies or technical inferiorities. We miss the kill, but have become addicted to the chase."[20] The fixed ideological boundary of the newly constructed Berlin Wall is contrasted with a spatial terrain where pursuit can take place.

In his discussion of the film, G. Thomas Couser argues that the "plot's organization as a hunt" broadens it beyond the Cold War, presents Finlander as an updated version of the Indian hater, and ironically undermines the whole ritualized mythology of the hunt.[21] Although Couser does not draw the comparison, Finlander resembles the figure of Ethan Edwards in John Ford's *The Searchers* (1956), who has been transformed by personal loss into a "demon of revenge."[22] One of the differences is historical, however. Finlander has experienced his traumatic injury, the source of his scar, from U-boats in the Second World War, in a totally different situation of overt combat. In effect he is still trying to act out the practices of that earlier era.

Captain Finlander tries to suppress this kind of dialogic doubling by suppressing those countervoices that question his enterprise. Ishmael represents the passive inverse to Ahab's monomania, while Spanos has questioned even this opposition as reinstating Cold War polarities and argues that Ishmael's is a "wandering" art that, far from being passive, actually takes apart the hegemonic impulses behind the classifications of the natural sciences and history. Thus, for Spanos Ishmael does not simply embody an "indeterminate freedom" but, rather, reveals the "relations between truth and power."[23]

There are many local resemblances between *The Bedford Incident* and Melville's novel. Rascovich names the sections of the novel as phases within an apparently inevitable sequence: "The War," "The Chase," "The Battle." The *Bedford* is first shown as a ghost ship looming out of the Arctic fog captained by a man with an awesome reputation. It is the surgeon of the *Bedford,* relieved of duty for unspecified reasons, but probably because he found disturbing signs in Finlander's medical file, who first draws a comparison between the latter and Ahab. Finlander himself insists to Munceford that the novel *Moby-Dick* (as distinct from the film, which Munceford *has* seen) is "not *all* about whaling."[24] The Melville comparisons are self-conscious and ambivalent. Once the chase begins, Finlander tells the crew that he has no gold doubloon to offer as prize, only encouragement. Finlander demonstrates a familiarity with the novel but explicitly denies any resemblance to Ahab. And if Finlander plays Ahab, Ben Munceford should play the role of Ishmael here, but his independence is compromised. Drafted to the *Bedford* by the navy's public relations office, Munceford is there to witness what is going on and to articulate the uncertainty of how to interpret Commander Finlander. He asks himself the very questions that have arisen from the earlier narrative: "Were matters aboard the *Bedford* really building toward a court-martial? Was the hounding of Moby Dick finally transgressing the accepted conduct of a cold war?"[25] The most radical possibility raised in the novel is that a U.S. commander might go beyond the limits of his authority, but Munceford draws back from this inference and decides instead to "play ball" by giving the crew a good write-up praising its vigilance. When James Hall was working on the movie adaptation he insisted on getting Sidney Poitier for this role and transformed Munceford into a stronger interrogating presence as a result. In short, the parallels between *The Bedford Incident* and *Moby-Dick* are skewed, intermittent, and ironic. They provide speculative cues to the reader to ask questions about Finlander's motivation, the nature of naval discipline, and the whole armed standoff prolonged by the Cold War.

Parallels with *Moby-Dick* were drastically reduced in the 1965 film. As Couser points out, Munceford is no Ishmael and remains marginalized, whereas "the film is ultimately dominated by Finlander." Couser continues: "The film's form is surprisingly conservative in its implications, for it tends to focus, literally, on the authoritarian Finlander; he is on screen, in close-up or two-shot, much of the time." He reads this focus as ultimately limited because, although he clearly wants to criticize the actions of this authoritarian captain, Harris "failed to devise an antiauthoritarian form for his movie."[26] This conclusion, however, does not do justice to the psychological themes of the film. One of the main questions hanging over the novel and film alike is the personal suitability of Finlander for such a responsible role. In the novel the disappearance of his medical file and the comparison with Captain Queeg in Herman Wouk's The "Caine" Mutiny, which is lodged in the reader's mind early in the narrative, open up further ominous possibilities for speculation.[27] In the latter, the captain is finally revealed to be a dangerous paranoiac, whereas Rascovich pursues a more ironic strategy in suggesting that Finlander is a kind of ultimate personification of naval efficiency. The film uses the confined space of scenic frames as an analogy for the claustrophobic interior of the Bedford and ultimately of Finlander's own consciousness. Thus, the interview that takes place between Munceford (Sidney Poitier) and the captain (Richard Widmark) is a set piece of psychological fencing.[28] The probing of the journalist and Finlander's cautious and defensive replies are played out through reverse shots, with the camera alternating between the carefully masked faces of each character. The true drama emerges only when the captain's mask slips just a little to give us a glimpse of the self-styled patriot frustrated by military and political bureaucracy.

Just as the crew of the Pequod is described as a microcosm of humanity, the Bedford's also has its representative significance. Captained by Eric Finlander, whose name echoes that of Eric the Red, the Norse chieftain who colonized Greenland, the crew also includes an Italian American, a Breton, a British officer on secondment, an African American steward who wants to become a medic, a Russian Jew, and others who hint at the ethnic diversity of America. The multiethnic nature of the crew reflects the ambiguous political position of the Bedford. All the crew members, including—albeit unwillingly—Commodore Schrepke, are participating in larger NATO patrolling exercises whose function Finlander hegemonically narrows down to the protection specifically of the United States. When commenting in the film on the Soviet submarine positions near Greenland, he reflects sardonically: "Might as well be on the bottom of San Francisco Bay." So much for the multinational membership of NATO. He gathers ethnic and professional difference into a single overriding purpose contradicted by the self-evident fact that the Bedford is a systems ship carrying specialists in chemistry, photography, code-breaking, and electronics.

The Bedford is bound into a network of interconnected areas of expertise, rather like a military-industrial complex in miniature, where all the crew members are enthusiastic participants. The technical details in the screenplay were revised on the advice of a U.S. naval officer.[29] Whereas the action of *Moby-Dick* and film reconstructions like *Sink the Bismarck* are dominated by the visual sense, *The Bedford Incident* packs much of its drama into periods of sonar monitoring, into the electronic "ears" of the destroyer. The narrative stresses the obscurity of the Arctic as the *Bedford* sails between patches of fog and sleet, often in darkness. A rare exception to this occurs one morning when frost transforms the *Bedford* into a morbid externalization of its commander's obsession: "All the familiar lines were subtly distorted by the frozen sheathing deposited by last night's sleet, all the solid battleship gray turned into a translucent and sickly pallor beneath the skin of ice."[30] Where Ahab can detach his boat from the larger enterprise of whaling, this separation is no longer possible in the electronic techniques of Cold War surveillance. Finlander can make no decisive move without checking with his superiors at the NATO command center. No event is singular, therefore. When the Soviet sub is caught within Greenland waters, it cannot be dealt with independent of, for example, a crisis in Berlin.

Rascovich ironically critiques the actions of Finlander by gradually revealing a process of mirroring, where Finlander projects imagined actions onto his Soviet opposite number. He personalizes the encounter between the two vessels as a duel of wits between rival warriors. Twilight is thus the "time of reconning for submariners and sub-hunter alike. The time to contest with each other for the ambush, to maneuver and countermaneuver for the weather gauge of darkness and light." When the *Bedford* meets the Soviet "mother ship," the *Novo Sibirsk*, crew members photograph each other. The symmetry is clear. But no encounter like that can take place with the submarine, which is only glimpsed electronically. For most of the novel and film it remains a hidden object, a space onto which Finlander can project his own "seething hatred" of submarines. Throughout *The Bedford Incident* Finlander registers an unconscious kinship with the submarine commander. When he calculates strategy, he imagines his opposite doing exactly the same; when he rigs his boat for silent running, he assumes the Russian is doing this too. The Soviet commander becomes a suppressed shadow self for Finlander, a dark double that he must hunt down and destroy. When he is accused of being too authoritarian, he retorts, "Say I've brainwashed my crew and turned them into a bunch of schizos." Any questioning of his methods is turned into a reflection on his patriotism and implies the construction of a "disowned, negative American self."[31] The two selves approach each other at the critical point when Finlander insists that he will never fire first. Perhaps in defiant bravado, he declares, "But if he fires a torpedo at me, then . . . then I'll fire one!"[32] His first words were partly smothered by the sounds on the bridge, and only his last two words are picked up by an officer who misinterprets them as an order to fire. By stating a tit-for-tat sequence of attack-and-response, Finlander actually performs by mistake the very act he projects onto the Soviet commander.

Examining the American practice of demonizing an enemy, Michael Rogin describes a process that sheds light on the representations in *The Bedford Incident*: "Cold War ideology . . . required America simultaneously to imitate practices attributed to the enemy and to demonize the subversive in order to defend against the resulting breakdown of difference. But looked at from outside the demonological system, the mirroring process blended the subversive into his countersubversive reflection."[33] America's ideological stance throughout the Cold War was a defensive one based on a premise that it would respond to, not initiate, aggression. This lesson has been learned by Finlander, who imagines the commander of the *Moby Dick* planning a nuclear attack on Western cities from "some secret fiord." One of his major addresses to the crew insists on a Soviet policy of aggressive intent from which all his own actions follow: "I am referring to the Russian submarine we call Moby Dick and I openly call him our enemy because he is intruding upon this part of the ocean with the objective of softening our defences and burying us."[34] Finlander's use of the pronoun "he" is symptomatic of an oscillation between identity and difference in his discourse; the hunt dehumanizes, the mirroring suggests kinship of sorts, and such contradictions are exposed by the countervoices in the novel and film.

Rogin argues that the contradictions of demonology become evident when looked at from the outside, and in the film version of *The Bedford Incident* there are three figures who perform this function: the journalist Munceford, the new surgeon, and the German commodore in the crew. Finlander tries to suppress the critical voices directed against him, including that of a Danish NATO admiral from the past. Munceford keeps deflating Finlander's insistence on the real by asking him what difference it makes to the outcome, thereby questioning the triumphalist narrative Finlander is trying to enact in his chases. Although Munceford's questions are addressed to Finlander, they are ultimately an interrogation of NATO defense discourse. When Munceford asks, "But how far would you go to destroy that enemy?" the captain retorts "All the way," to which the journalist next asks: "Does that mean all-out nuclear attack?" Finlander finally falls back on the generalities of deterrence, but the question persists. The new surgeon on the *Bedford* begins to suspect that Finlander is inducing a collective neurosis in his crew by keeping them at battle stations for such long periods. He diagnoses a dangerous state of mind in the crew, an unrelieved hate syndrome built up by their relentless pursuit of the enemy. He declares: "This is nothing new for Americans at war, of course, only we are *not* at war. The natural release of war's tremendous pressures—*killing*—is denied. Frustration builds and compounds the pressure until it begins to make men unpredictably aggressive, withdrawn, volatile, lethargic." The more Finlander keys his men to the highest level of attention, the more danger he risks of them losing control. And, to confirm the surgeon's point, Finlander himself bursts out in fury when he feels his purposes are being questioned.

More is at stake than Finlander's authority or pathology here. Rascovich is demonstrating how the crew has to negotiate contradictory possibilities—war and not-war. This paradox informs commentaries of the period, like the report on the U.S. Polaris submarines that appeared in *Look* magazine in 1961 and proclaimed in bold: "There are Americans at war today." Throughout the piece the text moves in and out of overt warfare, specifying the destructive capabilities of the Polaris missiles and yet denying that there is anything routine about their operations: "These submariners are men back from war—a non-shooting one, so far. Theirs has been no mere training exercise. They have risked death in a battle that might never be reported to the world."[35] In the same way, Finlander dangerously instills a feeling in his crew that he is leading them into actual combat. When the crisis mounts as they close in on Moby Dick, he insists to an officer, "It is *not* only an exercise . . . There's a real, live Commie submarine down there."[36] The only alternatives he can imagine are exercises—self-evident practices on the one hand and his "real" actions on the other. Insistence on the reality of the *Bedford*'s actions becomes his way of authenticating events by distinguishing them from the inconclusive acts of the Cold War that constantly head toward critical confrontation and then back off. In effect, Finlander is trying to construct the kind of narrative the Cold War has made impossible.

The Bedford Incident is a palimpsest narrative, written doubly over *Moby-Dick* and over events from the Second World War. On the novel's first pages Rascovich originally printed a map of the *Bedford*'s maneuvers, with the DEW line omitted, superimposed on a British admiralty chart—in other words, on a sea area already appropriated by one of the leading members of NATO. The very fact that Rascovich acknowledges permission to reproduce the chart aligns him with the institutions of NATO member countries, and the drawings the author supplied for the novel fail to show the Soviet submarine at all. The sub operates as a hidden sign, an unseen trigger for action by the *Bedford* on the surface of the sea. The cover of one reprint of the novel shows the *Bedford* in the foreground driving through the sea while the submarine begins to submerge in the opposite direction. But in the novel there is no scene like this. The sub is never named, only given nicknames: Moby Dick in the novel and Big Red in the film. The sub is only glimpsed through its garbage or its schnorkel or heard through sonar. And the very fact that it remains hidden beneath the sea adds to the drama of the novel by encouraging the U.S. captain and his crew to project a hostile identity onto it.[37] The novel's graphics, in other words, actually reinforce the Cold War ideology Rascovich is attempting to question.

Finlander's crew includes the German commander Schrepke, whose presence raises a number of ironic questions about Finlander's execution of his duties and the nature of Cold War combat. As a member of the *Bedford*'s crew he is a physical reminder of the shift in political relations between the USA and Germany since the Second World War. He is the former enemy turned ally who has experienced East as well as West in being conscripted into the East German submarine yards before he made his escape. And again he denies an implicit analogy between the present and the Second World War that Finlander tries to foist on his crew. The action of the novel takes place on the site of the 1941 Battle of the Denmark Strait, when the German battleship *Bismarck* sank the HMS *Hood*. The connection between the two events is unmistakable, especially when the Soviet sub hides next to the sunken wreck of the *Hood*. But that battle took place on the surface and under totally different conditions. As one of the *Bedford*'s crew explains, military technology has changed so much since then that now the stark alternatives are "total obliteration or total survival."[38] The officer here echoes Finlander's strategy of foreclosing all dissent in order to rationalize the destroyer's strategy.

The endings of the novel and film are strikingly different in the kind of closures they suggest. Within the logic of the frontier discourse applied by Finlander, hunt entails kill; in other words, the hunt analogy builds up a very strong expectation of death. The last time that the submarine is located on a plotting board, it appears as a sign already under erasure: a "white X edged in black." However, when Moby Dick blows up, it marks a symbolic death of the *Bedford* as well as the submarine: "The speaker erupted in a horrible cacophony of grating, tearing, ripping sounds. It gradually diminished to a crackling patter, but then the shock wave of a tremendous underwater explosion hit the *Bedford*'s steel hull, making her tremble and ring with a ghostly boom, like the tolling of a huge bell."[39] It is only at this point that Finlander seems to accept Schrepke's diagnosis of general insanity in the East-West nuclear standoff. But that comes too late for him. Schrepke has, in effect, become Finlander's second double through his identification with the Soviet commander, and he acts on their shared guilt for the firing by detonating the *Bedford*'s own weapons and destroying the destroyer.

When Ishmael survives by clinging to Queequeg's coffin, his survival authenticates the provenance of his narrative, but the status of *The Bedford Incident* is more ambiguous. Much of the narrative revolves around the secrecy institutionalized during the Cold War. The very presence and subsequent survival of Munceford teases the reader toward the possibility of exposure, but Munceford has already toyed with dressing up a report that will benefit both himself and Finlander and reassure his American readership: "If the whole story was presented from the point of view of the brave, dedicated American naval officer maintaining a vigil in the cruel Arctic, inspiring his valiant crew to endure all the hardships of the patrol, then Captain Finlander would come out of it smelling like a budding vice-admiral." But this is exactly the account that Rascovich's narrative belies. Finlander demonstrates his authoritarianism in suppressing the different critical voices that question his single-minded purpose in stalking Soviet submarines: a Danish admiral's from the past, his new doctor's diagnosis of induced neurosis, Munceford's suggestions of an institutional bitterness in the captain, and Schrepke's criticism of his war games. Munceford's doubts about what to write *before* the final crisis cast a general uncertainty over *The Bedford Incident* because the reader is left wondering what, if anything, will trickle through to the public. The ending of the novel echoes the conclusion to *Moby-Dick* in describing a sole survival—that of Munceford: "It was the devious cruising *Novo Sibirsk,* who, in her retracing search after missing children, found only another orphan." Where Melville emphasizes the common humanity of seafarers, Rascovich has never allowed the Soviet "weather ship" to develop a human dimension. It remains Other, and so ambiguities over this ending persist. Unlike Ishmael, Munceford has taken no part in the novel's narrative construction and has in fact shown to be too hesitant to be a reliable channel of reportage. The novel therefore contains its climax as a mystery with no larger implications since each vessel has been destroyed. In the sense proposed by Alan Nadel in his 1995 study *Containment Culture,* the ending attempts to contain the event—the status quo will presumably continue—and also the contradictions and dangers within Cold War military practice.

The film presents a different, altogether bleaker ending. In the novel nuclear weapons are discussed; in the film they are actually used. It was the first film to be directed by James B. Harris, who had ended his collaboration with Stanley Kubrick just before the release of *Dr. Strangelove.* That film had used the repeated image of the nuclear mushroom cloud as an emblematic ultimate ending. Within its sexual discourse, the death-orgasm represents the culmination of the characters' subconscious desires. In contrast, *The Bedford Incident* flirts with risk. Overt combat remains a constant danger throughout, which is gradually approached by events. Once Big Red blows up, Finlander is silenced as if part of himself has died. He is reduced to a mute subject. Thus, the last speech utterance of the film is Munceford's angry shout "Answer me, damn you!" But there is no answer because dialogue has halted. The last act of the Soviet commander has been to launch nuclear torpedoes at the *Bedford,* which strike a series of four still frames as if they burn themselves out in series. These strikes are followed by a single mushroom cloud image at the end. This is the sign of visibility; this event *cannot* be hidden. In the novel, concealment of the incident remains a possibility, and there is no sign of the status quo being altered.

At the end of the film the camera points us to a symbolic postnarrative, a notional view of nuclear destruction where survival has become a virtual impossibility. The film, therefore, but not the novel, exemplifies a narrowing-down of the Cold War subject, as described by Donald Pease, "to a melodrama with an anticipated last scene . . . the Moment of Final Annihilation."[40]

CHAPTER 10

Nuclear Safety Procedures in *Fail-Safe*

It is one of the major premises of this study that the nuclear bomb is not a single object, however feared, but the most dramatic weapon within a whole military system. We have seen how Mordecai Roshwald satirizes the dehumanizing effects of such a system because it reduces the human operative to an extension of the larger machine. One of the main ironies of *Level 7* is that no individual makes any important military decisions; war breaks out and ultimately humanity is destroyed by mistake. We turn now to narratives that take us to the nuclear brink and that dramatize different problems of control in preventing situations from tilting over that brink. One of the most important narratives to deal with the issue of systems malfunction was Eugene Burdick and Harvey Wheeler's 1962 novel *Fail-Safe*, which takes as its title a strategy or devices designed to make malfunction impossible.

In the wake of the Korean War, President Eisenhower ordered a major increase in U.S. defense spending, but the nuclear buildup of the late fifties received a double shock in 1957 when the Russians launched their first ICBM and the Sputnik satellite. The U.S. Strategic Air Command (SAC) promptly reduced its threat reaction time to fifteen minutes or less and by the end of the decade was maintaining a round-the-clock airborne alert force. During the 1950s both super powers had been developing complex systems of weaponry (including surveillance, delivery, monitoring, etc.), which were being designed to respond rapidly and automatically. The sociologist C. Wright Mills outlined the probable sequence as baldly as possible: "Should accident or breakdown occur, S.A.C. drops its stuff. Or the missile is launched. The Americans have massively retaliated. The Russians retaliate massively. A few hours later the world is a radioactive shambles, a chaos of disaster."[1] In 1958 Eisenhower announced details of the new fail-safe defense system, an engineering term which signified that the system had built-in safeguards against accident. The most prominent of these, the one novelists immediately picked up, was whether it was possible or not for a renegade bomber for whatever reason to go past its fail-safe point and thus trigger a nuclear holocaust. Mills, for one, was unimpressed by the new system and argued that neither malfunction nor human error could be ruled out.

These developments had a number of consequences that bear directly on the fiction of nuclear accident. First, the principle of Mutual Assured Destruction (with its appropriate acronym MAD) made triumphalist rhetoric absurd. Second, the refinement of the American defense machine meant that a potential technological sequence of strike, response, and counterresponse was taking shape, a sequence that might happen more rapidly than human response. Mordecai Roshwald satirized both of these factors in *Level 7* by divorcing political rhetoric from actuality and by streamlining his defense bunker to the last extreme. Mills had similarly identified a military ethos that used "men as 'functions' of a social machinery and which was rapidly developing its own impetus," apparently diminishing the role of human action within this new context.[2]

A foretaste of the sort of narrative that would be created by these new military circumstances was given by a dispatch that appeared in the *New York Times* on 19 April 1958:

> Imagine that you are the commander of a B-52 jet bomber of the United States Strategic Air Command. You are in flight toward an enemy target. You are carrying thermonuclear bombs capable of more destructive force than the combined American and British Air Forces delivered in all of World War II.
>
> This is not practice. Eight minutes ago you were dispatched from base. You are bound northward across the Pole, flying faster than the speed of sound.
>
> Fourteen minutes ago your base, and every other Strategic Air Command base in the world, received a flash from the DEW line (distant early warning) network across northern Canada that the radarscopes indicated a convergence of foreign objects flying swiftly toward the United States.
>
> Your aircraft was the last of the sortie off the runway; you were airborne in six minutes; you have been flying for eight minutes. Enemy missiles that must have passed you in flight would be due to strike North America in one minute. Other United States bombers are in the air all over the world with reprisal bombs.

But this is one thing you alone do not know: Since your take-off, the foreign objects picked up on the radar scopes turned out to be a shower of meteorites . . . [All the other bombers turn back.]

Do you proceed to your target, does your bombardier press the button and does the first nuclear bomb go "down the chimney" to start World War III?

All this because one of the Strategic Air Command's vast fleet failed to received a turn-back order?

Not so. You are saved, you and many others, by a powerfully simple plan called "Fail Safe." It is proof against error, human or mechanical.[3]

The overwhelming emphasis in this narrative falls on action, specifically speed of action, but we should also note its heavy ideological coding. All the specifics fall on the American side and underline that the action is responsive against a rather coyly unnamed "enemy." The reference to World War II appears partly for descriptive purposes, to convey scale; but the meta-message is that America finds itself in an analogous situation of threat. Although the crux of the passage lies at the point where World War III might break out, the whole vocabulary of the dispatch suggests that a state of combat already exists. A similar contradiction informs the dispatch's reference to attack and defense. When the United States is under attack, the missiles "converge" on the country as if from a hostile area of undefined extent. However, when America gears itself up for military response, the scale reverses. Now bombers set off "all over the world." The political implications of this rhetoric are clear. When the United States is under attack, it is reduced to a spatially limited and therefore vulnerable entity. When the United States responds, when it is acting in self-defense, it is spearheading a worldwide reaction to aggression. Indeed the "world" is not conceived as having alternative political systems but only figured as a huge spatial area of strategic value. Furthermore, most of the dispatch consists of a narrative that takes the reader to the brink of disaster and then draws back, no doubt with the intention of reassuring the reader that mistakes do not happen. But the narrative later returns to the same scenario (reader as bomber commander, flying toward fail-safe point, etc.), this time with the crucial difference being that the order to attack has been given. The dispatch uses narrative initially to reassure the reader of the system then to confirm it. Since the U.S. defense system is depicted as preventive, however, the hypothetical sequence of attack is given to prove that America means business and to simultaneously demonstrate the failure of that same system.

Although the fear of accidental nuclear war dates back to 1946, that fear had greatly increased by the end of the 1950s and was also being subjected to dramatic analysis through war games. One of the leading proponents of these games was Herman Kahn, the technical adviser to the U.S. government on nuclear weapons who admitted that popular fiction like Neville Shute's *On The Beach* had "picked up the idea of ultimacy" and that writers such as Pat Frank, Philip Wylie, or Stephen King-Hall were considering serious scenarios of unilateral disarmament or accidental war.[4] One of the best-known narratives of nuclear accident from this period is Eugene Burdick and Harvey Wheeler's *Fail-Safe*, which, though published in 1962, had its germ several years earlier.

In 1959 Wheeler published "Abraham '59—A Nuclear Fantasy" under the pseudonym F. B. Aiken. Originally written in 1956, he was trying out a hypothesis: "There is an accidental SAC thermonuclear bomber squadron attack on Moscow. We cannot call it back. The Russians cannot shoot it down. We cannot even shoot it down. Would the Russians say, oh, just an accident eh? Only going to destroy Moscow, eh? Well, glad that's all—but don't let it happen again! Or, as they'd warned, they'd launch the massive 'Doomsday' destruction of the U.S. Then, as we'd promised, we'd finish off the rest of the world."[5] The story recounts the growth to retrospective wisdom experienced by the unnamed narrator, who has witnessed a mutinous nuclear attack on Moscow by a SAC squadron. The narrator has been involved in developments in his capacity as a Russian interpreter for the U.S. president and is called in to assist the commander in chief in a crucial telephone call to Krushchev.

The story's opening lines establish a theme of missed signs: "Now that it is all over it is easy to think back and realize that today's events had been well prefigured, even before the Soviet launching of Sputnik 1 in October of 1957."[6] The frame of the narrative is established as a mistaken opposition the narrator takes to the new methods of analytical projection developed for Cold War strategy from the mid-1950s on. He dismisses the new discourse of "lead-times" (the times "from the point when the 'go ahead' on research and development is given to the attainment of appreciable numbers in inventory") and the dispassionate examination of scales of destruction as being a matter of "paper logic," but the story revolves around the narrator's later recognition of the need for such discourse.[7] Time is a central preoccupation in the narrative, which establishes a present moment of consequence and realization toward which all earlier events point. The "it" of the opening sentence gestures toward a climax that is hypothesized by Cold War analysts and later by the U.S. president but which is deferred beyond the ending of the story. The narrator is summoned to the president's office and told that in approximately four hours Moscow will be obliterated. The president decides that New York must be sacrificed, since for Krushchev "nothing short of this could prove to him our sincerity." The story then breaks off at the point where the president reaches for the telephone.

The narrator functions here largely as a witness, since the story stresses that no exchange takes place between himself and the president. Rather, the president uses the narrator's presence to rehearse events and consider possibilities. By so doing the very language of hypothesis ("suppose A . . . then would B?" etc.) the narrator had earlier been mocking now becomes valorized by its reutterance by the president. The story therefore tacitly attaches a very special status to the president and also draws an analogy between Abraham's son and the president's country, specifically New York. The president stands in a quasi-paternal relation to his fellow citizens, and a number of questions follow that *Fail-Safe* develops in detail: Are events being focused on the president as a test of his political "faith"? Will there be a last-minute reprieve provided the president shows his willingness to act? The short story does not answer these questions, instead concentrating on feeding the reader's speculative imagination. The "fantasy" of the title becomes questioned by the matter-of-fact neutral style so that presumptions of unlikely events find themselves replaced by a suspicion that all-too-familiar fears are being realized. Indeed, the elision of the climax in the narrative suggests a suppression more powerful than explicit description, because the absence of a clear climax leaves the reader speculating about exactly what did happen.

"Abraham '59" implicates the American military as a whole in the blindness of the narrator. The policy of SAC is to train its bomber crews into a state of "fanatical devotion" that dehumanizes them and alienates them from national norms: "At the moment they rose into the air with their 'pistols cocked' they were in effect demoniac anti-Communist janissaries."[8] Paradoxically, the procedures designed to safeguard against human error actually increase that likelihood by creating human automata. The cultural encoding of the crew as figures from a Western culture is erased and transformed into a symbolic opposition between the bombers and America (human/devilish; native/oriental; rationally questioning/blindly responsive, and so on).

Fail-Safe elaborates on the issues raised in Wheeler's original story. Cowritten by Wheeler and Eugene Burdick, this novel describes how in 1967 a minute electrical fault misdirects a group of American nuclear bombers to set a course for Moscow. Although American and Russian fighters destroy most of them, two manage to make their way to the Russian capital, and the world seems poised on the brink of nuclear holocaust. It is only telephone negotiations between the Russian premier and the American president and the president's sacrificial gesture of bombing New York in compensation for the destruction of Moscow that avert an even larger nuclear catastrophe.[9]

Burdick and Wheeler make it clear in their preface that *Fail-Safe* was intended to address an issue only raised by implication in such works as *Level 7* and *Dr. Strangelove*: the information gap between military activity and public awareness. The fundamental journalistic purpose of the novel is to close this gap. *Fail-Safe*, therefore, puts a high premium on descriptive data. Whereas in *Level 7* Mordecai Roshwald was concerned with portraying any technological defense system, Burdick and Wheeler specify names and other details to make it clear that this is an American system. They use the device of newcomers to each location to rationalize exposition or the kind of rapt attention to guards, procedures, and equipment that situates the narrative and highlights the importance of the screen in the headquarters bunker.

Also, the secret must repeatedly be related to the familiar. The progression of the translator Peter Buck at the beginning of the novel from the Washington streets into the White House and then down into the nuclear bunker sets the keynote for similar sequences in the novel where the strange is contextualized in relation to places the reader would know. Burdick and Wheeler follow a similar strategy with the crisis they are narrating, which is compared to the outbreak of the Korean War or the U2 incident, as well as with the political figures described. *Fail-Safe* can be read as a roman à clef in so far as several of the main characters are clearly modeled on contemporary figures. The president is a thinly disguised version of Kennedy, several reviewers thought Swenson was based on Secretary of Defense Robert McNamara, and so on. Once again, as with place and historical event, the aim is to take the reader into an extension of the familiar. Otherwise, as the authors admit, "a fictional portrayal employing declassified information may seem like science fiction to the layman."[10] The novel also had a clear psychological purpose. As Wheeler later explained, "No one has provided them [the public] with a means or the vocabulary for discussing the deep secret horror. We hope the book does just that."[11] The close coincidence of time between the novel's publication and the Cuban missile crisis that same year ensured that *Fail-Safe* was widely discussed in the media.[12]

The novel's engagement with secrecy through what is, by definition, a public and publicizing medium is expressed within the narrative by a spatial opposition between surface and depth. At one point, as the crisis mounts, this opposition is made absolutely explicit:

Now the world was living on two levels. There was an overt public level and a covert secret level. On the overt level the world's business proceeded serenely, innocently, and in its normal fashion: men worked, died, loved, and rested in their accustomed ways. But alongside this normal world, and ignored by it, the covert world went about its huge task of bringing two war plans to readiness. At that moment the covert, counterpoised world of war was in a waiting stage; its war dance had come to a high level of preparation and then stood arrested, held in a miraculous balance, a marvellous intricate suspension brought about by suspicions, intentions, information, and lack of information.[13]

This passage sums up the nexus of contrasts that pervade the novel. Although its surface is characterized by openness, normality, and civilian life, the novel's subsurface is a place of concealment, secrecy, burial, and military operations. Two key locations in *Fail-Safe* are the SAC headquarters at Omaha, Nebraska, and the nuclear bunker under the White House, which are both placed, literally, below the level of civilian awareness. In so far as the quoted passage gives a split image, it summarizes the authors' perception of contemporary American life as a civilian top layer covering an enormously elaborate military machine. The description of a Colorado missile base in chapter 4 follows a similar pattern; the surface (ground level) shows nothing, while below the crews live a bizarre, estranged existence. *Fail-Safe* introduces a series of analogies that represent the base under different aspects: as a collective coffin (in relation to impending death) and as a monastic order (to stress the enclosed obedience of their lives). The confining interiors that define most scenes suggest the limitations of an ideology and also encode depths with the suppressed fear, the authors imply, underlying the American military posture. A less striking feature of this passage is its global reach. Whatever individual event occurs carries worldwide implications, and for this reason one of the main locations in the novel, Offutt Air Force Base in Omaha, is presented as the nerve center of a global military system of monitoring by SAC.

The novel begins with a preliminary narrative of crisis followed by resolution. Chapter 2 describes the detection of a UFO on the SAC screen and the resultant rise in "conditions" (levels of preparedness) and punctuates the attempts to identify the UFO with a gradual countdown to the fail-safe point. In miniature, this chapter raises the problems the novel as a whole will then develop: the efficiency of procedures, the role of the human element, the capacity operatives have to distinguish a commercial airliner from the "countless war games" they have experienced. The ultimate issue here, however, is the relation of man to his technology. In one of the shrewdest reviews of the novel, Norman Cousins made this very point, arguing that "it is about the ultimate war between man and his machines. . . . It shows how the things men worship determine who they are, how they behave, and how they will die."[14] Burdick and Wheeler skillfully plant the seed of this theme in chapter 2. Immediately after an officer arrogantly claims that the system is infallible, a tiny fault occurs: "At that moment in Machine No. 6 a small condenser blew. It was a soundless event. There was a puff of smoke no larger than a walnut that was gone instantly."[15] This description gives us an event so reduced in time and size that it is virtually undetectable. And yet it will be the trigger to a sequence leading ultimately to mass destruction.

The false alarm in the second chapter demonstrates an ideal of professional competence which implies that the novel's treatment of technology is not as straightforwardly antagonistic as Cousins suggests. The commander of the SAC War Room reflects, "He was not the faceless servant, an automatic cog, in an elaborate machine. The War Room was the most delicate of man-machines." At first, the term "mechanism" can be used as a synonym for "system" without any negative connotation, but when bombers fly past their fail-safe point and head for Russia, the system fractures with one part trying to neutralize the other. The foregrounding of procedure constantly reminds us that a patterned, predictable sequence has been initiated. Most of the novel's subsequent action consists of discussions of how to retard that sequence. Whereas the unexpected is traditionally a source of plot interest, in this novel the appalling predictability of events emerges as a virtual dissociation of action from human control. And whereas in traditional cinematic or fictional narratives of bombing missions the control center gives guidance and moral support to the pilots, that communication is now cut by radio silence. The very emphasis on command centers in this novel reveals their helplessness. *Fail-Safe* thus presents an action within an action and narrates the struggle (through the framing plot) to regain the human initiative over events. This struggle emerges partly as a series of calculations at every phase of the technological sequence. So the Pentagon experts calculate that of the group of bombers two should be able to elude both the American fighters sent to shoot them down and the Russian defense network. Sure enough, two armed bombers do get through and head for Moscow. The novel reverses the usual chronological sequence of the thriller genre where hypotheses are formed about an already completed action; now the hypotheses are predictive, expressions of the most likely turn of events.

The hyphenated term "man-machines" suggests an ideal balance between man and technology, where the novel repeatedly celebrates such a balance in its depiction of procedures. For Rupert Wilkinson this is only one of three contradictory stances the novel takes toward technology; the other possibilities are that "advanced technical systems will diminish rather than enhance individual power" and that technology and its operators become invested with "intense aesthetic qualities."[16] The last is an obvious correlative of the first in that smoothly operating procedures are described as an "orchestration," a beautiful spectacle of efficiency. The second attitude Wilkinson notes represents the existential cost of the technology where operatives register estrangement both from ordinary civilian life and, at times, even from their own bodies as if they themselves have become mechanized. At no point, however, does the novel allow us to forget our dependence on the media. There is, for example, an important cinematic dimension to the action. The Big Board in SAC headquarters "resembled a gigantic movie screen," and the analogy is repeated as the screen dissolves or closes up on a scene filmed from a spy satellite. In combat the description alternates between electronic signals and their explanation: "A small blip fell away from the No. 6 plane . . . It was a Bloodhound . . . In the next second there was a great mushrooming blotch on the scene. The warhead of the Bloodhound had gone off." The description here alternates between sign and signification angled through the perspective of a military adviser, and the novel thereby preserves a close connection between technology and human consequence.

In addressing the balance between man and machine, Sidney Lumet's 1964 movie adaptation stressed human priority at every point, not least in giving his cast very strong roles to play. Thus, Walter Matthau plays the icily precise nuclear scientist Groteschele, Larry Hagman the Russian translator, and Henry Fonda the president. Fonda is given a whole series of scenes where he explicitly states the authority of his office and the fact that he is making all the crucial decisions. The president's translator, Peter Buck, is given the unenviable task of decoding the nuances of tone in the Soviet premier's voice to try to assess what he is leaving unspoken. The novel makes extensive use of the telephone and radio throughout, with the nature of the printed medium temporarily blanking out appearances. Lumet's adaptation reinstates print in such a way that the viewer is constantly reminded of the physical acts of communication rather than their abstracted content.

We saw earlier how the preliminary narrative of chapter 2 foregrounded the passage of time. In a philosophical moment, the president explains to Peter Buck that an emergency is nothing more than "time and a decision," and all the major themes of the novel are ultimately focused on time. Several reviewers agreed that the novel managed its action with great skill. John Phelps praised its "steadily mounting suspense," and Norman Cousins noted that the reader was "quickly subdued into staying with it until he finishes it."[17] One source of this power lay in the novel's combination of reminders that time is running out with characters' heartfelt but futile attempts to slow down the action. There are constant references to clock-time throughout, but that does not mean that the novel follows a simple linear chronology. The entire first half (more than a hundred pages) covers a time span of about seven minutes by introducing analeptic accounts of characters' earlier lives or by suspending the action in one location and repeating the discovery of crisis at another. We thus often encounter a case of narrated time greatly exceeding story time. The different sequences all come together in chapter 11, where time headings are placed in a sequence: "1044 hours: Omaha," "1044: the Skyscrappers," and so on. Technology gives the action its time limits, and as each moment takes on a heightened value, duration is drawn out to emphasize the comparative helplessness of those in the command centers. The nuclear strike on Moscow gradually becomes identified with the inevitable progression of time itself, and the eschatological implications become stronger until Buck imagines an "End of the World" scenario where the Russian premier's fingers are poised over a row of buttons.

One obvious way that the fear of a nuclear Armageddon can be conveyed is through such manipulations of time and through gearing the reader's expectations to those of the characters. Clock-time offered a potential way of conveying the urgency of the period. The cover of the *Bulletin of the Atomic Scientists,* for instance, carried a clock face with the clear implication that time was running out. A similar device to the timing of narrative segments is used more crudely in the U.S. historian William Craig's 1971 novel *The Tashkent Crisis.* This fantasy attacks the retrenchment of the Carter years, depicting the American military establishment as frustrated by the lack of appropriations. A hawk in the Russian Politburo seizes power and trains a new laser weapon on Washington, giving the United States an ultimatum to surrender. The novel's main ironies are leveled against a naive and malleable public that fails to recognize the Soviet threat. As the minutes tick by (each section is introduced by clock faces), the world seems to drift nearer to a holocaust, until the Russian moderates regain control of the situation and bundle their renegade off to a "comfortable dacha" on the Black Sea.

Fail-Safe does far more than whip up suspense, however. As events are unfolding, the narrative also devotes considerable space to the discussion of defense strategies. This fact is significant in itself, since Robert M. Hutchins, a mentor to both authors, argued that the Cold War had made statesmen suspicious of discussion; but "discussion implies that there is more than one point of view. The notion that the truth may be arrived at by discussion is peculiarly applicable to practical, political, economic matters."[18] Within the specific context of the novels of nuclear accident, discussion and debate counter two tendencies of the Cold War ideology, namely suppression in the name of secrecy and an authoritarian view of truth as singular and fixed. The academic adviser to the military, Groteschele, plays a special role in *Fail-Safe.* Partly based on Herman Kahn, he personifies a certain way of considering nuclear strategy by breaking it down into abstract quantifiable problems, and his name was "intended to call up the image of a gross careerist, climbing up Washington's power structure on The Bomb."[19] But it is not so much the specific details of Groteschele's advice that stand out as a dispassionate, even mathematical approach to nuclear confrontation.[20] In his 1960 study *On Thermonuclear War,* Kahn discussed the dispatch from the *New York Times* quoted above. He argued that the fail-safe system could be dangerous if the Russians employed a similar one and if "either of the two sides is so careless in his operating practices that a 'self-fulfilling prophecy' is set in motion." The solution, he continued, is to build the accident factor into the system, although there could be no fail-safe for ICBMs.[21] More generally Kahn takes the liberals and idealists in the United States to task for not thinking through the issue of nuclear confrontation and for believing that a thermonuclear war would destroy the entire planet. The latter belief he notes as being encouraged by popular novels like *On the Beach.*

In *Fail-Safe* Groteschele represents a similar way of thinking, which the novel as a whole refutes. His arguments are justified, as Derek C. Maus has noted, by his "fervent anti-Communism," a position shared by his audience, but he takes this as license to use willfully mystifying strategic jargon, whose apparent scientific objectivity masks dangerous presumptions.[22] One method followed by Burdick and Wheeler is to set up dialogue scenes where strategic issues are debated rather than simply expounded. Another is to privilege a character like General Black, who focalizes a Pentagon briefing and who registers an estrangement from the scene: "They had lost contact with reality, were free-floating in some exotic world of their own . . . They were caught in a fantastic web of logic and illogic, fact and emotion."[23] Groteschele personifies this *Catch-22* spiral of hypothesis and counterhypothesis that traps the Americans within a proof threshold where it becomes virtually impossible for them to demonstrate to the Russians the true situation. They fall victim to the naive acceptance of game theory parodied in *Dr. Strangelove.* Groteschele, in short, sums up the hawkish side of the American defense system, and that is why the main chapter dealing with him (written by Wheeler) should be called "The Organized Man" in ironic echo of William H. Whyte's stereotype of corporatism, the "organization man."

It is important to note that *Fail-Safe* starts from a position of ideological separation between East and West. In an interview Burdick explained: "One of its central themes is the paralyzing immobility into which both sides are frozen and the fact that we are now duplicating each other—not only in weaponry but in stereotyped thinking about each other."[24] The SAC missile crews have a similar perception that on the other side of the world "there was another set of silos, another pattern of hard sites, another organization of men—almost, they assumed, precisely like theirs." This disturbing, but for the moment neutral, professional insight suggests a parallelism between East and West that the action gradually confirms. Groteschele, however, speaks as an ideologue committed to denying this similarity. For him the Russians are qualitatively different: "The Russian leaders are Marxist ideologues . . . not normal people." In fact they are not people at all but, rather, as he puts it, "human calculating machines." Groteschele is by no means the sole spokesman for a hawkish military posture combining opportunism and latent fascism, only its most articulate representative. The chapter dealing with his past shows him disposing of liberal opposition in favor of an austerely "realistic" recognition of Russian aggression. Burdick and Wheeler use the "hot wire" between Washington and Moscow to reject this assertion and bring the two leaders together into a common predicament. The telephone humanizes Krushchev by giving him a voice, and the novel as a whole increases the number of recognized similarities between the two sides. In each case, for instance, an officer collapses under the strain of the crisis. One of the novel's many ironies lies in the fact that the recognition of these similarities occurs too late to prevent the bombing.

Groteschele declares that the Soviets are aggressive robots who do not possess the capacity to think rationally, whereas both novel and film gradually reveal a mirrorlike resemblance between the military establishments of each super power. The fact that each premier has to cope with hawkish generals who want to plunge into nuclear war presents each regime as the partial prisoner of its military system, and, although all the scenes contain American personnel, the narrative humanizes the Soviets as possessing the same anxieties as their U.S. counterparts. Discussion of nuclear war by figures like Groteschele hypothesize huge casualty figures inconceivable from their sheer size, but both the novel and film counteract this abstraction by positioning figures like the president's wife within the bombed areas. Lumet ingeniously avoided a simulated blast by giving what he later called "little pieces of life" from New York, filmed as a sequence of stills with zooms.[25]

The role of the communications media in the novel and film is thus central, since it literally bridges the ideological gap between East and West. Historically, the "hot line" between Washington and Moscow was established in the wake of the Cuban missile crisis in June 1963, but even earlier a number of writers had pointed out the laborious process of sending messages between the super powers. The British writer Stephen King-Hall, for instance, describes in his imagined scenario *Men of Destiny* how mounting tension between East and West Germany take the world to the nuclear brink because the situation is constantly being exacerbated by the sheer difficulties of communication, not least the Soviets' vulnerability before their own radar-jamming "Device X." The telephone and radio perform a crucial function in communication between the premiers and the public at large.

Burdick and Wheeler have gone on record as stating that they wanted an effect similar to a Greek tragedy in *Fail-Safe,* and to a certain extent the novel does conform to a tragic pattern, but with the system itself as protagonist. The tiny flaw in one of the activation machines reveals itself immediately after an officer declares the system to be "infallible." In other words, the collective hubris within the defense establishment is thrown into relief by a sequence of action, a tragic mechanism triggered by the initial fault. There then follow a series of peripeteia, or narrative cruxes, particularly those points where the U.S. Air Force is ordered to fire on its own bombers and where the Americans establish direct communications with their Russian opposite numbers. From chapter 14 on, the novel traces out a developing crisis that concentrates the action on the two national leaders negotiating over the "hot wire." In these sections, nuances of speech become crucially important within a drama of negotiation between the two premiers. Rupert Wilkinson has stated sweepingly that "nearly all the main characters in *Fail-Safe* receive great hero-worship," but, in fact, special heroic status is reserved for the U.S. president and his Russian counterpart because they take the destinies of their respective countries in their hands.[26] The translator, Buck, bears witness to the president's face reflecting the "ageless, often repeated, doomed look of utter tragedy,"[27] but the novel reserves the role of tragic spokesman for Krushchev. Their tragic testimonials are the signs of suffering they display as they negotiate with each other over a damage-limitation exercise.

It becomes obvious in the last chapters of the novel that each leader is boxed in by the ideological assumptions of his respective military establishment as much as by the sheer momentum of events, and here the novel's principal irony emerges. Again and again, gaps open between expectations and actuality, especially once a technical state of war exists between the two super powers. The constant references to World War II give us a measure of scale (the destructive potential of the new bombs) and a series of bearings from other depictions of warfare, but then an important intertextual reference to *The Naked and the Dead* signals a crucial difference. A pilot reflects on his crew: "No good war novel here. The whole damn crew is Anglo-Saxon. What we should have is a Jew in it and an Italian to give color."[28] Not only does the new system of selection ensure uniformity and thus wipe out one staple source of novelistic interest, the commander is also aware of his own historical demise, aware that bombers are on the verge of obsolescence to be replaced by ICBMs. If the analogy with World War II is precarious, it collapses completely in the final chapters, because the American war room is directing Russian pilots on how to bring down their own bombers. This reversal ironically blocks the patriotic responses of the Americans and shows their military machine being turned against itself. The crowning irony comes in the denouement, when American planes drop H-bombs on New York.

It was a measure of the public interest in *Fail-Safe* that in 1963 Sidney Hook published a book-length review of the novel. The *Fail-Safe Fallacy* sets out to refute what Hook sees as a "conjunction of unrelated improbabilities," even though the director of the Massachusetts Institute of Technology had confirmed that such a sequence of events was quite possible. Hook rejects in turn all the technical elements of this sequence and complains that the main danger is human not mechanical. For that reason he found Peter George's *Red Alert* (the base text for *Dr. Strangelove*) "more intelligent." In contrast, *Fail-Safe* was positively dangerous because its "alarmist and hysteria-producing picture" could increase the already evident mood of political defeatism in the United States. Nor was Hook impressed by the characterization. The American military was presented as "inhuman" and "fanatical," Groteschele was a monstrous travesty, and Krushchev was glorified as a "noble Roman senator."[29]

On the first of these characterizations, Hook was simply wrong. General Black, for instance, is a key figure in the humanizing direction of the action. In the other areas, Hook's general approach is to measure the novel against actuality without doing any justice to the novel's specific procedures. Whereas Hook exudes confidence in the American defense system, Burdick and Wheeler question such confidence as a kind of hubris, a pride in power that is symbolically brought into question by a mechanical fault. The novel replaces a calculation of casualties by numbers with individual victims known to the operating authorities as a means of reminding the reader of the potential human toll any nuclear explosion would take. There is no record of the widespread defeatism predicted by Hook; yet there is evidence that the U.S. military tightened up its fail-safe procedures after the novel was published. Not surprisingly, one reviewer took Hook to task for the patent absurdity of denying the possibility of mechanical failure and then combining this dogma with a blinkered anticommunism, an "advocacy of policy by ultimatum."[30] Hook does, though, pay backhanded tribute to Burdick and Wheeler's novel in his review by placing it within a new politically engaged genre: "There was a time when the themes of science fiction in novel and cinema were pure fantasies. Today a new genre has developed which prides itself on its concern with important and grim truths underlying the fictional detail."[31] This genre straddles realism and science fiction in extrapolating imminent hypotheses from the state of world politics and giving them fictional form.

Burdick and Wheeler responded to Hook's criticisms in an article which attempted to move away from personalities and stress the elaborate delivery systems that helped make accidental war a real danger. They survey likely causes as miscalculation, the accidental dropping of a device, unintended escalation, technological fault, and the "madman" theory (this directly applicable to *Dr. Strangelove*). What complicates the situation is the complex interrelation between human operatives and technology: "Our systems experts, we must remember, no longer deal with men and machines, they deal with man-machine systems, a 'bio-mechanical' linkage system between Presidential command and thermonuclear operations."[32] Although this is a symbiotic relationship, Burdick and Wheeler echo Mordecai Roshwald and other writers in arguing that the "discretionary functions" must be trained out of operatives to make them more reliant on their computers. The role they spell out for their own novel is that of investigative journalism, publicizing the dangers and deceptions of a secretive military establishment.[33]

Although Burdick and Wheeler pack *Fail-Safe* with specific technical and political data to situate the novel within a critical period of the Cold War, their narrative raises the broader question of public knowledge about the U.S. defense system. In a draft of their introduction they state, "We wish only to call attention to a reality of present day life which is little known to the American public."[34] Nineteenth-century novels took their reader into socially unfamiliar areas, and Burdick and Wheeler follow exactly the same strategy in the military and political domains and, in the process, dramatize the vulnerability of the military to political dissent and its dependence on strong leadership. Similar points were made by the journalists Fletcher Knebel and Charles W. Bailey II in their 1962 novel *Seven Days in May*, which described an attempted coup by the American military. Second, Burdick and Wheeler and all the novelists who dealt with nuclear holocaust were writing out of a technological situation as well as a political one. For the first time in history, mankind possessed the means, it was feared, of destroying all life on the planet. Although Herman Kahn argued that even the worst-case scenario would not have this result, inevitably the stakes in military action were massively raised. Both the novel and the film *Fail-Safe* were closely involved in contemporary political issues. When Sidney Lumet was planning his production, not only was he refused cooperation with the U.S. Army but the government even prevented him from using process Air Force footage from movie rentals. Perhaps one reason was that the scriptwriter Walter Bernstein had been blacklisted during the McCarthy era.

Fail-Safe demonstrates not only the need for rational communication with an enemy but also a conviction that such communication is possible. Therefore, it becomes a matter of some consolation that the Russian defense system is perceived as a mirror image of the U.S. system. The novel projects a basic conviction that self-interest will ensure a basic rationality in both super powers. This is not by any means the case with all narratives of nuclear brinkmanship. Bill Meyer's *Ultimatum*, for instance, describes a direct challenge posed by the Soviet premier to America, flushed with confidence that his regime has perfected an antimissile missile. He tells his ministers (prematurely) that "the world of capitalism is at this moment in a cold sweat. Our enemies are about to learn the power of Soviet Russia."[35] Meyer retains a conviction of the similarity of situations between the two premiers, using verbal repetitions to emphasize the point, but he presents a very different view of the political elites from that of Burdick and Wheeler. Both are riven by internal tensions, between the Joint Chiefs of Staff in the United States and between rival ministries in Moscow. There is far more disagreement in *Ultimatum* than in *Fail-Safe* and very little faith that the "hot-line teletype" between Moscow and Washington will defuse tensions.

In the Cold War context of *Ultimatum*, challenge is met by counterchallenge. The United States threatens to detonate a missile within Russian territory, secretly smuggling it into the Arctic by sleigh. The president then sends a secret request to the British prime minister to negotiate a surrender of the United States to Russia, and, finally, bogus radio messages are broadcast to American forces to give the Russians an impression of mobilization. The smuggled missile is detonated in Siberia, and the Soviet threat is thereby neutralized, although one predictable result is that the top Russian officials turn against their leader. Although he had spoken in the crudest terms of victory when he issued his challenge, it is not part of Meyer's purpose, unlike Burdick and Wheeler, to question the conduct of Cold War politics. Quite simply, the United States wins because it is more ingenious than the Soviet Union. The basic ground rules stay unchanged, and the teletype between the premiers plays only a minor part in the action by transmitting official messages between the two sides. There is no dialogue at all between the leaders.

Jeff Sutton's second novel about military satellites, *H-Bomb over America*, is far closer in spirit and method to *Fail-Safe* than *Ultimatum*, this time set in 1973.[36] Sutton had a long experience working in the aerospace industry but does not overburden the novel with technical detail. A Stalinist commander in the Soviet military launches an ICM armed with a hydrogen bomb in an attempt to scupper detente talks taking place between the U.S. president and Soviet premiers. Unknown to him, Chinese agents have taken over this plot and intend to use the bomb to trigger a nuclear war between the United States and Soviet Union that would leave China triumphant on the world scene. China gives both powers four days to capitulate to their demands, and the fate of the world is only saved by U.S. technology when an experimental high-altitude plane makes it possible to disarm the missile. The renegade Soviet officer is executed and the Chinese premier replaced.

This brief summary simplifies what is a complex sequence of guesses and counterguesses by the United States as to what is happening and what action to take. Although many developments take place on the world scene, like massive troop movements toward the frontiers in China, the main action operates on the level of dialogue. The following exchange between a hawkish U.S. senator and the president is typical. The senator tries to cut through the discussion:

> "The presence of the bomb in our skies speaks for itself . . . Instead of sneaking missiles back into Cuba, they've hung them over our fair cities. That bomb is living proof of their perfidy, gentlemen . . . The question is, what are we going to do about it?" He let his gaze rove around the table.
> "We're trying to resolve that," the President commented.
> "Time is running short, Mr. President."
> "I'm aware of that, Senator."
> "He could be pushing the button while we sit here."
> "Yes, he could."[37]

As in *Fail-Safe* and *Dr. Strangelove*, the president's voice is one of rational caution. In this passage the analogy with the Cuban missile crisis implies the need for decisive action and also pluralizes the single bomb causing the threat. The senator even echoes Roosevelt's charge of perfidy against Japan after Pearl Harbor, again with the same implication. Essentially, then, the president has to keep the brakes on such dangerously hasty hypotheses and at the same time take some action. His main decision is to move the military readiness to Red Alert One, the ultimate state before war breaks out. Again as in *Fail-Safe*, *Ultimatum* uses headings instead of chapter titles to give time and place. Duration becomes crucial and the method also effectively evokes the secretive nature of the Soviet and Chinese regimes, a factor which means that the U.S. authorities always have to operate on the basis of fragmentary information.

Where *Fail-Safe* projects the need for rational discussion between the U.S. president and the Soviet premier, the journalist William Prochnau's 1983 novel *Trinity's Child* presents an overblown system that rapidly collapses into disorder. Published soon before the end of the Cold War, the novel describes a preemptive but limited nuclear strike launched by the Soviet Union in desperation over its imminent economic collapse. A message from the Soviet premier explains its rationale and promises an end to hostilities if the United States launches a proportionate rejoinder. However, events very quickly spiral out of control with renegade officers on both sides launching strikes and a proliferation of launches by other countries. One of Prochnau's sharpest ironies lies in the inability of the U.S. military machine to halt the resulting escalation. The novel fails to evoke suspense or a recognition of the absurdity of events, but at one point a SAC general wonders what term can be used to describe the indiscriminate slaughter of some hundred million in the ensuing holocaust. "Genocide" is considered and discarded for being too specific and directed; but then "he realized that words were for the living, connectors between anthropoids, connectors between the past, the present, and the future."[38]

CHAPTER 11

Uncovering the Death Wish in
Dr. Strangelove

Where *Fail-Safe* focuses on technological malfunction, one of the most famous treatments of the U.S. nuclear defense system engages with human failings. *Dr. Strangelove* gives particularly bizarre expression to what had become known as the "mad man" scenario, where an individual pathological officer launches an attack on the Soviet Union.[1] The United States had introduced psychological screening in order to make this case virtually impossible, but once again we encounter the problem of the military machine, specifically the problem of preventing the dreaded outcomes from a renegade officer's actions.

This subject had already appeared in fiction as early as 1955 in the journalist Flora Lewis's *One of Our H-Bombs Is Missing*. Ingeniously cast in a whodunit framework, this narrative deals with events following a rumor that an H-bomb has gone missing from a U.S. base in Alaska. Because this base is so isolated, the chances of a Soviet assault are minimal, and so the guilty party must be a member of the American personnel. Accordingly, the investigation juggles with the two possible explanations: that someone suffered a nervous crisis or that an officer responded to the tensions of life on an Arctic base by taking his own action. Two factors make this narrative quite different from *Dr. Strangelove*, however. The action takes place during the premiership of Stalin, when Soviet aggression was more blatant; at one point, missiles are fired at the U.S. base. And the narrative predates the U.S. introduction of psychological screening for its officers. Indeed, most of the military personnel seem to be suffering from one kind of severe tension or another. It transpires that the culprit is an officer who is convinced that U.S. policy is one of supine appeasement. As he explains to his superior, the bomb "might mean saving the lives of a hundred million Americans. You know it means the future of your country. Yet you stand here and chicken. You give the world to the Commies. You want to wait for them to wipes us out!"[2] Although the mystery paradigm is cleverly handled, it is premised on a paradox. The action treats the theft as an isolated event, whereas in practice this could never be the case, nor could the scenario that a single officer could steal a bomb and fly toward Russia with the intention of dropping it. Even though this officer experiences a change of heart and returns to the base with the bomb intact, his actions would have instantly become part of a larger system, just as a single detonation would have produced instant escalation. As one character reflects, "The H-bomb could not be thought about. It was like trying to imagine infinity. The immensity, the horror of even one H-bomb explosion shocked the mind into defensive rejection of the truth, fatalistic indifference, and final disbelief."[3]

In this chapter we remain on the nuclear brink, which is approached by *One of Our H-Bombs* but then conveniently defused by the return of the renegade officer. The most famous treatment of this scenario remains the 1964 film *Dr. Strangelove*, which raised the nuclear stakes by including a doomsday device within its narrative and which was made against a background of military change where ballistic missiles were replacing nuclear bombers.[4] The film carried triple credits of authorship to Stanley Kubrick, Terry Southern, and Peter George, although the novel was published that same year under the latter's name only. The attribution of the movie was the more accurate of the two because it appropriately reflected how methods of black humor had been superimposed onto the realist base of Peter George's 1958 novel *Red Alert*. Kubrick's adaptation of this novel involved a fundamental shift in narrative mode so that rather than dramatizing a crisis within the Cold War, he could direct a comic assault on an entire political stance. George's novel, then, point for point supplied Kubrick with materials for parody or travesty.

Red Alert carried a brief foreword explaining that it described events which could easily happen and, more importantly, that it presented a battle on two fronts: military combat and one "in the minds of men." The events are triggered when the commander of a strategic air command base orders a "red alert," a state of maximum readiness to respond to Russian attack, and dispatches his bombers in retaliation to a nonexistent offensive, thus overriding the "fail-safe" system.[5] George explores the possibility of such action and examines the reasons behind it. Accordingly, it is crucial that General Quinten should not emerge as the kind of grotesque paranoid depicted in *Dr. Strangelove*. As the American president points out, Quinten is a typical casualty of the Cold War, pushed to the brink of nervous collapse by the permanent state of tension between the super powers, and in that respect he anticipates the officer who accidentally fires missiles from an American destroyer, thereby precipitating the nuclear climax to Mark Rasco-vich's *The Bedford Incident*. Furthermore, he articulates a distrust of politicians that spreads throughout the higher ranks of the military establishment.[6]

Quinten is in fact a Christian and paradoxically launches his bombers to bring about "peace on earth," one of his cherished slogans; an even more pointed irony is set up by the recurrence of the SAC slogan "Peace Is Our Profession" throughout *Dr. Strangelove*. Taking on himself the prerogative to play destiny, Quinten plans to break through the current super power impasse and create a new world order. This apocalyptic purpose is justified in two lengthy discussions he holds with his deputy officer where he forces the latter to survey world events since 1945 as a history of Communist conspiracy. Where Russia is presented as a single-minded aggressor, the United States is criticized for blindness, hesitation, and a failure to inspire any ideological counter to communism. Quinten's argu-ment, which his deputy finds "utterly convincing," for Merritt Abrash "does not run counter to deterrence but follows channels marked out by the logic of that policy."[7] Its very rationality becomes part of its force. Quinten simply reverses the United States' refusal to initiate a first strike in order to secure ultimate peace. Be-ing well-read as well as eloquent, he backs up his account with an analogy drawn from Kipling's *Jungle Book* story "Rikki-Tikki-Tavi," about the mongoose killing the cobra's eggs. He glosses this as a parable of decisive action: "He doesn't have to ask for proof—his instinct tells him a mongoose doesn't live with a snake. He kills the snakes, or the snakes kill him. So he acts, and he lives."[8] The progressive simplification of the syntax reduces the issue to stark alternatives, but the par-able carries an equally weighted meta-message that Communists belong to an alien threatening species and that right action can be dictated by the instinct for survival. These hidden assumptions are never addressed by the novel.

The foreword to *Red Alert*, like other narratives of nuclear accident, stresses the accelerated pace of events, which only covers a two-hour span, and chapters consist, for the most part, of five- or ten-minute blocks headed by the equivalent Greenwich mean, Washington, or Moscow times. The novel, however, never achieves the sophistication of Burdick and Wheeler's *Fail-Safe* in its handling of time during a comparable crisis between the super powers. George crudely exploits cliff-hanging chapter endings to whip up suspense, closing off the narrative just where a character is beginning to speak or just when a crucial event is on the verge of happening. The action moves toward an Armageddon that might be triggered by a multiple cobalt bomb—what will be called in *Dr. Strangelove*, after Herman Kahn, the "Doomsday Machine." It is the Russian ambassador who melodramati-cally points out this crisis: "Not just two hours to bomb time. But two hours to doom."[9] In fact, the novel draws back from total destruction and then sets up a series of diminishing crises as a tit-for-tat bombing of one city is agreed, but then even that proves unnecessary. The cinematic image of the "familiar mushroom cloud" is a suppressed presence in the narrative that attempts to maintain a known and familiar scale by constantly drawing comparisons with World War II. This is yet another strategy that will be undermined in *Dr. Strangelove.*

Red Alert anticipates *Fail-Safe,* although on a much smaller scale, and repeats the film *Strategic Air Command* (1955) in allowing its narrative to grow out of brief expositions of the U.S. defense system: "At a hundred listening posts throughout the free world, in hot climates and in cold, out of scorching desert and arctic tundra, the slender radio masts lift their receiving aerials high into the air. These are the stations which maintain a guardian watch, picking up signals from airborne bombers, and sometimes signals from the ground to those bombers. They are the junction points of the invisible spider's web of radio. They cover the whole of the northern hemisphere and ninety per cent of the southern. They never sleep."[10] There is no reservation at all about this passage's celebration of military technology. The connection between radio masts and bombers is presented as a miracle of collaboration articulated through an animating metaphor that suggests at once harmony, vigilance, and a posture of defense. Again and again the descriptive present gives way to the narrative past as if to remind the reader how easily these events might take place. And this transition even applies to the opening section, which takes the crew of the *Alabama Angel* out of a repeated routine flight into the sequence they have all been dreading. The bomber crew is carefully assembled out of a range of regional and ethnic types who are humanized by their incomplete attempts to block out of their consciousness memories of their families. They are the professionals of the novel, idealized case studies in discipline and resourcefulness, and ultimately the ironic victims of Quinten's obsession.

The possibility of adapting George's novel for the cinema was introduced to Kubrick by an article in the *Bulletin of the Atomic Scientists,* to which he subscribed.[11] In the September 1960 issue the economist Thomas Schelling discussed the outbreak of nuclear war through the medium of three novels: Nevil Shute's *On the Beach,* Pat Frank's *Alas, Babylon,* and *Red Alert.* He singled out the latter for special praise for its realistic embodiment of a possible scenario but also for its indictment of the limited public discourse about nuclear war.[12] When Kubrick started work on the screenplay for *Dr. Strangelove,* his original intention was to produce a serious adaptation of George's novel. Then, by his own account, he ran up against a difficulty: "I found that in trying to put meat on the bones and to imagine the scenes fully one had to keep leaving things out of it which were either absurd or paradoxical, in order to keep it from being funny, and these things seemed to be very real."[13] This blocked his true sense of a scenario: "After all, what could be more absurd than the very idea of two mega-powers willing to wipe out all human life because of an accident, spiced up by political differences that will seem as meaningless to people a hundred years from now as the theological conflicts of the Middle Ages appear to us today?"[14] It is possible that Kubrick's final method was suggested by a passing remark in Schelling's article, where he observed that "one thing that currently keeps the balance of deterrence somewhat stable is the sheer inertia, lack of initiative, lack of imagination about the reality of war."[15] When Kubrick chose a method of "nightmare comedy" as being most appropriate to the subject, he might have been acting on Schelling's perception that nuclear war simply was not understood by creating dialogue that repeatedly falls grotesquely short of the sheer scale of imminent actions.[16] The style of the film is indicated by a note on the cover of the shooting script that declares, "The story will be played for *realistic* comedy—which means the essentially truthful moods and attitudes will be portrayed accurately, with an occasional bizarre or super-realistic crescendo. The acting will never be so-called 'comedy' acting."[17]

One result of this comedy is, as we shall see, to estrange the reader, and a difference from *Red Alert* immediately presents itself. George introduces his narrative with a brief foreword that stresses the plausibility of the events to be recounted. The film *Dr. Strangelove* opens with a precredit voice-over about rumors of a Soviet doomsday device. In common with earlier films, like *Strategic Air Command,* this introduction incorporates documentary into its narrative, whereas the novel pushes the convention of future history so far forward that its introductory frame virtually presents the narrative as a documentary program called "The Dead Worlds of Antiquity." Just as Kurt Vonnegut uses the planet Tralfamadore to set up a remote, external, and therefore critical perspective on events on Earth in *Slaughterhouse 5* (1969), so an editorial note in the novel *Dr. Strangelove* establishes the convention of the found manuscript and also a huge unspecified chronological gap between the date of events and the date of the narrative frame. This alienating device prevents the reader from accepting anything within the narrative as "natural" and places us at an ironic remove from the Cold War. The anonymous narrator expresses bewilderment over the hostility between East and West: "They were not on friendly terms, and we find this difficult to understand, because both were governed by power systems which seem to us basically similar."[18] This description estranges us equally from both sides, inviting the reader to identify with the "we-group" referred to in the introduction. A similar alienating rhetoric is used in Albert Bermel's 1964 story "The End of the Race," which opens: "At that time the nations known as America and Russia had set off 2,500 nuclear explosions, pulverized every small island in the Pacific, Arctic and Indian Oceans, blown out of the earth lumps of great magnitude and little mineralogical value, and saturated the enclosing atmosphere and stratosphere with new elements, from Strontium-90 to Neptunism-237."[19] The story's title puns on human extinction and the culmination to the arms race, which is described as a futile, self-mystifying process of wanton destruction. As in *Dr. Strangelove,* "The End of the Race" prevents the reader from identifying with either national group by exploiting a notional future point from which these activities will seem absurd.

Kubrick brought Terry Southern in to work on the script, and the film subsequently appeared with credits to both as well as to George, although it has been argued on the basis of its style that the novel *Dr. Strangelove* was entirely the work of Southern, despite being published under George's name.[20] By 1962–1963, Southern had to his credit three novels: *Flash and Filligree* (1958), *The Magic Christian* (1959), and *Candy* (Paris 1958, U.S. 1964). Peter Sellers liked *The Magic Christian* so much that he bought the movie rights, and he might have had the original idea of bringing in Southern. Whatever the particular circumstances, critics have repeatedly linked the film and novel with the black humor of the sixties. Bruce Jay Friedman's 1965 anthology *Black Humor* included a piece by Southern, and in his introduction Friedman characterized the new mode as exploiting a blurred border between fantasy and reality and possessing a "nervousness, a tempo, a near-hysterical new beat."[21] The critic Max Schulz unduly narrowed his survey of the mode by trying to concentrate too much awareness into the protagonist, who was, he argued, "at once observer of, and participant in, the drama of dissidence detached from and yet affected by what happens about him."[22] "Dissidence," however, strikes a useful note in this context, because the new comedy trespassed on previous taboo areas creating humor out of death (*Catch-22*), sex (*Candy*), and, in the case of *Dr. Strangelove,* the fear of nuclear holocaust.

Where Burdick and Wheeler's *Fail-Safe* draws on the pattern of Greek tragedy for its action, *Dr. Strangelove* at once magnifies the human cost of accident and depicts the action as comic, partly to emphasize the helplessness of the human agents. George W. Linden has written that the "plot of the film is the accelerating technological inevitability of modern society, an acceleration that has as its products social stupidity and ultimate political impotence."[23] One sign of this impotence is the discontinuity within the action, where cross-cutting between scenes only emphasizes that communication has been lost. The three main settings are interiors, by implication sealed against an outside world of rationality; the most obvious case is General Ripper's office with its shuttered windows. Again in keeping with black comedy fiction, continuity of plot temporarily disappears. One hallmark of Southern's novels is that local episodes sketch out an initial situation that is then brought to a peak of disorder, and this same pattern recurs in *Dr. Strangelove*. As the crisis mounts, the president is blocked from entering the War Room by an overzealous guard who insists on seeing his pass even though he recognizes him. The farce is only resolved when secret service officers overcome the guards in a "fracas." Since the whole action of *Dr. Strangelove* concerns the workings of a procedure beyond the limits of human control, this particular scene makes a facetious comment on such limits. Similarly, violence breaks out between the Russian ambassador and General Turgidson within the War Room's already "highly explosive" atmosphere when the former is caught taking photographs through a spy camera. Both scenes revolve around a comedy of diminution—super power confrontation being reduced to an undignified brawl. This scene was originally designed as a "free-for-all fight with custard pies" to show the jealousy "between the rival branches of the U.S. military."[24] Kubrick cut this scene for the following reason: "I decided it was farce and not consistent with the satiric tone of the rest of the film."[25]

Discontinuity performs a function in *Dr. Strangelove* similar to that of *Catch-22* in making it impossible to view the American military as a collective entity. The innovation in *Two Hours* of introducing a displaced RAF officer as General Ripper's deputy immediately sets up a disparity of idiom and style between the two officers. This repeats itself in the relief of Burpelson Base, when Colonel Bat Guano bursts in on Mandrake mumbling to himself: "Guano was becoming convinced now that he was facing a lunatic. Besides, he was suspicious of Mandrake's strange uniform and long hair. Perverts let their hair grow long, he knew. They liked to dress up in fancy clothes, too."[26] Like General Ripper, he identifies the unknown with the alien and therefore with potential threat. Briefly Mandrake becomes another Yossarian (chosen by Heller precisely to be an outsider and a misfit). In the quoted passage Guano focalizes the scene, but the narrative voice remains studiedly deadpan, another hallmark of Southern's writings. His sketch "The Moon-Shot Scandal" (collected in *Red Dirt Marijuana*), for instance, describes the launch of the spaceship in pseudo-reportorial style and then introduces more and more ludicrous matters of "fact" (one of the crew might have been a woman, a control room officer reduced the scene to chaos by dancing around in feminine dress, etc.). The Swiftian facade of solemnity masks an impulse to disrupt an occasion of public reverence for technology. In the novel *Dr. Strangelove*, several chapters begin in a comparable documentary style of factual exposition that sets up a register against which the spoken idioms of the characters can play to ironic effect.

Another consequence of the isolation of scenes is their incongruous relation to the context of crisis. Kubrick has pointed this out as a central effect: "Most of the humor in *Strangelove* arises from the depiction of everyday human behavior in a nightmarish situation."[27] Whereas in *Red Alert* and *Fail-Safe* the hot line performs an important function in bringing the leaders of the super powers together, one of the many ironies of *Dr. Strangelove* is that the military machines function only too well while the means of communication constantly break down.[28] The comic business of Mandrake running out of coins when he tries to phone in the recall code is one example, where one machine has to be "shot" (a Coca-Cola dispenser) in order to give access to another, the telephone. In scenes like the first conversation between the president and the Russian premier, a different issue emerges: the inadequacy of language. Kubrick allowed Peter Sellers to improvise a number of scenes in the movie, one probably being where the president first speaks to Premier Kissof.[29] This masterpiece of repetition draws out polite banality to a ridiculous extreme as the critical moments tick by: "Listen, I can't hear too well. Do you suppose you could turn the music down just a little. Ah ha, that's much better . . . yes, fine. I can hear you now, Dimitri, clear and plain and coming through fine . . . I'm coming through fine too, eh? Good, then . . . Well then, as you say, we're both coming through fine . . . Well, it's good that you're fine and I'm fine. It's great to be fine, ha-ha-ha."[30] One thing the speakers are not is "fine." The resemblance to a phone call between two friends and the bland repetitions sound particularly absurd when we remember that a technical state of war exists between the two countries. Again and again speech breaks down before the enormity of the events themselves. After the Doomsday Machine goes off, the different members of the War Room speak aloud rather than to each other—"It's *wrong*," "It's not right," "It isn't *right*," and so on.[31] Cliché and banality reflect not only a limit to verbal expression but also the inability of the authorities to conceive of their own war machine in action.

Incongruity is the feature common to all the examples given above. At every point there is a clear disparity between the particular situation and the language used to describe it. Absurdist technique emerges from a profound pessimism about the very possibility of *discussing* the Bomb, let alone doing anything about unfolding events. When General Turgidson tries to convince the president to launch an all-out attack against the Soviet Union, his language betrays him. He insists: "I'm not saying we wouldn't get our hair mussed, Mister President, but I do say not more than ten to twenty million dead depending on the breaks."[32] In a facade of rationality he reduces the probable fate of millions to a minor personal inconvenience. The mentality he is articulating colloquially is indicated imagistically through the folder on the table in front of him, which lists casualties as "megadeaths." Southern was well aware of terminology when working on the script: "Sophisticated nuclear strategists also speak a language all their own. They are gradually evolving a terminology which is free of moral, or even human, connotation. They do not, for example, use any form of the word attack, but use instead the term pre-empt—which, of course, sounds like something in a bridge game rather than what it is."[33] One such word was "megadeath" on Turgidson's folder. This is a coinage from the 1950s by Herman Kahn to mean one million deaths; it suggests an anonymous statistic and also minimizes the impact of figures. "Ten megadeaths" sanitizes the notion of ten million deaths. Similarly, toward the end of the narrative Dr. Strangelove proposes a plan to "preserve a nucleus of human specimens."[34] The terms "nucleus" and "specimens" grotesquely run together nuclear physics and biological experimentation. Strangelove draws an implicit (fascistic) distinction between himself (and like-minded scientists) and the rest of humanity at his disposal.

Linguistic incongruity lies behind Kubrick's subtitle, which paradoxically echoes Dale Carnegie's *How to Stop Worrying and Start Living*. As befits the apostle of positive thinking, Carnegie offers a series of recommendations for stress management. Writing within an American tradition of self-help, he argues that each individual can change her life situation by changing attitude and gives the following advice about hatred, which bears directly on General Ripper: "When we hate our enemies, we are giving them power over us: power over our sleep, our appetites, our blood pressure, our health, our happiness."[35] Add to the list "precious bodily fluids" and we have his case exactly. Ripper's visceral hatred of communism is rationalized by him as self-defense against a sinister conspiracy partly revealed in the campaign for the fluoridation of drinking water.[36] A welfare measure is inverted by him into an attack, just as Kubrick's modification of Carnegie's title is a reversal. The lexical shift from "live" to "love" sounds innocuous until we register the object of the second verb as "the bomb," by which point we understand that the love impulse has become diverted to death. In that respect the subtitle of *Dr. Strangelove* cues in the sexual subtext of a collective death wish.

The scenic method of *Dr. Strangelove* establishes a series of alternations between key settings, underlining the lack of communication between them. Although Kubrick felt that *Two Hours to Doom* was a "very good suspense novel," he did not use alternation only for such an end.[37] There is an accelerating montage of shorter scenic units as *Leper Colony* approaches its target, but more is involved than establishing suspense. While time is referred to constantly, countdowns of different kinds recur in the action. More importantly, there is a striking structural difference between the novel and the film which confirms that the former was no mere routine adaptation. The novel contains approximately twice the number of scenes as the film, which are cleverly juxtaposed to bring out the main themes. In the novel sections 5–10 run as follows:

5. Burpelson Base is sealed. Ripper delivers a pep talk.
6. Kong itemizes the survival kits in *Leper Colony.*
7. The president enters the War Room with difficulty.
8. The news is announced in the War Room.
9. The crew of *Leper Colony* check their equipment.
10. Mandrake realizes Ripper is mad.[38]

Section 5 concludes and section 10 opens with Mandrake entering Ripper's office. This action is carefully repeated to suggest simultaneity between the embedded scenes the reader is invited to consider in juxtaposition to each other. Juxtaposition in turn suggests similarity: The crew of *Leper Colony* seal off their aircraft against enemy radio traffic; the War Room also might be just as sealed off as Burpelson. Similarly, when Kong is trying to free the bomb doors of *Leper Colony,* the sexual connotations of the action are brought out more clearly by Miss Foreign Affairs phoning Turgidson twice to make sure their relationship is not just physical. High and low drama alternate, the lack of communication is stressed, and the disruption to the mounting suspense blocks the reader from a simple involvement in the action's suspense.

The preamble to the movie explains that a single bomber's load is "about equivalent to fifteen times the amount of explosives dropped during World War Two." Such comparisons recur throughout the novels, essays, and films dealing with nuclear weapons to introduce an analogy between the active combat of the past and the latent combat of the present. In *Strategic Air Command* one character declares proudly: "With the new family of nuclear weapons one B-47 and a crew of three carries the destructive force of the entire B-29 force we used against Japan." Such a crude celebration of size and technical efficiency is mimicked in the opening lines of the narrative proper of *Dr. Strangelove* and then undermined with increasing irony. *Strategic Air Command* and *Two Hours to Doom* use connections with World War II in order to draw audience and reader into a collective group continuously under threat. Both works capitalize on the films and novelistic memoirs of the war that were published or reissued during the fifties. Works like Guy Gibson's *Enemy Coast Ahead* (1946) set up a tension between home base (the command center) and the heroism, versatility, and ultimate isolation of the bombers in coping with enemy action. In George's novel there are many echoes of such narratives in the references to hostile territory, for instance, and explicit comparisons with enemy flak. These connections familiarize the action for the reader despite Quinten's declaration that anything is possible in the new era of thermonuclear war.

Dr. Strangelove rejects such analogies with World War II by presenting them as absurd anachronisms. The first instance of this process is "King" Kong's statement to his crew, in spite of objections, that they are entering a phase of combat "toe-to-toe with the Russkies."[39] Where Kong hopes to continue a family line of soldiering, the technical facts of the new situation exclude just the sort of physical confrontation he is relishing. Again, the itemized survival kit ridiculously suggests possibilities of contact with enemy nationals when the very idea of survival is being brought into question. The flight of *Leper Colony* then resembles a displaced bombing mission without a supporting context, and the narrative simultaneously invites recognition of stereotyped expressions and characters from war movies or fiction and at the same time renders those stereotypes doubly absurd by their incongruity. Charles Maland rightly notes that Kong's pep talk to his crew (excluded from the novel) is a staple scene in World War II movies, and exactly the same point could be made about Ripper's address to the men on his base.[40] He concludes his telephone message to SAC headquarters in ringing tones that collapse bathetically into psychosis: "God willing we shall prevail in peace and freedom from fear and in true health through the purity and essence of our natural fluids."[41] The fact that Ripper lights up a cigar after he seals his base only confirms the role he is adopting as the director of national destiny, but the lofty abstractions in these lines are unconsciously deflated by Ripper's physical obsessions.

Group Captain Mandrake has a crucial role to play in the possible analogies with World War II and represents another major innovation on Kubrick's part since he can play their styles against each other. Where Mandrake is an immaculate and correct master of understatement, Ripper is flamboyantly gung-ho; the former acts as the perfect foil to the latter's paranoia. Partly an ineffectual voice of sanity, Mandrake is also associated with patriotic images of war. As a prisoner of war he was involved in building railway lines for "Japanese puff-puffs," a detail that could hardly fail to be linked to *The Bridge on the River Kwai* (1957). Defined entirely by his accustomed official procedures, once Mandrake realizes what has happened in the film he comes to attention and adopts an especially pompous tone of voice to announce the recall of the wing. But the whole point of the film and novel is that such procedures go wrong. Mandrake's presumption of order makes him into a surrogate reader/spectator at times, and it is an important detail that he is the only character who laughs, however nervously. Part of Ripper's "evidence" for the international Communist conspiracy is the World War II slogan "Joe for king," and Mandrake in vain tries to point out that it was a joke. Ultimately, the bizarre possibility emerges that the whole world might have been destroyed because one officer lacked a sense of humor.

One of the principles operating throughout *Dr. Strangelove* is discontinuity, whether within or between scenes, and this further erodes the analogies with earlier wars. The disparity between events and their stylistic rendering suggests that there are no fixed points of bearing because nuclear holocaust has no precedent. Thus, it is appropriate for the film to end with nuclear explosions, over which Vera Lynn sings "We'll Meet Again." The contradiction between soundtrack and image (a nuclear "sunset" is synchronized with the words "some sunny day") makes a fitting coda to a motif running right through the narrative that has denied any conceivable resemblance between nuclear war and any earlier kind of warfare. The present, in other words, cannot be read as a logical outcome of the past. It should be obvious from the foregoing that *Dr. Strangelove* possesses many similarities with *Catch-22*. As in that novel, the notion of "enemy" is revised as American pitted against American. The glamour of patriotic action is repeatedly ridiculed, and there are a number of points where potential logical spirals are introduced; for instance, when one soldier asks how they know those attacking Burpelson Base are "saboteurs," he is answered by the counterquestion, "How do you know they're not?"[42] As in Heller's novel, such circularity insulates those in authority from rational scrutiny. *Catch-22* is peopled with paranoids who find conspiracies everywhere and who personify different aspects of McCarthyism, like Captain Black, who mounts a Glorious Loyalty Oath Crusade, or General Dreedle, who finds Yossarian's name alien and therefore subversive. General Ripper similarly finds "evidence" for his conspiracy theory in 1946, marking both the beginning of a fluoridation campaign and the Cold War. Combining a double suspicion of welfare programs and communism, his words repeat the essential oppositions of McCarthyite rhetoric: "A foreign substance is introduced into the precious bodily fluids, without the knowledge of the individual and certainly without any free choice. That's the way the commies work."[43] The alien is pitted against the familiar, the unknown against the known, and national health strategy becomes recoded as a subversion of the body. The transposition of political subversion onto the body is a tactic common to *Catch-22*, and it is likely that Heller's novel offered Kubrick a model for burlesquing the McCarthy era, since on 30 July 1962 Kubrick wrote to Heller inviting him to draft a screenplay for *Dr. Strangelove*.[44] Heller declined, but the very fact of the invitation suggests an analogy between the comic treatment of combat in both works.

The comedy of both *Catch-22* and *Dr. Strangelove* is directed against institutional solemnity, and in the latter it is underpinned by many references to sexuality. This was first recognized by F. Anthony Macklin, who earned Kubrick's approval by describing the film as a "sex allegory," "from foreplay to explosion in the mechanized world."[45] Macklin argues that this sequence can be observed particularly clearly in the flight of *Leper Colony,* as its commander "King" Kong progresses from "reading" *Playboy,* through arming the bombs (which then become "potent") and preliminary combat, to the orgasmic launch of the bombs, one of which is ridden by Kong to his death. Norman Kagan has further fleshed out this reading, adding more glosses on characters' names and pointing out that the B-52 bomber is itself "phallic, particularly in its indefatigable race to coitus."[46]

The novel and film both use sexual innuendo to suggest that the American military machine is being fed by a distorted sexual impulse—hence, the appropriateness of the title—that has diverted Eros onto Thanatos. To establish this theme, *Dr. Strangelove* travesties a motif in *Strategic Air Command,* namely the attribution of femininity to a military technology that has to be controlled and operated by men. The most dramatic moment in *Strategic Air Command* occurs not when "Dutch" Holland's baby is born but when he is taken into a hangar to see a prototype bomber. He gasps, "She's the most beautiful thing that I've seen in my life." The language of the family is transposed into a military context to suggest that the family unit must take second place to the larger entity of the military, which represents the nation itself.[47] *Dr. Strangelove* takes over such discourse and foregrounds sexuality from the very first scenes. The film opens with a sequence of a bomber refueling in midair taken straight from *Strategic Air Command* but wrenched out of context so that it resembles two gigantic metal insects copulating in midair. The novel is slower to establish the theme, but it is just as marked. Indeed, a significant revision of the film is that one of the bombs is named Lolita. In both versions the centerfold figure from *Playboy* is Miss Foreign Affairs (who later appears as General Buck Turgidson's secretary) sprawled under a sunlamp. This scene echoes the movie *Lolita* and clearly uses throw-away visual details like the fact that she is wearing a bikini, named after Bikini Atoll, the location of the H-bomb tests. While Kong is contemplating the earlier image, he reflects complacently on his own good taste in women ("prime cut and double grade-A premium") in terms that encode them as items of food. To take a slightly different example, the scene between Turgidson and his secretary concludes with him telling her, "You start your count down right now and old Buckie will be back before you can say re-entry."[48] The concluding ribald pun (the film uses the more decorous "blast-off") confirms an analogy between sexual activity and the operation of weaponry. In short, the puns, innuendoes, and metaphors that recur throughout *Dr. Strangelove* establish an intricate series of connections between scenes and figures that focus on three interlocking areas: sex, food, and military hardware. Casual colloquialisms like "shoot" (Kong's exclamation) or "blast" (telephone call, Turgidson's term) cannot be read in innocence because the novel and film repeat them in different contexts. In case we miss the pun on Miss Foreign Affairs, the Russian ambassador stresses that his premier is also a man of "affairs." Thomas Nelson is the only critic to date who has spotted the "primal importance" Kubrick gives to food and eating, but he fails to point out how consumption meshes in with sex, consumerism (the assault on the Coke machine, etc.), and even technology, since the bomber "drinks" fuel.[49]

The attention to double entendre and the metaphors of slang all come to bear on one recurring target, the macho postures of the military hawks. The rather solemn commentary that some critics have made on characters' names under-states their absurdity. Kong casts himself as a latter-day warrior, a new "top gun," drawing his roles from westerns; but his name recasts him as an ape. Similarly, Turgidson's name renders his aggressive posture absurd, and several scenes sug-gest that the only thing swollen is his rhetoric. Such names then become comic labels that operate at their wearers' expense. They function collectively as an alienation device that incidentally burlesques the convention of nicknames in war narratives. Macklin lapses into solemnity and sexism when he explains that Merkin Muffley's name shows the "feminity of the President, illustrated by his lack of action," when the most obvious ribald significance is the ironic contrast between slang connotations of pubic hair and the president's baldness.[50] One of the main targets of black humor was the decorum of realism, and these labels, like the blatant bad joke of Jack D. Ripper's name, undermine the potential solemnity of the subject and perform the verbal equivalent of the fights noted earlier. In *The Magic Christian* the billionaire protagonist Guy Grand takes a delight in inserting scenes into films that make criminal or sexual connotations unmistakeable, and a similar process occurs in *Dr. Strangelove*. The allusions to *Strategic Air Command* and casual gender terms in war narratives (like referring to the bomber as "she") are now pushed to an extreme, where the sexual connotations of language almost take over as a subject in their own right.

Almost, but not quite. The comedy of *Dr. Strangelove* is, after all, a comedy ultimately about death, and destruction turns out to be the true aphrodisiac. When the bombers head for the Soviet Union, Dr. Strangelove's eyes gleam with excitement and Turgidson becomes "almost feverish." Similarly, the sexual mime of Kong forcing open the bomb doors leads directly to his own annihilation. General Ripper functions in the narrative not only as a trigger to the action but as a particular instance of a general pathology. *Dr. Strangelove* clearly draws on

Freud's theory of the death wish here, since the impulse to dissolve living units and "bring them back to their primæval, inorganic state" finds its most literal demonstration in Kong dissolving into raw matter. Freud declares that "man's natural aggressive instinct . . . is the derivative and the main representative of the death instinct which we have found alongside of Eros and which shares world-dominion with it."[51] At the time when Kubrick and Southern were working on the film script, an article appeared in the *Bulletin of the Atomic Scientists* that applied Freud's theory to contemporary warfare. Mortimer Ostow speculates on the unconscious motives behind war, suggesting that the death instinct might be subject to "discharge pressure" like Eros: "In the case of some of the more aggressive and bold leaders of the past, it is likely that their belligerence served to deflect their inward directed death impulses to the outer world."[52]

General Ripper rationalizes a fear of ejaculation as a triple conspiracy by women, crypto-Communists in the American administration, and the Soviet Union to rob him of his "essence." Self-defense inverts into preemptive attack and projects his sexual fears onto the world scene. In that respect he offers a case study of the death instinct determining military conduct, and the novel's subtext repeatedly hints at the sexual motives to his action. Once he seals off his base he lights up a cigar, a celebratory act and also a metaphorical hint that the sexual tempo is rising. Cigar leads into pistol and machine gun as a mini-sequence of phallic symbols that build up to an orgiastic climax when he fires the machine gun out of his office window. Once his men surrender, however, postcoital gloom descends on him. His cigar goes "dead," his eyes glaze over "almost dead," and he seems to age unnaturally. Peter George naturalized Quinten's impending death as an incurable disease, and the last time we see him he is sorting out his last formalities. In the film *Dr. Strangelove*, however, Ripper walks toward his bathroom while Mandrake carries on an absurd monologue of cliché phrases ("wash and brush up," "water on the back of the neck," etc.), which halt abruptly with the sound of a shot. The novel, again in contrast, makes greater play of the weapon he is carrying: "Ripper began to walk slowly across the office, the empty bullet cases clinking as his dragging feet moved through them. He was trailing the machine gun in his left hand."[53] Verbal description selects and therefore highlights details that would otherwise merge into a whole visual scene in the cinema and thereby suggests that Ripper's fears of emptiness have been realized. In a sense, it is more appropriate for him to simply exit from the scene rather than shoot himself as he does in the film, because metaphorically he is already dead. The recurrence of conspiratorial rhetoric and the cigar motif beyond Ripper prevents us from taking his obsessions as a matter of only individual pathology and extends them into a collective political mentality.

At the time when *Dr. Strangelove* was being completed, George H. Smith's 1963 novel *Doomsday Wing* described a very similar scenario, with the difference being that the ballistic missiles are launched by a Soviet officer convinced that his nation needs protecting. The moment of his launch has a clear personal symbolism for him as he appears in full dress uniform. Like Ripper, he loses contact with actuality at the moment of crisis, his eyes taking on a "glassy look" as his hand moves toward his red button.[54] The psychological screening implied in *Dr. Strangelove* is made explicit in the Soviet military, and General Aristov is actually pronounced insane by a psychologist before hostilities break out, but the rigidly authoritarian structure of the army prevents any action from being taken. Again like Ripper, Aristov is a superpatriot gathering support from a Stalinist clique that is almost responsible for a total war. In the event, even though nuclear strikes take place, the two premiers negotiate a compromise armistice that prevents the launch of a U.S. "doomsday wing" of ballistic missiles carrying cobalt bombs. The main difference between *Doomsday Wing* and *Dr. Strangelove* lies in Smith's conservative treatment of Cold War politics. The melodrama of nuclear rivalry goes unquestioned, since the first strike is initiated by a Russian general, whereas Kubrick uses a nuclear launch to satirize collective mentality of the U.S. military.

If Ripper represents the pathological extreme of a hawkish mentality, Dr. Strangelove expresses its scientific facade. The film delays introducing Strangelove until the Doomsday Machine is mentioned so that his scientific explanations are associated from the very start with death. The novel merely identifies him as a watchful presence and thereby loses the sudden visual impact of the film as he wheels slowly toward the president. In the film the image of the evil scientist has barely registered before Peter Sellers's exaggerated pronunciation shifts it toward comedy by dramatizing him as a parody Nazi. The novel keeps the comedy in a lower key, quietly hinting at his myopia (literal and metaphorical) and alerting the reader to his crippled hand, which throws out implicit allusions to the scheming scientists of *Metropolis* and *Doctor No*.[55] Charles Maland has suggested that he also combines aspects of Edward Teller, Henry Kissinger, and Herman Kahn in articulating an analytical approach to nuclear war based on disinterested calculation.[56] Once again, no individual possesses unique characteristics, however, because General Turgidson half-quotes from Kahn, whose study *On Thermonuclear War* certainly stands behind the name and discussion of the Doomsday Machine, although the idea for such a device dated back to 1950, at least, when it was explained by Leo Szilard at a Chicago Round Table discussion.[57] Essentially, this weapon was a "dirty" H-bomb containing cobalt that, as radioactive fallout, had the capacity to kill all life on earth and as such represented the ultimate extreme of a rapidly developing technology of destruction. Strangelove's exposition is far more extreme than Kahn's and describes the device as cheap and reliable, both qualities Kahn questions. Strangelove can only take a positive role in the action once the Doomsday Machine has fired. Until that point his very presence as an ex-Nazi casts an ironic light on the president's refusal to go down in history as the "greatest mass murderer since Adolf Hitler" (which Sellers plays for laughs in his uncontrollable fascist salutes) while Strangelove, like Wernher von Braun, is participating in a military program whose scale dwarfs anything from World War II.

Dr. Strangelove clearly addresses a reader/viewer who is alert to Freudian psychology and who will pick up the many hints of transference of the sexual onto the military domain of experience. As Norman O. Brown pointed out during a lengthy application of the theory of the death wish, art makes the unconscious conscious and converts symptom into play: "The neurotic mechanism involves repression and a shutting of the eye of consciousness, and a resultant psychic automatism . . . Art does not withdraw the eye of consciousness, does not repress, and attains some freedom."[58] The characters of *Dr. Strangelove*, especially, but not uniquely, Kong, Turgidson, and Strangelove himself, are determined by clear obsessions and compulsions. The comedy of the narrative reveals these compulsions as a form of ignorance and in every case presents psychic automatism as a mechanization of the self.

Understanding *Dr. Strangelove* involves identifying a pathological subtext, a series of verbal and symbolic links embedded in the characters' discourse that they themselves hardly glimpse. The humor of the work is therefore quite different from Jules Feiffer's satirical cartoons on the arms race from the late fifties. In "Boom!" (collected in *Passionella*, 1960) Feiffer rewrites the arms race as a graphic fairy tale that ridicules public apathy and that culminates with a scientist inventing the ultimate bomb. The story ends with a radioactive cloud over the caption "and it worked," ironically playing the subject against the generic expectations of the narrative mode. *Dr. Strangelove*, by contrast, repeatedly refers to different levels of signification and uses its comedy to attack the collective mystification of East-West nuclear confrontation.

Dr. Strangelove, as Maland has argued, attacks the ideology of liberal consensus head on. The film "uses nightmare comedy to satirize four dimensions of the Cold War consensus: anti-Communist paranoia; the culture's inability to realize the enormity of nuclear war; various nuclear strategies; and the blind faith modern man places in technological progress."[59] The film's most striking setting, the War Room, reinforces our sense of inadequacy as the huge screen and table dwarf the human figures. The latter resembles an immense poker table, and this analogy makes an implicit (and again ironic) comment on those grouped round it. Once the news of the crisis breaks, the president goes around to some of the members asking them to "bid" an opinion. Some "see" his suggestion, another passes, and all the time the hypotheses we encounter in other narratives of nuclear disaster are reduced to a game of chance.[60] More strikingly, the war table is shot from a very high angle downward, whereas the usual direction of shots in comparable nuclear films is upward toward the screen—from the perspective of human observers. Kubrick's high downward angle on the table reduces the humans to adjuncts to a huge wheel, an effect that sums up one of the film's main themes: the sheer difficulty of human operatives in controlling a military machine of their own making. Despite the existence of the hot line, *Dr. Strangelove* presents a sequence of events moving remorselessly toward ultimate destruction. The blackest aspect of its comedy is that it grows out of humanity's perverse capacity to wipe itself out, as evidenced in the final montage of nuclear blasts. This makes a grimly appropriate conclusion to a narrative whose action has focused on a supposed control center—the War Room. In the final sequence Kubrick spliced together archival footage of the bomb blasts, and a nuclear holocaust could not be experienced as spectacle. Yet again the satirical point is made that strategic controllers are detached in every sense from the real-life consequences of their actions.

CHAPTER 12

Mapping the Postnuclear Landscape

Narratives of nuclear war regularly evoke it as a massive rupture that might or might not open up possibilities of survival. Because the normal continuity to life has been so damaged, these novels describe attempts by characters to decode the shattered landscape in an attempt to understand what has happened. This process involves narrative reconstruction and also exploration of the terrain, since mapping constitutes a spatial exercise of understanding.

In Robert Heinlein's 1964 novel *Farnham's Freehold,* the impact of a massive thermonuclear bomb throws the family in their fallout shelter forward in time to a strangely empty but still recognizable landscape. Farnham's reaction is typically practical: "Oh, we'll survey it first." When another character objects that they don't even have a spirit level, Farnham retorts, "The Egyptians invented surveying with less, Joe."[1] Not even translation in time can damage Farnham's confidence in his capacity to overcome difficulty through practical inventiveness. On a small scale, his plan to survey the terrain, build a house, and construct a dam is essentially a plan to appropriate the landscape and create—or rather *re*-create—the country his family has left. There is a chronological irony in his optimism, because the landscape resembles terrain before settlement, whereas Farnham's house has been moved into a totalitarian future. The misguided attempt to appropriate this landscape is made possible by its chronological distance from the novel's present, which has erased the signs of nuclear war. When the family returns to the opening situation, they respond quite differently to the urgencies of nuclear attack. Heinlein establishes a rapid tempo through scenes where the characters hunt for supplies from place to place before taking refuge in an abandoned mine. The novel concludes with an image of survival taken from earlier American history, that of a trading post; but it is an embattled image, since the post is surrounded by mines to protect against possible attack. The signs on the freehold offering nursery facilities, blacksmithing, and bridge lessons suggest a reconstituted society, which Heinlein's brief allusion to "disorders" makes problematic.

Nuclear war is always imagined as a major rupture, a fissure that challenges survivors' capacity for reconstruction and even understanding. What mutes Heinlein's dramatization of war is his protagonist's unshaken confidence that the same processes of territorial acquisition were applied in the original formation of the United States. However, this confidence is an exception in geographical representations of postnuclear America, where typically the shattered terrain challenges not only would-be travelers' mobility but also their capacity to understand what has taken place. In his classic introduction to cultural geography, *Maps of Meaning*, Peter Jackson discusses the ways in which "social practices . . . take place in historically contingent and geographically specific contexts." Specifically, he considers how geography has fed into literary criticism to produce original new readings of regional novelists, and as part of the way in which analysis of the "symbolic representation of place in literature" might proceed, he asks speculatively: "How do science fiction novels, like all utopian works, project contemporary social relations on to the imagined geographies of the future?"[2] What follows is an attempt to answer part of that question by examining the construction of place in some postnuclear war U.S. narratives, taking a lead from Jackson and incorporating John Agnew's useful division of the concept of space into three aspects: locale ("the settings in which social relations are constituted"), location (the "effects upon locales of social and economic processes operating at wider scales"), and sense of place (the local "structures of feeling").[3] In examining nuclear war novels, we shall see that the recurring casualty in these accounts is location as connections are lost between the immediate setting and the nation at large. Following the massive rupture of war, the landscape has to be reexplored or reappropriated, whether in the immediate or distant aftermath of war. Neal Barrett's choice of the title *Through Darkest America* for his 1986 postnuclear novel directly reflects this theme of the postwar landscape having reverted to wilderness.[4]

Mapping will be addressed in its double sense of cartography and, more generally, of organizing perceptions of postwar America into a meaningful set. Bernard Wolfe's *Limbo* attempted both modes of representation but then warned the reader about risks within the very process of representation. Dr. Martine attempts an exploratory return to his nation, which he had fled during a nuclear war, and to his birth place, synchronizing an investigation both of his own past and of the current state of his nation. For his travels he consults a road map that depicts a truncated

United States, now known merely as the Strip: "The picture was complicated . . . by the skinny irregular arms which stretched out more or less laterally from each side of the Strip, rather like the pseudopods of an amoeba."[5] The term "picture" estranges us from a habitual reading of a map, transforming it into an image then made analogous to an organism. In other words, the map gives us a nudge toward the sort of holistic thinking recommended in a lecture Martine attends on Korzybski's General Semantics, summed up as projecting "man-as-a-whole-in-his-environment." The lecture warns against too closely identifying the representation with its referent, quoting Korzybski's famous statement that "the map is not the territory."[6] Although Wolfe facetiously sums up his novel as a "spurious map of the future," its anxious attempts to organize disparate areas of knowledge in order to understand humanity's self-destructive impulse remain one of the most striking instances of mapping through narrative in the Cold War period.[7]

It is one of the most pointed ironies of U.S. nuclear war narratives that the discovery of America has to be recapitulated. Aldous Huxley's *Ape and Essence* gives us one of the earliest instances with its narrative starting at the point where a group of scientists land on the coast of southern California in the wake of World War III. The New Zealand Re-Discovery Expedition to North America is led by a naive botanist named Poole, whose sole purpose is to investigate local flora. Within the fictitious film script, Huxley gives us a general shot of Los Angeles where the sands of time have obliterated the cityscape: "What was once the world's largest oasis is now its greatest agglomeration of ruins in a waste-land. Nothing moves in the streets. Dunes of sand have drifted across the concrete. The avenues of palms and pepper trees have left no trace."[8] Instead of placing it with his scientist, Huxley establishes a perspective that demands memory: "We dissolve to the corner of Fifth Street and Pershing Square. As of old, the Square is the hub and centre of the city's cultural life. From a shallow well in front of the Philharmonic Auditorium two women are drawing water in a goatskin, which they empty into earthenware jars for other women to carry away."[9] The reversion to a primitive way of life both bemuses and fascinates Poole, who becomes attracted to a nubile local girl. In a very American ending, Poole and his newfound partner head off into the desert with their knapsacks, convinced that they can find a better world elsewhere.

Where Huxley uses the fiction of a scientific expedition to set up his satire of Hollywood, Leo Szilard draws on the science fiction trope of Earth being visited by inhabitants of another planet to depict the grim consequences of nuclear weapons. "Report on 'Grand Central Terminal'" (1948) describes the arrival of travelers in New York after a ten-year space voyage only to find the city (and apparently the rest of the world) completely devoid of life but the city buildings undamaged. A leading member of the Manhattan Project who, after the bombings of Hiroshima and Nagasaki, tried to organize scientists in the cause of disarmament, Szilard grimly predicted in 1947 that "ten or fifteen years from now giant bombs which disperse radioactive substances in the air may be set off far away from our cities. If such giant bombs were used against us, the buildings of our cities would remain undamaged, but the people inside of the cities would not remain alive."[10] His tale embodies this possibility and describes the travelers exploring a key landmark in New York—Grand Central Station, or Terminal, as he puns. The layout of this structure is explored in a quasi-anthropological investigation of the extinct culture that produced it, and a dialogue develops between the narrator and his associate Xram (Marx), who formulates the hypothesis that humanity has destroyed itself in a massive war. One piece of evidence lies in the traces of uranium found in the city, but the narrator is not convinced: "This sounded pretty unlikely indeed, since uranium is not in itself explosive and it takes quite elaborate processing to prepare it in a form in which it can be detonated. Since the earth-dwellers who built all these cities must have been rational beings, it is difficult to believe that they should have gone to all this trouble of processing uranium just in order to destroy themselves."[11] The internal contradiction between cultural signs of intelligence and the demise of humanity is the sticking point here. In effect, Szilard's extraterrestrial visitors perform an autopsy on humanity itself by applying the reason that should have prevented humanity's extinction. The same sort of process is carried out in the frame to Mordecai Roshwald's *Level 7*, where the Martian Institute for Archaeological Excavations in the Solar System unearths the diary narrative of a nuclear holocaust, and in the frame to the novel version of *Dr. Strangelove*, which summarizes the action as one in the series *The Dead Worlds of Antiquity*.

For his narrative Szilard extrapolates from the bombs of Hiroshima and Nagasaki, imagines a more powerful weapon, and then transposes its effects onto the American scene. Similarly, in his contribution to the American scientists' polemic against the bomb, the physicist Philip Morrison transposed accounts of Hiroshima onto the American scene by having a bomb explode over Manhattan, at the corner of Third Avenue and East 20th Street:

> From the river west to Seventh Avenue, and from south of Union Square to the middle thirties, the streets were filled with the dead and dying. The old men sitting on the park benches in the square never knew what had happened. They were chiefly charred black on the side toward the bomb. Everywhere in this whole district were men with burning clothing, women with terrible red and blackened burns, and dead children caught while hurrying home to lunch.

[He then turns to the buildings and continues:] Closer to the centre nothing much was left . . . Here and there collapsed buildings had piled a great heap of pitiful debris, all the wares and effects of living, into a useless and smouldering jumble.[12]

Unfortunately, Morrison's very care over his descriptions undermines their impact. Essentially he gives the reader snapshot images of the different zones of damage where the observer's point of view is taken for granted as unproblematic. Because he wants to measure the range of damage according to the city grid, his clarity over setting and position gives us an abstracted image of that damage because it excludes one of the most likely psychological effects, namely confusion.

Morrison's sketch was an exercise in future reportage that did not place the bombing within a narrative context and in that sense is not typical of the procedures followed by postnuclear fiction. Characteristically, nuclear war was repeatedly imagined as bringing about a massive destruction or disruption of the landscape so severe that those terrains have to be explored afresh. The typical scenario in this fiction is of a solitary male making his way laboriously across a devastated landscape, which has to be explored partly for physical progression and partly since it carries within its own destruction the physical clues to what has happened. Alfred Coppel's *Dark December* follows the pattern in having as protagonist an officer who was serving in a far north underground bunker when war breaks out. He is literally out of the landscape, and the novel describes his attempts to return to his San Francisco home in an extended journey south loosely modeled on the *Odyssey*. This journey falls into three phases according to his means of transport: plane, truck, and horse. By plane he gets a unique view of the landscape round the Columbia River: "The further south we flew, the more trees were down until by the time we were within thirty miles of the Columbia River, there was not a tree standing. They lay like blackened jackstraws on the seared earth, and from the air you could see the pattern clearly." That pattern points him toward ground zero, which, as usual in this fiction, is described negatively, as an absence: "When I looked ahead of us to where the Columbia River should be I see only a vast muddy lake that shouldn't be there at all, a monstrous inland sea with raw beaches of churned rock and mud and yellowish substratal earth."[13] The effect is as if violence has been done to the landscape itself, partly erasure in the disappearance of the river and partly displacement in the substitution of an inland sea. But the view remains safely distant and free from human casualties. Once he is down on the ground, Major Gavin experiences a regression back through historical time: "Redmond looked like some kind of frontier town," he notes.[14] The military convoy he joins pulls up every night in a circle modeled on the wagon trains to protect themselves against "bandits." And once Gavin penetrates the area south of any military control, the landscape changes yet again into areas of radiation, biological pollution, or local militia rule. Following U.S. Route 97 gives a misleading impression of orderliness that every episode questions. Gavin's move into the "moonscape" of the south is figured as a gradual loss of orientation that results in his physical collapse. He literally loses the capacity to distinguish hallucinatory dream images from any external landscape. At the very stage of his journey where he should be approaching more and more familiar places, his estrangement becomes most severe. His journey south in that sense shows him moving gradually away from any notion of location, and as the signs of national activity become less, he can scarcely maintain any concept of locale either, since there are scarcely any traces of communities for him to enter. Gavin's journey is set up as a kind of homecoming where both he and the reader expect the terrain to become more familiar the closer he gets to home but whereas the very opposite takes place. The last stages of his journey show his disorientation reaching a gradual peak; he loses his ability to construct any sense of place. There is no Homeric homecoming with the status quo being reestablished, and this gives Coppel's narrative its austere strength.

The conclusion to Coppel's narrative makes a striking contrast with Wilson Tucker's *The Long Loud Silence,* where the United States has been sharply divided along the Mississippi River into eastern and western sections. Russell Gary, a World War II veteran, wakes up after a drinking binge to find himself on the wrong side of the river after the eastern part of the country has been laid waste by nuclear and biological weapons. His first shock is that the imagery of European warfare he saw in Italy has become transposed onto the United States: "bombs here, in Illinois!" he exclaims. "Who would bomb Illinois? Who would make war on the United States?"[15] And similarly, when he reaches Chicago, he finds the city in flames and is shocked by its transformation: "The image of the flames persisted . . . It shouldn't be! Chicago was different from those cities in Europe, big and little cities that had undergone brutal destruction from the skies. Chicago was *ours* . . . and *our* cities were not meant to be touched."[16] This novel as a whole depicts Gary's dislocation within his own country, which has become transformed into a place of danger. The action focuses on a sequence of chance encounters with other fugitives searching for safety. Traversing the country he comes back again and again to the single issue of how to cross the river, which is no longer a highway but a barrier or frontier manned by armed soldiers who will shoot on sight: "This was the only bridge left intact along a six or seven hundred mile stretch of the Mississippi, and American troops would be concentrated in strength on the other end."[17] The novel opens with a bridge, a classic image of joining, and inverts it into a sign of division. *The Long Loud Silence* shows a United States divided, like postwar Germany, into two zones whose separation is strictly enforced by the military. What limits this account, however, is Tucker's inability to do anything with the division he describes. It remains a geographical given that neither changes nor challenges the protagonist's sense of the real. Despite his references to nuclear and biological bombs, Tucker attempts a transposition of the imagery of World War II onto the American landscape, whose separation remains an essentially practical problem for his protagonist. The end result of his search is not safety but an ultimate estrangement—"the world was gone."[18]

These examples focus on attempts to return to safety in the immediate aftermath of nuclear attack. However, another group of novels set farther into the future describe how postnuclear locations have changed and become institutionalized. The reformed American nation is often a divided and internally hostile area resulting from a reversion back to preindustrialized historical eras. Ironically, the control, or in some cases the suppression, of history becomes a charged issue. In Leigh Brackett's *The Long Tomorrow*, set two generations after a nuclear war, the U.S. Constitution has been amended to forbid cities. This amendment stands as an epigraph to the novel: "No city, no town, no community of more than one thousand people or two hundred buildings to the square mile shall be built or permitted to exist anywhere in the United States of America." This change privileges the legal model of the local rural community that enforces its own values through tight social bonding. Like Ray Bradbury's 1963 story "To the Chicago Abyss," where Chicago has become an enormous crater, Brackett's novel presents a future society that forbids any reference to the time before what they call the "Destruction." Brackett's New Mennonites view nuclear destruction as God's punishment of humanity for its sins, and so any attempt to investigate the causes of the war becomes construed as questioning divine retribution. Both works describe an attempt at historical erasure where the exercise of either memory or curiosity has become illegal. Remembering obviously carries the potential symbolic importance of bridging the gap between prewar and postwar. Brackett's protagonist, a young boy named Len, who is loosely modeled on Huckleberry Finn, comes across a radio and a history book, symbolic pointers to an outside culture, and from that point on is consumed by a desire to leave his community. Thus, Brackett runs together the impulse to learn, curiosity about the outside world, and a specific desire for access to a suppressed history, which are all enacted in Len's journeys.

The radio and book function as catalysts to Len's latent dissatisfaction with the isolation from the rest of America enforced by his society. His father tries unsuccessfully to drum into him the lesson that cities made technology and nuclear war possible and that "when the cities went they were not possible any more."[19] Desire is expressed topographically as a growing fascination for Len of the "magical" names of other places, especially the legendary Bartorstown, a mysterious secret installation built before the war. A pivotal moment comes soon after he leaves home and reaches the town of Refuge on the Ohio River: "It had come by the name, Len understood, because people from a city farther along the river had taken refuge there during the Destruction. It was the terminus now for two main trading routes stretching as far as the Great Lakes, and the wagons rolled day and night while the roads were passable, bringing down baled furs and iron and woollen cloth, flour and cheeses. From east and west along the river came other traffic."[20] Here Len's horizons literally open up as he simultaneously discovers the past and the topography of the present. His perception of trade routes is symptomatic of a new and growing perception of the American landscape. When he finally reaches Bartorstown, an underground facility disguised as an abandoned mine in the Rocky Mountains, he enters the suppressed archive of his culture and encounters the technology his parents' generation had been trying to conceal from him.

In the narratives by Coppel and Tucker, the maps of their respective landscapes function like a subtextual grid onto which are projected the details of the action. Within the new time bearings, these maps codify the reader's present as an imagined past, partly erased by war, and give us approximate bearings to keep track of the protagonist's movements across the American landscape. The recognition of place is historicized, however, in *The Long Tomorrow* and in Edgar Pangborn's *Davy*, which describes a neo-feudal America centuries after a nuclear war. Cultural memory persists of the "Old Times," and there are even maps stored in a regional museum that give the narrator a "fair picture of the world as it was some four hundred years ago."[21] Davy maps out the territory for the reader in this way: "The republic of Moha [Mohawk] . . . is a nation of small lonely farms and stockaded villages in the lake and forest and grassland country north of the Katskil Mountains and the rugged nation that bears the mountains' name . . . I was born in one of Moha's three cities, Skoar [Scotia]." The area is characterized by newly cleared roads, of which we are told: "There's a raw splendour to these roads, except when wartime makes folk more than ever afraid of travel and open places."[22] Pangborn's place names are identifiable but estranging so as to convey the transformation of America into a patchwork of new kingdoms ranging from ecclesiastical states to the far distant "Misipa" empire.

Davy serves a spell as King of the Fools and was planned by Pangborn to be a character restive against limits. During the composition of the novel he wrote, "All through the reign Davy has become increasingly interested in exploration—the Foreign Lands across the Atlantic and the unknown country west of the Wilderness. He tries to search history, to understand the Old Time as no one has done before."[23] As in *The Long Tomorrow,* local social restrictions trigger the protagonist's desire for discovery, exploring the terrain, collecting and decoding unfamiliar cultural artifacts, and acting on his conviction that the past has a continuity in the present. So, once again, cultural exploration is carried out through space and the historical time, to which the new religious authorities are trying to limit access. The image that best sums up Davy's historical enterprise is him sailing his ship *The Morning Star* through fog, a traditional representation of confusion, across a raised sea level he is exploring with the help of surviving maps from the Old Time.

In Pangborn's 1966 novel *The Judgment of Eve,* memories of a prewar era are focused specifically on the roads of America. When the eponymous Eve hears her mother's stories of how life used to be, they appeal to her imagination quite separately from her memory. She "could picture buses moving on the roads, since the dulled body of one was serving as a section of their brush fence and had done so ever since she could remember."[24] The narrative traces out the laborious rediscovery of the roads by Eve and other characters. Indeed, central chapters are devoted to the journeys of each main character in turn, journeys that involve unexpected encounters. The road for Mikhail Bakhtin is one of the main chronotopes in fiction, since, as he explains, "on the road . . . the spatial and temporal paths of the most varied people . . . intersect at one spatial and temporal point."[25] Bakhtin is of course making a general point about narrative encounters, but his concept of chronotope is especially applicable to this body of fiction, which is uniquely conscious of time. Postnuclear fiction is always retrospective, looking back to a period before the rupture of war. Thus, the meetings between Pangborn's travelers always carry significance beyond themselves in suggesting possibilities of new social groupings and communities. On one journey a self-appointed guide explains the history of a city street overgrown with vines and vegetation: "This road . . . was called State Street. It had that name, this same road, in another city it enters a long way to the west of here. You might wind up there, I suppose."[26] Despite its ruin, the road is still invested with potential for future travel, which would simultaneously be a means of recapturing the past.

The classic phase of postnuclear fiction was during the 1950s and 1960s. With the end to atmospheric nuclear tests and the easing of other Cold War tensions, the number of novels devoted to the nuclear theme diminished strikingly. When it was revived during the debate over Star Wars in the 1980s, it recurred in new and self-conscious forms. For example, the very notion of a tour might seem oddly anachronistic to a postwar America, and yet it was applied in one of the most original postnuclear narratives of the eighties.

For their book *Warday and the Journey Onward,* Whitley Strieber and James Kunetka drew on the tradition of the tour to survey the state of the nation, similar to that we find in John Gunther's *Inside USA* (1947) or John Steinbeck's *Travels with Charley: In Search of America* (1962). The idea for *Warday* grew out of Strieber and Kunetka's mounting anxiety over the nuclear arms race. Kunetka had both a personal and a scientific interest in the subject. His father had participated in the Manhattan Project, and he himself had written studies of Los Alamos and J. Robert Oppenheimer and had met with Edward Teller, who indicated that he was in favor of a limited nuclear war.[27] They jettisoned the idea of a story narrative, preferring a combination of travelogue and scientific report, and published *Warday* against a background of heightened public discussion of nuclear war. As they were completing the book, ABC television released its docudrama *The Day After* in November 1983, which dramatized a full-scale nuclear exchange between the United States and the Soviet Union.[28] *Warday,* by contrast, addressed a limited exchange. Also, President Reagan had recently announced his controversial Strategic Defense Initiative (SDI) involving laser-armed satellites in space. Star Wars, as SDI was dubbed, is exactly the system that causes war in *Warday:* In 1988 (a very near future) the United States launches new satellites in a "Spiderweb" system; this provokes the Soviets to launch their own satellites, which are destroyed but not before they launch missiles at America. In short, *Warday* joined other writings designed to show that SDI would be an inadequate deterrent. Indeed, the book carried an endorsement from Senator Edward Kennedy, who fiercely opposed SDI.

The division of labor in *Warday* was that Strieber would supply the narrative and Kunetka the scientific tables and reports. The result is a work of fictional reportage describing the United States five years after a limited nuclear war. The two investigators trace out a circular route starting in Dallas, moving westward to the Hispanic Free State of Aztlan in El Paso, detouring to Los Alamos, then traveling cross-country by train to Los Angeles. In California they visit San Francisco and Oakland, then back east follow a route through Chicago, Cleveland, Pittsburgh, and arriving finally in New York. In a brief coda they return to Dallas. Apart from the fact that some cities (San Antonio, Washington, D.C., and others) have been completely destroyed, the mere fact that they can travel by rail on most of their journey suggests that communication has not collapsed despite the effects of the massive electromagnetic pulse sent out by nuclear blasts. Thus, early in *Warday* it is clear that we are not being offered an apocalyptic scenario: "The issue was not Armageddon. It was consequences."[29]

At one point in *Warday* the travelers interview an economist called Walter Tevis, who gives his version of the war and who explains how the value of money collapsed. Walter Tevis was in fact a novelist who coincidentally died the year the book was published. It is possible that Strieber and Kunetka were using him as meta-fictional reinforcer of their nuclear theme. Tevis's famous 1963 novel *The Man Who Fell Down to Earth* describes a humanoid alien fleeing from a planet that has been devastated by five nuclear wars. He is thus a survivor and a fugitive, but one with a grim message to humanity: "We are certain beyond all reasonable doubt that your world will be an atomic rubble heap in no more than thirty years, if you are left to yourselves."[30] *Warday* shares the same purpose of warning. On the dust jacket of the first edition, the publisher declares that the book "reveals the hard, scientific truth of what really happens after such a ["limited"] war, what the planners are afraid to tell us."

Before the travelers set out on their journey proper, they visit one of the Dead Zones of what used to be San Antonio. One of the craters, "even two years after the explosion, still shimmered in the sunlight from the fusion of soil, metal, concrete, and other materials."[31] Because the terrain is still too radioactive to cross on foot, they approach in a helicopter, tracing in reverse the effects of a blast until they reach ground zero, a place of total erasure. The episode is designed to have a special poignancy because the travelers (like Strieber and Kunetka themselves) grew up in San Antonio, but it is difficult to avoid a projected spectacle here, even a grim kind of tourism. The episode does, however, demonstrate the new classification of areas into color-coded zones reflecting their varying threats to life.

Strieber and Kunetka give an account of a fragmented country broken into states and regions each affected in varying degrees by nuclear fallout and each dependent for its survival on foreign aid. Survival is a real issue for the two travelers, who face a whole series of dangers. First, there is the hostility of the Hispanic Free State of Aztlan, which extends over the eastern part of Texas, where we first encounter a new regional territoriality in action. It seems as if the Hispanic American dream of a "Nation of Aztlan" has been realized, and the travelers encounter their first hostility as alien "gringos." The new regime in this region is nothing compared to the travelers' experiences of California, where military authorities have established a strict system of controls and passes to exclude immigrants. Briefly following the route of the migrants in *The Grapes of Wrath*, the travelers reach the California border where notices warn: "ILLEGAL ALIENS LIABLE TO BE SHOT." California has established hegemony over the west, demonizing the rest of the country as hostile or diseased. In other words, here and elsewhere the nation has fragmented either into areas of deadly radiation or into local fiefdoms.

This is where the new meaning to "zoning" comes in. Elsewhere zones are color-coded according to their degrees of radiation. Manhattan, for instance, is a red zone, as it's used for salvage. San Antonio is a dead zone, which can only be visited from the air, with its own grisly "souvenirs." In California, by contrast, travel zones are coded in order to maximize police surveillance of travelers. The travelers are told, "You have Red Zones, Yellow Zones, Blue Zones, and Green Zones. Stick to the Greens. They lead to the intrastate tracks . . . Yellow Zones are for incoming trains from our sister restricted-immigration states, Washington and Oregon. Red Zones are for trains arriving from abroad, which means the rest of the United States. Don't even look as if you might be interested in them."[32] Here zones are extrapolated from transport maps and given a new, sinister significance. At another point in *Warday* we learn that European powers are planning to divide what is left off the United States into zones, thereby reversing the process of occupation that took place in Germany at the end of World War II.

At this point we encounter a contradiction at the heart of *Warday*. Toward the end of the book Jim (Kunetka) reflects, "We belong to one another," a sentiment that makes explicit the quasi-documentary method the authors have been using.[33] To alternate their own narrative with interviews, official documents, and tables implies that the travelers and the people they encounter are all participating in the larger collective of the nation, however much it is damaged. Paul Brians, nevertheless, sees a more austere moral to the book, stating that the authors' "point is undoubtedly to establish that even a limited nuclear war from which the United States suffered little damage would destroy it as a nation."[34] We have to negotiate between directly contrasting interpretations of *Warday*. The book's full title suggests survival and hope, whereas the narrative details evoke regional and ethnic antagonisms that the war has brought to the surface with a vengeance. The maps of the United States that chart fallout dispersal might be consistent with the nuclear strikes that took place and at the same time codify a scientific overview of the country, but the latter is exactly what is usually missing from postnuclear fiction. Strieber and Kunetka excel at conveying the sheer anxiety of travel within a country divided by stringent immigration laws. It is an unconscious irony of the title that the journey onward, as witnessed by the narrators, is fraught with the danger attendant on the rigid policing of state boundaries.

Warday, in common with many postnuclear narratives, depicts a landscape that has become a kind of palimpsest written over by postwar events but where the traces of an earlier world are discernible. In this respect the authors are continuing an older tradition where "American topography became a geographical palimpsest beneath which the Old World discerned traces of Atlantis and the Elysian

Fields, the Garden of Eden and the Promised Land."[35] This can be seen clearly in Walter M. Miller's *A Canticle for Leibowitz*, which recapitulates the whole of Western history from the new Dark Age ushered in by nuclear war back up to the present, where nuclear war breaks out yet again. The novel opens on a road in a desert: "Perhaps, in earlier ages, the road had been a portion of the shortest route from the Great Salt Lake to Old El Paso; south of the abbey it intersected a similar strip of broken stone that stretched east and westward. The crossing was worn by time, but not by Man, of late."[36] This is a landscape bearing the traces of an America that has receded into a new medieval age where the most advanced features of nuclear technology, like a fallout shelter, have become inscrutable ruins. The novel describes a gradual historical loop so that the reader is taken back to a present, where the technology is understood and used once again, but at that point the cycle of war and destruction begins to repeat itself. Against a landscape containing recognizably American place names, like Utah and Denver, a series of historical situations, like the struggle between church and state, play themselves out. By the time we reach the new present, Miller carefully avoids using any designation for the nation being described, implicitly cuing in the reader's recognition of earlier historical events within the novel's descriptions. By that stage, the nation has become departicularized into one of a series in an "unending sequence of rise and fall," which includes France, Britain, and America.[37]

Miller builds his narrative on the historical ignorance of his characters and consistently puts the reader in a position of greater awareness. That enables us to "map" the historical changes as they occur, but at the same time it implies the inevitability of these large processes. The expatriate Russell Hoban's *Riddley Walker*, which was directly influenced by Miller's novel, similarly centers on a journey but once again problematizes travel. Hoban has recorded how much of the research he did for the novel consisted of familiarizing himself with the detailed layout of southeast England: "Ordnance Survey 1:25,000 maps were my constant companions; nautical charts also."[38] Apart from informing the narrative detail, Hoban's research resulted in a map being included in every edition of the novel, where place names have morphed: Canterbury into Cambry, Folkestone into Fork Stoan, Sandwich into Sams Itch, and so on. The map retains the spatial locations of towns but little else; broken lines suggest lost or former routes of communication. Hoban is thus constructing his narrative over a lost system of routes that were themselves partially constructed over Roman roads. Hoban's new names project a theme of physical violence onto the landscape itself ("Bernt Arse," "Ram Gut") and become incorporated into the narration that describes a gradual movement toward Canterbury. Hoban has produced his own sequence of postnuclear Canterbury tales.

Set centuries after nuclear war has devastated southeast England, the novel describes a circuitous journey by the young Riddley Walker to Cambry (Canterbury). Riddley's name suggests a process, suggests in fact that the whole landscape is "riddled" with the traces of the past he tries to decipher. But Riddley's very name suggests a cryptic narrating process where meaning might be withheld. Is he "walking" riddles, as he says, or is he himself a walking riddle? This kind of ambiguity is fed into his journey that "ghosts" the Canterbury pilgrimage to a definite destination. Riddley's progression across the country is fraught with difficulty; every location presents fresh dangers and fresh riddles. With his companion, they "Souf and Eastit then for Fork Stoan which that put the wind on our lef side in stead of in our faces. The wind it jus kep fulling on and the rain like sling stoans in our faces." Riddley constantly shifts bearings and direction and repeatedly sets up chains of analogy. Fork Stoan has literally become a place of stones and rubble, a collection of ruins that typifies the whole landscape. As Riddley struggles forward, he constantly encounters the traces of lost features. For instance, he records: "Nearing on to Burnt Arse outers we come thru some old burnt over common it use to be a fents there long time back."[39] Among the many puns the novel sets up, Riddley's "Eusa" story is of what used to be. Every detail of the landscape carries a sign of temporal loss, just as every word in Hoban's text reads like a deformation of English, as if nuclear war has attacked the language itself, not just the terrain and its inhabitants.

Cutting across Riddley's desire to reach Cambry is the recurring figure of the circle, sometimes signifying a ring of "dead towns," sometimes suggesting confusion. At one point as he approaches Cambry we are told: "My head begun to feal like it wer widening like circels on water I dint know if it wud ever stop I dint know where the end of it wud be."[40] Commenting on this passage, Peter Schwenger has argued that this figure is identical with the concentric diagram of a nuclear explosion and that this identity bears on the difficulty of expressing the nuclear subject. Not only does it blur distinctions between inner and outer, but when we apply it to Cambry the location becomes a presence (a goal or "senter") and an absence since the city suffered a nuclear blast.[41] Riddley's journey enacts this ambiguity by combining circularity with progression, describing an extended loop from a point up the River Sour (Stour), down through Fork Stoan, and then northwest toward what Riddley calls Zero Groun. By reversing the nominalization of "ground zero," the ambiguous nature of Cambry is increased even further to a possible "no-place." But then we don't have the grounds to decide, and neither does he. In his search for meaning he may himself be tracing out yet another fools circle, a spatial figure for an apparently pointless and repetitive story. Nevertheless, walking for Riddley offers a means of recall. Hoban has stated that "every history is a palimpsest of geographies, whether great or tiny," and the complex search pursued by his protagonist clearly embodies this principle.[42]

As postnuclear narratives became more numerous and established their own clichés, later instances of this fiction have demonstrated an increasing self-consciousness of reference. Where Edgar Pangborn estranges the reader from the postnuclear American landscape by modifying his place names, Kim Stanley Robinson's *The Wild Shore* retains the original names for the ruins of Californian cities, as if he rejects what had become a rather tired convention of this fiction by the 1980s. Another reason for this difference might be the writers' presentation of time. *Davy* describes a period far removed from the reader's implied present, whereas Robinson's retention of place names helps to substantiate the possibility that America might imminently rebuild itself. Names in *The Wild Shore* thus retain their connection with actual locales, albeit ruined ones. Although Robinson bases his narrative on a journey, once again, by a boy named Hank Fletcher, his text establishes a terrain full of echoes from earlier SF. Allusions to Aldous Huxley, Jerry Sohl, and Jules Verne punctuate the narrative, and it can be no coincidence that the author of a fictional work within the novel should be called Glen Baum. This is not to argue that Robinson is depicting a new Oz, but, rather, that like Russell Hoban he presents a landscape filled with the traces of earlier fiction. Hank's progress through the California landscape thus supports an ongoing dialogue with the people he meets about the kinds of stories, historical and otherwise, that have been circulating. Like Huck Finn (echoed in his initials), Hank simultaneously shows a skepticism toward stories and a fascination with them, because they act as pointers toward possible histories and raise disturbing questions about whether Hank belongs in any national group. His older companion, Tom (another Twain analogue), constantly relates the travelers' experiences to external events, at one point declaring, "We're like Japs after Hiroshima."[43] Traditionally, journey narratives head toward a goal or point of achieved knowledge. This does not happen in *The Wild Shore*, which denies any final resolving certainty: "I don't have a dog's idea what it meant," we are told.[44]

Exploration rather than excavation characterizes Denis Johnson's *Fiskadoro,* set mainly in a postnuclear Florida, in which a central character performs a ritual recitation to preserve memory of prewar America. In his "The Fifty States in Alphabetical Order" routine, all the names are linked to a "series of mental pictures, and each picture joined to the next in a chain of imagined sights and sounds."[45] Through his recitals of this list, the Declaration of Independence, a description of the bombing of Nagasaki, and other texts, Mr. Cheung denies the popular description of nuclear war as the End of the World.[46] By organizing reading groups, he attempts to link these recitals to the local community to induce an awareness of location within the locale, but it remains an open question throughout the novel whether this attempted remembering of place and history will succeed. The stark alternative is a "totally blank screen" memory. Cheung feels himself to be a walking anachronism, and the physical beauty of the Florida Keys distracts the locals from larger questions of their relationship to the outside world. His place names constantly risk becoming free-floating terms without any shared referents. Here, as in Hoban and Robinson, the problem of making sense of the postnuclear world has become one of language itself.

Similarly, David Brin's *The Postman* also retains actual place names in its Oregon setting, which in this case has a slightly different effect. Brin's protagonist stumbles across the dead body of a postman, dons his uniform, and even quixotically tries to revive his civic function. Thus, he becomes a walking palimpsest himself, attempting to reenact the functions of following set routes and conveying messages to different recipients. Brin's Oregon has lapsed into different domains, including one centered on a sentient computer (the Cyclops) housed in the former state university at Corvallis. When the Cyclops offers to help the protagonist by offering him an itinerary codified in a map, "it was covered with an impressive array of computer graphics, charting out in fine symbols the path he should take in establishing a postal network in northern Oregon. He had been told the itinerary was designed to take him most efficiently around hazards such as known lawless areas and the belt of radioactivity near Portland." As Gordon scrutinizes it, his suspicions grow: "The longer he examined the map, the more puzzled he grew . . . Against his will he began to suspect it was designed instead to take him far *out* of his way. To waste his time, rather than save it."[47] At this point he realizes that the map is an exercise in deception designed to damage his own mental mapping of the state for fear that he might establish a rival power base. Brin's narrative also describes the experiences of a character on the ground, embedded in the concrete signs of a nuclear aftermath.

Mapping out postnuclear landscapes presents the physical acts of exploration or excavation as a search for a lost social whole. The terrain in these narratives is scarred, ruptured, and, in many cases, scarcely recognizable, posing unpredictable dangers for the protagonists. The land thus raises basic issues of survival that had previously been taken for granted. The landscape also carries its own history, which the reader unpicks through the actions of the protagonist in a tortuous attempt to discover how the nuclear disaster came about.

CHAPTER 13

Future Reportage on World War III

In one form or another, all the narratives examined in this volume have dealt with war. In many cases the duration of combat is telescoped into a single day known variously as "X-Day," "Doomsday," or just "The Day." However, the Cold War also saw the emergence of a quasi-documentary subgenre that described a conduct of the war that was repeatedly imagined but never actually took place. The roots of this subgenre lie in the future histories that became popular in the late nineteenth century, particularly after the success of George Tomkyns Chesney's *The Battle of Dorking* (1871). This body of writing has been definitively examined by I. F. Clarke in his pioneering study *Voices Prophesying War,* where he shows that the main impetus behind its development was the imperial rivalry between European powers and the United States.

In the wake of World War II, the expectation of yet another war very soon became a routine ingredient within Cold War discourse. James Burnham, for instance, dramatically opened his 1947 study *The Struggle for the World* with "The Third World War began in April 1944" and went on to outline a prolonged super power confrontation between the United States and the Soviet Union. The nuclear age for Burnham signified an indefinitely prolonged state of war readiness, especially as the Cold War had entered an "explosive state" where hostilities could break out any time over the next five years.[1] Although George Orwell ridiculed Burnham for being "too fond of apocalyptic visions," he nevertheless incorporated many of the latter's ideas into *Nineteen Eighty-Four.*[2] Burnham was playing his part in making familiar the concept of an imminent war, and the message seemed to be getting through, because soon after the Communist takeover of Czechoslovakia in 1947 a Gallup poll found that 73 percent of Americans believed a third world war was inevitable.³ This public expectation obviously arose from a number of factors, but one important source was the literature of imminent nuclear holocaust that became increasingly prevalent in the postwar period.

Within months of the end of the Second World War, *Life* magazine was preparing its readers for the next international conflict. "The 36-Hour War," which appeared in the 19 November 1945 issue, was about just that subject: preparedness. The article was designed as a commentary on and fictional extrapolation of the warnings expressed by General Henry H. Arnold, commander of the Air Corps, for the United States never to let itself slide into a state of military vulnerability. Nowhere is mention made of Pearl Harbor, but its shadow falls right across American defense deliberations of the late 1940s and beyond: "Weeks and weeks of congressional hearings in 1945 laid bare the scandalous negligence before the Japanese attack on Pearl Harbor; and God knew, the Republicans cried, that the same Democrats were still in office and showing nothing like the required alertness against the new perils."⁴ The perception of danger, paradoxical as it sounds for an America with its economy buoyant and its monopoly of the atomic bomb, is written into "The 36-Hour War" as a sneak attack from enemy bases located, bizarrely, in equatorial Africa. The article raises the problem of defense against atomic rockets—virtually impossible, even with interceptor rockets—and argues that the best defense is the promise of overwhelming retaliation. Despite the deaths of some forty million citizens and massive devastation, the essays insist that the United States can win the war, but this assertion is offset by the grim graphic of New York in ruins.

From the same period Will F. Jenkins (Murray Leinster) narrated similar unprovoked attacks in *The Murder of the U.S.A.* and *Fight for Life* (1947) by an unnamed enemy. The first of these is a strangely abstracted narrative where the origin of the attack is left unexplained. Most cities are destroyed, and survivors use a system of underground bunkers called "Burrows" that ultimately prove to be ineffective. Leinster's major purpose is to document the physical and psychological effects of the attack: "The nation they had believed they guarded was dead; its cities not even heaps of debris, but merely hollowed chasms in which poisonous radioactive gases formed and seeped out upon the countryside. The Burrows were useless, and doomed. The nation was a chaos of tiny, isolated hamlets and small towns, united only in their hatred of the unknown enemy."⁵ Leinster's narrative sets the tone for subsequent accounts of nuclear attack, presenting it as unexpected, well-planned (cities and Burrows are targeted), and delivered over the North Pole. Since the only country to possess such sophisticated military technology is the United States, the attack constitutes a fantasy reversal, where American know-how is turned against the United States.

Accordingly, for H. Bruce Franklin the novel presents a "glorification of the doctrine of nuclear deterrence" regardless of the civilian casualties involved.[6] The fact that the enemy is initially unknown is an important consideration since Leinster's novel predated the souring of relations between the United States and the Soviet Union. Unfortunately, he awkwardly attempts to combine reportage with the detective genre as his hero tracks down the aggressors. The result is that some sections describe the arrival of bombs with the omniscient clarity of a chronicle, and other chapters focus tightly on the investigation. The latter uncovers spies at the heart of the U.S. military establishment, revealing that Leinster's narrative is one of betrayal. In both these cases, American military technology was projected onto a hostile nation and then directed against itself, as if expressing the fear that this technology might slip all too easily out of Western hands.

Life magazine by 1945 had established itself as a leading source that exploited the interaction between graphics and written text. It is the sequence of imagery that conveys the immediacy of the war, but, more importantly, the illustrations make it clear that the conflict is playing itself out symbolically through the destruction of stylized images of the American nation. Tom Shippey has examined the related cases in American science fiction of disfigurement to the Statue of Liberty, which represents iconically the fate of the United States. Thus, in one of Shippey's examples the statue has fallen on its side and is excavated later as a neglected artifact, and in the second (from Norman Spinrad's 1973 story "A Thing of Beauty") the statue has lost its head. Shippey comments, "Evidently, the Statue is America, showing a light to the rest of the world, unable to see that light itself, self-blinded self-mutilated."[7] Such images might carry far more force than the text, which in the *Life* narrative is rather understated. There are seven illustrations in all, each one supplementing the basic narrative of sneak attack, response, and final victory. The first shows an aerial view of Washington, D.C., with an atomic blast superimposed. In the foreground stands a shape resembling an enormous glowing blade pointed at the United States. Then a two-page spread extends the panorama to Earth viewed from the stratosphere, showing the trajectory of rockets falling on American cities. By this point a disturbing possibility has crept into the narrative, one voiced by General Arnold, that the enemy can, "without warning, pass over all formerly visualized barriers and can deliver devastating blows at our population centres and our industrial, economic or governmental heart."[8] In other words, there may be no defense against such an attack. This issue proved to be one of the longest-running controversies of the Cold War, from the civil defense debates of the 1950s right up to Star Wars in the 1980s.

If *Life* evokes an America shattered by a preemptive atomic strike, the reader obviously wonders about the national means of retaliation. Illustrations then show a radar installation (a "spotty defense in future wars") and an enemy rocket being intercepted, then another two-part spread showing an underground A-bomb factory and launching bunker. Here the text begins to diverge from the graphic material in an interesting way. The caption to the spread reads "US Makes Its Counterattack," but the picture shows no activity. Its very stasis reinforces the ideological depiction of "fortress America" that has been emerging. Pictorially, the United States is shown passively as the victim of aggression, nowhere more clearly than in the penultimate illustration. This depicts masked invading troops repairing the telephone exchange of a small town. Sprawled in the wreckage of the switchboard is a buxom blonde, while near her in the middle ground a soldier appears to be aiming a phallic bazooka at the ground. If the small town is a synecdoche of the nation, the blonde is its personification, metaphorically violated by the invading enemy. The final illustration shows technicians testing for radioactivity in the ruins of New York. As far as the eye can see, the city is destroyed—except for the two lions at the entrance to New York Public Library. These creatures traditionally symbolize bravery or an indomitable spirit, but once again the image is totally static. By the end of "The 36-Hour War," a total disparity has become evident between the textual narration of military triumph and the graphic narration of vulnerability and destruction. We actually *see* no evidence of America's stated capacity to achieve victory in an atomic war.

Understandably Hiroshima functions as a major reference point throughout writings on nuclear war, explicitly so in Philip Morrison's contribution to the 1946 *Federation of Atomic Scientists* symposium publication *One World or None*. Morrison played his part in the Manhattan Project and was sent to Japan to report on the Hiroshima bombing. As he explains in the preamble to his essay "If the Bomb Gets Out of Hand," the streets of Hiroshima are rather remote for American readers, and so he engages in an experiment in transposition, literally bringing the atomic bomb home to Americans by imagining a strike on Manhattan. The result he describes in graphic detail:

> From the river west to Seventh Avenue, and from south of Union Square to the middle thirties, the streets were filled with the dead and dying . . . They were chiefly charred black on the side toward the bomb. Everywhere in this whole district were men with burning clothing, women with terrible red and blackened burns, and dead children caught while hurrying home to lunch . . . The parapets and the porches tumbled into the streets, the glass of the windows blew sometimes out and sometimes in, depending on the complex geometry of the old buildings.[9]

Morrison is caught in something of a double-bind here. On the one hand, he wants to be as precise as possible about effects so as to avoid the charge of alarmism; on the other hand, the very orderliness of his description would have been unavailable to an eyewitness, whose experiences would have been locally vivid but confusing. Possibly to counteract this effect, Morrison follows John Hersey's strategy of giving grim vignettes of casualties: "The man who saw the blast through the netting of the monkey cage in Central Park, and bore for days on the unnatural ruddy tan of his face the white imprint of the shadow of the netting, was famous."[10] Shadowing was one of the peculiar characteristics of photographs of Hiroshima, where the atomic blast had imprinted on the ground shadows of objects and even of a human being apparently sitting on the steps of a bank. This effect became central to Ray Bradbury's 1950 story "There Will Come Soft Rains," where a bomb blast has imprinted the shadows of a family on the wall of their house, like a photographic negative.[11]

The persistence of Hiroshima as a point for measuring the scale of subsequent imagined nuclear wars is demonstrated in the 1960 pamphlet *Community of Fear*, published by the Center for the Study of Democratic Institutions. Here the example is a ten-megaton bomb dropped on downtown Los Angeles. The firestorm of Hiroshima gives the precedent for what would happen:

> The area would be one great sea of fire, which would burn until there was nothing more to consume. A good proportion of the metropolitan area's three-and-a-half million cars and trucks would be lifted and thrown like grotesque Molotov cocktails, to spew flaming gasoline, oil, and automotive shrapnel onto and into everything in their paths. In an instant most underground gasoline and oil tanks would rupture and explode within the blast area, and a large proportion of the remainder of the firestorm radius would follow, each in its own particular manner—pumps and pies sheered and, finally, higher and higher ambient temperatures which would soon expand, rupture, and explode the remainder.[12]

There is no attempt here to dramatize the event through an eyewitness or to symbolize survival through iconic buildings. Instead, a remorseless chain of explosions is described in order to evoke a local spectacle of total destruction.

A perception of the disproportion between the brief duration of a nuclear attack and its consequences is expressed ironically in the condensation of a third world war into a short story. Murray Leinster's "Short History of World War Three" ironically telescopes its action into a little more than twenty-four hours for its mock reportage on the war that never happened. A Soviet submarine in the Bay of California is welcomed by the Americans as if on a friendly visit, and similar events occur where apparent aggression is smothered by friendly behavior thinly masking military superiority. The climax comes when the United States demonstrates a new computer that can set its rockets to intercept any incoming missiles. At this point the Soviets give up and even abandon communism. Leinster's coda declares that "World War Three was a psionic war, instead of an atomic one, and people ought to realize it."[13] "Psionic" is a misnomer here, referring to the paranormal; Leinster seems to mean simply "psychological." But more importantly, the preamble to his story reflects on how difficult it is to pin down an exact meaning to "war." The reason is that by the late 1950s the term had become thoroughly assimilated into Cold War discourse. In 1958 the sociologist C. Wright Mills commented that "the drift and the thrust toward World War III is now part of the contemporary sensibility—and a defining characteristic of our epoch."[14] Indeed, the very fact that Leinster adopted a drily humorous tone in his short story suggests that the next world war had become a routine fear. Mills argues that the sheer expectation of war runs the risk of turning into a self-fulfilling prophecy.

The Cold War was a period of extended emergency with the specter of nuclear war symbolized in one of the most famous icons of the time: the doomsday clock on the cover of the *Bulletin of the Atomic Scientists,* which showed only a few minutes to midnight. Time itself took on a special importance as imminence or warning time, and, correspondingly, scenarios of World War Three usually stressed brevity as well as scale. The time scale might vary from a matter of hours to a month, but the duration is closely connected to the projected destruction of nuclear weapons. Just as Leinster diminishes the status of the event he describes, so J. G. Ballard reduces world war to an incidental background event taking second place to the health of the American president in "The Secret History of World War 3" (1988). Narrated by a pediatrician living near Washington, D.C., the story facetiously combines eyewitness reporting with a satirical perception that even nuclear war has become a media event. The war lasts "barely four minutes," and the narrator confesses that he is "virtually the only person to know that it ever occurred."[15] Ballard satirizes the U.S. preoccupation with its own president—the aging Ronald Reagan, "this robotic figure with his eerie smiles and goofy grins"— and the media distortion of priority in giving Reagan's blood pressure and bowel movements priority over mounting tensions between the super powers. Hostilities finally break out with nuclear launches from both sides, but to uninhabited areas, and a ceasefire comes into operation almost immediately. By this time Reagan has become completely identified with his TV image, so much so that the narrator isn't sure that he is alive. It is a measure of the fact that the Cold War was about to end when Ballard published his story and reduced the whole issue of nuclear warfare to such black humor.

Although Leonard Engel and Emanuel S. Piller's *World Aflame* was published in 1947, their narrative accepted it as inevitable that the Soviet Union would construct (and, if necessary, use) an atomic bomb. *World Aflame* is presented as a U.S. government report on the Russian-American War five years after it breaks out in 1950. It is framed partly as a new plan that "coordinates every last detail of our national life into the war effort."[16] The complaint that became increasingly voiced during the Cold War that U.S. life was becoming militarized has become literally true under the pressure of the war, where survival is critical. Like Leonard Engel himself, the main narrator is a journalist given special status as a government spokesman, and it falls to him to summarize the history of the war. His account, however, glosses over the specific event—a military confrontation over the Black Sea—that triggers hostilities. Furthermore, although the Soviets are presented as aggressive and war-mongering, it is the United States that launches the first major air strike against 143 Russian cities. In response the Red Army overruns West Germany and South Korea. The United States begins to deploy biological weapons, and in reprisal the Soviets bomb a number of American cities. This is the point where eyewitness detail begins to enter the narrative in its account of the destruction of Chicago: "Entire sections of Chicago appeared to be evaporating into pillars of dust which were rising into the atom cloud overhead. Behind these pillars, the sky was red with flame. As I watched, the glow became brighter. The dust columns themselves seemed to be catching fire."[17]

The description presents an apocalyptic reversal of the imagery in Exodus 13, where pillars of cloud and fire providentially guide the Israelites toward the promised land. Here the effect is of erasure and spectacle. The description gradually closes in on buildings nearer to the observer: "Several buildings about 600 yards up the bank of the river were burning, great sheets of flame rising out of their walls, up into the sky . . . And a huge slick of oil was blazing in midstream." The journalistic authenticity of such accounts grows out of their echoes of World War II, but with a further extrapolation signaled when the narrator summarizes, "This was Hersey's *Hiroshima*—ten times worse—in my own country."[18]

World Aflame is an unusual description of a war that drags on for five years and is continuing even at the moment of the fictional report. It describes a process of escalation seemingly without end as each side develops more and more drastic weapons. Essentially it is a war in the air where infantry campaigns prove inconclusive, and despite the U.S. deployment of "counter-bomb rockets," plague virus, and radioactive dust, the Soviet Union appears to be indestructible. In fact, the Soviets have a relatively abstract role to play in *World Aflame,* where they function as an anonymous belligerent regime compulsively attacking the United States with any means to hand. The book accordingly gives an account primarily of American war damage and survival. The national morale is the true protagonist here, embodied in the journalist observer who records his astonishment at the destruction of downtown Boston: "Before me stretched block after block of petrified waste. Where there had been old stone buildings there were now disorderly piles of rocks, bricks, and rubble. Where there had been more modern buildings, there was now a strange collection of skeletons."[19] In common with other accounts of World War III, *World Aflame* packs its main impact into such images of urban destruction familiar in Europe at the end of the last world war. And again like similar accounts, the narrative conveys its cautious stoicism imagistically through the survival of the dome of the Capitol and the White House, providentially saved amid the surrounding destruction of Washington.

Surveying publications such as this, Paul Boyer has explained: "These orchestrations of fear were undertaken quite consciously and deliberately. To many post-Hiroshima social observers, *fear* represented a potent lever of social change. From mass terror would spring a mass demand for the radical transformation of the international order upon which survival depended."[20] Boyer goes on to cite Philip Morrison's sketch "If the Bomb Gets Out of Hand."[21] In this case, no doubt the purpose was to shock readers into recognizing the appalling destruction that the bomb could bring. But even Morrison joins the more sensational narratives of nuclear attack in presenting America as the potential victim of unprovoked aggression. Despite the United States' temporary possession of a nuclear monopoly, these early narratives demonstrate a surprising degree of anxiety and vulnerability. For Burnham the whole fate of Western civilization depended on American preservation of that monopoly, but his very insistence thinly masks a recognition that the advantage would soon pass. Reports of the Third World War would have played their part in the creation of a public atmosphere of crisis favorable to a steady rise in defense expenditure. A rare exception to such narratives was John Lear's "Hiroshima, U.S.A.," which was an exercise in demystification. Lear admits that he was "under the persuasive spell of five years of propaganda to the effect that the A-bomb was all-powerful."[22] He then visited the British Civil Defence School at Easingwold near York and realized that a partial defense was possible after all against such attack (still the same premise) and applauded the first signs of a national civil defense policy taking shape. The kind of organization Lear endorsed was based closely on analogies with World War II and on a sense of scale derived from Hiroshima and Nagasaki, but the creation of the hydrogen bomb very soon rendered such measures obsolete.

The use of a periodical format to "report" on a future war was further developed in the special issue of *Collier's* of 27 October 1951, which was devoted to the "Unwanted War," took some ten months to prepare, and was addressed—notionally, at least—to Stalin and his Politburo. Its premises, as described by the editor, were "that the U.S. is supposed to have been hurt but not crippled by atomic bombs, and that internal revolutions in the Balkans and Russia itself played a part in the downfall."[23] The issue counters present threat (the "ominous substance of Soviet aggression") with the future warning of a narrative of World War III (starting in 1952) that is triggered by a failed assassination attempt on Tito and the invasion of Yugoslavia (a fictional actualization of a threat leveled by the Cominform in 1949). The Soviets drop atomic bombs on key American cities and then invade Western Europe and Turkey. The West, for its part, retaliates in kind until the Soviet Union collapses and a new era of peace begins presided over by the United Nations. As in *Life*, this issue contains strategic maps and aerial charts of Chicago and Detroit showing bomb damage. Now, however, the sequence of articles does not correspond to the chronology of future events. Thus, the most distinguished contributor to the three journalistic dispatches, Ed Murrow (who had reported on the London Blitz), describes the bombing of Moscow before we learn of the event to which this is a response. The Third World War is described throughout this issue as a familiar process all the easier to recognize from comparisons with World War II. Similarly, Murrow presents an implicitly familiar bombing sequence from briefing to encounter with shore defenses and bomb drop. The bombing of Moscow is a brief event and one without affect: "I saw it—something I can only describe as the flame of a gigantic blowtorch filtering through dirty yellow gauze. We felt nothing."[24] Murrow avoids the by then conventional icon of the mushroom cloud and the whole sublime dimension to the blast, minimizing its impact and diverting the reader from the contradiction between this event and the Western claim not to have bombed any Soviet civilian centers.

Murrow's laconic account sets up the next dispatch, the supposed "first eyewitness account" of Washington, D.C., after the bombing, which has a totally different style and which possibly draws on John A. Siemes's "Hiroshima: Eye-Witness" (*Saturday Review*, 11 May 1946). In order to strengthen the United States' status as victim of unprovoked aggression, Washington is described as a composite casualty, the personification of the nation itself. This report by an Associated Press columnist is placed under a vivid two-page spread graphically rendering the destruction of Washington. A sequence of present-tense statements draw out the importance of the attack: "The American capital is missing in action," "Washington is burning to death," and so on.[25] In fact, this description has a special symbolic force in showing the desecration of the "shrines that unite the American people." Thus, the dome of the Capitol—the metaphorical keystone of the capital—has been shattered, and for exactly the same reasons of symbolic restoration the rebuilding of Philadelphia's Independence Hall is given priority in a later sketch. Here again a contradiction emerges within the issue. The sequence of reports, dispatches, and journal narratives describes a stark confrontation between tyranny and freedom, represented nationally by the Soviet Union and the United States. Although a real effort is made to show that a new period of internationalism is being ushered in—an illustration for the Moscow Olympics of 1960 shows a multiethnic group of smiling competitors—the major role in the war and its aftermath is clearly played by the United States.

It is only partly true to describe this issue as a war narrative, since many sessions are devoted to the transformation of life in the Soviet Union once the war has finished. A future-retrospective diagnosis is thereby made of Stalin's Russia, whose collapse triggers a resurgence of economic productivity, religion, and artistic activity. Among the more famous contributors, J. B. Priestley (who had visited the Soviet Union in 1945–1946 on a lecture tour) punned in his title "The Curtain Rises . . ." to survey the phases of the arts since the revolution. He saw the postwar phase as the most deadening, characterized by uncritical adulation of Stalin and breaking links with the West. Arthur Koestler ironically applied the revolutionary paradigm against the supposed revolutionaries to demonstrate, with other contributors, the benefits of Ukrainian separation and the heroism of Siberian political prisoners who rose up against their guards. Koestler returned to the central trope of *The God That Failed* (1949) to reaffirm that communism was only faith to its followers outside the Soviet Union while internally it represented a system of robotization and repression. Koestler gives real substance to the periodical's analysis of Soviet society in his depiction of displaced children. Finally, Philip Wylie, in 1951 serving as an expert consultant to the Federal Civil Defense Agency, contributed a political sketch ("Philadelphia Phase") articulated as a romantic tug of attractions for an army major between a Russian conscript laborer and his American fiancée. Uniquely among the contributors, Wylie expresses doubt about the demise of communism. In 1951 he had published a novel about Communist saboteurs secretly assembling a bomb in New York, *The Smuggled Atom Bomb,* and in "Philadelphia Phase" has his narrator wonder about the Russian woman, "She would be an ideal agent for some plan to infiltrate post-war America with new discontents, new cells of Communists, a new underground."[26]

Most of the pieces in *Collier's,* however, were much more confident about the final defeat of Stalinism, and for that reason Paul Brians has described the issue as constituting the "ultimate cold war fantasy."[27] The columnist Walter Winchell addresses the Russian people in glowing millenarian terms to declare that a "golden age" had been realized now that the UN possessed supreme power, while John Savage in "Trouble at Tuaviti" describes how a Soviet platoon violates the idyllic peace of a South Pacific atoll to attempt to establish a missile guidance base there. This mythic "fall" into history is prevented by the quick thinking of an islander who tricks the Soviets into withdrawing under the impression that warships are on their way. Most of the sketches contrast Western material plenty with Soviet austerity, and the very format of *Collier's* helps this process. Koestler's account of deprivation and starvation in the gulags, for instance, is punctuated on its margins by a whole series of advertisements for everything from wringer-washers to aftershave and electric organs. These reminders of the cornucopia of American consumerism reinforce the political positions adopted by Koestler and the other contributors. Here the medium really is part of the message.

The original plan of *Collier's* editors was to convert the issue into book form, but that was dropped as a result of hostile reactions in the European, especially French, press. Their hostility was explained by Koestler as a demonstration of a prevailing neurosis, an unwelcome reminder of what public fears were suppressing. The special issue "was unmistakeably intended to act as a warning and deterrent from war," Koestler continued; "the critics in the French press described it as an encouragement to war and an act of provocation."[28]

The documentary method pursued in *Life* and *Collier's* represented an attempt to "tell it like it was," except that, paradoxically, they were describing a kind of war that had never taken place and that, it was hoped, never would. Not surprisingly, covert political judgments find their way into this "future documentary" mode, like the anxieties over vulnerability in *Life*. *Collier's* by contrast is more triumphalist, although its ostensible internationalism—it is being produced by the UN Historical Commission—is somewhat offset by the self-evident military superiority of the United States. Also, the issue mounts a retrospective diagnosis of the faults of Stalinism, exploiting echoes of 1945 to present the West as both benign and generous in its aid. The true fantasy of *Collier's* lies in its expression of the desire for a conclusion to the Cold War. The hoped-for demise of Soviet aggression, however, was premature and world war continued to be a routine perception of the world political scene right through the fifties. Thus, C. Wright Mills's *The Causes of World War Three* mounts an inquest into the rise of parallel military machines in East and West, and Harry Welton's *The Third World War* displaces the concept of warfare on to trade, which is the new battlefield.[29]

The scenarios described in *Life* and *Collier's* had their military parallel in the institution of war-gaming, which became more and more important during the postwar period. This practice drew on the then-nascent field of game theory and developed into a major dimension to military planning, later to be ridiculed in *Dr. Strangelove* as a grotesquely elaborate form of poker.[30] Thomas B. Allen has described the ramifications of war-gaming, showing how it became the special province of certain planning groups and organizations like the RAND Corporation. Out of this context grew the second kind of "reportage" to be considered here: the future history of the Third World War. Allen shows how, since the late 1940s, NATO has been testing out scenarios where Warsaw Pact forces invade Western Europe, and this is the same pattern followed in a work written by a former NATO commander.[31] In General John Hackett's *The Third World War, August 1985* war breaks out when the Soviet Union invades West Germany and Yugoslavia with the aim of bringing about the collapse of NATO. At first overwhelming superiority of arms and men give them victories, until the Western allies rally and force the armies back toward the Russian border. At this point the hawks in the Kremlin bring about the launch of a single nuclear device, which explodes over Birmingham. The West responds with four devices (two American and two British) that destroy Minsk, and in the aftermath the Soviet Union collapses.

Unlike the works discussed previously, Hackett does not explain how he has managed to assemble his narrative. His volume does include some eyewitness accounts, and his sequel, *The Third World War: The Untold Story*, contains a number of letters from soldiers and salvaged documents, but essentially the effect of confusion that is central to most nuclear fiction is lacking here. Essentially, Hackett's 1978 history presents a description of the strategy of both sides, appearing in the process to "make a case for preparing for a conventional war in Europe."[32] This sidesteps the major issue of whether nuclear weapons were so dangerous as to make war obsolete, a view held by Linus Pauling, for example. Most of the volume describes campaigns rather similar to World War II but with updated technology, and it's liberally illustrated with photographs of modern weaponry.

Nuclear weapons are the wild card in the pack, since "nobody, anywhere, knew what would happen" if they were used in battle.[33] Leaving aside the inherent implausibility of the Soviets launching a single missile, the destruction of Birmingham is described from the periphery inward following the sequence of heat-wave, blast, and firestorm: "Within a second or so of the detonation the blast-wave hit the city centre beneath the fireball. The enormous pressures had the effect of instantly crushing all buildings below it so that what remained was only a levelled mountain of rubble . . . Within three kilometres of Winson Green [ground zero] nothing survived, every building and structure being reduced to rubble and strewn across the roads so that the entire area looked like a gigantic rubbish heap."[34] The implicit presence of a witness/observer is never made explicit or referred to the perceptual limits of any individual casualties, unlike John Hersey's *Hiroshima,* which traces out the experiences of six survivors. Hackett minimizes affect in his attempt to maximize clarity, specifying exactly what damage is caused at different distances from the blast center. Thus, he relates that "the human casualties resulting from the detonation of the nuclear weapon were horrific" because people's light dress gave them no protection; the account continues that "approximately 300,000 were killed within minutes by the heat and blast effects of the weapon or were subsequently to die unattended by any medical or rescue team."[35] The description stays safely general, on the level of discursive statistics, so that the claims of tragedy are neutralized by the even, matter-of-fact tone where nothing impedes the process of explanation. The event is further scrutinized by Hackett's dismissal of the electromagnetic pulse and by his minimalization of one of the worst aspects of such explosions: fallout.

The two nuclear strikes do not receive equal attention because Hackett is so intent on hammering home the point that the Soviet Union was a "grim totalitarian system whose extension worldwide was the openly avowed intention of its creators."[36] So Minsk receives four missiles (proof of Western resolve), whose effect, as the four fireballs combine, is described as follows: "What seemed about to form huge mushrooms was now writhing in promethean patterns, turning, twisting and whirling, beginning within one minute to form a single colossal cloud rising to a height of some 25 kilometres across a span of 30 or 40 and now spreading in one single blanket across the sky. The blinding light from the central pillar lasted a full twenty seconds even in the clarity of an August afternoon sky."[37]

The differences between the nuclear strikes have ideological implications. In Birmingham the battered rescue services pull themselves together to reestablish some kind of order and to confirm to the reader that the spirit of the Blitz is not dead, whereas in Minsk the city becomes ringed with KGB units to prevent the locals from leaving the area. The Birmingham description notes human and civic casualties; the account of Minsk returns to the nuclear sublime of early descriptions of the atomic bomb. The cloud over the latter city is a spectacle implicitly testifying to Western military capability. That being the case, Hackett's concluding remarks on this episode are somewhat disingenuous. He wonders "why such an appalling disaster should ever have been invited and who was to blame," continuing: "There will probably never be an answer."[38]

Hackett was taken to task by some reviewers for the tendentious premise of the Soviets launching a single missile, for the blatant imbalance of nuclear destruction (and of attention to that destruction on both sides), and for a sequence of events favorable to the West: "By portraying the Russians as losing the conventional war in Europe, Hackett avoids having the West use nuclear bombs first. Had he let the war go against the West, he would have had to deal with the well-known NATO doctrine that stipulates the United States will use nuclear weapons rather than lose to the Soviet Union in a conventional war in Europe."[39] In short, the choice of scenario was dictated by the adverse image of the West that would have been presented by a first nuclear strike. One of the most enthusiastic readers of Hackett's first volume was Ronald Reagan, for a number of reasons: It suggested that a limited nuclear war was possible; it projected an image of the Soviet Union as despotic and aggressive; and it anticipated Reagan's subsequent Star Wars initiative.[40]

Hackett's future chronology was elaborated on in Dean Ing's *Systemic Shock,* which takes the year 1996 as its crisis point, this time between a Chinese-Indian alliance and between Russia and the United States. A series of further nuclear attacks follows on from the first assault on "Dead Day," but Ing devotes relatively little attention to military strategy or the terrain after nuclear strikes, which function as an abstract background to the main action in this hybrid work that focuses on the training of the protagonist to become an expert warrior. Ing's heavy emphasis on individualism has its anachronistic side, since Ted Quantrill develops into a latter-day "gunsel" and is named after the organizer of a group of Confederate guerrilla fighters in the American Civil War. By the end of *Systemic Shock,* a new "streamlined" America has emerged thanks to its Mormon leadership and the assistance of Standard Oil.

The same year that Hackett's first volume was published there appeared a similar exercise in projection, *World War 3,* edited by the British physicist Shelford Bidwell. Like Hackett, Bidwell was a former officer in the British Army and coordinated a team of contributors who produced a survey of postwar military and political history and an account of a world war that breaks out in 1983. Bidwell rejects the position adopted by Burnham and others that World War III had already started, distinguishing between situations of actual combat and armed readiness by calling the latter a "world-wide state of warfare."[41] The trigger to war in Bidwell's case is West Germany's development of its own nuclear weapon. This is unacceptable to the Soviets, who, after an ultimatum, invade West Germany in a "police action," an ironic echo of the United States' rationalized intervention in Korea in 1950. Initially the move is a success thanks to NATO divisions and the hesitancy of the U.S. president. Once these are corrected, valiant resistance is offered by the sheer weight of Warsaw Pact forces, which makes it look as if their victory is assured. At this point we move into a more speculative dimension: "What a nuclear attack of even moderate heaviness would mean for *society* is anyone's guess and as much the domain of science fiction as of science."[42] With great honesty the climactic chapter, "Doomsday," refuses the impetus toward nuclear holocaust by abandoning the previous narrative and simply rehearsing some consensus information about such a war. Although we are told that the imagined scenario of nuclear war "seeks to highlight important detail rather than attempt a complete, self-contained narrative," the second part scarcely presents a narrative at all, offering factual data instead, probably in an effort to contain the subject and exclude any emotive aspects.

The persistence of such genre assumptions is revealed in Michael A. Palmer's *Arctic Strike!* billed as a "visual novel of the war of tomorrow."[43] This work describes the Arctic campaign of the Third World War when the Soviets launch an invasion of Norway from the Kola Peninsula, crossing Finnish and Swedish territory in the process. After their advance is halted, the offense crumbles and a peace treaty restores the status quo. Palmer's narrative acknowledges its debt to Hackett and similarly uses as illustrations photographs taken from the U.S. Department of Defense publication *Soviet Military Power.* Accordingly, part of the novel is taken up with the description of NATO and U.S. military tactics, minimizing references to civilian casualties and recording military fatalities abstractly as numbers. The reader is thus buffered against the physical suffering of war while being invited to "witness" vicariously a future campaign given actuality by quoted statements from the participants and sample diagrams of the terrain. Most crucial of all, the novel describes a nonnuclear war, basing itself on an arbitrary premise that allows for comparisons with World War II, while the overwhelming majority of nuclear fiction refuses such analogies as deceptive and anachronistic. The novel's use of documentary paraphernalia—photographs, battle plans, quotations from "documents," etc.—thus turns out to be an imposture and a pretext for supplying the reader with information about armaments.

The application of documentary methods to the nuclear subject ultimately fails because of the sheer number of unknown factors. The various works considered here have all been selective in the extreme and, as often as not, more interesting for their exclusions and implications than for what they state explicitly. This gives these works their abiding value as cultural documents from different phases of the Cold War. Since they are speculative narratives, their generic status remains ambiguous, somewhere between reportage and fiction. And it is no coincidence that novelists should contribute to them (Koestler and Wylie to *Collier's*) or that fiction should supply them with points of reference (Nevil Shute's *On the Beach* in Bidwell). Even Dropshot, the U.S. plan for war with the USSR drawn up in 1949 immediately after the latter exploded its first A-bomb, is described by its editor as a probable failure: "It would have meant that America would have been in for a very long war that would have been fought in all likelihood, much as George Orwell thought it would be fought in his novel *1984*: two exhausted giants hurling missiles at each other from time to time in an interminable and inconclusive war that ruined the world."[44] Yet again, probable future turns out to resemble fictional extrapolation.

The end of the Cold War did not by any means see the end of extrapolations of future war narratives. One of the most complex is Eric L. Harry's *Arc Light,* which describes the holocaust triggered by an invasion of South Korea by the North, Russian deployment of nuclear weapons against an expansionist China, and a near-coup by a renegade Soviet general. Like *Fail-Safe* and *Dr. Strangelove,* Harry's novel assembles a montage sequence of narrative segments located variously in command centers, special installations, airports, and infantry bases. It combines graphic descriptions of individual and group deaths, like that of a U.S. commander once his base is struck and he endures the sudden rise in atmospheric pressure: "As the pressure exceeded thirty pounds per square inch, his lungs were emptied of air and his organs began to burst and hemorrhage in a rapid progression towards death. He mercifully lost consciousness before the radiant heat of the fireball, now shining directly onto his body, raised the temperature of first his skin and then the bone and tissue that composed his body above their burning points, reducing much of him to the elements."[45] Harry uses a strategy we have seen earlier of slowing down an instantaneous process of destruction in order to identify the mini-phases within the literal disappearance of the victim. Graphic as such descriptions are, Harry's novel has a more ironic point to make about nuclear combat—namely, its potential for confusion. Whether a local action is taking place in a command center or in a civilian location, no one has an adequate grasp on what is happening. The situation is made all the more complex by the rivalry within the U.S. and Russian establishments alike, between hawks and doves, but ultimately, yet again, nuclear forces escape human control.

CHAPTER 14

Beyond the Cold War

The 1980s marked the last major wave of fiction dealing with nuclear war. Once the Soviet Union collapsed, the Cold War ended. But of course nuclear weapons continued to exist. A number of novels were published over the following decades that still address the nuclear threat but that reflect considerable difficulty in identifying the new enemies of the United States and in setting up speculative narratives of nuclear conflict. Alternate histories articulate a different kind of hypothesis from the novels discussed in this volume, which dramatize wars that might happen in the imminent or far future. Alternate history fiction asks instead not what might happen but what might have happened *if* a given sequence of events had taken a different route.

One such novel is Brad Ferguson's *The World Next Door,* which describes the United States in the aftermath of nuclear war. Like David Brin's *The Postman* and many other nuclear novels, it situates its action in a very specific area—the Adirondacks in Upstate New York—and describes the desperate efforts citizens are making to rebuild some kind of civic order. The lapse into a pretechnological economy, the physical dangers presented by wandering looters, and the emptying of urban centers are all familiar aspects of this fiction, as are the efforts of characters to understand what has happened to the United States, done partly by examining a map where all the major cities have been X'd out. The unusual dimension to Ferguson's narrative emerges when characters register strange dreams of push-button phones, government health warnings on cigarette packets, and other cultural details that would have been contemporary reality to the first readers of the novel. It gradually becomes clear that the United States has endured not one but two nuclear strikes, one when the 1962 Cuban crisis erupted into war and the other in the 1980s when

231

the Soviet Union invaded Western Europe. The characters in the novel are thus picking their way through a landscape destroyed twice over.

Another novel that takes the Cuban missile crisis as its reference point is Brendan DuBois's *Resurrection Day*, whose action takes place during 1972 in the aftermath of a nuclear war that has reduced the United States to a minor player on the world scene despite the fact that it still possesses nuclear weapons. The narrative is focused primarily through Carl Landry, a reporter for the *Boston Globe* who was serving in Vietnam when the war broke out. The choice of a journalist as protagonist is a shrewd one because it gives a very strong investigative impulse to the plot. Throughout the novel Landry is trying to answer exactly the questions that would be presenting themselves to the reader: How did the war break out, and how is the United States coping with its newly diminished stature in the world? His search for information leads him to discover that there is an underground network of survivors living in the ruins of New York City and that Britain is colluding with sections of the U.S. Army to introduce a militaristic dictatorship—hence the irony of the novel's several allusions to *Nineteen Eighty-Four*.

One of the main points of the novel is its investigation, retrospectively, of the United States' handling of the nuclear threat. DuBois even quotes at one point from the 1961 Department of Defense booklet *Fallout Protection—What to Know and Do About Nuclear Attack*.[1] The latter is ridiculed by Landry for its bland reassurances against despair. More importantly, Landry unconsciously repeats the exposés of the 1970s when he discovers the secret history of the Cuban crisis, namely the covert roles played by the military both in the United States and the USSR, which was opposed to appeasement. It emerges that the nuclear strikes against Cuba and its invasion were ordered by General Ramsey Curtis against the wishes of President Kennedy. Curtis is an obvious version of Curtis LeMay, the head of Strategic Air Command who did recommend preemptive nuclear strikes and an invasion of Cuba and whose notorious speech about gelding the Russian bear is quoted in the novel. Landry, who clearly functions as an author surrogate in the novel, reflects on the crude polarities of the Cold War, which precluded rational thought: "Everything was black and white. We were good, they were bad. Our nuclear weapons were good. And of course, we ringed the Soviet Union with bombers and troops and spy planes and missiles and submarines because we were going to 'contain' them."[2] Landry actually meets with General Curtis and engages in a dialogue with him and with other representatives of the nationalist cause, but ultimately the main source of hope in the novel comes with the decision of the *Globe* to flout military censorship and publish the story about Curtis's actions. The novel has very little to say about how this exposure will defeat the forces of crude nationalism; it is enough that the publication reasserts the cherished national ideal of freedom of the press. It is surely no coincidence that the main events of the novel should take place in the same year as the Watergate scandal.

William R. Forstchen's *One Second After* represents the rare case of a novel that explicitly situates itself within the tradition of Cold War nuclear fiction. Although Forstchen includes several allusions to Pat Frank's *Alas, Babylon* in his text, there is one major difference from the earlier novel. Frank describes the gradual spread of radiation and the illnesses that induces. Forstchen, in contrast, describes an attack on the United States through an electromagnetic pulse that knocks out electricity everywhere. Where Frank identifies the aggressor as the Soviet Union, Forstchen leaves the identity of the aggressors unknown. Like Frank, he describes the difficult process of survival, but it is a relatively sanitized process and one that tests out the hypothesis of removing electricity from daily life. Again like Frank (and like the 1983 film *Testament,* set in a township near San Francisco), he explores the difficulties of survival by focusing on a small-town community, that of Black Mountain, North Carolina, a "Norman Rockwell town" at least initially. As refrigerators cease to work, the problem of a food source becomes acute, and then disease increases dramatically as medicines become exhausted. The problem of fending off attacks from outside becomes increasingly difficult, and in such situations the role of the protagonist becomes crucial.

John Matherson saw military service in World War II, and his role is not simply to apply organizational skills to maintain some semblance of community life but also to serve as the carrier of cultural memory. It is through his perspective that a whole sequence of references are made to older films and fiction, some bearing on the Cold War, like *The Twilight Zone,* and others emerging from a tradition of westerns: When thieves are summarily tried and condemned, one character condemns the action as lynch law; a group of looters becomes known as the Posse; and so the analogies multiply. The problems of survival enable Forstchen to examine aspects of contemporary American culture in order to demonstrate its vulnerability at virtually every level. In former crises the media had bonded the nation, but now the media has been removed in one fell swoop. Survival in American culture has been traditionally linked to mobility, but now there are virtually no means of transport. The persistence of allusions to film cumulatively suggest a culture of the spectacle, whereas the urgencies of the new situation demand inventive action.

The novel takes on a semi-official status with a foreword by former Speaker of the House Newt Gingrich, who insists that the novel's future history effectively counters national indifference to the subject. "Few in our government and in the public sector have openly confronted the threat offered by the use of but one nuclear weapon, in the hands of a determined enemy, who calibrates it to trigger a massive EMP burst."[3] In a similar spirit, U.S. Navy captain Bill Sanders supplies an afterword that draws the reader's attention to the 2004 U.S. government report of the Commission to Assess the Threat to the United States from Electromagnetic Pulse (EMP) Attack. The latter mounted an investigation of the catastrophic damage to national life that could be done by a single nuclear device whose provenance, since the end of the Cold War, could be uncertain: "What is different now is that some potential sources of EMP threats are difficult to deter—they can be terrorist groups that have no state identity, have only one or a few weapons, and are motivated to attack the U.S. without regard for their own safety. Rogue states such as North Korea and Iran may also be developing the capability to pose an EMP threat to the United States and may also be unpredictable and difficult to deter."[4] *One Second After* is clearly attempting to flesh out this perceived threat and reflects the report's difficulty in identifying America's enemies by omitting any narrative backstory that would contextualize the attack. The latter thus comes as a bolt right out of the blue, and its suddenness is implied in the title. It is likely that Forstchen had in mind the doomsday clock and related titles from the Cold War, where midnight figured as a symbolic moment of ultimacy.[5] Even in these bleak narratives there is a tentative hope of restoration after a nuclear war, but Forstchen austerely closes his text by denying such a possibility: "The world had changed forever, the America they knew . . . never to return."[6] Although he focuses his action on a small town, the fate of Black Mountain is the fate of the nation itself.

Where Forstchen describes an event almost as impersonal as an act of nature, a number of novels have engaged with the conspiratorial dimension to nuclear terrorism. Tom Clancy's 1991 novel *The Sum of All Fears* still evokes a relatively stable world of super powers, although the power blocs are beginning to collapse. With explicit acknowledgment of his debt to Thomas Harris's *Black Sunday* (1975), where terrorists plan to detonate a bomb at a New Orleans sports arena, Clancy describes how a group of Islamists secure the assistance of an East German nuclear technician to repair and arm a device salvaged from the Golan Heights on the Syrian-Israeli border. They also place the device in a sports stadium, this time in Denver. Despite the fact that the KGB has now adopted a relatively benign stance toward the West, and despite the suspicious nature of the machine tools ordered up, the process of construction goes undetected, and the only thing that prevents a massive blast is a minor fault in the bomb's construction. Clancy points to a clear moral at the end of the novel when a character declares, "Nuclear weapons cannot be un-invented." But the novel also demonstrates the comparative ease with which such a device could be constructed and placed.[7] He has stated in an interview that the development of nuclear technology means that a handful of scientists could now do what in the past it took a whole team to achieve and also that the proliferation of information has opened up the process still further, commenting that "information is the universal solvent of secrecy . . . The more that is known, the less remains that can be kept unknown."[8]

Interviewed while he was working on his novel *America,* Stephen Coonts was asked about the weapons left over from the Cold War: "Biological weapons are certainly horrific, but to my mind, the forty thousand nuclear warheads lost somewhere in the former Soviet Union are the most dangerous items on this planet today. Control of these weapons ought to be America's Number One foreign policy objective, and it isn't."[9] This urgency has informed Coonts's three novels, which explore the possible consequences of nuclear weapons falling into the hands of terrorists. *Final Flight* takes one of the least likely cases of such a loss—the theft of devices from a U.S. aircraft carrier—to hammer home the point about danger. Here the conspiracy is mounted by Islamic terrorists and almost succeeds were it not for the initiative of a pilot while the theft is in progress. It is not surprising that Coonts, who served as a naval pilot in the Vietnam War, should privilege the actions of his serial protagonist Jake Grafton, but the latter's actions expose a second target in these novels. While the terrorists present a clear and unambiguous danger, there is a second latent threat nearer to home, namely the sluggishness of official responses to danger. The ultimate nightmare scenario would be the destruction of an American city, but in *America,* where a U.S. nuclear submarine is stolen from under the eyes of military observers, Manhattan and Washington are e-bombed, acts that demonstrate the power of the terrorists to strike where they please. As we have seen in Forstchen's *One Second After,* the result of such an attack is not destruction but total disempowerment. Luckily the attacks were localized in this case.

Liberty addresses a different danger: the inadequate supervision by the Russians of their own nuclear weapons. Four devices are sold again to Islamic terrorists and shipped to the United States from Pakistan in disguised containers. In a remarkably convenient coincidence, an ex-KGB officer who is a friend of Jake Grafton's tells him of the sale, and the search for them—the central action of the novel—begins. Again, luckily Grafton is given carte blanche by the U.S. president to take whatever measures are necessary to find the bombs. What makes this novel more complex in its treatment of the nuclear subject are the negative, retarding effects of U.S. bureaucracy, interagency rivalry, and the hostility displayed toward Grafton's quickly assembled team of hackers, former thieves, and other "specialists" by the FBI and local police forces. In that sense, the novel makes an implicit case for the existence of the Bureau of Homeland Security. In another way, however, it demonstrates that there is a threat at home from domestic dissidents, terrorist cells inside the United States, and even renegade CIA agents. The climax takes place at the Statue of Liberty, where the terrorists have mounted a nuclear weapon within the torch. The national symbolism could hardly be clearer.[10]

One of the most forceful fictional commentaries on 9/11 is *King of Bombs* by the Canadian journalist Sheldon Filger, who actually lived through the World Trade Center bombings. Filger has written frequently on the dangers of nuclear terrorism and has accused the Clinton and Bush administrations of being blind to that threat. In a 2009 article he argues that "the 9/11 attack displayed ruthless execution and bold planning. It also established a benchmark for future attacks on America, with a far higher threshold of destruction."[11] He claims that the most likely target would be an urban center and that there would not be much difficulty in obtaining fissile materials from Russian sources, concluding grimly that "this vital issue of national survival has barely seeped into the public consciousness."

Filger had already given narrative form to this warning in his novel *King of Bombs*, whose title alludes to the massive Soviet Tsar Bomba that was detonated in 1961. This conspiracy is mounted by al-Qaeda, whose agents salvage fissile material from a U.S. bomber that crashed in a Canadian lake in the 1960s. With the help of a former Soviet nuclear machinist (who is beheaded after his services are no longer required), the group constructs a powerful H-bomb in Canada and then ships it in a disguised crate to New York where it is housed in a Korean cleaning company ready for detonation. Filger impressively combines the suspense of the investigation with step-by-step explanations of the emerging information necessary to understand the magnitude of the threat; the bomb could potentially kill some eighty million people. In that sense, the novel is intensely didactic, being directed toward an uninformed reader who is willing to assimilate the information. In a contrast so striking that it approaches satire, the U.S. president and vice president and the directors of the CIA and the Office of Homeland Security are shown to be ridiculously complacent about nuclear terrorism. Indeed, at one point the president declares, "Homeland Security is a PR package to make the American people feel more secure. In reality, all the different parts of it, the FBI, Customs, Immigration, they'll all continue to function normally as they always have."[12]

"Normally" here means separately, and the novel makes a powerful case that the conspiracy is only thwarted thanks to those intelligence agents capable of synthesizing and drawing together information from quite diverse fields ranging from nuclear technology to Islamist rhetoric and banking practices. Although the immediate action is played out in Canada and the United States, the novel's field is global, just as the conspiracy is multinational, involving the active support of Iran and North Korea. A key figure linking these groups is a Pakistani named Pervaz Khan, a very thinly disguised version of Abdul Qadeer Khan, who was responsible for the proliferation of nuclear technology in the Middle and Far East.[13] The reader follows the gradual piecing together of snippets of information to assemble a plot working simultaneously on the levels of banking, technology, and espionage. The traditional resolution of a thriller narrative is the last-minute neutralization of the danger, and sure enough the bomb is discovered. But Filger refuses to close his novel so reassuringly and finally reveals that there is a second bomb, also timed to detonate very soon—so soon that the president's only recourse is to drop a preemptive device to stop the larger detonation. The novel ends with the president ordering the bombing of Los Angeles.

The role of the president is also a factor in Whitley Strieber's *Critical Mass,* in which another Islamist conspiracy takes place. The plotters detonate a nuclear device over Las Vegas, presumably as a demonstration of their ability to strike anywhere rather than from their hostility to gambling. After this object lesson, the president is compelled to state publicly his "conversion" to Islam. Strieber's narrative is unusual in the high profile given to religion. Indeed, he presents the reader with a Western Christian mirror image of the conspirators' ideology of a worldwide spiritual struggle. The fact that the Vatican is also attacked demonstrates that their target is not exclusively the United States. The novel also evokes an American intelligence community riddled with traitors, and therefore agencies like the CIA present the most immediate enemy to the protagonist, who is himself a serving CIA officer.

The fact that several novelists have written about the terrorist threat, especially since 9/11, reflects a level of public concern that was shared by the SF author and nanotechnology specialist Arlan Andrews Sr. In 1992, while working in the White House Science Office, he was struck by the rigidity of government thinking on terrorism and as a result organized SIGMA, an independent think tank of SF writers that now advises the Department of Homeland Security on potential threats. Its membership includes figures like Ben Bova, David Brin, and Jerry Pournelle.[14] The organization forms a symbolic link between fiction, politics, and the technological specialties of its members, a link that emerges in the repeated allusions nuclear novels make to related nonfictional texts.

Undoubtedly, the most sustained and elaborate depiction of nuclear terrorism to date has been Robert Ferrigno's Assassin trilogy that began in 2006 with *Prayers for the Assassin.*[15] As he has stated in an interview, the immediate trigger for the novel was 9/11, which Ferrigno saw as exposing weaknesses in the U.S. system. Hence, he has extrapolated possible global consequences of an Islamist conspiracy: "The US could never be defeated militarily within the near future, but the actions of the nineteen illustrated our Achilles heel, the disparity between the power of faith in a liberal western democracy and a fundamentalist Islamic world. In a war that will likely go on for decades, which power bloc do you think will tire first?"[16] *Prayers* takes as its starting point the premise that the United States has lost this struggle and the nation has divided mainly between the Islamic Republic of America and the Christian Bible Belt (roughly equivalent to the southern states in the Civil War), with the western states maintaining varying degrees of independence. The crisis year when this transformation started was 2015, when Zionist conspirators detonated nuclear weapons in New York, Washington, and Mecca. The resulting status quo is only achieved after years of internal strife.

Ferrigno was clearly aware of the risks in depicting an Islamic version of the United States but manages to avoid a crude demonization of the faith. What differentiates his novels from other treatments of nuclear terrorism is his exploration of long-term consequences and the importance he attaches to religion as a test of will.

The action is pushed forward by two protagonists—Rakkim, a martial arts specialist, and his lover Sarah, an academic historian. They thus combine the two impulses central to the plot: the retrospective investigation of the nuclear bombings and the exposure of a conspiracy to maintain the public version of events. As in earlier Cold War accounts of nuclear war, the bombings figure as a rupture with the past, a rupture visualized through the surveillance photographs of the bombed cities: "Rakkim stared at the stark, black-and-white wreckage of New York City and Washington, D.C., trying to take in the miles of shattered concrete and twisted metal, but it was impossible. The photo from ground zero at Mecca was dramatic, but equally devastating. The nuclear bombs that had been smuggled into New York and Washington, D.C., had been city busters, but Mecca had better security. The device detonated at the height of the hajj had been a suitcase nuke, a dirty bomb."[17] The difference is that the latter religious sites have been preserved, although heavily polluted with radiation. Mecca is hardly visualized at all, whereas the photographs of the American cities surely carry implicit analogies with those of Hiroshima. The final revelation in *Prayers for the Assassin* is that the terrorists who planted the bombs, including one in China that failed to detonate, were themselves Moslems, and therefore the regime and official history alike have been founded on deception and bad faith.

The two possibilities considered so far have been alternate histories and accounts of nuclear terrorism. However, there is a third scenario—nuclear war between the United States and Russia—and this is the one explored in Eric L. Harry's *Arc Light*. The novel opens with the North Koreans invading the South in a reprise of 1950, the difference being that overt hostilities break out between China and Russia. When the United States goes on to a higher alert, a Russian general is so outraged that he launches a coup and sends missiles against America. General Zorin appropriately carries the same name as the ex-KGB villain in the 1985 James Bond film *A View to a Kill,* since his ambitions for a Greater Russia are comparable. The novel follows a method very similar to that in Burdick and Wheeler's *Fail-Safe,* where suspense is maintained through a rapid montage of scenes, each with its own location and time heading. Harry also demonstrates that one complicating factor is belief, neither side being willing to trust the other. If anything, the situation is even worse in *Arc Light,* because at least the Cold War gave a set of guiding parameters to the action. Now bewilderment is as strong as mistrust, and the constant jumps between scenes put the reader in a position to identify with some of the characters who are experiencing great difficulties in piecing together the sequence of action. The multistranded plot makes it virtually impossible to get an overview of events.

Arc Light continues the tradition of most nuclear war fiction in using its action to turn an ironic spotlight on American political attitudes. One of the more enlightened Russian generals, for instance, points out a problem in U.S. reaction to nuclear war: "Nothing like this has happened to them since the Civil War ended in 1865! They have forgotten what war is like, and instead of concluding . . . that war, any war, is a human disaster of unparalleled magnitude—the Americans are choosing instead to attribute their civilian dead to villainies, to atrocities, to *us!*"[18] In other words, he accuses the United States of engaging in a collective attribution strategy where they deflect responsibility for these events onto a demonized Other. Harry's novel demonstrates another general characteristic of post–Cold War fiction in its evocation of a continuity between past and present. Its very title does this, since Operation Arc Light was the name originally given to a 1965 campaign deploying B-52 bombers over Vietnam and thereafter to any similar campaign of air support. In that respect, *Arc Light,* like other narratives produced since the end of the Cold War, continues to investigate the United States' own nuclear past.

Notes

Introduction

1. Leinster, *Fight for Life,* 4.
2. Ibid., 53.
3. Amis, *Einstein's Monsters,* 9.
4. *Diacritics* 14 (Summer 1984) on nuclear criticism; *Science Fiction Studies* 13.ii (July 1986) on nuclear war and science fiction; *PLL: Papers on Language and Literature* 26.i (Winter 1990) on nuclear criticism.
5. Derrida, "No Apocalypse, Not Now (full speed ahead, seven missiles, seven missives)," 20–31.
6. Norris, *Derrida,* 164.
7. Hinds and Windt, *The Cold War as Rhetoric,* 6. The other major study in this area is Medhurst et al., *Cold War Rhetoric.*
8. Williams, "Nuclear Criticism," 246–48.
9. Schwenger, *Letter Bomb,* 31.
10. Dowling, *Fictions of Nuclear Disaster;* Mannix, *The Rhetoric of Antinuclear Fiction.*
11. Berger, "Nuclear Energy," 121.
12. Jacobs, *The Dragon's Tail,* 120–21.
13. Ruthven, *Nuclear Criticism,* 82.
14. Bush, *Modern Arms and Free Men,* 171.
15. Klein, "The Future of Nuclear Criticism," 77.
16. Clarkson, *The Last Day,* 183.
17. Stone, *Literary Aftershocks;* Cordle, *States of Suspense;* Jacobs, *Dragon's Tail.*
18. Cordle, "Cultures of Terror," 1186–99. Further commentary on this subject can be found in Norris, "'Nuclear Criticism' Ten Years On," 130–38.

1. The Atom—From H. G. Wells to Leo Szilard

1. Kuhn, *The Structure of Scientific Revolutions*, 111.
2. Weart, *Nuclear Fear*, 55.
3. Cromie, *The Crack of Doom*, 1.
4. Priestley, *The Doomsday Men*, 207. The book was originally subtitled *An Adventure* and then, in the 1949 edition, *A Thriller of the Atomic Age*.
5. Cromie, *The Crack of Doom*, 177–78.
6. Soddy, *The Interpretation of Radium*, 8.
7. Ibid., 233, 221.
8. Frederick Soddy's "Lecture to the Royal Engineers, 1904," quoted in Carlisle, *Scientific American Inventions and Discoveries*, 373.
9. Soddy, *The Interpretation of Radium*, 4, 33.
10. Ibid., 246.
11. Ibid., 247, 249.
12. The full dedication reads "To Frederick Soddy's 'Interpretation of Radium' / This Story, Which Owes Long Passages to the Eleventh Chapter of That Book, Acknowledges and Inscribes Itself." An alternative American title for the novel is *The Last War: The World Set Free*.
13. Wells was, however, well aware of how new technology could change the paradigm of war and designed *The War in the Air* to demonstrate that air forces would compel us to replace the notion of war fronts with that of areas.
14. Haynes, *H. G. Wells*, 78.
15. Canaday, *The Nuclear Muse*, 231.
16. Wells responded to Soddy also in revising his statement in his 1902 essay "The Discovery of the Future" to say that the "most insistently convincing" nightmare involved the extinction of life in a far-future ice age. In 1925 he added a footnote stating that "the discovery of radio-activity has changed all that." Wells, *The Discovery of the Future*, 34, 37.
17. Wells, *The World Set Free*, 56. Unless otherwise stated, subsequent page references are to the 1988 edition.
18. Wells, *The World Set Free* (1924), 9.
19. Ibid. (1924 ed.), 10.
20. Wells, *The World Set Free*, 139.
21. Ibid., 137.
22. Ibid., 71.
23. *The Hell Bomb* was the title of the journalist William L. Laurence's 1951 book about the hydrogen bomb. Wells, *The World Set Free*, 86.
24. Graves, "Fiction," 837.
25. Brians, *Nuclear Holocausts*, 3.
26. Wells, *An Experiment in Autobiography*, 569.
27. Wells, *The World Set Free*, 176, 172.
28. Bartter, "Nuclear Holocaust as Urban Renewal," 150–51.
29. Soddy's comments of 1915 are quoted in Weart, *Nuclear Fear*, 29; Wells, *Experiment in Autobiography*, 569.

30. Sinclair, *The Millennium,* 33.

31. Ibid., 47.

32. Capek, *Krakatit,* 15.

33. Meek, "The Red Peril," 492. The passage continues: "The vacite bombs destroyed the air and would produce a complete vacuum for several hundreds of yards around their place of explosion or 'point of burst,' and it was confidently expected that they would destroy any aircraft within the radius of this action. Uranite was a substance somewhat allied to the common radite, but immensely more powerful. Its action was to start a progressively atomic disintegration in anything other than air with which it came in contact."

34. Vanny, "The Radium Master," 271.

35. Dickson, *H. G. Wells,* 362.

36. David C. Smith, *The Correspondence of H. G. Wells,* 531. Wells had already used the planned title for his film in 1928 for a collection of journalistic pieces entitled *The Way The World Is Going: Guesses and Forecasts of the Years Ahead.* In 1938 Korda had made the film *Things to Come* in collaboration with Wells.

37. Kirchwey, "When H. G. Wells Split the Atom," 154.

38. Merricks, *The World Made New,* 163.

39. Soddy, *The Story of Atomic Energy,* 35, 117–18.

40. Ibid., 124.

41. Ibid.

42. Quoted in Berger, *The Magic That Works,* 76.

43. Campbell, *The Atomic Story,* 231.

44. Ibid., 279.

45. Ibid.

46. Weart and Szilard, *Leo Szilard,* 16. Szilard also read Wells's *The Open Conspiracy* (1928), which called for a general revolution in ways of thinking.

47. Lanouette, *Genius in the Shadows,* 179.

48. Canaday, *The Nuclear Muse,* 206, 20.

49. Szilard, "President Truman Did Not Understand," 68–71.

50. Szilard, "The Physicist Invades Politics," 7.

51. Lanouette, *Genius in the Shadows,* 318. The film, directed by Norman Taurog, was made with the blessing of President Truman, who had unwittingly supplied its title at a White House meeting. The MGM press kit described the film as "the story of the men and women who solved the atomic mystery, and who helped America win a life and death race to become the first nation to build an atom bomb. And, possibly most important of all, it is a story that tells all the peoples of the world just what they face today—the crucial problem of whether atomic energy is to be used for good or evil" (http://www.atomicbombcinema.com/english/image_gallery/beginning/begin_end_intro.htm). One of the major special effects in the film was the elaborate duplication of the atomic bomb's lightning flash.

52. Lanouette, *Genius in the Shadows,* 362.

53. Szilard, "The Diary of Dr. Davis," 52.

54. Ibid., 51.

55. Szilard, *The Voice of the Dolphins and Other Stories,* 143.

56. Ibid., 135.
57. Ibid., 160.
58. There is a historical irony in Szilard's subject, since in the very year when *The Voice of the Dolphins* was published the U.S. Navy began a program of experiments in the military uses of dolphins for mine detecting and other purposes. The 1973 film *The Day of the Dolphins*, based on Robert Merle's 1963 novel *Un Animal doue de raison* [A Sentient Animal], incorporates aspects of Lilly's work and describes how dolphins could be used in a plot to kill the U.S. president.
59. Lanouette, *Genius in the Shadows*, 415.
60. Canaday, *The Nuclear Muse*, 234–35.
61. Szilard, *The Voice of the Dolphins*, 98.
62. Canaday, *The Nuclear Muse*, 236. In his review of this collection, Robert M. Hutchins more ironically pointed out that although the dolphins are intelligent, they are "unable to advance any ideas for the salvation of the world that had not been previously put forward by Leo Szilard" ("Szilard and the Dolphins," 290).

2. The Dawn of the Atomic Age—The Bomb and Hiroshima

1. "The Atomic Bomb," 87B.
2. Boyer, *By the Bomb's Early Light*, 5. One of the first such accounts was *The Murder of the U.S.A.* by Murray Leinster writing as Will F. Jenkins, which describes the destruction of one-third of the nation in only forty minutes.
3. Groves, *Now It Can Be Told*, 326. Laurence had started reporting on nuclear research as early as 1940 with his article "The Atom Gives Up" in the *Saturday Evening Post* for 7 September. The FBI subsequently attempted to remove all copies of this issue from circulation.
4. Cooper, "The Whiteness of the Bomb," 105.
5. Laurence, "My Life in Atomland," in *Men and Atoms*, 97, 98.
6. Laurence, "The Atomic Age Begins," in *Dawn Over Zero*, 9–10. Laurence reinforces the biblical parallels in his account by heading his opening chapter "Genesis." The report originally appeared in the *New York Times* on 26 August 1945. Laurence revised this description extensively for his collection *Men and Atoms*.
7. Laurence's books were *Dawn Over Zero*, *We Are Not Helpless* (1950), *The Hell Bomb*, and *Men and Atoms*.
8. "The Bomb," 19.
9. McCullough, *Truman*, 443, 455, 456. In public Truman was more upbeat in announcing that the bomb was a "harnessing of the basic power of the universe" and declaring America's custodial responsibilities: "We must constitute ourselves trustees of this new force—to prevent its misuse."
10. General Farrell, one of the witnesses to the Alamagordo test, declared frankly, "Words are inadequate tools for the job of acquainting those not present with the physical, mental, and psychological effects. It had to be witnessed to be realized" (Jungk, *Brighter Than a Thousand Suns*, 184). For commentary on this iconography, see Gleick, "After the Bomb."

11. Thomas and Morgan-Witts, *Ruin from the Air,* 326.

12. Laurence, "12:01 over Nagasaki," in *Men and Atoms,* 159–60.

13. Ferguson, "The Nuclear Sublime," 9.

14. Laurence, *Men and Atoms,* 197; and *The Hell Bomb,* 113. The Four Freedoms were enunciated by Roosevelt in his annual message to Congress on 6 January 1941 and consisted of freedom of expression and of worship and freedom from want and from fear.

15. George Burchett, *Rebel Journalism,* 2.

16. Wilfred Burchett, "The Atomic Plague," 23–24.

17. Laurence, "U.S. Atom Bomb Site Belies Tokyo Tales," 4.

18. Weller, *First into Nagasaki,* 18. Weller later recorded that "what remained fascinating for me was the constant revision of my own ideas of total-devastation and no-escape-from-the-bomb" (20). In 1943 he had received the Pulitzer Prize for reporting on the war in the Pacific.

19. Donovan, "U.S.: 60 Years Later."

20. Weller, *First into Nagasaki,* 302–3.

21. For information on responses to Hersey's *Hiroshima,* see Yavenditti, "John Hersey and the American Conscience," 24–49; and Boyer, *By the Bomb's Early Light,* 204–10.

22. Siemes, "Hiroshima: Eye-Witness," 24. Siemes's account was extensively summarized in Laurence's *Man and Atoms.*

23. Siemes, "Hiroshima: Eye-Witness," 41.

24. Hersey, *Interview.*

25. Brother Juniper reflects: "If there was any plan in the universe at all, if there were any pattern in a human life, surely it could be discovered mysteriously latent in those lives so suddenly cut off. Either we live by accident and die by accident, or we live by plan and die by plan" (Wilder, *The Bridge of San Luis Rey,* 5).

26. Laurence, *Men and Atoms,* 115; Weart, *Nuclear Fear,* 147–48.

27. Sanders, *John Hersey,* 46. Stressing the representative nature of these characters, Robert A. Jacobs has argued that "individuality is erased as a critical factor survivors" (*The Dragon's Tail,* 79).

28. Hersey, *Hiroshima,* 23. The book won a Pulitzer Prize in 1945.

29. Mas'ud Zavarzadeh has helpfully described disruptive moments in *Hiroshima* as making a "dislodging of consciousness" (*The Mythopoeic Reality,* 96).

30. Boyer, *By the Bomb's Early Light,* 208.

31. Yavenditti, "John Hersey and the American Conscience," 35; Boyer, *By the Bomb's Early Light,* 208.

32. Nadel, *Containment Culture,* 55–57.

33. Wilder, *The Bridge of San Luis Rey,* 129.

34. Quoted in Boyer, *By the Bomb's Early Light,* 206.

35. Hersey, *Hiroshima,* 15, 30.

36. Ibid., 44–45. Some details from this passage bear a striking similarity to Hemingway's description of political executions in the vignette to chapter 5 of *In Our Time.*

37. Hersey, *Hiroshima,* 66.

38. Scheick, "The Bi-Nuclear Voice of Hersey's *Hiroshima,*" 5.

39. Hersey, *Hiroshima,* 88.

40. Tanimoto was adopted as a cause by Norman Cousins, the editor of the *Saturday Review*, and on 11 May 1955 the hapless Tanimoto found himself transformed into a media personality on the NBC program *This Is Your Life*, which opened with predictable shots of the rising mushroom cloud.

41. Hersey, *Hiroshima*, 118.

42. Cordle, *States of Suspense*, 73.

43. The scientist was Louis Slutin, and the accident happened at Los Alamos in 1946, not during the initial Manhattan Project. Masters co-edited with Katherine Way *One World or None*, a collection of statements against the use of atomic bombs. He took a steadfastly negative view of the Japanese bombings, which he felt had no justification at the time other than as the beginning of the Cold War with Russia.

44. Masters's negotiations with David O. Selznick to make a film of *The Accident* were blocked by the State Department. Masters, "Foreword," *The Accident*, vii–viii. Masters and his wife left the United States after being dogged by the FBI and took up residence in England.

45. Morris, *The Flowers of Hiroshima*. Morris's son served in U.S. naval intelligence and visited Hiroshima soon after the bombing. Morris and her husband, Ira, founded the Hiroshima Foundation for Peace and Culture.

46. Cantor states of the Holocaust and the bomb that "we must re-understand ourselves as people who are capable of such acts." Capobianco, "An Interview with Jay Cantor," 6.

47. Cantor, *Krazy Kat*, 242.

48. Morrow, "How I Slouched Towards Hiroshima."

49. Sontag's essay appeared in *Against Interpretation*. Morrow's novel was issued by Tachyon in 2009.

50. Lydia Millet herself visited Hiroshima and Nagasaki while researching her novel. Her brief report, "The Humblest of Victims," appeared in the *New York Times* on 7 August 2005, and she incorporated details from it into the novel.

51. Millet, *Oh Pure and Radiant Heart*, 4. In the passage she echoes the creation of the world in Genesis, which is punctuated by the refrain "and God saw that it was good."

52. Jernigan, "The Nuclear Sublime."

53. Ferguson, "The Nuclear Sublime," 7.

54. Thackara, *America's Children*, 8.

55. Ibid., 174–75.

56. Ibid., 265–66.

57. Robinson, "A Sensitive Dependence on Initial Conditions," 440–51.

58. Boyer, "Exotic Resonances," 159.

3. The Debate over Nuclear Refuge

1. Levine, "Civil Defence vs. Public Apathy," 27.

2. Boyer, *By the Bomb's Early Light*, 175–77, 326. See Oakes, *The Imaginary War*, for an excellent overview of American civil defense during the Cold War.

3. Boyer, *By the Bomb's Early Light*, 321. Urban replanning was discussed in Lapp, *Must We Hide?*

4. Lang, *Early Tales of the Atomic Age*, 113. Mine shafts used as nuclear shelters made a ludicrous reappearance at the end of *Dr. Strangelove*, and underground automated factories were featured in Frederik Pohl's 1959 postholocaust story "The Waging of the Peace," where automated production methods have become the new enemy.

5. Grossman, *Neither Dead nor Red*, 42.

6. Quoted in Rose, *One Nation Underground*, 59.

7. Weart, *Nuclear Fear*, 206.

8. Spencer, "Fallout," 86.

9. Quoted in Edward James, *Science Fiction in the Twentieth Century*, 89.

10. For a discussion of Wylie and Caidin's relevant fiction, see Seed, *American Science Fiction and the Cold War*, 19–22.

11. Bradley, *No Place to Hide*, 165, 16.

12. Boyer, *By the Bomb's Early Light*, 92.

13. Bradley, *No Place to Hide*, 106–7.

14. Ibid., 92–93.

15. Among the many examples, see Chernus, *Dr. Strangegod*; and Cohn, "Sex and Death in the Rational World of the Defense Intellectuals," 687–718.

16. The case was described in Lapp, *The Voyage of the Lucky Dragon*.

17. Shute, *On the Beach*, 158.

18. Ibid., 187.

19. Weart, *Nuclear Fear*, 219.

20. U.S. Information Agency, "Infoguide 60–24, December 4, 1959; *On the Beach*," in White House Cabinet papers for December 7, 1959; Cabinet Series, Dwight D. Eisenhower Library, Abilene, KS.

21. "Possible Questions and Suggested Answers on the Film 'On the Beach,'" 8 December 1959, Eisenhower Library.

22. Teller and Brown, *The Legacy of Hiroshima*, 239, 241.

23. In that respect, Gerstell anticipates the Federal Civil Defense Authority's "Grandma's Pantry" campaign later in the fifties, which was promoted through images of old-fashioned kitchens and slogans like, "With a well-stocked pantry you can be just as self-sufficient as Grandma was" (May, *Homeward Bound*, 91–92).

24. Gerstell, *How to Survive an Atomic Bomb*, 105.

25. Ibid., 121–22.

26. Caidin at that time was working with the New York State Civil Defense Commission.

27. Morrison, "If the Bomb Gets Out of Hand," 3.

28. Lear, "Hiroshima, U.S.A.," 11, 15.

29. Tenn, *The Wooden Star*, 14.

30. Grossman, *Neither Dead nor Red*, 77–78, 102–3. Grossman rejects May's view (*Homeward Bound*) of a "hegemonic paternalism" in the FCDA as being based on insufficient data.

31. Rose, *One Nation Underground*, 130.

32. The full title of the 1945 Smyth Report was *Atomic Energy for Military Purposes: The Official Report on the Development of the Atomic Bomb Under the Auspices of the United States Government*.

33. Dearborn, "She'd Give up Everything for a Trip to the Moon," 7.
34. Merril and Pohl-Weary, *Better to Have Loved,* 89. The story was rejected by *Collier's* because it caused "revulsion" in the readers.
35. "That Only a Mother" was collected in Merril's *Out of Bounds* (1960). For valuable critical commentary on this story, see Cummins, "Short Fiction by Judith Merril," 202–14.
36. Judith Merril, letter, 19 February 1949, Merril Collection, National Archives of Canada, Ottawa.
37. *Six Steps to Survival,* a government pamphlet on civil defence, available in the 'Virtual Atomic Museum" at http://tinyurl.com/7nfxg3k.
38. In fact, this appropriateness was probably coincidental, because the title was chosen by Merril's publishers despite her preference for more explicit references to nuclear war. Merril and Pohl-Weary, *Better to Have Loved,* 99.
39. This story, collected in *The Martian Chronicles,* draws an explicit analogy between the outlines of the family members and photographic negatives, as if they are memento images of the family long after the family itself has been destroyed.
40. According to Peter Tate, Merril was a member of the United World Federalists and also a supporter of Gary Davis's World Citizen Movement ("The Fantastic World of Judith Merril," 7).
41. For commentary on the increasing prominence of doctors in the debate over fallout from the mid-1950s into the following decade, see Boyer, *Fallout,* 81–86.
42. Merril, The *Shadow on the Hearth,* 21.
43. Here Merril reflects the "mania for finding spies everywhere" (Brians, *Nuclear Holocausts,* 17). Brians's survey is an invaluable guide to this body of fiction.
44. Merril, *The Shadow on the Hearth,* 39.
45. Dowling, *Fictions of Nuclear Disaster,* 59.
46. Merril, *The Shadow on the Hearth,* 131–32.
47. Poore, "Books of the Times," 29.
48. In that sense it is not helpful to lump Merril's novel in with other narratives under the heading "The 'Civil Defence' Plot," as Martha A. Bartter does (*The Way to Ground Zero,* 122–23).
49. Merril, *The Shadow on the Hearth,* 192.
50. Robert Heinlein, letter to Merril, 7 November 1962, Merril Collection.
51. English-language transcript of interview with Elisabeth Vonarburg and Luc Pomereau in *Solaris* 69 (1986): 2, Merril Collection.
52. The TV play script was written by David Davidson and the production directed by Ralph Nelson.
53. This and subsequent passages transcribed from video recording of *Atomic Attack.*
54. Merril registered misgivings about this simplification when she saw the film and later recalled, "For the first time I became aware of the major differences in the media" (Merril and Pohl-Weary, *Better to Have Loved,* 100).
55. Merril, letter, 19 August 1958, Merril Collection.
56. Wylie, "A Better Way to Beat the Bomb," 42.
57. Peterson, "They Said It Would Never Happen," 4–5. Wylie had written to Truman to stress the importance of people remaining in the cities while under nuclear attack and sent an advance copy of *Tomorrow!* to Eisenhower. This novel and Wylie's other writings are discussed in chapter 5.

58. Grossman, *Neither Dead nor Red,* 62.

59. Foster, *The Rest Must Die,* 150.

60. Ibid., 120.

61. Blish, *So Close to Home,* 63.

62. "The Box" was also collected in Blish, *So Close to Home.*

63. Deer, "The Unavoidable Shelter Race," 66–67.

64. Blish, *A Case of Conscience,* 92. In his 1956 story "To Pay the Piper" (collected in *Galactic Cluster,* 1959), Blish dealt further with the neurosis-inducing conditions of living in underground shelters in the aftermath of a nuclear and biological war.

65. Ketterer, *Imprisoned in a Tesseract,* 99.

66. Kennedy's shelter campaign is discussed in Weart, *Nuclear Fear,* 253–58.

67. For a discussion of these and similar works, see Seed, *American Science Fiction and the Cold War,* chap. 11. In Berriault's novel preachers promote the cause of shelters by giving them an epic grandeur—"the greatest migration in the history of mankind is to be the migration underground into the shelters"—and by convincing their audience that descent really constituted a spiritual ascent (*The Descent,* 110–11).

68. Berriault, *The Descent,* 111.

69. Ibid., 165.

70. Dyson, *Weapons and Hope,* 88–89, 92.

71. Boyer, *Fallout,* 110–22. Among other reasons for the reduction of concern after 1963, Boyer cites the remoteness and abstraction of nuclear reality, the tranquillizing effect of the "peaceful atom" program, and the emergence of the New Left in the United States.

4. Do-It-Yourself Survival

1. Schelling, "Meteors, Mischief, and War," 293. The article also discussed Peter George's *Red Alert.*

2. Stone, *Literary Aftershocks,* 49.

3. Boyer, *By the Bomb's Early Light,* 260.

4. Frank, "Hiroshima: Point of No Return," 25. In the same article Frank notes that Nevil Shute fell into the "time trap" of postulating cobalt bombs after their obsolescence, expresses his interest in Andrew Sinclair's *The Project* (describing the launch of a missile against the Soviet Union by an unhinged scientist), and praises the satire in Gina Berriault's *The Descent.*

5. Frank, *Alas, Babylon,* xv.

6. Among other related works to draw on this book of the Bible, Ray Bradbury's *Fahrenheit 451* quotes from Revelation 22.2 on the tree of life immediately after a nuclear strike.

7. Frank, *Forbidden Area,* 20.

8. Frank, *How to Survive the H-Bomb,* 32.

9. Frank, *Alas, Babylon,* 85.

10. The missile in question is a heat-seeking Sidewinder, like those used against the Chinese during a crisis over Taiwan. When the novel was published, an officer in the military told Frank that such an error could not happen. However, in 1961 a Sidewinder homed in on the exhaust of a bomber from Biggs Air Force Base in Texas and the resulting detonation

caused fatalities. Frank noted with grim satisfaction that the event only confirmed his scenario. Frank, *How to Survive the H-Bomb,* 45.

11. Frank, *Alas, Babylon,* 87.
12. Ibid., 94–95.
13. Ibid., 98.
14. Frank, *How to Survive the H-Bomb,* 106.
15. Frank, *Alas, Babylon,* 117.
16. Ibid., 117–18.
17. Frank, *How to Survive the H-Bomb,* 88.
18. The film was directed by Ray Milland, who also played the lead role. In *How to Survive the H-Bomb* Frank identified Los Angeles as the city where the citizens would have the least chance of survival.
19. Owen, *End of the World,* 35. This novelization stays close to the script of the film.
20. Ibid., 109.
21. Frank, *Alas, Babylon,* 126.
22. The same echo of Pearl Harbor occurs in the 1952 film *Invasion USA,* where the U.S. president describes the attack by an unnamed Communist force as "another day of infamy."
23. Frank, *Forbidden Area,* 33. The title for the serial and UK edition of this novel was *Seven Days to Never.*
24. Frank, *How to Survive the H-Bomb,* 81.
25. Frank, *Alas, Babylon,* 161.
26. Frank, *How to Survive the H-Bomb,* 42, 10.
27. Ibid., 96.
28. Frank, *Alas, Babylon,* 144.
29. Frank, *How to Survive the H-Bomb,* 111.
30. Frank, *Alas, Babylon,* 316.
31. Brin, "Foreword," in ibid., xi.
32. Heinlein, *Expanded Universe,* 168. This was the first publication of the essay.
33. Ibid., 174.
34. Heinlein, *Farnham's Freehold,* 314.
35. Ibid., 40.
36. Clayton, "Planning for the Day After Doomsday," 49–53.
37. Clayton, *Life After Doomsday,* 142.
38. A connection between Dean Ing and Clayton can be found in the work of the survivalist Mel Tappan, whose book *Survival Guns* Clayton consulted. Ing contributed to Tappan's *Personal Survival ("P.S.") Letter,* a survivalist newsletter that was published between 1977 and 1982.
39. Ing, "Nuclear Survival," 167. In 1984 Ing published with Jerry Pournelle the nonfiction *Mutual Assured Survival,* which reverses the Cold War doctrine of Mutual Assured Destruction (MAD).
40. Endorsement in Ing, *Pulling Through,* i.
41. Frank had general recommendations to make about equipping the home as a potential shelter and singles out for praise the "subterranean fortress" at Sylvan Shores in Florida,

which accommodated twenty-five families on a private subscription basis. Frank, *How to Survive the H-Bomb*, 25.

42. Ing, *Pulling Through*, 30.
43. The main guide mentioned is Kearny, *Expedient Shelter Construction and Occupancy Requirements*.
44. Ing, *Pulling Through*, 142.
45. LeClair and McCaffery, *Anything Can Happen*, 271.
46. O'Brien, *The Nuclear Age*, 124. For critical commentary on this novel, see Schwininger, "Ecofeminism, Nuclearism, and O'Brien's *The Nuclear Age*," 177–85.

5. Philip Wylie on the State of the Nation

1. Wylie, "Science Fiction in an Age of Crisis," 234.
2. Wylie appreciated the "mordant scenery" of *Ape and Essence*, which he saw as a "logical extension of current events," and approved of Huxley's satirical inversions of Christianity (*Opus 21*, 198).
3. Wylie, "Science Fiction in an Age of Crisis," 239.
4. Bendau, *Still Worlds Collide*, 6.
5. When Wylie first submitted this story for publication, he was reportedly visited by an officer from Army Intelligence who threatened his life if he caused a "leak." Wylie agreed to shelve the story until the end of the war. Barshay, *Philip Wylie*, 68. This story resembles a similar investigation by Army Intelligence of SF writer Cleve Cartmill, whose 1944 story "Deadline" described a uranium-235 bomb in some detail. See Silverberg, "Reflections," September 2003 and October/November 2003, respectively.
6. In Derleth, *Strange Ports of Call*, 377 (ellipsis points in original).
7. Wylie, *Opus 21*, 256.
8. Wylie, "A Better Way to Beat the Bomb," 42.
9. Condon, "The New Technique of Private War," in Masters and Ways, eds., *One World or None*, 40. Condon later ran into trouble with the House Un-American Activities Committee. For full details, see Wang, *Science, Security, and the Cold War*.
10. In 1950 the U.S. Senate approved a bill granting the Coast Guard powers to stop and search suspect vessels. In that same year the *Bulletin of the Atomic Scientists* carried advertisements for devices like the "R-gun," which could be used to detect bombs.
11. Wylie, *The Smuggled Atom Bomb*, 107.
12. Wylie, *The Disappearance*, 49, 52.
13. Wylie's fear of the U.S. seaboard being mined by Soviet H-bombs led him in 1961 to send a detailed inquiry to Kennedy, whose presidential campaign Wylie had actively supported. Kennedy took the possibility seriously enough to pass Wylie's letter on to his military advisers.
14. Wylie, *The Disappearance*, 117.
15. Wylie was a strong supporter of the 1946 Baruch Plan for the international control of atomic weapons, which the Soviets turned down. The cover of *The Answer* carried the following endorsement by Baruch: "What Philip Wylie has said so interestingly and

beautifully I have tried to say in the proposals for an International Atomic Development Authority." Wylie also sent a copy of *The Answer* to J. Edgar Hoover, who had given personal attention to consolidating Wylie's security clearance in 1951.

16. Wylie, *The Answer,* 15–16.

17. Ibid., 47.

18. Wylie, *The Innocent Ambassadors,* xiv. In "Communism: A Mental Illness" Lindner and Wylie describe the Marxist state as basing itself on "institutionalized *paranoia*" (Wylie Papers, Princeton University Library, Princeton, NJ). In *The Innocent Ambassadors,* an account of a journey round the world with his wife, Wylie found himself constantly having to counter the abrasive effects of John Foster Dulles's visits. Wylie, who knew Dulles through his father, thought the latter had made a serious error in identifying communism with atheism rather than with the fate of humanity itself.

19. Wylie, "Panic, Psychology, and the Bomb," 40.

20. Wylie's contribution was "Philadelphia Phase." This issue is discussed in chapter 13.

21. Wylie, "The Bomb: Introduction," p. A, Wylie Papers.

22. Wylie, "The Bomb," pp. 60–61, Wylie Papers.

23. Bradbury, *Fahrenheit 451,* 160.

24. Wylie to Eisenhower, letter, 19 November 1953; and "The ABCs of the H-Bomb," p. 1, Wylie Papers.

25. Wylie, *Tomorrow!* 124–25, 49.

26. Ibid., 268.

27. Ibid., 298.

28. In a 1951 essay, "Terror—and the Terror Weapons," Wylie discusses popular hysteria and recommends that the mass media show "atomic bomb casualties from nudity through the most grisly burns to evisceration, decapitation, and the like" (p. 21, Wylie Papers). There is no evidence that they took up Wylie's suggestion.

29. Wylie, *Tomorrow!* 267.

30. Oakes and Grossman, "Managing Nuclear Terror," 367, 368. They point out that complimentary copies of *Tomorrow!* were sent out to state governors and civil defense directors and that the FCDA actively promoted the volume. For all his reservations about its grisly detail, Oakes himself admits that *Tomorrow!* "reproduces without significant exaggerations the basic assumptions of Cold War emotion management" (*The Imaginary War,* 77). FCDA director Val Peterson reviewed the novel, praising it for embodying the "new language" of atomic warfare" ("They Said It Would Never Happen," 4).

31. Wylie, *Tomorrow!* 353–54.

32. Eugene Rabinowitch to Philip Wylie, letter, 18 January 1954; and Wylie to Rabinowitch, letter, 27 January 1954, Wylie Papers.

33. Martin Caidin to Wylie, letter, 18 July 1954, Wylie Papers.

34. Caidin, *The Long Night,* 43.

35. Wylie to Eugene Rabinowitch, letter, 17 June 1960, Wylie Papers.

36. Wylie, "Why I Believe There Will Be No All-Out War," 22.

37. Ibid., 25.

38. Wylie, *Triumph,* 96. When Wylie had completed the novel he sent an advance copy to Eugene Burdick (coauthor of *Fail-Safe*), who praised the work to the *Saturday Evening*

Post: "In a remarkable and compelling manner Wylie takes his reader through the searing moments of atomic cataclysm. The pages describing what a world-wide atomic war will look like are utterly unique" (Eugene Burdick to James Perkins, letter, 6 November 1962, Wylie Papers).

39. Brians, *Nuclear Holocausts*, 347.
40. Wylie, *Triumph*, 39–40.
41. Ibid., 46.
42. Ibid., 240 (ellipsis points in original).
43. Wylie, "McNamara's Missile Defense," 182.
44. Orwell's *Nineteen Eighty-Four* is cited within the future timeline of Wylie's narrative as predicting that the world would be split between two "absolute dictatorships." Though by Wylie's 1984 there was still a democracy in the United States, the larger threat to the environment was going unheeded. Wylie, *The End of the Dream*, 197–98.
45. Wylie, "Deliverance or Doom," 80.
46. Wylie, "The Atomic Age—A Recapitulation," 1. Compare with Wylie's assertion in 1953 that "all 'freedom' depends basically on an absolute freedom to know" ("Knowledge for Man's Sake," 331).
47. Wylie, *The End of the Dream*, 95.
48. Carson, *Silent Spring*, 22.
49. Wylie, *The End of the Dream*, 158, 162.
50. Barshay, *Philip Wylie*, 67.
51. Wylie, *The End of the Dream*, 184.

6. Cultural Cycles in Walter M. Miller's *A Canticle for Leibowitz*

1. Brians, *Nuclear Holocausts*, 69.
2. These novellas were all published in *The Magazine of Fantasy and Science Fiction*. The differences between these texts and the final novel are examined in Secrest, *Glorificemus*, 103–7.
3. Senior, "From the Begetting of Monsters," 330.
4. Miller, *The Best of Walter M. Miller, Jr.*, 181–82.
5. For a critical discussion of Miller's short stories, see Samuelson, "The Lost Canticles of Walter M. Miller, Jr.," 3–26.
6. Miller, *A Canticle for Leibowitz*, 33.
7. Spencer, "The Post-Apocalyptic Library," 337.
8. Secrest, *Glorificemus*, 3.
9. Miller, *A Canticle for Leibowitz*, 206.
10. "The parchment codex was adapted to large books in emphasizing facility of reference and consequently lent itself to religion and law in the scriptures and the codes" (Innis, *Empire and Communications*, 140).
11. "Since the material of an earlier culture must be required, an extensive censorship emerged in which material suited to religion and law was given enormous emphasis" (ibid., 141).

12. Probably Miller's coinage, the term "autoscribe" has since become assimilated into computer software and company naming.

13. Miller and Greenberg, *Beyond Armageddon,* 10–11. The subtitle to the U.S. edition was *Twenty-One Sermons to the Dead.*

14. Miller, *A Canticle for Leibowitz,* 267–68. The space station is a probable allusion to the Soviets' first launch of Sputnik in 1957.

15. Hutcheon, *A Poetics of Postmodernism,* 125.

16. Percy, "Walker Percy on Walter M. Miller," 263.

17. Both stories are collected in Miller, *The Best of Walter M. Miller, Jr.,* 82–119, 332–87.

18. Miller, *A Canticle for Leibowitz,* 156.

19. Griffin, "Medievalism in *A Canticle for Leibowitz,*" 112–25.

20. Ibid., 114.

21. Miller, *A Canticle for Leibowitz,* 273. A similar shift occurs between different meanings for fire in Bradbury's *Fahrenheit 451,* between destructive power and the capacity to warm. The abbot in Book III of *A Canticle* is the third in a series of protagonists who, for Secrest, are "in conflict with authority and the world" (*Glorificemus,* 16).

22. Galouye, *Dark Universe,* 9.

23. Ibid., 123.

24. Ibid., 178.

25. Frye, *The Great Code,* 106.

26. Miller, *A Canticle for Leibowitz,* 266.

27. Eco, *The Middle Ages of James Joyce,* 45.

28. Cross, *The Oxford Dictionary of the Christian Church,* 235. David Dowling ingeniously glosses this term as a Joycean compositional metaphor suggesting a short discrete narrative unit (*Fictions of Nuclear Disaster,* 194).

29. Walker, "Reciprocity and Exchange in *A Canticle for Leibowitz,*" 67.

30. Miller, *A Canticle for Leibowitz,* 236. While the style of the passage partly echoes Auden's "Spain," the specific allusion here is to Tennyson's poem "Merlin and the Gleam," a monologue by the dying Merlin on a whole lifetime spent pursuing a will-o'-the-wisp, a fluctuating and fugitive goal that always lies just "over the margin."

31. Boucher, "The Quest for Saint Aquin," 379.

32. Miller, *A Canticle for Leibowitz,* 67. Miller's Flame Deluge conflates two biblical accounts of destruction and was probably influenced by Stephen Vincent Benét's 1937 story "By the Waters of Babylon," which describes a world laid waste by the "Great Burning." Miller respected this story enough to include it as a postholocaust narrative before the fact in *Beyond Armageddon.*

33. Miller, *A Canticle for Leibowitz,* 235.

34. Manganiello, "History as Judgement and Promise in *A Canticle for Leibowitz,*" 161.

35. The Russian protagonist in this story is a young woman who seeks revenge on the Americans for causing her to lose her baby in the invasion due to her poisoned breast milk. The invasion in the story is carried out with tactical atomic bombs. The use of Lucifer (the H-bomb) is considered.

36. Miller, *A Canticle for Leibowitz,* 255.

37. Percy, "Walker Percy on Walter M. Miller," 267.

38. Miller, *A Canticle for Leibowitz*, 143–44.

39. Scholes and Rabkin, *Science Fiction*, 225.

40. Miller and Greenberg, *Beyond Armageddon*, 13.

41. Ibid., 14–15.

42. Bisson describes his experience working on the project in "A Canticle for Miller: Or, How I Met Saint Leibowitz and the Wild Horse Woman but Not Walter M. Miller, Jr.," http://www.sff.net/people/tbisson/miller.html.

43. Miller, *Saint Leibowitz and the Wild Horse Woman*, 4.

7. The Pathology of Warfare in Bernard Wolfe's *Limbo*

1. Wolfe, "Author's Notes and Warnings," *Limbo*, 438.

2. In a roundtable discussion of the hydrogen bomb, Leo Szilard warned that American coastal cities would be the most vulnerable to attack. Bethe et al., "The Facts about the Hydrogen Bomb," 107.

3. It is mentioned, for instance, in Warrick, *The Cybernetic Imagination in Science Fiction*, and Dunn and Erlich, *The Mechanical God*.

4. Ballard, "From Shanghai to Shepperton," 119.

5. Mendelson, "Encyclopedic Narrative," 1270.

6. For a discussion of this aspect of *Gravity's Rainbow*, see Wolfley, "Repression's Rainbow," 99–123.

7. Koestler and Wiener are named in *Limbo*. Mumford's general discussion of the mechanization of humanity and his references to Wells, Toynbee, and Adelbert Ames and to William James's essay "The Moral Equivalent of War" make it virtually certain that Mumford was one of Wolfe's sources.

8. Hayles, *How We Became Posthuman*, 116.

9. Freud, *Civilization and Its Discontents*, 28–29.

10. Wiener, *Cybernetics*, 27.

11. Wiener, *The Human Use of Human Beings*, 214.

12. Hayles, *How We Became Posthuman*, 120.

13. Vonnegut, *Player Piano*, 105.

14. In identifying this process, Wolfe explicitly follows the argument of industrial rationalization put forward in James Burnham's *The Managerial Revolution* (1941), which helped Orwell shape *Nineteen Eighty-Four*.

15. Wolfe, *Limbo*, 140.

16. Toward the end of *The Human Use of Human Beings*, written during the height of the McCarthy witch hunts, he notes, "We have attempted to synthesize a rigid system to fight fire by fire, and to oppose Communism by institutions which bear more than a fortuitous resemblance to Communistic institutions" (229).

17. Mumford, *Programme for Survival*, 4; and *The Conduct of Life*, 223.

18. Wolfe, "Self Portrait," 72. Hayles notes the link in this story between cybernetics and McCarthyism (*How We Became Posthuman*, 308).

19. Agee's piece was first published in *Politics* (April 1946) as "Rough Sketch for a Moving Picture" and reprinted in Fitzgerald, *The Collected Short Prose of James Agee.*

20. Boyer, *By the Bomb's Early Light,* 278.

21. Mumford, *Programme for Survival,* 27; and *The Conduct of Life,* 5.

22. Wolfe, *Limbo, 191,* 162.

23. Ibid., 311.

24. Geduld, *Bernard Wolfe,* 45.

25. James proposed, "Instead of military conscription a conscription of the whole youthful population to form for a certain number of years a part of the army enlisted against *nature*" (*Essays in Religion and Morality,* 171).

26. Wolfe, *Limbo,* 93.

27. Walsh, *From Utopia to Nightmare,* 150.

28. Geduld, *Bernard Wolfe,* 47–48.

29. Wiener, *The Human Use of Human Beings,* 262, 141.

30. Wolfe, *Limbo,* 413.

31. Wolfe, *The Great Prince Died,* 395.

32. Wolfe, *Limbo,* 172.

33. Koestler, *Insight and Outlook,* 25.

34. Ibid., 36.

35. Wallace, "The Operation of the Last Resort," 24. The Soviet Union banned these operations in 1950.

36. The controversy is commented on by Wiener (*Cybernetics,* 148–49). A similar anxiety emerges over the function of electrotherapy in novels such as Ralph Ellison's *Invisible Man,* Sylvia Plath's *The Bell Jar,* and Ken Kesey's *One Flew Over the Cuckoo's Nest.* Wolfe knew Ellison well and would certainly have been familiar with Kesey's novel.

37. Wolfe, *Limbo,* 10, 11, 412.

38. Ibid., 176.

39. Ibid., 136.

40. Szilard, "The Diary of Dr. Davis," 57.

41. Wolfe, *Limbo,* 214–15.

42. Wylie, "After the Hydrogen Bombs," 11.

43. Brians, *Nuclear Holocausts,* 71.

44. Samuelson, "*Limbo:* The Great American Dystopia," 79.

45. Bukatman, *Terminal Identity,* 293.

46. Wiener, *Cybernetics,* 24.

47. Hayles, *How We Became Posthuman,* 114.

48. Wiener, *The Human Use of Human Beings,* 209. The reference is to John von Neumann, coauthor of *Theory of Games and Economic Behaviour* (1944).

49. Wolfe, *Limbo,* 331.

50. Ibid., 211. Martine bolsters his argument by drawing an analogy with Kafka's "Metamorphosis," written during World War I. The terminology here derives from Groddeck's *The Book of the It.*

51. Wolfe, *The Great Prince Died,* 268.

52. Wolfe, *Limbo,* 355.

53. This famous statement was made in 1931 by the Polish American founder of general semantics, Alfred Korzybski, and is further discussed in chapter 12.

8. Push-Button Holocaust in Mordecai Roshwald's *Level 7*

1. Ley, "Push for Pushbutton Warfare," 87–105.
2. Campbell, "The Place of Science Fiction," 17, 18–19.
3. Campbell, "The Real Pushbutton War," 5. One of the earliest occurrences of the phrase "push-button warfare" comes in a description of the V-2 guided missiles. Lang, *Early Tales of the Atomic Age*, 145.
4. Bone, "Triggerman," in Campbell, *Analog Anthology*, 207. Bone was a professor of veterinary medicine.
5. The Distant Early Warning radar system extending from Alaska to Baffin Island was completed in 1957.
6. Martino, "Pushbutton War," in Campbell, *Analog Anthology*, 266–67.
7. Ibid., 273.
8. Mumford, *The Myth of the Machine*, 187, 192, 225.
9. Conklin, *Great Science Fiction by Scientists*, 288.
10. Curtis C. Smith, *Twentieth-Century Science-Fiction Writers*, 613.
11. Roshwald, *Level 7*, xlvi.
12. Roshwald, *Dreams and Nightmares*, 206.
13. Cook, *The Warfare State*.
14. Roshwald, "Who Will Bury Whom?" 249. The primacy Roshwald gives to automation here signals an interest he pursued in a study to be called *Modern Technology: The Promise and the Menace*, which was typeset by the Borgo Press before it went bankrupt. This work is listed in the U.S. National Union Catalog.
15. Roshwald, *Level 7*, xxxviii.
16. Roshwald, "Quo Vadis, America?" 198.
17. Roshwald, "Confusion of Spheres," 243–51.
18. Roshwald to H. Bruce Franklin, letter, 15 September 1988, quoted in Franklin, "Afterword" to *Level 7* (Chicago: Lawrence Hill, 1989), 190.
19. Roshwald, "Order and Over-Organization in America," 38. John R. Raser echoed Roshwald's sentiment, specifically arguing that the nuclear warrior is "expected to be a servomechanism to electronic devices, a brain plugged into a vast machine, a single circuit in an endlessly complex chain of command" ("The Failure of Fail-Safe," 134).
20. Scortia and Zebrowski's *Human-Machines* collects stories relevant to cybernetics, mostly from the 1940s and 1950s.
21. Huxley, *Complete Essays*, 222, 235.
22. Roshwald, *Level 7*, 93.
23. Ibid., 79.
24. During the fifties the phrase "the button" became incorporated into the debate over nuclear war and was often used to refer to the dangerous ease with which such a war could be triggered. For a general discussion of offensive war technology, see Ford, *The Button*.

25. Fromm, *The Sane Society,* 110. Donald Barthelme describes the psychologically estranging effects of life in a nuclear control center in his short story "Game" (1965).

26. Roshwald, *Level 7,* 118.

27. Ibid., 186. The essay is reprinted in this edition as an appendix.

28. Roshwald, "The Cybernetics of Blunder," 335–36.

29. Roshwald, *Level 7,* 125–27.

30. Ibid., 188.

31. Roshwald, letter to author, 6 December 1990.

32. Roshwald, *Dreams and Nightmares,* 197.

33. Deer, "The Unavoidable International Shelter Race," 66–67. The impact of Deer's article on James Blish is discussed in chapter 3. The Holifield Committee report was entitled *Civil Defense for National Survival: Hearings Before a Subcommittee of the Committee on Government Operations* (1956) and was reviewed that same year by Mary Simpson for the *Bulletin of the Atomic Scientists.*

34. Roshwald, *Level 7,* 143.

35. Ibid., 179.

36. Roshwald, letter to author, 10 April 1991.

37. Bartter, "Still on the Level," 414.

38. Priestley, "Britain and the Nuclear Bombs," 554, 556.

39. Priestley, "Best Anti-Bomb Story Yet," 4.

40. Ryan, *Bertrand Russell,* 175.

41. Notes for 1953 speech to the Authors' Club, in Feinberg, *The Collected Stories of Bertrand Russell,* 13.

42. Russell, *Common Sense and Nuclear Warfare,* 37.

43. Feinberg, *Collected Stories of Bertrand Russell,* 318.

44. *The "Lomokome" Papers* was written in 1949 and published in periodical form in 1956 and as a novel in 1968. The description is Wouk's own, from his introduction to the Pocket Books 1968 edition. A traveler from Earth to the moon learns that nuclear war has been going on there for centuries.

45. Russell, *Common Sense and Nuclear Warfare,* 27, 47.

46. Russell, *Has Man a Future?* 31.

47. Roshwald, *A Small Armageddon,* 14. Roshwald wove the nuclear theme into a later SF novel called "Anno Hiroshimae 155," so far unpublished. Roshwald, letter to author, 15 June 2003.

48. Roshwald, *A Small Armageddon,* 108.

49. Roshwald, "My Encounters with Bertrand Russell," 152.

50. Roshwald, *Level 7,* 183.

9. Whales, Submarines, and *The Bedford Incident*

1. Peter George's 1965 novel *Commander-1* describes how a U.S. submarine manages to survive a nuclear war through extended submersion in the Arctic.

2. Thule Air Base was used by Dan Brown in his 2001 novel *Deception Point.*

3. Piette, *The Literary Cold War*, 79. In 1955, during the construction of the DEW line, the poet Allen Ginsberg served on a military transport that passed through the area. Surprisingly, the Arctic has only rarely been used in Cold War narratives, but *Ice Station Zebra* (novel 1963, film 1968) would fit Piette's description exactly. Its location is a meteorological station in the Arctic Circle, which a U.S. nuclear submarine is trying to reach in order to retrieve film dropped from a surveillance satellite.

4. Herbert, *The Dragon in the Sea*, ix. The serial title was "Under Pressure."

5. Herbert's technical detail outraged a retired admiral who wrote to complain that Herbert was clearly a Communist agent and should be investigated for betraying the nation's secrets. Letter from "Necessarily Anonymous," *The Dragon in the Sea*, correspondence file, Herbert Papers, University of California at Fullerton.

6. Herbert, *The Dragon in the Sea*, 112.

7. Ibid., xi.

8. Hampton, "Atomic Submarine," 7.

9. Ibid., 77.

10. Ibid., 69.

11. Mydans, "Here the U.S. Fights the Coldest War," 18, 23. The DEW line was closed down in 1993.

12. Kennedy, "Address of Senator John F. Kennedy."

13. Slotkin, *Gunfighter Nation*, 503. The discourse of the frontier applies awkwardly to submarines, which were valued for their mobility. Tropes of combat tend to become divorced from actual locations, as happens in the post–Cold War film *Crimson Tide* (1995), in which the commander of the USS *Alabama* tells his crew, "We constitute the front line and the last line of defense."

14. Bucher, *Bucher: My Story*, 17. The *Pueblo* was seized in international waters.

15. Wilson, "Moby Dick and the Atom," 195, 196, 197. Wilson made a short film of *Moby-Dick* that won a prize at the 1955 Venice Film Festival.

16. Bradbury, *Bradbury Speaks*, 184. Bradbury discusses his adaptation (ibid., 16–22) and made the filming the subject of his 1992 film *Green Shadows, White Whale*. On the strength of his performance in *Moby-Dick*, Forrest J. Ackerman suggested to Herbert that Gregory Peck play the lead role in a film adaptation of *The Dragon in the Sea*. Letter, 2 March 1956, *The Dragon in the Sea*, correspondence file, Herbert Papers.)

17. Mumford, *The Myth of the Machine*, 376. Mumford saw Ahab as a figure of obsession and amoral compulsion in his 1954 essays "Irrational Elements in Art and Politics" and "The Uprising of Caliban."

18. Pease, *Visionary Compacts*, 44.

19. Rascovich, *The Bedford Incident*, 69–70. Arne Axelsson comments on the hunt: "Strictly nothing more is at stake than the prestige of captains and crews involved" (*Restrained Response*, 127).

20. Rascovich, *The Bedford Incident*, 68.

21. Couser, "The Hunt for 'Big Red,'" 34.

22. Slotkin, *Gunfighter Nation*, 462.

23. Spanos, *The Errant Art of "Moby-Dick,"* 226. Geraldine Murphy gives valuable commentary in "Ahab as Capitalist."

24. Rascovich, *The Bedford Incident*, 75.

25. Ibid., 228.

26. Couser, "The Hunt for 'Big Red,'" 35, 36.

27. Wouk's novel won a Pulitzer Prize on publication and was adapted for the cinema in 1954, with Humphrey Bogart playing the role of Queeg. The relation of the novel to the Cold War is discussed in Swados, "Popular Taste and *The Caine Mutiny.*"

28. By 1965 Richard Widmark had established his credentials as a Cold War warrior in the cinema, playing leading roles in *Take the High Ground!* (1953) and *Time Limit* (1957), both dealing with the Korean War. The most relevant predecessor to *The Bedford Incident* was *Hell and High Water* (1954), in which Widmark played a submarine commander uncovering a conspiracy by the Chinese to start World War III. Anticipating a similar quasi-documentary opening in *Dr. Strangelove,* a pre-credit sequence announces: "In the summer of 1953, it was announced that an atomic bomb of foreign origin had been exploded somewhere outside of the United States. Shortly thereafter it was indicated that the atomic reaction, according to scientific reports, originated in a remote area in North Pacific waters, somewhere between the northern tip of the Japanese Islands and the Arctic Circle. This is the story of that explosion" (http://tinyurl.com/6uuyn8z). This authenticating strategy implies, paradoxically, that the film will take the viewer behind the scenes of international drama. Widmark is called in to head up a submarine expedition supported clandestinely by a group of businessmen and politicians which sets off from Japan and sails north to find proof that the Chinese Communists have constructed a secret atomic base. Their plan was to use an American bomber to drop an atomic bomb on either Korea or Manchuria and thereby trigger a nuclear war. The plot is thwarted, but the bomb actually detonates on the secret base. Although the Chinese did not make the decision to develop nuclear weapons until 1955, the film clearly reflects the anxieties of the period that they might upset the precarious nuclear status quo. Perhaps for this reason the U.S. government supplied footage of an atomic bomb blast, and perhaps, too, that explains the film's double layer of secrecy. On the one hand, viewers are allowed to see an action so secret that not even the U.S. government can admit its existence; on the other hand, this supposed violation of secrecy is rationalized by the greater good of revealing the Chinese conspiracy.

29. Suid, *Sailing on the Silver Screen,* 167. The director James Harris and the screenwriter James Poe took a five-day cruise on a destroyer before the screening started. Deadlock ensued when the U.S. Navy wanted further changes made to the script, so a British destroyer was used in the film's opening shots.

30. Rascovich, *The Bedford Incident,* 173.

31. Rogin, "Ronald Reagan," the Movie and Other Episodes in Political Demonology, 284.

32. Rascovich, *The Bedford Incident,* 123, 220, 262.

33. Rogin,"Ronald Reagan," the Movie and Other Episodes in Political Demonology.

34. Rascovich, *The Bedford Incident.* The allusion here is to Soviet premier Krushchev's notorious warning to the West in an address of 1956, when he declared, "We will bury you."

35. Moskin, "Polaris," 17, 19.

36. Rascovich, *The Bedford Incident,* 252. Although Rascovich foregrounds the problematic meaning of Finlander's term "real" in this context, he too presents the Arctic as an actualization of the political situation through the rather easy congruence between cold ocean and Cold War.

37. In that respect *The Bedford Incident* differs strikingly from Tom Clancy's late–Cold War

thriller *The Hunt for Red October* (1984), which alternates between American scenes and those within the renegade Soviet submarine, thereby distinguishing the latter from the ultimate enemy—the Soviet military/political system.

38. Rascovich, *The Bedford Incident,* 149.
39. Ibid., 261, 267.
40. Pease, "*Moby-Dick* and the Cold War," 115.

10. Nuclear Safety Procedures in *Fail-Safe*

1. C. Wright Mills, *The Causes of World War Three,* 52.
2. Ibid., 83–84.
3. "This Is Article Cited by Soviet in Its Criticism of U.S. Flights," 4.
4. Kahn, *On Thermonuclear War,* 9.
5. Wheeler, "Fail-Safe Then and Now." His pen name, F. B. Aiken, was chosen from the seventeenth-century scientist Francis Bacon. This story enabled Burdick and Wheeler to win the suit for infringement of copyright brought against them in 1963 by Stanley Kubrick and Columbia Pictures. One outcome was that Columbia took over production of the film adaptation.
6. Wheeler, "Abraham '59," 18.
7. Kahn, *On Thermonuclear War,* 316.
8. Wheeler, "Abraham '59," 20.
9. Both Burdick and Wheeler were political analysts, though Burdick did have some novel-writing experience (famous for his 1958 collaboration with William Lederer, *The Ugly American*), and they composed *Fail-Safe* following the pattern that "every 'heavy' chapter be interspersed with a fast-moving or montage chapter" (Wheeler, "The Background of *Fail-Safe,*" box 41, Burdick Papers, Mugar Library, Boston University).
10. Burdick and Wheeler, *Fail-Safe,* 7.
11. Harvey, "A Novel of World War III," 23.
12. One of the novel's most enthusiastic readers was President John Kennedy, who invited Burdick to the White House to discuss it. Harvey Wheeler, letter to author, 5 August 1992. Another appreciative reader was Philip Wylie, who wrote to Burdick to express his enthusiasm and to thank him for his letter about his own novel *Triumph.* Wylie to Burdick, letter, 14 December 1962, Burdick Papers.
13. Burdick and Wheeler, *Fail-Safe,* 199.
14. Cousins, "Fallible Man and His Infernal Machines," 22.
15. Burdick and Wheeler, *Fail-Safe,* 44.
16. Wilkinson, "Connections with Toughness," 233, 235.
17. Phelps, "The Grim Possibility," 28; Cousins, "Fallible Man and His Infernal Machines," 22.
18. Hutchins, *The University of Utopia,* 90.
19. Wheeler, "Fail-Safe Then and Now."
20. Wheeler confirmed that Groteschele was partly based on Kahn. (Wheeler, letter to author, 5 August 1992.) After the novel was published, he met with the physicist Edward Teller to discuss it and in his memorandum of the meeting recorded that Teller probably

recognized aspects of himself in Groteschele, but Wheeler categorically denied that he had drawn on Teller for the characterization. Teller pointed out that by 1967 the U.S. military would no longer be relying on manned aircraft. He praised the power of the novel but declared that it would produce the "defeat of everything he stood for and believed in" ("Wheeler Recollections of the Dinner Discussion with Edward Teller," Burdick Papers).

21. Kahn, *On Thermonuclear War*, 205, 209, 259.
22. Maus, *Unvarnishing Reality*, 154.
23. Burdick and Wheeler, *Fail-Safe*, 152.
24. Harvey, "A Novel of World War III," 23.
25. Schwarz, *Revisiting "Fail-Safe."*
26. Wilkinson, "Connections with Toughness," 227.
27. Burdick and Wheeler, *Fail-Safe*, 225.
28. Ibid., 137.
29. Hook, *The Fail-Safe Fallacy*, 11, 19, 26.
30. "A Professor's Accident," 19.
31. Hook, *The Fail-Safe Fallacy*, 32.
32. Wheeler and Burdick, "The Politics of Destruction," 83.
33. It was an ironic testament to the accuracy of *Fail-Safe* that soon after its publication Burdick and Wheeler were investigated by military intelligence to ascertain where the "leaks" of data were coming from, although all the information they used was declassified.
34. Burdick and Wheeler, "Introduction," May 1962, Burdick Papers.
35. Meyer, *Ultimatum*, 87.
36. Sutton's 1959 novel *Bombs in Orbit* describes a state of armed hostility between the United States and the Soviet Union. When the latter puts a number of satellites into orbit armed with hydrogen bombs, the U.S. sends up a special craft with technicians to disarm them. An air force colonel explains the military context as one of undeclared war, "war in which aircraft, submarines and even troops are like spies—operating without identifying marks of nationality—battle units for which no nation can take responsibility" (14). Accordingly, even near space has become militarized, and a bomb launched from such a satellite seems invincible: "Men would wait its coming, crouched behind batteries of push-buttons, prepared to hurl countermissiles skyward," but these would be anticipated by the device's radar. Thus, "cities would vanish in sun-hot heat, states would perish under a radio-active blanket, the heart of a nation would shrivel and die" (107). The novel draws suspense out of a simple question: Can the protagonist disarm the satellite bombs before the Soviets activate them? The terms of Cold War confrontation are unquestioned and unexamined, whereas Sutton's later novel pursues a far more sophisticated enquiry into hypotheses and consequences.
37. Sutton, *H-Bomb over America*, 115.
38. Prochnau, *Trinity's Child*, 253. Prochnau's title presents the nuclear standoff as an inheritance of the very first atomic blast, code name Trinity. His novel depicts how widely the nuclear subject had penetrated U.S. culture through allusions to *Dr. Strangelove*, *Star Wars*, the TV series *Mission Impossible*, etc. His president is a thinly disguised version of Ronald Reagan. One of the most striking absences in this novel is any description of the destruction produced by the nuclear missiles.

11. Uncovering the Death Wish in *Dr. Strangelove*

1. For Lewis Mumford the general nuclear stance of the United States reflected an inert willingness "to accept the indiscriminate extermination of human life, by atomic and bacterial means" (*In the Name of Sanity*, 5). In other words, the insanity was collective and endemic.
2. Lewis, *One of Our H-Bombs Is Missing*, 133.
3. Ibid., 102.
4. The film was ready for release in 1963 but was delayed until the following year because of the Kennedy assassination. The novel was published in 1963 as an advance movie tie-in.
5. The term "red alert" was borrowed from engineering in the late fifties and applied to a system of checks within the U.S. system of air defense. The *Oxford English Dictionary* credits George's novel with the first civilian use of the term. The novel was first published by T. V. Boardman in 1958 under the pen name Peter Bryant with the title *Two Hours to Doom;* later that same year the Ace Books reprint changed the title to *Red Alert.* The 1961 Corgi edition retains the original title. George returned to the subject of nuclear war in his novel *Commander-1,* where an all-out exchange of missiles between the United States and the Soviet Union is triggered by the launch of a Chinese device. George gives a grim picture of crude triumphalism persisting on the Chinese and American sides, even after the majority of the world's population has perished. When George committed suicide in 1966 he was working on a novel to be called *Nuclear Survivors.*
6. This distrust subsequently became the subject of a novel by the Washington journalists Fletcher Knebel and Charles W. Bailey, *Seven Days in May,* which describes an attempt by hawkish elements of the U.S. military to mount a coup. The strategist Herman Kahn admired George's depiction of how an officer could circumvent the safeguards in the military system and used his novel in RAND training courses for officers. P. D. Smith, *Doomsday Men,* 416.
7. Abrash, "Through Logic to Apocalypse," 131.
8. George, *Red Alert,* 93.
9. Ibid., 137. The novel was praised by Herman Kahn as a clever presentation of the "clever way the general negates the elaborate system set up to prevent unauthorized behavior" (*On Thermonuclear War,* 44).
10. George, *Red Alert,* 31.
11. Terry Southern has stated that *Red Alert* was drawn to Kubrick's attention in 1961 by Alistair Buchan, the director of the Institute for Strategic Studies in London ("Check-Up with Dr. Strangelove"). This piece started life as a profile of Kubrick written by Southern for *Esquire* in 1963 and then was subsequently shelved. Needless to say, one source does not preclude the other.
12. Schelling, "Meteors, Mischief, and War," 293.
13. Kubrick, "How I Learned to Stop Worrying and Love the Cinema," 12.
14. Gelmis, *The Film Director as Superstar,* 309.
15. Schelling, "Meteors, Mischief, and War," 296.
16. Kubrick later declared that "the present nuclear situation is so totally new and unique that it is beyond the realm of current semantics; in its actual implications, and its infinite

horror, it cannot be clearly or satisfactorily expressed by any ordinary scheme of aesthetics. What we do know is that its one salient and undeniable characteristic is that of the *absurd*" (Southern, "Check-Up with Dr. Strangelove").

17. Ibid.
18. George, *Dr. Strangelove*, 1.
19. Albert Bermel, 'The End of the Race," in Pohl, *The Eighth Galaxy Reader,* 77.
20. Richard Gid Powers, "Introduction," in George, *Dr. Strangelove,* xvi.
21. McKeen, "Terry Southern," 413; Friedman, *Black Humor,* viii.
22. Schulz, *Black Humor Fiction of the Sixties,* 12. Nancy Pogel and William Chamberlain find self-reflexivity a common feature of black comedy films but do not discuss *Dr. Strangelove* in their survey "Humor into Film," 187–93.
23. Linden, "Dr. Strangelove," 58.
24. "Strangelove Outtake: Notes from the War Room," in Southern and Friedman, *Now Dig This,* 83.
25. Gelmis, *The Film Director as Superstar,* 309.
26. George, *Dr. Strangelove,* 103. In the movie Guano accuses Mandrake of being a "prevert."
27. Gelmis, *The Film Director as Superstar,* 309.
28. The description of the hot line in *Red Alert* led Thomas Schelling to suggest to the Eisenhower government that they set one up. The same recommendation was made to Krushchev by Leo Szilard in 1960. P. D. Smith, *Doomsday Men,* 429.
29. Kagan, *The Cinema of Stanley Kubrick,* 112.
30. Transcribed from the film. The comic detail of the Soviet premier's partying resembles the scenario in Herbert Gold's 1961 story "The Day They Got Boston," where a Soviet officer gets drunk and breaks a rubber band holding computer cards, thereby triggering a launch that destroys Boston. The resulting bargaining whereby Leningrad is nuked as compensation superficially resembles *Fail-Safe* but on a far more ludicrous level.
31. George, *Dr. Strangelove,* 138.
32. Ibid., 49.
33. Southern, "Check-Up with Dr. Strangelove."
34. George, *Dr. Strangelove,* 139.
35. Carnegie, *How to Stop Worrying and Start Living,* 142. The subtitle of *Dr. Strangelove* also conflates the title of Szilard's article "How to Live with the Bomb and Survive," where he proposes a Pax Russo-Americana. The March 1962 issue of *Playboy* carried a satirical piece entitled "How to Stop Worrying About the Bomb."
36. Every detail of *Dr. Strangelove* has its basis in history and Ripper's hostility to fluoridation is no exception. In 1955 the Keep America Committee of Los Angeles issued a flyer urging citizens to resist "Communistic World Government" by opposing the "Unholy Three": fluoridated water, polio serum, and mental hygiene. The latter was described as a "subtle and diabolical plan of the enemy to transform a free and intelligent people into a cringing horde of zombies" ("Ron Paul War Room," http://tinyurl.com/74nfssb). The context of this measure is discussed in Freeze and Lehr, *The Fluoride Wars.*
37. Ciment, *Kubrick,* 157.
38. The reader is now able to compare novel and film. See "*Dr. Strangelove:* A Continuity Transcript," http://www.visual-memory.co.uk/amk/doc/0055.html/.

39. George, *Dr. Strangelove*, 19.

40. Maland, "*Dr. Strangelove* (1964)," 707. The use of hand-held cameras for the shots of soldiers storming Burpelson Base similarly imitate documentary footage from World War II.

41. George, *Dr. Strangelove*, 38. Turgidson's message echoes Franklin D. Roosevelt's 1941 State of the Union address where he named the four freedoms, the last being freedom from fear. The analogy with Roosevelt implies a worldwide situation of actual war and, ironically, Turgidson's action contradicts Roosevelt's utopian plea for a general disarmament that would preclude any "act of physical aggression" against a neighbor. One of his key terms here, "prevail," is singled out for comment by Herman Kahn: "Because its use is ambiguous, the reader does not know whether the author is serious about his goal or is just making a meaningless concession to old-fashioned thinking" (*On Thermonuclear War*, 24).

42. George, *Dr. Strangelove*, 56.

43. Ibid., 81.

44. Manuscript note to Joseph Heller, 30 July 1962, Heller Archive, Special Collections, Brandeis University Library, Waltham, MA.

45. Macklin, "Sex and Dr. Strangelove," 55.

46. Kagan, *The Cinema of Stanley Kubrick*, 137.

47. Biskind, *Seeing Is Believing*, 68.

48. George, *Dr. Strangelove*, 25.

49. Nelson, *Kubrick*, 92.

50. Macklin, "Sex and Dr. Strangelove," 56.

51. Freud, *Civilization and Its Discontents*, 55–56, 59.

52. Ostow, "War and the Unconscious," 27.

53. George, *Dr. Strangelove*, 95.

54. George H. Smith, *Doomsday Wing*, 69.

55. In the 1962 movie *Doctor No* the eponymous villain has lost his hands due to radioactivity. For details on the similarities between these figures, see Stillman, "Two of the MADdest Scientists."

56. Maland, "*Dr. Strangelove* (1964)," 202–3.

57. P. D. Smith, *Doomsday Men*, 20–21. The science journalist William L. Laurence discussed the possibility of a cobalt bomb in his *The Hell Bomb*. By the mid-1950s the "C-bomb" had become a standard item in discussions of nuclear weaponry.

58. Norman O. Brown, *Life Against Death*, 62, 65.

59. Maland, "*Dr. Strangelove* (1964)," 198.

60. The satirical allusion here is to the application of game theory to nuclear strategy like that promoted by John McDonald, who concludes *Strategy in Poker, Business and War* with the statement that the H-bomb "simply represents a higher pay-off for a hit. War is chance and minimax must be its modern philosophy" (112).

12. Mapping the Postnuclear Landscape

1. Heinlein, *Farnham's Freehold*, 98.
2. Jackson, *Maps of Meaning*, 23, 22.
3. Agnew, "Representing Space," 263.
4. Barrett has described *Through Darkest America* and its follow-up, *Dawn's Uncertain Light* (1989), as "extremely dark pictures of tomorrow" but adds that "none of us can write even the boldest, most far-out picture of the future without a strong cord, or at least a flimsy thread, to the past" (Nick Gevers, "In a Genre of His Own: An Interview with Neal Barrett, Jr.", http://tinyurl.com/78rvu49.
5. Wolfe, *Limbo*, 269.
6. Ibid., 135, 136.
7. Ibid., 478.
8. Huxley, *Ape and Essence*, 45.
9. Ibid., 66.
10. Szilard, "The Physicist Invades Politics," 7.
11. Szilard, *The Voice of the Dolphins and Other Stories*, 144.
12. Morrison, "If the Bomb Gets Out of Hand," 3–4.
13. Coppel, *Dark December*, 38–39.
14. Ibid., 43.
15. Tucker, *The Long Loud Silence*, 13–14.
16. Ibid., 38–39.
17. Ibid., 5.
18. Ibid., 136.
19. Brackett, *The Long Tomorrow*, 35.
20. Ibid., 71–72.
21. Pangborn, *Davy*, 9.
22. Ibid., 11.
23. Pangborn, undated synopsis of *Davy*, p. 3, Pangborn Collection, Boston University Library.
24. Pangborn, *The Judgment of Eve*, 9.
25. Bakhtin, *The Dialogic Imagination*, 243.
26. Pangborn, *The Judgment of Eve*, 81–82.
27. Swaim, "Wired for Books Audio Interview with Whitley Strieber." Strieber and Kunetka actually completed a companion volume to be called "Warday: Europe and Russia," but the book was never published owing to a lack of interest from publishers.
28. This film is discussed in relation to its British counterparts *The War Game* and *Threads* in Seed, "TV Docudrama and the Nuclear Subject," 154–63.
29. Strieber and Kunetka, *Warday and the Journey Onward*, 39.
30. Tevis, *The Man Who Fell Down to Earth*, 134.
31. Strieber and Kunetka, *Warday and the Journey Onward*, 75.
32. Ibid., 164.
33. Ibid., 365.
34. Brians, *Nuclear Holocausts*, 44–45.

35. Jarvis, *Postmodern Cartographies,* 1.

36. Miller, *A Canticle for Leibowitz,* 12.

37. Ibid., 255.

38. Hoban, *Riddley Walker,* 226.

39. Ibid., 90.

40. Ibid., 120.

41. Schwenger, *Letter Bomb,* 37–40.

42. "1975 by Russell Hoban," http://www.ocelotfactory.com/hoban/1975.html.

43. Robinson, *The Wild Shore,* 102.

44. Ibid., 370.

45. Johnson, *Fiskadoro,* 11.

46. Among other works, Frank W. Chinnock's *Nagasaki: The Forgotten Bomb* was consulted.

47. Brin, *The Postman,* 152, 153. This novel carried an endorsement by Whitley Strieber, among others.

13. Future Reportage on World War III

1. Burnham, *The Struggle for the World,* 9, 229. Even before the Soviet Union possessed its own atomic bomb, Burnham was recognizing the inevitable need for a preemptive strike "in order to defend ourselves" (p. 44). Burnham's dating of World War Three was more or less echoed in Pournelle and Possony, *The Strategy of Technology,* which applies the notion of warfare to all aspects of technology developed since 1945.

2. Orwell, "Burnham's View of the Contemporary World Struggle," 102.

3. Solberg, *Riding High,* 105.

4. Ibid., 128.

5. Leinster, *The Murder of the U.S.A.,* 52. Leinster quotes John W. Campbell's *The Atomic Story,* which supplied the idea of a sneak attack on America, and also dedicates his novel to Campbell.

6. Franklin, *War Stars,* 160.

7. "The Fall of America in Science Fiction," in Shippey, *Fictional Space,* 116.

8. "The 36-Hour War," 28.

9. Morrison, "If the Bomb Gets Out of Hand," 3. Other contributors to the symposium included Leo Szilard, Albert Einstein, and Louis N. Ridenour. Morrison recalled of Hiroshima, "It was the magnitude of the damage that was so appalling . . . Most of us who hadn't dropped out of this atom project during the last two or three years had developed our own private justifications for staying in it" (Lang, *Early Tales of the Atomic Age,* 70).

10. Morrison, "If the Bomb Gets Out of Hand," 5.

11. The story first appeared in *Collier's* and was collected in *The Martian Chronicles* (1950).

12. Brown and Real, *Community of Fear,* 15.

13. Leinster, "Short History of World War Three," 83

14. Mills, *The Causes of World War Three,* 9. Mills cites Huxley and Orwell as examples of the "images of sociological horror" being promoted in fiction about the future (99). In 1959

Harry Welton published his own account of super power confrontation, *The Third World War*, with an opening chapter that echoes Burnham's title *The Struggle for the World*. In this case the war is commercial and ideological but universal: "In every inhabited part of the world the forces of Communism and Democracy are locked together in combat" (*The Third World War*, 1).

15. Ballard, *War Fever*, 23.
16. Engel and Piller, *World Aflame*, 8.
17. Ibid., 32.
18. Ibid.
19. Ibid., 76.
20. Boyer, *By the Bomb's Early Light*, 69.
21. Masters and Way, *One World or None*. Morrison's scenario was subsequently incorporated into Merril's *Shadow on the Hearth*. In order to test out civil defense capability, the *Bulletin of the Atomic Scientists* ran an article in their January 1950 issue on "The City of Washington and an Atomic Attack."
22. Lear, "Hiroshima, U.S.A.," 64.
23. Knox Burger to Philip Wylie, letter, 27 May 1951, Wylie Papers. In addition to Wylie, Burger also invited the novelists Howard Maier and Kurt Vonnegut to contribute.
24. Edward R. Murrow, "A-Bomb Mission to Moscow," *Collier's*, 27 October 1951, 19.
25. Hal Boyle, "Washington Under the Bomb," *Collier's*, 27 October 1951, 20.
26. Philip Wylie, "Philadelphia Phase," *Collier's*, 27 October 1951, 42.
27. Brians, *Nuclear Holocausts*, 161.
28. Koestler, *The Trail of the Dinosaur and Other Essays*, 150.
29. The dust jacket to Welton's *The Third World War* declares, "It is not science fiction, nor a warning of horrors to come. *The Third World War is already in progress.*"
30. This most probably alludes to McDonald's 1950 introduction to game theory, *Strategy in Poker, Business and War*.
31. Allen, *War Games*, 77–88.
32. Brians, *Nuclear Holocausts*, 34.
33. Hackett, *The Third World War, August 1985*, 137.
34. Ibid., 291–92.
35. Ibid., 294.
36. Ibid., xvii.
37. Ibid., 383–84.
38. Ibid., 387.
39. Dugger, "*The Third World War:* The President's Favorite Book," 414. The president in question was Ronald Reagan. The precision of Hackett's military detail is discussed in Clarke, *Voices Prophesying War*, 198–201. Clarke notes how quickly the political premises of the volume dated. Two related projections that followed Hackett's were John Bradley's *Illustrated History of World War Three* and David Fraser's *August 1988*.
40. Chapter 18 of Hackett's first volume, "The War in Inner Space," opens with a passing reference to Star Wars and discusses the super power rivalry over interceptor satellites.
41. Bidwell, *World War 3*, xvii.

42. Ibid., 272.
43. Palmer, *Arctic Strike!* The cover shows an Arctic sea battle removed from human habitation and proclaims, "Awesome machines of war clash in an explosive engagement at the top of the world!"
44. Brown, *Operation: World War III*, 29. The hypothetical date for the outbreak of hostilities in this plan was 1957. The Dropshot scenario is discussed by John J. Reilly in "World War III in 1957," which argues that according to this plan a nuclear strike against the Soviet Union would not have been decisive.
45. Harry, *Arc Light*, 139.

14. Beyond the Cold War

1. The full text of *Fallout Protection* is found at http://tinyurl.com/7b8jpfv. It was in this report that President Kennedy's 1961 speech is quoted where he recommended a program of shelter construction, which never really took off.
2. DuBois, *Resurrection Day*, 214.
3. Newt Gingrich, "Foreword," in Forstchen, *One Second After*, 12.
4. *Report of the Commission to Assess the Threat to the United States from Electromagnetic Pulse (EMP) Attack*. Volume 1: *Executive Report 2004*, http://tinyurl.com/7oddab6.
5. Compare with H. Bruce Franklin's choice of *Countdown to Midnight* as the title of his 1984 collection of nuclear war stories.
6. Forstchen, *One Second After*, 345.
7. Clancy, *The Sum of All Fears*, 802. Harris's novel was inspired when he saw the Palestinian attack on the Israeli athletes in the 1972 Munich Olympics.
8. Tom Clancy and Russell Seitz, "Five Minutes Past Midnight—and Welcome to the Age of Proliferation," in Greenberg, *The Tom Clancy Companion*, 95, 105.
9. "St. Martin's Press: An Interview with Bestseller Stephen Coonts," http://tinyurl.com/72oxakl.
10. The ending might carry homage to the 1959 Hitchcock thriller *North by Northwest*, whose climax plays itself out at Mount Rushmore. Here too national survival is at issue.
11. Filger, "Will Al-Qaeda Nuke America?"
12. Filger, *King of Bombs*, 147.
13. For a discussion of Khan's network and the threat of nuclear terrorism, see Kazi, "Nuclear Terrorism."
14. For a list of members, see http://tinyurl.com/75gkuy5.
15. The other volumes in the trilogy are *Sins of the Assassin* (2008) and *Heart of the Assassin* (2009).
16. Judd, "One Nation, Under Allah."
17. Ferrigno, *Prayers for the Assassin*, 18.
18. Harry, *Arc Light*, 280.

Bibliography

Abrash, Merritt. "Through Logic to Apocalypse: Science-Fiction Scenarios of Nuclear Deterrence Breakdown." *Science-Fiction Studies* 13.ii (1986): 129–38.

Agnew, John. "Representing Space: Space, Scale and Culture in Social Science." In *Place/Culture/ Representation*. Ed. James Duncan and David Ley. London: Routledge, 1993. 251–71.

Allen, Thomas B. *War Games*. New York: Berkley Books, 1989.

Amis, Martin. *Einstein's Monsters*. London: Jonathan Cape, 1987.

"The Atomic Bomb." *Life*, 8 August 1945, 87B.

Axelsson, Arne. *Restrained Response: American Novels of the Cold War and Korea, 1945–1962*. Westport, CT: Greenwood Press, 1990.

Bakhtin, M. M. *The Dialogic Imagination: Four Essays*. Ed. Michael Holquist. Trans. Caryl Emerson and Michael Holquist. Austin: U of Texas P, 1981.

Ballard, J. G. "From Shanghai to Shepperton." *Re/Search* 8/9 (1984): 112–24.

———. *War Fever*. London: Collins, 1990.

Barrett, Neil, Jr. *Through Darkest America*. London: New English Library, 1988.

Barshay, Robert Howard. *Philip Wylie: The Man and His Work*. Washington, DC: UP of America, 1979.

Bartter, Martha A. "Nuclear Holocaust as Urban Renewal." *Science-Fiction Studies* 13.ii (July 1986): 148–58.

———. "Still on the Level." *Science-Fiction Studies* 17.iii (1990): 414.

———. *The Way to Ground Zero: The Atomic Bomb in American Science Fiction*. Westport, CT: Greenwood Press, 1988.

Bendau, Clifford P. *Still Worlds Collide: Philip Wylie and the End of the American Dream*. San Bernardino, CA: Borgo Press, 1980.

Bennett, Spencer Gordon, dir. *The Atomic Submarine*. Allied Artists, 1959.

Berger, Albert I. *The Magic That Works: John W. Campbell and the American Response to Technology*. San Bernadino, CA: Borgo Press, 1993.

———. "Nuclear Energy: Science Fiction's Metaphor of Power." *Science Fiction Studies* 6.ii (1979): 121–28.

Bermel, Albert. "The End of the Race." In *The Eighth Galaxy Reader*. Ed. Frederik Pohl. London: Victor Gollancz, 1966. 77–81.

Berriault, Gina. *The Descent*. London: Arthur Barker, 1961.

Bethe, Hans, Harrison Brown, Frederick Seitz, and Leo Szilard. "The Facts About the Hydrogen Bomb." *The Bulletin of the Atomic Scientists* 6.iv (1950): 106–9, 126–27.

Bidwell, Shelford, ed. *World War 3*. Rev. ed. London: Hamlyn, 1980.

Biskind, Peter. *Seeing Is Believing: How Hollywood Taught Us to Stop Worrying and Love the Fifties*. New York: Pantheon, 1983.

Bisson, Terry. "A Canticle for Miller: or, How I Met Saint Leibowitz and the Wild Horse Woman but Not Walter M. Miller, Jr." http://tinyurl.com/7l9v9lz.

Blish, James. *A Case of Conscience*. New York: Ballantine, 1958.

———. *So Close to Home*. New York: Ballantine, 1961.

"The Bomb." *Time*, 20 August 1945, 19.

Boyer, Paul. *By the Bomb's Early Light: American Thought and Culture at the Dawn of the Nuclear Age*. 2nd ed. Chapel Hill: U of North Carolina P, 1994.

———. "Exotic Resonances: Hiroshima in American Memory." In *Hiroshima in History and Memory*. Ed. Michael J. Hogan. Cambridge: Cambridge UP, 2009. 143–67.

———. *Fallout*. Columbus: Ohio State UP, 1998.

Brackett, Leigh. *The Long Tomorrow*. Garden City, NY: Doubleday, 1955.

Bradbury, Ray. *Bradbury Speaks: Too Soon from the Cave, Too Far from the Stars*. New York: William Morrow, 2005.

———. *Fahrenheit 451*. New York: Ballantine, 1991.

———. *The Martian Chronicles*. New York: Bantam, 1979.

Bradley, David. *No Place to Hide*. Boston: Little, Brown, 1948.

Bradley, John. *Illustrated History of World War Three: The Cause and Effect of a Final Confrontation*. London: Windward, 1982.

Brians, Paul. *Nuclear Holocausts: Atomic War in Fiction, 1895–1984*. Kent, OH: Kent State UP, 1987. Rev. ed. 2008 at http://public.wsu.edu/~brians/nuclear/.

Brin, David. *The Postman*. New York: Bantam, 1988.

Brown, Anthony Cave, ed. *Operation: World War III*. London: Arms & Armor Press, 1979.

Brown, Harrison, and James Real. *Community of Fear*. Santa Barbara, CA: Center for the Study of Democratic Institutions, 1960.

Brown, Norman O. *Life Against Death: The Psychoanalytic Meaning of History*. New York: Random House, 1959.

Bucher, Lloyd M., with Mark Rascovich. *Bucher: My Story*. New York: Doubleday, 1970.

Bukatman, Scott. *Terminal Identity: The Virtual Subject in Postmodern Science Fiction*. Durham, NC: Duke UP, 1993.

Burchett, George, ed. *Rebel Journalism: The Writings of Wilfred Burchett*. Cambridge: Cambridge UP, 2007.

Burchett, Wilfred. "The Atomic Plague." In *Tell Me No Lies: Investigative Journalism and Its Triumphs*. Ed. John Pilger. London: Vintage, 2005. 10–25.

Burdick, Eugene, and Harvey Wheeler. *Fail-Safe*. New York. McGraw-Hill, 1962.

Burnham, James. *The Managerial Revolution*. Harmondsworth, UK: Penguin, 1962.

———. *The Struggle for the World*. London: Jonathan Cape, 1947.

Bush, Vannevar. *Modern Arms and Free Men: A Discussion of the Role of Science in Preserving Democracy.* New York: Simon & Schuster, 1949.

Caidin, Martin. *The Long Night.* New York: Dodd Mead, 1956.

Campbell, John W. *The Atomic Story.* New York: Henry Holt, 1947.

———. "The Place of Science Fiction." In *Modern Science Fiction, Its Meaning and Its Future.* Ed. Reginald Bretnor. New York: Coward-McCann, 1953. 4–22.

———. "The Real Pushbutton War." *Astounding Science Fiction* 44.v (1950): 4–5.

———, ed. *Analog Anthology.* London: Dobson, 1966.

Canaday, John. *The Nuclear Muse: Literature, Physics and the First Atomic Bombs.* Madison: U of Wisconsin P, 2000.

Cantor, Jay. *Krazy Kat: A Novel in Five Panels.* New York: Collier, 1988.

Capek, Karel. *Krakatit.* Trans. Lawrence Hyde. London: Geoffrey Bles, 1925.

Capobianco, Ken. "An Interview with Jay Cantor." *Journal of Modern Literature* 17.i (Summer 1990): 3–11.

Carlisle, Rodney B. *Scientific American Inventions and Discoveries.* Hoboken, NJ: John Wiley, 2004.

Carnegie, Dale. *How to Stop Worrying and Start Living.* Kingswood, UK: World's Work, 1972.

Carson, Rachel. *Silent Spring.* New York: Penguin, 2000.

Chernus, Ira. *Dr. Strangegod: On the Symbolic Meaning of Nuclear Weapons.* Columbia: U of South Carolina P, 1986.

Chinnock, Frank W. *Nagasaki: The Forgotten Bomb.* New York: World, 1969.

Ciment, Michel. *Kubrick.* Trans. Gilbert Adair. London: Collins, 1983.

Clancy, Tom. *The Sum of All Fears.* London: Harper Collins, 1991.

Clarke, I. F. *Voices Prophesying War: Future Wars, 1763–3749.* 2nd ed. Oxford: Oxford UP, 1992.

Clarkson, Helen [as Helen McCloy]. *The Last Day.* New York: Dodd, Mead, 1959.

Clayton, Bruce D. *Life After Doomsday.* Boulder, CO: Paladin Press, 1980.

———. "Planning for the Day After Doomsday." *Bulletin of the Atomic Scientists* 33.7 (1977): 49–53.

Cohn, Carol. "Sex and Death in the Rational World of the Defense Intellectuals." *Signs: Journal of Women in Culture and Society* 12.iv (1987): 687–718.

Conklin, Groff, ed. *Great Science Fiction by Scientists.* New York: Collier Books, 1962.

———, ed. *17 X Infinity.* London: Mayflower-Dell, 1964.

Cook, Fred J. *The Warfare State.* New York: Macmillan, 1962.

Coonts, Stephen. *America.* London: Orion, 2001.

———. *Final Flight.* New York: Dell, 1989.

———. *Liberty.* London: Orion, 2003.

Cooper, Ken. "The Whiteness of the Bomb." In *Postmodern Apocalypse: Theory and Cultural Practice at the End.* Ed. Richard Dellamora. Philadelphia: U of Pennsylvania P, 1995. 79–106.

Coppel, Alfred. *Dark December.* 1960. London: Coronet, 1971.

Cordle, Daniel. "Cultures of Terror: Nuclear Criticism during and since the Cold War." *Literature Compass* 3.vi (2006): 1186–99.

———. *States of Suspense: The Nuclear Age, Postmodernism and United States Fiction and Prose.* Manchester, UK: Manchester UP, 2008.

Couser, C. Thomas. "The Hunt for Big Red: *The Bedford Incident,* Melville and the Cold War." *Literature/Film Quarterly* 24.i (1996): 32–38.

Cousins, Norman. "Fallible Man and His Infernal Machines." *Saturday Review* 45 (20 October 1962): 22.

Craig, William. *The Tashkent Crisis*. London: Hodder & Stoughton, 1971.

Cromie, Robert. *The Crack of Doom*. London: Digby, Long, 1895.

Cross, F. L. *The Oxford Dictionary of the Christian Church*. London: Oxford UP, 1974.

Cummins, Elizabeth. "Short Fiction by Judith Merril." *Extrapolation* 33.iii (1992): 202–14.

Dearborn, Dorothy. "She'd Give Up Everything for a Trip to the Moon." *Evening Times-Globe* [Saint John, New Brunswick], 10 April 1971, 7.

Deer, James W. "The Unavoidable International Shelter Race." *Bulletin of the Atomic Scientists* 13.ii (1957): 66–67.

Derleth, August, ed. *Strange Ports of Call*. New York: Pellegrini & Cudahy, 1948.

Derrida, Jacques. "No Apocalypse, Not Now (full speed ahead, seven missiles, seven missives)." *Diacritics* 14 (Summer 1984): 20–31.

Dickson, Lovat. *H. G. Wells: His Turbulent Life and Times*. Harmondsworth, UK: Penguin, 1972.

Dikty, T. E., ed. *The Best Science Fiction Stories and Novels: 1956*. New York: Frederick Fell, 1956.

Donovan, Jeffrey. "U.S.: 60 Years Later, Nagasaki Witness Is Finally Heard." *Radio Free Europe*, 24 June 2005. http://tinyurl.com/7gjej63.

Dowling, David. *Fictions of Nuclear Disaster*. Basingstoke, UK: Macmillan, 1987.

DuBois, Brendan. *Resurrection Day*. London: Warner Books, 2000.

Dugger, Ronnie. "*The Third World War:* The President's Favorite Book." *The Nation*, 27 October 1984, 413–14, 416.

Dunn, Thomas P., and Richard D. Erlich. *The Mechanical God: Machines in Science Fiction*. Westport, CT: Greenwood Press, 1982.

Dyson, Freeman. *Weapons and Hope*. New York: Harper & Row, 1984.

Eco, Umberto. *The Middle Ages of James Joyce*. Trans. Ellen Esrock. London: Hutchinson Radius, 1989.

EMP Commission. *Report of the Commission to Assess the Threat to the United States from Electromagnetic Pulse (EMP) Attack*. Vol. 1: *Executive Report 2004*. http://tinyurl.com/7oddab6.

Engel, Leonard, and Emanuel S. Piller. *World Aflame: The Russian-American War of 1950*. New York: Dial Press, 1947.

Fallout Protection: What to Know and Do About Nuclear Attack. Washington DC: Office of Civil Defense, 1961.

Feinberg, Barry, ed. *The Collected Stories of Bertrand Russell*. London: George Allen & Unwin, 1972.

Ferguson, Brad. *The World Next Door*. New York: Tor, 1990.

Ferguson, Frances. "The Nuclear Sublime." *Diacritics* 14 (Summer 1984): 4–10.

Ferrigno, Robert. *Prayers for the Assassin*. New York: Scribner's, 2006.

Filger, Sheldon. *King of Bombs*. Bloomington, IN: Author House, 2006.

———. "Will Al-Qaeda Nuke America?" *Huffpost Politics*, 13 May 2009. http://tinyurl.com/7pkqctt.

Fitzgerald, Robert, ed. *The Collected Short Prose of James Agee*. New York: Houghton, 1968.

Ford, Daniel. *The Button: The Nuclear Trigger—Does It Work?* New York: Simon & Schuster, 1985.

Forstchen, William R. *One Second After*. New York: Tom Docherty, 2009.

Foster, Richard [as K. F. Crossen]. *The Rest Must Die.* New York: Fawcett, 1959.

Frank, Pat. *Alas, Babylon.* New York: Harper Perennial, 2005.

———. *Forbidden Area.* Philadelphia: J. B. Lippincott, 1956.

———. "Hiroshima: Point of No Return." *Saturday Review of Literature* 43 (24 December 1960): 25, 40.

———. *How to Survive the H-Bomb—And Why.* Philadelphia: J. B. Lippincott, 1962.

Franklin, H. Bruce. "Fatal Fiction: A Weapon to End All Wars." *Bulletin of the Atomic Scientists* 45.ix (1989): 18–25.

———. *War Stars: The Superweapon and the American Imagination.* Rev. ed. Amherst: U of Massachusetts P, 2008.

Fraser, David. *August 1988.* London: Collins, 1983.

Freeze, R. Allen, and Jay H. Lehr. *The Fluoride Wars: How a Modest Public Health Measure Became America's Longest Running Political Melodrama.* Hoboken, NJ: Wiley- Blackwell, 2009.

Freud, Sigmund. *Civilization and Its Discontents.* Trans. Joan Riviere. Ed. James Strachey. London: Hogarth Press, 1975.

———. *Jokes and Their Relation to the Unconscious.* Trans. and ed. James Strachey. London: Routledge & Kegan Paul, 1960.

Friedman, Bruce Jay, ed. *Black Humor.* New York: Bantam, 1965.

Fromm, Eric. *The Sane Society.* New York: Fawcett, 1967.

Frye, Northrop. *The Great Code: The Bible and Literature.* London: Routledge & Kegan Paul, 1982.

Fuller, Samuel, dir. *Hell and High Water.* Twentieth Century Fox, 1954.

Galouye, Daniel F. *Dark Universe.* New York: Bantam, 1961.

Garrison, Dee. *Bracing for Armageddon: Why Civil Defence Never Worked; The Myth of Civil Defense in the Nuclear Age.* New York: Oxford UP, 2006.

Geduld, Carolyn. *Bernard Wolfe.* New York: Twayne, 1972.

Gelmis, Joseph. *The Film Director as Superstar.* London: Secker & Warburg, 1971.

George, Peter. *Commander-1.* London: Heinemann, 1965.

———. *Dr. Strangelove: Or, How I Learned to Stop Worrying and Love the Bomb.* Boston: Gregg Press, 1979.

George, Peter [as Peter Bryant]. *Red Alert.* New York: Ace Books, 1958.

Gerstell, Richard. *How to Survive an Atomic Bomb.* Washington, DC: Combat Forces Press, 1950.

Gevers, Nick. "In a Genre of His Own: An Interview with Neal Barrett, Jr." http://tinyurl.com/78rvu49.

Gleick, James. "After the Bomb, a Mushroom Cloud of Metaphors." *New York Times,* 21 May 1989. http://tinyurl.com/7r3ahum.

Goodman, Amy, and David Goodman. *The Exception to the Rulers: Exposing Oily Politicians, War Profiteers, and the Media That Love Them.* New York: Hyperion Books, 2004.

Graves, C. L. "Fiction." *The Spectator,* 16 June 1915, 836–37.

Greenberg, Martin H., ed. *The Tom Clancy Companion.* London: Harper Collins, 1992.

Griffin, Russell M. "Medievalism in *A Canticle for Leibowitz.*" *Extrapolation* 14.ii (1973): 112–25.

Groddeck, Georg. *The Book of the It.* New York: Vintage, 1949.

Grossman, Andrew D. *Neither Dead nor Red: Civil Defense and American Political Development during the Early Cold War.* New York: Routledge, 2001.

Groves, Leslie M. *Now It Can Be Told: The Story of the Manhattan Project.* New York: Da Capo Press, 1983.

Hackett, John. *The Third World War: The Untold Story.* London: Sidgwick & Jackson, 1982.

———. *The Third World War, August 1985: A Future History.* London: Sidgwick & Jackson, 1978.

Hampton, Orville H. "Atomic Submarine: Screenplay." Allied Artists, 1959. http://leonscripts.tripod.com/scripts/ATOMICSUB.htm/.

Harris, James B., dir. *The Bedford Incident.* Columbia/Bedford Productions, 1965.

Harry, Eric L. *Arc Light.* London: Hodder & Stoughton, 1995.

Harvey, Mary Kersey. "A Novel of World War III." *Saturday Review* 45 (October 20, 1962): 23.

Hayles, N. Katherine. *How We Became Posthuman: Virtual Bodies in Cybernetics, Literature and Informatics.* Chicago: U of Chicago P, 1999.

Haynes, Roslynn D. *H. G. Wells: Discoverer of the Future.* London: Macmillan, 1980.

Heinlein, Robert A. *Expanded Universe.* New York: Ace, 1980.

———. *Farnham's Freehold.* London: Dennis Dobson, 1974.

Henriksen, Margot A. *Dr. Strangelove's America: Society and Culture in the Atomic Age.* Berkeley: U of California P, 1997.

Herbert, Frank. *The Dragon in the Sea.* Boston: Gregg Press, 1980.

Hersey, John. *Hiroshima.* Exp. ed. Harmondsworth, UK: Penguin, 1986.

———. *Interview.* Columbia, MO: American Audio Prose Library, 1988.

Hinds, Lynn Boyd, and Theodore Otto Windt Jr. *The Cold War as Rhetoric: The Beginnings, 1945–1950.* New York: Praeger, 1991.

Hoban, Russell. *Riddley Walker.* Exp. ed. Bloomington: Indiana UP, 1998.

Hook, Sidney. *The Fail-Safe Fallacy.* New York: Stein & Day, 1963.

Hutcheon, Linda. *A Poetics of Postmodernism: History, Theory, Fiction.* New York: Routledge, 1988.

Hutchins, Robert M. "Szilard and the Dolphins." *Bulletin of the Atomic Scientists* 17.iii (1961): 290.

———. *The University of Utopia.* Chicago: U of Chicago P, 1953.

Huxley, Aldous. *Ape and Essence* London: Chatto & Windus, 1949.

———. *Complete Essays: 1956–1963.* Vol. 5. Ed. Robert S. Baker and James Sexton. Chicago: Ivan R. Dee, 2002.

Ing, Dean. "Nuclear Survival: Part Two, Living Under Pressure." *Destinies: The Paperback Magazine of Science Fiction and Speculative Fact* 2.iv (1980): 147–67.

———. *Pulling Through.* New York: Ace, 1983.

———. *Systemic Shock.* New York: Ace, 1981.

Innis, H. A. *Empire and Communications.* Oxford: Clarendon Press, 1950.

Jackson, Peter. *Maps of Meaning.* London: Routledge, 1995.

Jacobs, Robert A. *The Dragon's Tail: Americans Face the Atomic Age.* Boston: U of Massachusetts P, 2010.

James, Edward. *Science Fiction in the Twentieth Century.* Oxford: Oxford UP, 1994.

James, William. *Essays in Religion and Morality.* Cambridge, MA: Harvard UP, 1982.

Jarvis, Brian. *Postmodern Cartographies: The Geographical Imagination in Contemporary American Culture.* London: Pluto Press, 1998.

Jernigan, Jessica Lee. "The Nuclear Sublime: Interview with Lydia Millet." http://tinyurl.com/777ctly.

Johnson, Denis. *Fiskadoro.* London: Chatto & Windus, 1985.

Joseph, Mark. *To Kill the Potemkin*. London: Souvenir Press, 1987.

Judd, Orrin C. "One Nation, Under Allah: An Interview with Robert Ferrigno." http://tinyurl.com/7579rch.

Jungk, Robert. *Brighter Than a Thousand Suns*. Harmondsworth, UK: Penguin, 1964.

Kagan, Norman. *The Cinema of Stanley Kubrick*. New York: Holt, Rinehart & Winston, 1972.

Kahn, Herman. *On Thermonuclear War*. 2nd ed. Princeton, NJ: Princeton UP, 1961.

Kazi, Reshmi. "Nuclear Terrorism: No Longer a Science Fiction." *Strategic Analysis* 32.iii (2008). http://tinyurl.com/7h2wp2v.

Kearny, Cresson H. *Expedient Shelter Construction and Occupancy Requirements*. Oak Ridge, TN: Oak Ridge National Laboratory, 1976.

Kennedy, J. F. "Address of Senator John F. Kennedy Accepting the Democratic Party Nomination for the Presidency of the United States." http://tinyurl.com/7ghac8e.

Ketterer, David. *Imprisoned in a Tesseract: The Life and Work of James Blish*. Kent, OH: Kent State UP, 1987.

King-Hall, Stephen. *Men of Destiny: Or, The Moment of No Return*. London: K-H Services, 1960.

Kirchwey, Freda. "When H. G. Wells Split the Atom: A 1914 Preview of 1945." *The Nation*, 18 August 1945, 154–56.

Klein, Richard. "The Future of Nuclear Criticism." *Yale French Studies* 97 (1990): 78–102.

Knebel, Fletcher, and Charles W. Bailey II, *Seven Days in May*. New York: Harper & Row, 1962.

Koestler, Arthur. *Insight and Outlook*. New York: Macmillan, 1949.

———. *The Trail of the Dinosaur and Other Essays*. London: Jonathan Cape, 1955.

Kubrick, Stanley. "How I Learned to Stop Worrying and Love the Cinema." *Films and Filming* 9 (June 1963): 12–13.

Kuhn, Thomas S. *The Structure of Scientific Revolutions*. 2nd ed. Chicago: U of Chicago P, 1970.

Lang, Daniel. *Early Tales of the Atomic Age*. New York: Doubleday, 1948.

Lanouette, William. *Genius in the Shadows: A Biography of Leo Szilard; The Man Behind the Bomb*. Chicago: U of Chicago P, 1994.

Lapp, Ralph E. *Must We Hide?* Boston: Addison Wesley, 1949.

———. *The Voyage of the Lucky Dragon*. New York: Harper, 1958.

Laurence, William L. *Dawn Over Zero: The Story of the Atomic Bomb*. London: Museum Press, 1947.

———. *The Hell Bomb*. London: Hollis & Carter, 1951.

———. *Men and Atoms*. London: Scientific Book Club, 1961.

———. "U.S. Atom Bomb Site Belies Tokyo Tales." *New York Times*, 12 September 1945, 1, 4. http://tinyurl.com/7nqs6m4.

Lear, John. "Hiroshima, U.S.A.: Can Anything Be Done About It?" *Collier's*, 5 August 1950, 11, 15.

———. "Hiroshima, U.S.A.: Something CAN Be Done About It." *Collier's*, 5 August 1950, 16, 64–69.

LeClair, Tom, and Larry McCaffery, eds. *Anything Can Happen: Interviews with Contemporary American Novelists*. Urbana: U of Illinois P, 1983.

Leinster, Murray. *Fight for Life: A Complete Novel of the Atomic Age*. New York: Crestwood, 1947.

———. "Short History of World War Three." *Astounding Science Fiction* 60.v (1958): 69–83.

Leinster, Murray [as Will F. Jenkins]. *The Murder of the U.S.A.* New York: Crown, 1946.

Levine, Murray S. "Civil Defence vs. Public Apathy." *Bulletin of the Atomic Scientists* 9.i (1953): 27–28.

Lewin, Leonard C. *Report from Iron Mountain on the Possibility and Desirability of Peace.* London: Macdonald, 1967.

Lewis, Flora [as Frederick Hazlitt Brennan]. *One of Our H-Bombs Is Missing.* Robbinsdale, MN: Fawcett, 1955.

Ley, Willy. "Push for Pushbutton Warfare." *Astounding Science Fiction* 40.i (1947): 87–105.

Linden, George W. "Dr. Strangelove: Or, How I Learned to Stop Worrying and Love the Bomb." In *Nuclear War Films.* Ed. Jack G. Shaheen. Carbondale: Southern Illinois UP, 1978. 58–67.

Lumet, Sidney, dir. *Fail-Safe.* Columbia Pictures, 1964.

Macklin, F. Anthony. "Sex and Dr. Strangelove." *Film Comment* 3 (Summer 1965): 55–57.

Maland, Charles. "*Dr. Strangelove* (1964): Nightmare Comedy and the Ideology of Liberal Consensus." In *Hollywood as Historian: American Film in a Cultural Context.* Ed. Peter C. Rollins. Lexington: UP of Kentucky, 1997. 190–210.

Manganiello, Dominic. "History as Judgement and Promise in *A Canticle for Leibowitz.*" *Science-Fiction Studies* 13.ii (1986): 159–69.

Mannix, Peter. *The Rhetoric of Antinuclear Fiction: Persuasive Strategies in Novels and Films.* Lewisburg, NY: Bucknell UP, 1992.

Masters, Dexter. *The Accident.* London: Faber, 1987.

Masters, Dexter, and Katherine Way, eds. *One World or None: A Report to the Public on the Full Meaning of the Atomic Bomb.* New York: Whittlesey House/McGraw-Hill, 1946.

Maus, Derek C. *Unvarnishing Reality: Subversive Russian and American Cold War Satire.* Columbia: U of South Carolina P, 2011.

May, Elaine Tyler. *Homeward Bound: American Families in the Cold War Era.* New York: Basic Books, 1988.

McCullough, David. *Truman.* London: Simon & Schuster, 1993.

McDonald, John. *Strategy in Poker, Business and War.* New York: Norton, 1996.

McKeen, William. "Terry Southern." In *Encyclopedia of American Humorists.* Ed. Stephen H. Gale. New York: Garland, 1988. 411–14.

Medhurst, Martin J., Robert L. Ivie, Philip Wander, and Robert L. Scott, eds. *Cold War Rhetoric: Strategy, Metaphor, and Ideology.* Westport, CT: Greenwood Press, 1990.

Meek, S. P. "The Red Peril." *Amazing Stories* 4.vi (1929): 486–503, 521.

Mendelson, Edward. "Encyclopedic Narrative: From Dante to Pynchon." *Modern Language Notes* 91.vi (1976): 1267–75.

Merricks, Linda. *The World Made New: Frederick Soddy, Science, Politics, and Environment* Oxford: Oxford UP, 1996.

Merril, Judith. *Homecalling and Other Stories: The Complete Solo Short SF of Judith Merril.* Farmington, MA: New England Science Fiction Association Press, 2005.

———. *Shadow on the Hearth.* London: Roberts & Vintner, 1966.

Merril, Judith, and Emily Pohl-Weary. *Better to Have Loved: The Life of Judith Merril.* Toronto: Between the Lines, 2002.

Meyer, Bill. *Ultimatum.* New York: New American Library, 1966.

Miller, Walter M. *The Best of Walter M. Miller, Jr.* London: Victor Gollancz, 2000.

———. *A Canticle for Leibowitz.* Boston: Gregg Press, 1975.

————. *Saint Leibowitz and the Wild Horse Woman*. London: Orbit, 1997.

Miller, Walter M., Jr., and Martin H. Greenberg, eds. *Beyond Armageddon: Survivors of the Megawar*. London: Robinson, 1987.

Millet, Lydia. *Oh Pure and Radiant Heart*. New York: Soft Skull Press, 2005.

Mills, C. Wright. *The Causes of World War Three*. London: Secker & Warburg, 1959.

Morris, Edita. *The Flowers of Hiroshima*. London: Macgibbon & Kee, 1959.

Morrison, Philip. "If the Bomb Gets Out of Hand." In *One World or None*. Ed. Dexter Masters and Katherine Way. New York: Whittlesey House/McGraw-Hill, 1946. 1–6.

Morrow, James. "How I Slouched Towards Hiroshima." *Futurismic*. http://tinyurl.com/7euu3jd.

————. *Shambling Towards Hiroshima*. San Francisco: Tachyon, 2009.

Moskin, J. R. "Polaris." *Look,* 29 August 1961, 17–31.

Mumford, Lewis. *The Conduct of Life*. London: Secker & Warburg, 1952.

————. *In the Name of Sanity*. Westport, CT: Greenwood, 1973.

————. *The Myth of the Machine: The Pentagon of Power*. New York: Harcourt Brace Jovanovich, 1970.

————. *Programme for Survival*. London: Secker & Warburg, 1946.

Murphy, Geraldine. "Ahab as Capitalist, Ahab as Communist: Revising *Moby-Dick* for the Cold War." http://tinyurl.com/6vw2fo6.

Mydans, Carl. "Here the U.S. Fights the Coldest War." *Life,* 1 March 1963, 18–29.

Nadel, Alan. *Containment Culture: American Narratives, Postmodernism, and the Atomic Age*. Durham, NC: Duke UP, 1995.

Nelson, Thomas Allen. *Kubrick: Inside a Film Artist's Maze*. Bloomington: Indiana UP, 1982.

Norris, Christopher. *Derrida*. Cambridge, MA: Harvard UP, 1988.

————. "'Nuclear Criticism' Ten Years On." *Prose Studies* 17.ii (1994), 130–38.

Nowlan, Philip Francis. *Armageddon 2419 A.D.* New York: Ace, 1962.

Oakes, Guy. *The Imaginary War: Civil Defense and American Cold War Culture*. New York: Oxford UP, 1994.

Oakes, Guy, and Andrew Grossman. "Managing Nuclear Terror: The Genesis of American Civil Defence Strategy." *International Journal of Politics, Culture, and Society* 5.iii (1992): 361–401.

O'Brien, Tim. *The Nuclear Age*. New York: Knopf, 1985.

Orwell, George. "Burnham's View of the Contemporary World Struggle." In *The Complete Works of George Orwell: It Is What I Think, 1947–1949*. Vol. 19. Ed. Peter Davidson. London: Secker & Warburg, 1998. 102.

Ostow, Mortimer. "War and the Unconscious." *Bulletin of the Atomic Scientists* 19.i (1963): 25–28.

Owen, Dean. *End of the World*. New York: Ace, 1963.

Palmer, Michael A. *Arctic Strike! A Visual Novel of the War of Tomorrow*. New York: Avon Books, 1991.

Pangborn, Edgar. *Davy*. New York: Ballantine, 1964.

————. *The Judgment of Eve*. London: Rapp & Whiting, 1968.

Pease, Donald E. "*Moby-Dick* and the Cold War." In *The American Renaissance Reconsidered*. Ed. Walter Benn Michaels and Donald E. Pease. Baltimore: Johns Hopkins UP, 1985. 113–55.

————. *Visionary Compacts: American Renaissance Writings in Cultural Context*. Madison: U of Wisconsin P, 1987.

Percy, Walker. "Walker Percy on Walter M. Miller, Jr.'s *A Canticle for Leibowitz*." In *Rediscoveries:*

Informal Essays in which Well-Known Novelists Rediscover Neglected Works of Fiction by One of Their Favorite Authors. Ed. David Madden. New York: Crown, 1971. 262–69.

Peterson, Val. "They Said It Would Never Happen." *New York Times Book Review,* 17 January 1954, 4–5.

Phelps, John. "The Grim Possibility." *Bulletin of the Atomic Scientists* 19.vi (1963): 28.

Piette, Adam. *The Literary Cold War, 1945 to Vietnam.* Edinburgh: Edinburgh UP, 2009.

Pogel, Nancy, and William Chamberlain. "Humor into Film: Self Reflections in Adaptations of Black Comic Novels." *Literature/Film Quarterly* 13.iii (1985): 187–93.

Pohl, Frederik, ed. *The Eighth Galaxy Reader.* London: Gollancz, 1966.

Poore, Charles. "Books of the Times." *New York Times,* 5 June 1950, 29.

Pournelle, Jerry, and Stephan T. Possony. *The Strategy of Technology.* http://www.jerrypournelle.com/slowchange/Strat.html.

"Preview of the War We Do Not Want." *Collier's,* 27 October 1951.

Priestley, J. B. "Best Anti-Bomb Story Yet." *Reynolds News,* 20 September 1959, 4.

———. "Britain and the Nuclear Bombs." *New Statesman and Nation,* 12 November 1957, 554–56.

———. *The Doomsday Men.* London: Corgi, 1963.

Prochnau, William. *Trinity's Child.* New York: Putnam, 1983.

"A Professor's Accident." *The Minority of One,* October 1963, 18–19.

Rascovich, Mark. *The Bedford Incident.* New York: Atheneum, 1963.

Raser, John R. "The Failure of Fail-Safe." In *Beyond Conflict and Containment: Critical Studies of Military and Foreign Policy.* Ed. Milton J. Rosenberg. New Brunswick, NJ: Transaction Books, 1972. 127–46.

Reilly, John J. "World War III in 1957." http://tinyurl.com/7junwkh.

Rein, Harold. *Few Were Left.* New York: John Day, 1955.

Robinson, Kim Stanley. *The Wild Shore.* London: Macdonald, 1986.

———. "A Sensitive Dependence on Initial Conditions." In *Remaking History and Other Stories.* New York: Tom Doherty, 1991. 440–51.

Rogin, Michael. *"Ronald Reagan," the Movie and Other Episodes in Political Demonology.* Berkeley: U of California P, 1987.

Rose, Kenneth D. *One Nation Underground: The Fallout Shelter in American Culture.* New York: New York UP, 2001.

Rosenberg, Milton J. ed. *Beyond Conflict and Containment: Critical Studies of Military and Foreign Policy.* New Brunswick, NJ: Transaction Books, 1972.

Roshwald, Mordecai. "Confusion of Spheres: A Comment on American Civilization." *British Journal of Sociology* 16 (1965): 243–51.

———. "The Cybernetics of Blunder." *The Nation,* 13 March 1967, 335–36.

———. *Dreams and Nightmares: Science and Technology in Myth and Fiction.* Jefferson, NC: McFarland, 2008.

———. *Level 7.* Ed. David Seed. Madison: U of Wisconsin P, 2004.

———. "My Encounters with Bertrand Russell." *Russell: The Journal of the Bertrand Russell Archives* 6.ii (1986–1987): 150–53.

———. "Order and Over-Organization in America." *British Journal of Sociology* 24.i (1973): 30–42.

———. "Quo Vadis, America?" *Modern Age* 2.ii (1958): 193–98.

———. *A Small Armageddon.* London: New English Library, 1966.

———. "Who Will Bury Whom?" *The Nation,* 14 October 1961, 248–49.

Russell, Bertrand. *Common Sense and Nuclear Warfare.* London: Allen & Unwin, 1959.

———. *Has Man a Future?* Harmondsworth, UK: Penguin, 1961.

Ruthven, Ken. *Nuclear Criticism.* Melbourne: Melbourne UP, 1993.

Ryan, Alan. *Bertrand Russell: A Political Life.* London: Penguin, 1990.

Samuelson, David N. "*Limbo:* The Great American Dystopia." *Extrapolation* 19 (1977): 76–87.

———. "The Lost Canticles of Walter M. Miller, Jr." *Science-Fiction Studies* 3.i (1976): 3–26.

Sanders, David. *John Hersey.* New York: Twayne, 1967.

Scheick, William J. "The Binuclear Voice of Hersey's *Hiroshima.*" *Nuclear Texts and Contexts* 11 (Spring 1995): 5.

Schelling, Thomas. "Meteors, Mischief, and War." *Bulletin of the Atomic Scientists* 16 (September 1960): 292–96, 300.

Scholes, Robert, and Eric S. Rabkin. *Science Fiction: History, Science, Vision.* New York: Oxford UP, 1977.

Schulz, Max F. *Black Humor Fiction of the Sixties.* Athens: Ohio UP, 1973.

Schwarz, Jeffrey, prod. *Revisiting* Fail-Safe. Columbia Tristar Home Video, 2000.

Schwenger, Peter. *Letter Bomb: Nuclear Holocaust and the Exploding Word.* Baltimore: Johns Hopkins UP, 1992.

Schwininger, Lee. "Ecofeminism, Nuclearism, and O'Brien's *The Nuclear Age.*" In *The Nightmare Considered: Critical Essays on Nuclear War Literature.* Ed. Nancy Anisfield. Bowling Green, OH: Bowling Green State U Popular P, 1991. 177–85.

Scortia, Thomas N., and George Zebrowski, eds. *Human-Machines: An Anthology of Stories About Cyborgs.* London: Robert Hale, 1977.

Secrest, Rose. *Glorificemus: A Study of the Fiction of Walter M. Miller, Jr.* Lanham, MD: UP of America, 2002.

Seed, David. *American Science Fiction and the Cold War: Fiction and Film.* Edinburgh: Edinburgh UP, 1999.

———. "TV Docudrama and the Nuclear Subject." In *British Science Fiction Television: A Hitchhiker's Guide.* Ed. John R. Cook and Peter Wright. London: I. B. Tauris, 2006. 154–63.

Senior, W. A. "From the Begetting of Monsters": Distortion as Unifier in *A Canticle for Leibowitz.*" *Extrapolation* 34.iv (1993): 329–42.

Shaheen, Jack G., ed. *Nuclear War Films.* Carbondale: Southern Illinois UP, 1978.

Shippey, Tom, ed. *Fictional Space: Essays on Contemporary Science Fiction.* Oxford: Blackwell, 1991.

Shute, Nevil. *On the Beach.* New York: William Morrow, 1957.

Siemes, John A. "Hiroshima: Eye-Witness." *Saturday Review,* 11 May 1946, 24–25, 40–44.

Silverberg, Robert. "Reflections: The Cleve Cartmill Affair; One." *Asimov's Science Fiction,* September 2003. http://www.asimovs.com/_issue_0310/ref.shtml.

———. "Reflections: The Cleve Cartmill Affair; Two." *Asimov's Science Fiction,* October/November 2003. http://tinyurl.com/5mapp.

———, ed. *Science Fiction Hall of Fame.* Vol. 1. Garden City, NY: Doubleday, 1970.

Simpson, Mary. "A Long Hard Look at Civil Defense: A Review of the Holifield Committee Hearings." *Bulletin of the Atomic Scientists* 12 (November 1956): 346.

Sinclair, Upton. *The Millennium: A Comedy of the Year 2000*. 1924. New York: Seven Stories Press, 2000.

Six Steps to Survival. Washington, DC: Federal Civil Defense Administration, 1957. http://tinyurl.com/7nfxg3k.

Slotkin, Richard. *Gunfighter Nation: The Myth of the Frontier in Twentieth-Century America*. New York: Atheneum, 1992.

Smith, Curtis C., ed. *Twentieth-Century Science-Fiction Writers*. 2nd ed. Chicago: St. James Press, 1986.

Smith, David C. ed. *The Correspondence of H. G. Wells: 1935–1946*. Vol. 4. London: Pickering & Chatto, 1998.

Smith, E. E. "Doc." *The Skylark of Space*. Providence, RI: Bison, 1946.

Smith, George H. *Doomsday Wing*. Derby, CT: Monarch Books, 1963.

Smith, P. D. *Doomsday Men: The Real Dr. Strangelove and the Dream of the Superweapon*. London: Allen Lane, 2007.

Soddy, Frederick. *The Interpretation of Radium*. London: John Murray, 1909.

———. *The Story of Atomic Energy*. London: Nova Atlantis, 1949.

Solberg, Carl. *Riding High: America in the Cold War*. New York: Mason & Lipscomb, 1973.

Sontag, Susan. *Against Interpretation, and Other Essays*. London: Eyre & Spottiswood, 1967.

Southern, Nile, and Josh Alan Friedman, eds. *Now Dig This: The Unspeakable Writings of Terry Southern, 1950–1995*. New York: Grove Press, 2001.

Southern, Terry. "Check-Up with Dr. Strangelove." *Filmmaker* (Fall 2004). http://tinyurl.com/83kmoqd.

Spanos, William V. *The Errant Art of "Moby-Dick": The Canon, the Cold War, and the Struggle for American Studies*. Durham, NC: Duke UP, 1995.

Spencer, Steven M. "Fallout: The Silent Killer." *Saturday Evening Post*, 29 August 1959 (Part 1): 26–27, 87, 89–90; 5 September 1959 (Part 2): 25, 84–86.

Spencer, Susan. "The Post-Apocalyptic Library: Oral and Literate Culture in *Fahrenheit 451* and *A Canticle for Leibowitz*." *Extrapolation* 32.iv (1991): 331–42.

Stillman, Grant B. "Two of the MADdest Scientists: Where Strangelove Meets Dr. No; Or, Unexpected Roots for Kubrick's Cold War Classic." *Film History: An International Journal* 20.iv (2008): 487–500.

Stone, Albert E. *Literary Aftershocks: American Writers, Readers, and the Bomb*. New York: Twayne, 1994.

Strieber, Whitley. *Critical Mass*. New York: Tor, 2009.

Strieber, Whitley, and James W. Kunetka. *Warday and the Journey Onward*. London: Hodder & Stoughton, 1984.

Suid, Lawrence. *Sailing on the Silver Screen: Hollywood and the U.S. Navy*. Annapolis, MD: Naval Institute Press, 1996.

Sutton, Jeff. *Bombs in Orbit*. New York: Ace Books, 1959.

———. *H-Bomb over America*. New York: Ace Books, 1967.

Swados, Harvey. "Popular Taste and *The Caine Mutiny*." *Partisan Review* 20 (March–April 1953): 248–56.

Swaim, Don. "Wired for Books Audio Interview with Whitley Strieber." 6 April 1984 and 23 October 1985. http://tinyurl.com/7ss3gcm.

Szilard, Leo. "The Diary of Dr. Davis." *Bulletin of the Atomic Scientists* 6.ii (1950): 51–57.

———. "How to Live with the Bomb and Survive." *Bulletin of the Atomic Scientists* 16.ii (1960): 59–73.

———. "The Physicist Invades Politics." *Saturday Review of Literature,* 3 May 1947, 7–8, 31–34.

———. "President Truman Did Not Understand." *U.S. News and World Report,* 15 August 1960, 68–71. http://tinyurl.com/7wgvtp8.

———. *The Voice of the Dolphins and Other Stories.* Exp. ed. Palo Alto, CA: Stanford UP, 1992.

Tate, Peter. "The Fantastic World of Judith Merril." *Western Mail* [UK], 14 October 1966, 7.

Teller, Edward, and Allen Brown. *The Legacy of Hiroshima.* London: Macmillan, 1962.

Tenn, William. *The Wooden Star.* New York: Ballantine, 1968.

Tevis, Walter. *The Man Who Fell Down to Earth.* New York: Dell, 1986.

Thackara, James. *America's Children.* New York: Overlook Press, 2002.

"The 36-Hour War." *Life,* 19 November 1965, 27–35.

"This Is Article Cited by Soviet in Its Criticism of U.S. Flights." *New York Times,* 19 April 1958, 4.

Thomas, Gordon, and Max Morgan-Witts. *Ruin from the Air: The Atomic Mission to Hiroshima.* London: Hamish Hamilton, 1977.

Tucker, Wilson. *The Long Loud Silence.* New York: Dell, 1954.

Vanny, Jim. "The Radium Master." *Wonder Stories* 2.iii (1930): 271.

Vonnegut, Kurt. *Player Piano.* London: Granada, 1969.

Walker, Jeanne Murray. "Reciprocity and Exchange in *A Canticle for Leibowitz.*" *Renascence* 33.ii (1989): 67–85.

Wallace, Irving. "The Operation of the Last Resort." *Saturday Evening Post,* 20 October 1957, 24.

Walsh, Chad. *From Utopia to Nightmare.* London: Geoffrey Bles, 1962.

Wang, Jessica. *Science, Security, and the Cold War: The Case of E. U. Condon.* MIT Working Paper No. 17. Cambridge, MA: Program in Science, Technology, and Society, 1991. http://tinyurl.com/7wgvtp8.

Warrick, Patricia S. *The Cybernetic Imagination in Science Fiction.* Cambridge, MA: MIT Press, 1980.

Weart, Spencer R. *Nuclear Fear: A History of Images.* Cambridge, MA: Harvard UP, 1988.

Weart, Spencer R., and Gertrude Weiss Szilard, eds. *Leo Szilard: His Version of the Facts.* Cambridge, MA: MIT Press, 1978.

Weller, George. *First into Nagasaki: The Censored Eyewitness Dispatches on Post-Atomic Japan and Its Prisoners of War.* Ed. Anthony Weller. New York: Crown, 2006.

Wells, H. G. *The Discovery of the Future.* Ed. Patrick Parrinder. London: PNL Press, 1989.

———. *An Experiment in Autobiography.* Boston: Little, Brown, 1962.

———. *The World Set Free.* London: Hogarth Press, 1988.

———. *The World Set Free.* London: Collins, 1924.

Welton, Harry. *The Third World War.* London: Pall Mall Press, 1959.

Wheeler, Harvey [as F. B. Aiken]. "Abraham '59—A Nuclear Fantasy." *Dissent* 6 (Winter 1959): 18–24.

Wheeler, Harvey. "Fail-Safe Then and Now." *The Idler: A Web Periodical* 2 (29 May 2000). http://tinyurl.com/7l74gwt.

Wheeler, Harvey, and Eugene Burdick. "The Politics of Destruction." *Saturday Review,* 9 November 1963, 25–27, 83–84.

Wiener, Norbert. *Cybernetics*. Cambridge, MA: MIT Press, 1961.

———. *The Human Use of Human Beings*. Boston: Houghton Mifflin, 1950.

Wilder, Thornton. *The Bridge of San Luis Rey*. London: Longmans, Green 1931.

Wilkinson, Rupert. "Connections with Toughness: The Novels of Eugene Burdick." *Journal of American Studies* 11 (1977): 223–39.

Williams, Paul. "Nuclear Criticism." In *The Routledge Companion to Science Fiction*. Ed. Mark Bould, Andrew M. Butler, Adam Roberts, and Sherryl Vint. London: Routledge, 2009. 246–48.

———. *Race, Ethnicity and Nuclear War. Representations of Nuclear Weapons and Post-Apocalyptic Worlds*. Liverpool: Liverpool UP, 2011.

Wilson, Gilbert. "Moby Dick and the Atom." *Bulletin of the Atomic Scientists* 8.vi (1952): 195–97.

Winkler, Allan M. *Life Under a Cloud: American Anxiety About the Atom*. Urbana: U of Illinois P, 1999.

Wolfe, Bernard. *In Deep*. London: Secker & Warburg, 1958.

———. *Limbo*. New York: Random House, 1952.

———. "Self Portrait." *Galaxy Science Fiction*, November 1951, 72.

———. *The Great Prince Died*. London: Jonathan Cape, 1959.

Wolfley, Lawrence. "Repression's Rainbow: The Presence of Norman O. Brown in Pynchon's Big Novel." In *Critical Essays on Thomas Pynchon*. Ed. Richard Pearce. Boston: G. K. Hall, 1981. 99–123.

Wouk, Herman. *The "Caine" Mutiny*. New York: Doubleday, 1951.

Wylie, Philip. *The Answer*. New York: Rinehart, 1955.

———. "A Better Way to Beat the Bomb." *Atlantic Monthly* 187 (February 1951): 42.

———. "After the Hydrogen Bombs." *New York Herald Tribune Book Review*, 14 December 1952, 11.

———. "Deliverance or Doom." *Collier's*, 29 September 1945, 18–19.

———. *The Disappearance*. New York: Rinehart, 1951.

———. *The End of the Dream*. Garden City, NY: Doubleday, 1972.

———. *The Innocent Ambassadors*. New York: Rinehart, 1957.

———. "Knowledge for Man's Sake." *Bulletin of the Atomic Scientists* 9 (November 1953): 330–31.

———. *The "Lomokome" Papers*. New York: Pocket Books, 1968.

———. *Los Angeles: A.D. 2017*. New York: Popular Library, 1971.

———. "McNamara's Missile Defense: A Multibillion Fiasco?" *Popular Science* 192.i (1968): 59–61, 182.

———. *Opus 21*. New York: Rinehart, 1949.

———. "Panic, Psychology, and the Bomb." *Bulletin of the Atomic Scientists* 10 (February 1954): 37–40, 63.

———. "Science Fiction in an Age of Crisis." In *Modern Science Fiction: Its Meaning and Future*. Ed. Reginald Bretnor. New York: Coward McCann, 1953. 221–41.

———. *The Smuggled Atom Bomb*, New York: Lancer Books, 1965.

———. *Tomorrow!* New York: Rinehart, 1954.

———. *Triumph.* Garden City, NY: Doubleday, 1963.

———. "Why I Believe There Will Be No All-Out War." *Rotarian* 97 (September 1960): 22–25.

Yavenditti, Michael J. "John Hersey and the American Conscience: The Reception of *Hiroshima.*" *Pacific Historical Review* 43 (1974): 24–49.

Zavarzadeh, Mas'ud. *The Mythopoeic Reality: The Postwar American Nonfiction Novel.* Urbana: U of Illinois P, 1976.

Index

Atomic Energy Commission (AEC), 81
The Atomic Story (Campbell), 18
The Atomic Submarine, 149
authenticity, from details, 2, 25

Bailey, Charles, II, 177, 265n6
Ballard, J. G., 3–4, 44–45, 113, 220–21
Barrett, Neal, Jr., 95, 200
Bartter, Martha, 140–41
Baruch, Bernard, 253n16
The Bedford Incident (Rascovich), 7, 262n37;
   contradictions within, 157–59; differences
   between novel and film, 153, 155–56, 160–62;
   effects of destruction of enemy in, 160–62;
   film version, 154, 262n28, 262n29; *Moby-
   Dick* and, 151, 153–55, 159, 161; psychological
   themes of, 154–56, 158–59; significance as
   Arctic frontier in, 147, 150
The Beginning or the End (film), 20, 245n51
Bendau, Clifford B., 76
Berger, Albert I., 4
Bermel, Albert, 185–86
Bernstein, Walter, 177
Berriault, Gina, 60–61, 251n67
"A Better Way to Beat the Bomb" (Wylie), 57, 77
Beyond Armageddon (Miller), 3, 110
the Bible, 78, 89, 93, 148, 248n50, 251n6; *Alas,
   Babylon* referring to, 63, 65; in *A Canticle
   for Leibowitz,* 103–4, 256n32
Bidwell, Shelford, 228
"The Big Flash" (Spinrad), 4
Bikini Atoll, 28, 44–45, 151–52
Bisson, Terry, 110–11
Black Humor (Friedman), 186
Blish, James, 58–60, 251n64
"Blunder" (Wylie), 76
Boardman, Tom, Jr., 145
Bombs in Orbit (Sutton), 264n36
Bone, J. F., 131
"Boom!" (Feiffer), 197
Bova, Ben, 237
"The Box" (Blish), 59
Boyer, Paul, 6, 24, 33, 40, 61–62; on cultural
   impact of atomic bomb, 42, 117; on fear of
   nuclear weapons, 222, 251n71
Brackett, Leigh, 205–7
Bradbury, Ray, 3, 52, 205, 219; *Fahrenheit 451*
   by, 82, 251n6; *Moby-Dick's* influence on, 152,
   261n16
Bradley, David, 44–46, 48, 51–52
Brave New World (Huxley), 132, 135

Brave New World Revisited (Huxley), 135–36
Brians, Paul, 14, 87
The Bridge of San Luis Rey (Wilder), 31–32
"The Brigadier and the Golf Widow" (Cheever),
   60
Brin, David, 71, 214, 237
Britain, civil defense in, 49–50, 57
Brown, Allen, 47–48
Brown, Norman O., 197
Bryans, Paul, 125
Bukatman, Scott, 125
Bulletin of Atomic Scientists, 184–85, 195, 220,
   270n21
Burchett, Wilfred, 28–29
Burdick, Eugene, 7, 144, 176, 254n38; *Fail-Safe*
   by, 167–76, 263n9, 264n33; goals for *Fail-
   Safe,* 175, 177; writing style of, 173, 263n9
Burnham, James, 215–16, 222, 269n1
By the Bomb's Early Light (Boyer), 24

Caidin, Martin, 44, 48, 85
"Calling All Stars" (Szilard), 21–22
Campaign for Nuclear Disarmament, 141
Campbell, John W., 18, 130–31, 269n5
Canaday, John, 12, 19, 22–23
Candy (Southern), 186
A Canticle for Leibowitz (Miller), 7, 72, 101;
   decoding theme in, 99–100; influence on
   Catholicism on, 106–7; interpretations
   of ending of, 109–10; "It Takes a Thief"
   preceding, 96; lack of progress in, 103–4,
   107–8; novellas of, 95, 99–100; repetition
   of history in, 107–9, 211; sequel to, 110–11;
   signification in, 100, 105; treatment of the
   past in, 107–9
Cantor, Jay, 38, 248n46
Capek, Karel, 11, 15
Carson, Rachel, 92
A Case of Conscience (Blish), 59–60
casualties, from nuclear war, 49, 52, 85–86,
   144, 202; *Arctic Strike!* minimalizing, 228; in
   doctrine of deterrence, 217; in *Dr. Strangelove,* 188–89; *Fail-Safe* humanizing, 176; in
   imagined attack on New York City, 218–19;
   Wylie on, 83, 254n28
Catch-22 (Heller), 186–87, 192–93
The Causes of World War Three (Mills), 225
Cheever, John, 60
Children of the Ashes (Jungk), 37
China, 112, 262n28, 265n5
Christmas Eve (Kornbluth), 84

Derrida, Jacques, 2–3
The Descent (Berriault), 60–61, 251n67
deterrence, 158, 216, 217
"The Diary of Dr. Davis" (Szilard), 20, 123
Dick, Philip K., 95
The Disappearance (Wylie), 78
disarmament, 7, 125, 267n41; movement
 for, 141–43, 202; opposition to, 28, 72; in
 Szilard's stories, 22–23
disaster narratives, 14, 31; ecological, 90–94;
 monster films as, 38–39
Doomsday for Dyson (Priestley), 141
Doomsday Wing (Smith), 196
Dowling, David, 3, 54
Dr. Strangelove, 7, 60, 161, 179, 202, 266n36;
 based on *Red Alert*, 144, 176, 184–85, 189;
 black humor of, 184–85, 186–87; communication breakdowns in, 186, 188; compared
 to *Catch-22*, 187, 192–93; credit for film *vs.*
 novel, 182, 186; discontinuity in, 186–89,
 192; film *vs.* novel, 183, 189–90, 193–94, 195,
 265n4; filming of, 198, 267n40; game theory
 parodied in, 173, 226; humor in, 182, 184–85,
 187–88, 196–98; narrator in, 133, 185–86;
 other nuclear fiction compared to, 145, 168,
 196; sexuality in, 190, 193–95; shelter race
 in, 139–40; "us" *vs.* "them" in, 190–91; use of
 documentary style in, 185, 187
The Dragon in the Sea (Herbert), 148–49,
 261n5, 261n16
Dropshot (U.S. plan for war), 229–30
DuBois, Brendan, 232
"Dumb Waiter" (Miller), 99
Dyson, Freeman, 61, 74
dystopias, 114–15, 119, 135

early warning systems (DEW line), 131, 147,
 164, 259n5, 261n11
ecology, Wylie on, 90–94
education: on civil defense, 50, 57, 73; on survival, 71–72
Einstein's Monsters (Amis), 2
Eisenhower, Dwight, 82–83, 134, 163–64, 266n28
electromagnetic pulse, in, 233–34
Empire and Communications (Innis), 98
encyclopedic narratives, *Limbo* as, 113–14
The End of the Dream (Wylie), 90–94
"The End of the Race" (Bermel), 185–86
enemy, in nuclear fiction, 5, 138, 218; in *Alas,
 Babylon*, 64, 68; in *The Bedford Incident*,
 150, 153–54, 157–62; demonization of, 52,

68, 158, 160; in *Dr. Strangelove*, 189–92;
 need for communication with, 178–79; own
 technology as, 91–92; Soviets as, 16, 64, 76,
 78–80, 85, 88, 153–54, 158–60; unknown,
 217, 231, 234
enemy, U.S., 68, 150, 216
Enemy Coast Ahead (Gibson), 185
energy, 9, 16, 18, 24–25
Engel, Leonard, 221–22
Eniwetok Atoll, nuclear testing on, 44–46,
 113, 152
entropy, and end of the world, 11–12
environment, effects of fallout on, 46
evacuation, 42, 48, 77
expectancy, 84, 101
explosions, nuclear, 65, 87; descriptions of,
 14–16, 26–28, 30, 64–65, 79–82, 198; effects
 of, 36, 43; in nuclear sublime, 45–46

Fahrenheit 451 (Bradbury), 82, 96, 251n6
Fail-Safe (Burdick and Wheeler), 7, 144, 167,
 179, 264n33; communications in, 174–75,
 178; defense strategies in, 172–73; film adaptation of, 171, 174, 177, 263n5; goals of, 168,
 175, 177; heroes of, 175–76; opposing levels
 in, 168–69; other nuclear fiction compared
 to, 183–84, 239; responses to, 169–71, 176–77,
 263n9; on similarities between U.S. and
 Soviets, 173–74; technology in, 170–71; time
 as theme in, 171–72
Fail-Safe Fallacy (Hook), 176
fail-safe systems, 173, 175–76, 182
fallout. *See* radioactive fallout
"Fallout: The Silent Killer" (Spencer), 43
Fallout Protection (Department of Defense),
 71, 232, 271n1
fallout shelters, 50, 87. *See also* civil defense;
 culture of, 60–61; effects of, 74, 251n64;
 futility of, 58–60, 103, 140, 144; lack of
 confidence in, 55, 60–61, 77; options for,
 42, 57–58, 249n4; promotion of, 48, 55,
 71, 251n67, 271n1; provisioning of, 249n23,
 252n41; race for, 139–40, 260n33; in survivability of nuclear war, 6–7
families: civil defense and, 52, 71; effects of
 nuclear attack on, 51–57, 72
Farnham's Freehold (Heinlein), 71–72, 199–200
Federal Civil Defense Authority (FCDA), 43,
 57, 144, 254n30; Wylie as consultant with,
 77, 82–83
Feiffer, Jules, 197

The Human Use of Human Beings (Wiener),
120, 126, 257n16

humanity, 186; capacity for self-destruction,
7, 198, 202; effects of stress on, 148–49; loss
of, 134–36, 141, 145–46, 167; mechanization
of, 257n7, 259n19; pessimism about fate of,
17–18, 21–22

humor: black, 182, 184–88, 192–94, 26622;
in *Dr. Strangelove,* 182, 184–88, 192–94,
196–98; theories of, 120–21, 127

hunting: as American tradition, 7; *The Bedford
Incident* as narrative of, 147, 153–55, 157, 160

Hutcheon, Linda, 99

Hutchins, Robert M., 172, 246n62

Huxley, Aldous, 90, 95, 135–36, 201

hydrogen bombs, 112, 257n2, 264n36. *See also*
nuclear weapons; effects of, 40, 42–43, 196;
impossibility of defense against, 86, 144,
223; testing of, 28, 113

"If the Bomb Gets Out of Hand" (Morrison),
218–19, 222, 269n9

"The Imagination of Disaster" (Sontag), 39

In Deep (Wolfe), 123

Ing, Dean, 72–74, 228, 252n38, 252n39

Innis, Harold A., 98

intelligence gathering, spying *vs.,* 150–51

International Society for the Study of Nuclear
Texts and Contexts (ISSNTC), 2

The Interpretation of Radium (Soddy), 11–13

The Invasion of the Body Snatchers (Wylie), 78

"It Takes a Thief" or "Big Joe and the Nth
Generation" (Miller), 96

Jackson, Peter, 200

Jacobs, Robert A., 4, 6

Japan, 32. *See also* Hiroshima; evaluation of
bombing of, 19–20, 38–39, 248n43; MacArthur's
security blackout of, 28, 35, 37; U.S.
on news of radiation sickness in, 29, 43

Jenkins, Will F. *See* Leinster, Murray

jeremiads, nuclear fiction as, 6

Johnson, Denis, 213–14

Jones, D. F., 116

journal fiction, 43; bearing witness in, 6, 123;
diary entries in *Level 7,* 133, 136, 138–39

The Judgment of Eve (Pangborn), 207

Jungk, Robert, 37

Kagan, Norman, 193

Kahn, Herman, 183, 196–97, 265n9; on effects

of nuclear war, 177, 189; Groteschele in *Fail-Safe* modeled on, 172–73, 263n20

Kennedy, John F., 150, 253n13; *Fail-Safe* and,
168, 263n9; promoting shelters, 60, 71, 271n1

Kennedy, Leigh, 37

Kermode, Frank, 141

Ketterer, David, 60

King-Hall, Stephen, 174–75

King of Bombs (Filger), 236–37

Klein, Richard, 5

Knebel, Fletcher, 177, 265n6

knowledge, 96, 168, 235; control of, 98, 205,
207; preservation *vs.* interpretation of,
97–98, 105, 111

Koestler, Arthur, 121, 127, 224–25

Korean War, 28, 112, 163

Kornbluth, C. M., 84

Krakatit (Capek), 11, 15

Kramer, Stanley, 47

Krazy Kat (Cantor), 38

Krushchev, Nikita, 134, 174, 262n34, 266n28

Kubrick, Stanley, 192, 263n5, 265n16; on adapting
Red Alert for film, 184–85, 265n11; *Dr.
Strangelove* and, 182, 186, 193–94, 198; on
humor in *Dr. Strangelove,* 185, 187–88

Kuhn, Thomas, 9

Kunetka, James, 208–11, 268n27

landscapes: cycles of history etched on, 211–13;
dislocation from, 203–5; efforts to retain sense
of place, 213–14; mapping of, 206–7, 211–13;
place names in, 211–14; reappropriation of,
199–200, 203, 206–7; in *Warday,* 210–11

Lang, Daniel, 42

language, 127, 129, 193–94, 246n10; effects of
nuclear war on, 3, 212–14; incompatibility
in causes of war, 115, 118; of nuclear weapons
and war, 24–25, 188–89; transferability,
122–23

Lanouette, William, 23

The Last Day (Clarkson), 5–6

Laurence, William L., 246n3, 246n6, 267n57;
chronicling Manhattan Project, 24–29; descriptions
of atomic bombs, 35–36; Hersey
compared to, 35–37

Lear, John, 49–50, 52, 222–23

The Legacy of Hiroshima (Brown and Teller),
47–48

Leinster, Murray, 1, 246n2, 269n5; "Short
History of World War Three," 219–20; on
unprovoked attacks, 216–17

LeMay, Curtis, 232

Letter Bomb (Schwenger), 3

Level 7 (Roshwald), 6–7, 116, 132, 168; bleak ending of, 146; diary entries in, 133, 136, 138–39; goal of, 168, 202; meaning of title, 140–41; nuclear launches in, 137–38, 163; psychological health in, 136–37; reviews and endorsements of, 141–42, 144; technology in, 133–34, 136–37; TV adaptation of, 145–46

Levine, Murray S., 42

Lewin, Leonard C., 60

Lewis, Flora, 181–82

Liberty (Coonts), 235–36

Life After Doomsday (Clayton), 72

Life magazine, 216–18, 225

Lifton, Robert Jay, 38

light, as deity, 102–3

Limbo (Wolfe), 7, 130; on aggression, 114, 117, 126; compared to *Player Piano,* 115–16; humor in, 119, 121, 125; influences on, 112–13, 113–14, 257n7; mapping in, 200–201; Martine's journals in, 123–24; meaning of bodies in, 125–26; morals of, 119–20; moving among genres, 113–14, 123–24; obsession with death in, 118, 121–22; Olympics in, 126–27; as postmodern, 123–24, 123–25; reviews of, 119–20, 125; wordplay in, 118–22, 125, 128–29

Linden, George W., 186

Lindner, Robert, 80

literature, and science, 19–20

The "Lomokome" Papers (Wouk), 143, 260n33

The Lonely Crowd (Riesman), 134

The Long Loud Silence (Tucker), 204–5

The Long Night (Caidin), 48, 85

The Long Tomorrow (Brackett), 205–7

Los Angeles: A.D. 2017 (Wylie), 90

Lucifer's Hammer (Pournelle and Niven), 72

Lumet, Sidney, 171, 174, 177

MacArthur, Douglas, 28, 37, 112

Macdonald, Dwight, 34

Macklin, F. Anthony, 193

The Magic Christian (Southern), 186, 194

Maland, Charles, 191, 196–97

Manganiello, Dominic, 108

Manhattan Project: imagined effects on designers, 39–40; Laurence chronicling, 24–29; Szilard in, 19, 202

Mannix, Patrick, 3

mapping: in nuclear fiction, 200–201, 210–11; in postnuclear fiction, 206–7, 214

Maps of Meaning (Jackson), 200

Martino, Joseph P., 131

Masters, Dexter, 37, 248n43, 248n44

materialism, U.S., 89

Maus, Derek C., 173

McCarthy era, 39, 192, 257n16

McDonald, John, 267n60

McNamara, Robert, 89–90, 168

media, 51; in nuclear fiction, 67–68, 88, 91, 98, 171, 174–75, 232–33; reporting on Hiroshima and Nagasaki, 28–35; speculating on effects of nuclear attack, 43, 225

Meeks, S. P., 16

Men of Destiny (King-Hall), 174–75

Mendelson, Edward, 113

Merril, Judith, 7, 50–51, 250n40, 270n21

metaphor, nuclear weapons treated as, 74

Meyer, Bill, 178–79

Middle East, imagined nuclear war starting in, 64, 66, 73

militarism: as pathology, 152, 156, 158–59; resistance to, 117

military, in nuclear fiction, 89, 167, 180, 187; forcing action, 175, 265n6; nuclear war triggered by rogue officer of, 181–83, 194–96, 239; postnuclear, 70

military, U.S., 136, 216, 226; intelligence gathering *vs.* spying by, 150–51; political relations with, 177–83; psychology of, 181, 184, 193–96; public and, 82–83, 168; secrecy of, 169, 177; superiority of, 36–37; technology of, 115, 176

military-industrial complex, 92, 98–99, 128, 146

Milland, Ray, 252n18

The Millennium (Sinclair), 15

Miller, Walter M., 3, 7, 105; on government control of information, 98–99; influence of, 72, 211; on Logos, 109–10; religion and, 106, 110; treatment of the past, 107–8, 211; writing style of, 98–102

Millet, Lydia, 39–40, 248n50

Mills, C. Wright, 163–64, 220, 225, 269n14

"The Mined Cities" (Szilard), 22

mirroring: in Cold War, 16, 142–43; of Soviet Union and U.S., 120, 139, 142–43, 150, 157–58, 173–74, 178

"The Misfortune of Being Out of Date" (Russell), 143

Mitchell, Greg, 38

Moby-Dick (Melville): *The Bedford Incident* and, 147, 151, 153–55, 159, 161; symbolism used during Cold War, 151–53 morale, 57, 73, 222

Morris, Edit, 37–38, 248n45

Morrison, Philip, 49, 202–3, 222, 269n9; influence on *Shadow on the Hearth,* 51–52; transposing Hiroshima to New York, 218–19

Morrow, James, 38–39

Mr. Adam (Frank), 62

Mumford, Lewis, 116–17, 132, 153, 257n7, 265n1

The Murder of the USA (Leinster), 216–17, 246n2

Murrow, Edward, 223–24

mushroom cloud, 65, 79, 227; as iconic image, 27–28, 39–40, 161; in nuclear sublime, 45–46

mutants, 104–5, 110

Mutual Assured Destruction, 164

Mutual Assured Survival (Ing and Pournelle), 72–73, 252n39

"My Trial as a War Criminal" (Szilard), 20–21

Nadel, Alan, 33, 161

Nagasaki, bombing of, 16; effects of, 27–28, 49; opposition to, 248n43; reports on, 25, 28–30

Naipaul, V. S., 141

narrators: lack of, 226–27; in *Level 7,* 140, 146; in nuclear fiction, 5–6, 133; off-planet, 76, 85, 143, 202

nationalism, 13

NATO: in *The Bedford Incident,* 153, 156–58; in *The Third World War, August 1985,* 226–27

nature, 122; as balanced system, 90–91, 93; desire to control, 10–11; nuclear energy as secret of, 9, 25; nuclear war compared to force of, 50; nuclear weapons' damage to, 26, 46, 48, 65, 70

Nelson, Thomas, 194

Nightmares of Eminent Persons and Other Stories (Russell), 142

Nineteen Eighty-Four (Orwell), 99, 108, 215, 232

Niven, Larry, 72

"No Apocalypse, Not Now" (Derrida), 2–3

No Place to Hide (Bradley), 44–46, 51–52

Nowlan, Philip Frances, 15–16

The Nuclear Age (O'Brien), 74

nuclear attacks, 68, 112, 149. *See also* nuclear war; alien attacks *vs.,* 52; casualties from, 30, 83, 85–86; chaos after, 48, 58, 65–66; destruction from, 87–88, 219–20; effects of, 30, 51–57, 69–70, 78–79, 218–19; lack of defense against, 89–90; morale as target of, 57; possibility of, 56, 84; preemptive, 179–80, 195, 217, 232, 269n1; prevention of, 52–53; psychological effects of, 80–84, 254n28; re-

sponses to accidental, 166–67, 227; shadowing from, 50, 219, 250n39; speed of, 219–20, 234; survivability of, 55, 71; unprovoked, 216–17, 222; Wylie's desire to depict, 81–82

nuclear brinkmanship, 178

nuclear criticism, 2–3, 6

Nuclear Criticism (Ruthven), 3

nuclear energy, 9, 18, 24–25

nuclear fiction: absence in, 3, 5; after the Cold War, 6, 221, 230, 238–39; confusion in, 199–200, 226, 230; destruction of American icons in, 217–18; documentary methods in, 208, 228; Frank on, 62, 251n4; goals of, 6, 143; mapping in, 200–201; other genres *vs.,* 14, 176, 231; popularity of, 207; reappropriation of landscapes in, 199–201; responses to, 166, 184–85, 216, 222; taking perspective outside Cold War, 143; themes in, 3–4, 47, 218; uncertainty over endings in, 5–6, 55

nuclear fission, energy from, 11–12, 18

nuclear-powered submarines, 148–50, 260n1; in *The Bedford Incident,* 147, 160–62

nuclear safety, debates over, 44

nuclear subject: challenging rationality, 4; effects on expression, 1; FBI trying to squelch, 246n3

nuclear sublime, 5, 40, 45–46, 80, 227

nuclear testing, 6, 61, 81. *See also* Alamagordo test; on Bikini Atoll, 151–52; effects of, 44–46, 113; nuclear fiction and, 79–80, 207; radioactive fallout from, 43, 46

nuclear war. *See also* nuclear attacks: accidental triggering of, 132, 138, 141, 144, 157–58, 167–68, 172, 177, 266n30; benefits attributed to, 14–15; causes of, 13, 46–47, 64, 67, 73; characters' efforts to understand, 203, 205, 214, 231–32; confusion in, 46–47, 239; ecological disaster compared to, 91–93; effects of, 4, 7, 44, 164, 184, 208–9, 221–22, 234; effects of electromagnetic pulse in, 233–34; fail-safe system supposed to prevent accidental, 164–65; game theory applied to, 117, 126, 267n60; government minimizing effects of, 43–44, 47–48, 89–90; as insanity, 60, 265n1; length of, 221–22; *Life* magazine's use of graphics and text to portray, 217–18; likelihood of, 64, 66, 74, 163, 198; limited, 208–9, 227–28; as major rupture, 199–200, 203; psychological effects of, 80, 82–83, 202–3; public discourse on, 184–85, 208, 233–34; public education on, 47–48, 63, 80–82; public response to threat of, 64, 74; representations of, 2–3, 50; in science fiction, 43–44, 51; speed of, 4, 64, 132, 163–64, 183–84; strategies in, 68, 226, 228; survivability of, 6–8, 59–61, 72–73, 162; triggered by rogue officer, 181–83, 194–96, 239, 265n6; triggered by satellite system, 208; winnability of, 43, 56–57, 70, 86–87, 144; winner of, 84–85, 218, 227–28; WWII *vs.*, 175, 184, 190–92, 204, 222, 228

nuclear weapons, 4, 16–17, 72, 248n46, 251n71, 264n38. *See also* atomic bombs; hydrogen bombs; accessibility of, 77, 234; cobalt in, 84, 267n57; control of, 15, 230; defenses against, 42, 59–60; destructiveness of, 87, 190, 269n9; development of, 26; giving U.S. power for global conquest, 18–19; lack of defense against, 49, 216–17; representations of, 2, 14, 74; response to possession of, 28, 61, 117; standoff with as insanity, 160, 265n1, 265n16; terrorists and, 234–38; unknown effects of, 226, 238; U.S. monopoly on, 18–19, 222

Oakes, Guy, 84, 254n30
O'Brien, Tim, 74
Oh Pure and Radiant Heart (Millet), 39–40, 248n50
On the Beach (Shute), 45–46, 87, 173, 184; ending of, 5, 69; "misconceptions" from, 47–48, 72
On Thermonuclear War (Kahn), 196
One of Our H-Bombs Is Missing (Lewis), 181–82
One Second After (Forstchen), 233–34
One World or None (Masters and Way, ed.), 248n43; Morrison's contribution to, 49, 53, 218–19
Operation Crossroads. *See* Eniwetok Atoll nuclear testing
Oppenheimer, Robert, 39–40, 77
Orwell, George, 215
Ostow, Mortimer, 195
other-directedness, 134

pacifism, in *Limbo*, 119, 124
Palmer, Michael A., 228
Pangborn, Edgar, 206–7, 213
"Panic, Psychology, and the Bomb" (Wylie), 80–81
Panic in Year Zero! (film), 67–68, 70
paradigm shifts, in science and narratives, 9
"The Paradise Crater" (Wylie), 76, 253n5
pathology, 7, 152, 197

patriotism, survival as, 68, 71
Pauling, Linus, 141, 226
Pease, Donald, 153
Pentagon of Power (Mumford), 132, 153
Percy, Walker, 99, 109
Peterson, Val, 254n30
"Philadelphia Phase" (Wylie), 224
Piette, Adam, 147, 261n3
Piller, Emanuel S., 221–22
Pilot Lights of the Apocalypse (Ridenour), 132, 146
"Planetary Effulgence" (Russell), 142–43
Player Piano (Vonnegut), 115–16, 122
Pohl, Frederick, 73, 249n4
polarities, 120, 134; Cold War, 5, 80, 116, 120, 134, 153, 155, 232; dual selves, 157–58
politics, 196, 224; around civil defense, 50; dissociation of, 118, 153; in *Limbo,* 120–21; military relations to, 177–83; science's relation to, 11, 17–19, 23
The Postman (Brin), 71, 214, 269n47
postmodernism, 99, 123–25
postnuclear fiction, 37, 207, 213; changed language in, 212–14; history in, 9, 95; isolated families in, 17–18; landscapes in, 203–6; *Limbo* as, 112, 125; rediscovery of U.S. in, 201–2; *Riddley Walker* as, 211–13; utopias in, 15; *Warday* as, 208–10
postnuclear world, 35, 37, 140, 205, 214, 231; isolation in, 66–67; landscapes in, 7, 200, 203–4; life in shelters in, 87, 102–3; pessimism about, 17–18; planning for, 72; politics in, 14–15, 57–58, 224; reestablishment of status quo in, 146, 161–62; social systems in, 68, 95–97; touring, 207–11
Pournelle, Jerry, 72–73, 237, 252n39
power, 10–11, 15, 118, 144–45
preparedness, 216; advice for, 48, 71; as key to survival, 57, 72–74; lack of, 66, 77, 82–83, 88–89
Priestley, J. B., 10, 141–42, 145–46, 224
Prochnau, William, 179–80, 264n38
progress, 114, 117
prosthesis, 114, 116–18
Protection in the Nuclear Age (government brochure), 73
Pugwash Movement, 143
Pulling Through (Ing), 73–74
"Pushbutton War" (Martino), 131, 146
pushbuttons: operatives and, 137–38, 146; symbolism of, 7, 259n24
Pynchon, Thomas, 114

Weart, Spencer, 9, 32, 43, 47

Weller, George, 28–30, 247n18

Wells, H. G., 6, 11–15, 72, 244n13, 244n16, 245n36; film scenario by, 16–17; influence of, 19, 22–23, 90

Welton, Harry, 225, 269n14, 270n29

Wheeler, Harvey, 7, 144, 166, 173, 263n5; *Fail-Safe* and, 167–76, 263n9, 264n33; goals for *Fail-Safe*, 168, 175, 177

When the Sleeper Wakes (Wells), 90

Widmark, Richard, 262n28

Wiener, Norbert, 114–16, 120, 125–26

The Wild Shore (Robinson), 213

Wilder, Thornton, 31–32

Wilkinson, Rupert, 170–71

Williams, Paul, 2, 6

Wilson, Gilbert, 151–52

Winchell, Walter, 225

Wolfe, Bernard, 7, 112, 120; influences on, 114, 258n36; on *Limbo* as encyclopedic narrative, 113–14; on mapping in *Limbo*, 200–201; writing style of, 118–19, 121–22, 124–25, 127

World Aflame (Engel and Piller), 221–22

The World Jones Made (Dick), 95

The World Next Door (Ferguson), 231–32

The World Set Free (Wells), 6, 12–15, 17–19

World War 3 (Bidwell, ed.), 228

World War I, 15

World War II, 77; compared to Cold War, 154, 160, 165; expectation of war following, 215–16; nuclear war *vs.*, 86, 175, 184, 190–92, 204, 222–23, 228

World War III, 4, 223; computers in, 115–16; expectation of, 112, 215–16, 220; future histories of, 7, 226; journalistic style writing about, 219–24, 225; in *Limbo*, 123–24; projected causes of, 225, 269n14

Wouk, Herman, 143, 260n33, 262n27

Wylie, Philip, 3, 7, 48, 224, 253n13, 254n38; background of, 75; on civil defense, 44, 76–77, 90; criticisms of Pentagon, 89–90; criticisms of science fiction, 75–76; declining popularity of, 75; dissemination of books, 250n47, 254n30; on ecology, 90–94; goals of, 57, 81–82, 95, 254n28; on other nuclear fiction, 125, 263n9; Soviets as enemy for, 78–80, 85, 88; writing style of, 76, 90–91